THE OLD SOUTH

New studies of society and culture

Edited by
J. William Harris

Routledge
Taylor & Francis Group

NEW YORK AND LONDON

Originally published in 1992 as *Society and Culture in the Slave South*

This edition published 2008
by Routledge
270 Madison Ave, New York, NY 10016

Simultaneously published in the UK
by Routledge
2 Park Square, Milton Park, Abingdon, Oxon OX14 4RN

Routledge is an imprint of the Taylor & Francis Group,
an informa business

Typeset in Palatino by RefineCatch Limited, Bungay, Suffolk
Printed and bound in the United States of America on acid-free
paper by
Edwards Brothers, Inc.

Library of Congress Cataloging in Publication Data
The old South : new studies of society and culture/ edited by
J. William Harris.
p. cm. – (Rewriting histories)
Originally published: London ; New York : Routledge, 1992. With
title: Society and culture in the slave South.
Includes bibliographical references and index.
ISBN13: 978–0–415–95728–1 (hbk. : alk. paper)
ISBN13: 978–0–415–95729–8 (pbk. : alk. paper)
ISBN10: 0–415–95728–1 (hbk. : alk. paper)
ISBN10: 0–415–95729–X (pbk. : alk. paper)
1. Southern States–Social conditions. 2. Southern States–Economic
conditions. 3. Slavery–Southern States–History. 4. Slavery–
Economic aspects–Southern States. 5. Women–Southern States–
Psychology. Slaves–6. Southern States–Psychology. I. Harris,
J. William, 1946– II. Society and culture in the slave South.
HN79.A13O43 2008
306.3'620975–dc22
2007025674

ISBN10: 0–415–95728–1 (hbk)
ISBN10: 0–415–95729–X (pbk)

ISBN13: 978–0–415–95728–1 (hbk)
ISBN13: 978–0–415–95729–8 (pbk)

CONTENTS

Series editor's preface   vii
Acknowledgments   ix

Introduction   1

1 **The dilemma**   12
   EUGENE D. GENOVESE

2 **Slavery and plantation capitalism in Louisiana's
   sugar country**   37
   RICHARD FOLLETT

3 **Ideology and death on a Savannah River rice plantation,
   1833–1867: paternalism amidst "A Good Supply Of
   Disease And Pain"**   58
   JEFFREY R. YOUNG

4 **Old South time in comparative perspective**   84
   MARK M. SMITH

5 **Slavery, freedom, and social claims to property among
   African Americans in Liberty County, Georgia,
   1850–1880**   113
   DYLAN C. PENNINGROTH

6 **The pleasures of resistance: enslaved women and
   body politics in the Plantation South, 1830–1861**   142
   STEPHANIE M. H. CAMP

CONTENTS

7 The management of negroes   170
   KIRSTEN E. WOOD

8 The slave trader, the white slave, and the politics of
   racial determination in the 1850s   195
   WALTER JOHNSON

9 Tippecanoe and the ladies, too: white women and
   party politics in antebellum Virginia   222
   ELIZABETH R. VARON

10 The sex of a human being   249
    MICHAEL O'BRIEN

11 To harden a lady's hand: gender politics, racial realities,
    and women millworkers in antebellum Georgia   272
    MICHELE GILLESPIE

12 Law, domestic violence, and the limits of patriarchal
    authority in the antebellum South   295
    LAURA F. EDWARDS

    Index   321

SERIES EDITOR'S PREFACE

Rewriting history, or revisionism, has always followed closely in the wake of history writing. In their efforts to reevaluate the past, professional as well as amateur scholars have followed many approaches, most commonly as empiricists, uncovering new information to challenge earlier accounts. Historians have also revised previous versions by adopting new perspectives, usually fortified by new research, which overturn received views.

Even though rewriting is constantly taking place, historians' attitudes towards using new interpretations have been anything but settled. For most, the validity of revisionism lies in providing a stronger, more convincing account that better captures the objective truth of the matter. Although such historians might agree that we never finally arrive at the "truth," they believe it exists, and that over time it may be better approximated. At the other extreme stand scholars who believe that each generation or even each cultural group or subgroup necessarily regards the past differently, each creating for itself a more usable history. Although these latter scholars do not reject the possibility of demonstrating empirically that some contentions are better than others, they focus upon generating new views based upon different life experiences. Different truths exist for different groups. Surely such an understanding, by emphasizing subjectivity, further encourages rewriting history. Between these two groups are those historians who wish to borrow from both sides. This third group, while accepting that every congeries of individuals sees matters differently, still wishes, somewhat contradictorily, to fashion a broader history that incorporates both of these particular visions. Revisionists who stress empiricism fall into the first of the three camps, while others spread out across the board.

Today the rewriting of history seems to have accelerated to a blinding speed as a consequence of the evolution of revisionism. A variety of approaches has emerged. A major factor in this process has been the enormous increase in the number of researchers. This explosion has reinforced and enabled the retesting of many assertions. Significant ideological shifts have also played a major part in the growth of revisionism. First, the crisis of Marxism, culminating in the events in eastern Europe in 1989, has given rise to doubts about explicitly Marxist accounts. Such doubts have spilled over into the entire field of social history, which has been a dominant subfield of the discipline for several decades. Focusing on society and its class divisions implied that these are the most important elements in historical analysis. Because Marxism was built on the same claim, the whole basis of social history has been questioned, despite the very many studies that directly had little to do with Marxism. Disillusionment with social history simultaneously opened the door to cultural and linguistic approaches largely developed in anthropology and literature. Multiculturalism and feminism further generated revisionism. By claiming that scholars had, wittingly or not, operated from a white European/American male point of view, newer researchers argued that other approaches had been neglected or misunderstood. Not surprisingly, these last historians are the most likely to envision each subgroup rewriting its own usable history, while other scholars incline towards revisionism as part of the search for some stable truth.

Rewriting Histories will make these new approaches available to the student population. Often new scholarly debates take place in the scattered issues of journals that are sometimes difficult to find. Furthermore, in these first interactions, historians tend to address one another, leaving out the evidence that would make their arguments more accessible to the uninitiated. This series of books will collect in one place a strong group of the major articles in selected fields, adding notes and introductions conducive to improved understanding. Editors will select articles containing substantial historical data, so that students—at least those who approach the subject as an objective phenomenon—can advance not only their comprehension of debated points but also their grasp of substantive aspects of the subject.

Fields continue to evolve. When the first edition of this book appeared, most scholars accepted Eugene Genovese's views of a patriarchal planter class as an overall paradigm, different from northern capitalists, who ruled over slaves with a personal relationship. Only a few scholars contested this view. Fifteen years later some things have changed little. Genovese has continued to defend and elaborate his view, but now more scholars contend that his view of paternalism overstates the extent of difference between planters and other elites. Yet an entirely new wave of studies, while often relating to the controversy, has appeared. Building on interest in women and gender as well as cultural history, these new studies consider subjects that were not central to Genovese or his detractors. This volume sums up the literature in antebellum southern history at a time of change and new directions.

ACKNOWLEDGMENTS

The editor and publishers wish to thank the following for their permission to reproduce copyright material:

Eugene D. Genovese, "The Dilemma," chapter 1 from *The Slaveholder's Dilemma: Freedom and Progress in Southern Conservative Thought, 1820–1860* (Columbia: University of South Carolina Press, 1992), 10–45.

Richard Follett, "On the Edge of Modernity: Louisiana's Landed Elites in the Nineteenth-Century Sugar Country," in Enrico Dal Lago and Rick Halpern, eds., *The American South and the Italian Mezzogiorno: Essays in Comparative History* (New York: Palgrave, 2002), 73–94. This was originally published in substantially the same form as "Slavery and Plantation Capitalism in Louisiana's Sugar Country," *American Nineteenth Century History*, vol. 1 (Autumn, 2000), 1–27.

Jeffrey R. Young, "Ideology and Death on a Savannah River Rice Plantation, 1833–1867: Paternalism amidst 'A Good Supply of Disease and Pain'," *Journal of Southern History*, 59 (1993), 673–706.

Mark M. Smith, "Old South Time in Comparative Perspective," *American Historical Review*, 101 (1996), 1432–69.

Dylan C. Penningroth, "Slavery, Freedom, and Social Claims to Property among African Americans in Liberty County, Georgia, 1850–1880," *Journal of American History*, 84 (Sept. 1997), 405—35.

Stephanie M. H. Camp, "The Pleasures of Resistance: Enslaved Women and Body Politics in the Plantation South, 1830–1861," *Journal of Southern History*, 68 (2002), 533–72.

Kirsten E. Wood, "The Management of Negroes," chapter 2 in Wood, *Masterful Women: Slaveholding Widows from the American Revolution through the Civil War* (Chapel Hill: University of North Carolina Press, 2004), 35–60.

Walter Johnson, "The Slave Trader, the White Slave, and the Politics of Racial Determination in the 1850s," *Journal of American History*, vol. 87, #1 (June 2000), 13–38.

Elizabeth R. Varon, "Tippecanoe and the Ladies, Too: White Women and Party Politics in Antebellum Virginia," *Journal of American History*, 82 (Sept. 1995), 494–521.

Michael O'Brien, "The Sex of a Human Being," chapter 6 in O'Brien, *Conjectures of Order: Intellectual Life and the American South, 1810–1860*, 2 vols. (Chapel Hill: University of North Carolina Press, 2004), 253–84.

Michele Gillespie, "To Harden a Lady's Hand: Gender Politics, Racial Realities, and Women Millworkers in Antebellum Georgia," in *Neither Lady Nor Slave: Working Women in the Old South*, ed. Susanna Delfino and Michele Gillespie (Chapel Hill: University of North Carolina Press, 2002), 61–84.

Laura F. Edwards, "Law, Domestic Violence, and the Limits of Patriarchal Authority in the Antebellum South," *Journal of Southern History*, 65 (1999), 733–80.

Every effort has been made to contact the copyright holders and relevant parties. The publishers would be very grateful for notification of any omissions.

INTRODUCTION

For more than forty years the Old South in the United States has been the focus of innovative and influential historical scholarship. Established and younger scholars continue to do exciting work, especially in the study of culture and the interaction of gender, race, and class in this slave society. The essays presented here include some of this diverse scholarship and introduce some of the central debates about the nature of society and culture in the Old South.[1]

I

A brief consideration of the historiography on slavery and the Old South will be helpful for a full understanding of current work. We may begin with Ulrich B. Phillips, whose work dominated the historiography of U.S. slavery in the first half of the twentieth century. Phillips was a scholar of great range and fine style, but his work, while based on deep research, was profoundly flawed by his racist assumptions about African Americans.[2] While Phillips did not repress all evidence of the cruelties of slavery, he argued that the system in the Old South was "essentially mild," and that slave plantations were "on the whole . . . the best schools yet invented for the mass training of that sort of inert and backward people which the bulk of the American negroes represented." Vigorous dissent from black scholars failed to have much impact on the general acceptance of Phillips's interpretation of the slave South.[3]

It should not be necessary to explain in detail why such interpretation of the Old South eventually lost its influence. As racial attitudes of scholars (and, of course, others) changed, so did their understandings of slavery. Attacks on Phillips's assumptions and evidence mounted, and in 1956 Kenneth Stampp published a new and comprehensive study of slavery, *The Peculiar Institution*. Stampp, like Phillips, was thoroughly at home with the documentary evidence on slavery. He stated at the outset his assumption that "Negroes are, after all, only

1

white men with black skins, nothing more, nothing less." Stampp portrayed slave masters not as kindly paternalists but as businessmen in an essentially dirty business. They ruled primarily by force and fear. The consequences for black slaves were indeed fearful, including a stripping away of their African culture without having it replaced by anything else substantial. "The Negro," therefore, "existed in a kind of cultural void . . . more or less in a bleak and narrow world." Three years later, Stanley Elkins, in another influential study, went even further in arguing that slaves in the U.S. had been psychologically infantilized by the slave experience, in effect turned into the "Sambos" depicted by apologists of slavery like Phillips.[4]

II

The work of Stampp and Elkins was but the beginning of a sustained outpouring of research and writing on the slave South that has continued to this day. A number of developments in the 1960s helped to spark this research, perhaps the most important being reassessment of black history that accompanied the rise of the Civil Rights Movement and the subsequent growth of black nationalism. This reassessment took several forms: a determination to see slaves as more than helpless victims of their own history; a greater awareness of evidence in the past of the kinds of pride and courage that were so prominent among black civil rights activists; and a search for the origins of what some saw as a separate African-American culture in the United States. This scholarship often included explicit rejection of the arguments of Stampp and Elkins about the effects of slavery on slaves. The new scholarship was also marked by the use of previously neglected sources and evidence, especially the many autobiographies of runaway or former slaves, the thousands of interviews with ex-slaves recorded in the 1930s by the Works Progress Administration Project, and the rich body of black song and folklore.[5] Much of this research reached fruition in the 1970s with the publication of major books by John W. Blassingame, Lawrence W. Levine, and Herbert G. Gutman. Each of these in its own way argued that slaves had created a partly autonomous culture that helped them resist white values and white oppression.[6]

III

A quite independent source of new directions in the study of slavery was the rise of the "new economic history"—the application of economic theory and statistical techniques to the study of the past. The "new economic history" was launched in large part by the publication in 1958 of "The Economics of Slavery in the Antebellum South", by Alfred H. Conrad and John R. Meyer.[7] Conrad and Meyer offered evidence that slave plantation agriculture was highly profitable; as profitable, for example, as investments in railroad stocks. The article sparked a number of subsequent studies of slavery, many of them based on massive sets of data collected from sources such as the manuscripts of the U.S. census, and analyzed with the aid of new computer technology.[8] This line of research, too, reached a climax of sorts in the 1970s, with the publication of *Time On the Cross*, by Robert William Fogel and Stanley Engerman.[9] Fogel and Engerman synthesized the work of the new economic historians of slavery and presented the results of their own large research project.

Time On the Cross included a number of highly controversial assertions. Going beyond the now accepted idea that slavery was profitable, Fogel and Engerman argued that slave plantations were actually more efficient than northern farms. They concluded from this that black slaves had been efficient and effective workers because they had, despite their bondage, adopted a strong work ethic. Planters, they claimed, had learned to use positive incentives, rather than punishment, to motivate slaves. (They also argued that abolitionists, as well as historians who had called slavery an inefficient and wasteful system, were helping to propagate a racist image of blacks as lazy and careless.) Fogel and Engerman made other surprising claims—that slaves had a more-than-adequate diet, that planters seldom divided slave families, and that slaves shared "Victorian" attitudes about sexual behavior and morality.

Criticism descended upon Fogel and Engerman from many directions. Economists faulted them for incorrect inferences from inadequate data and for inappropriate applications of economic theory. To many, their portrayal seemed to show slavery as an even more benign system than the one portrayed by Phillips, and hardly the "time on the cross" implied by their title.[10] Some historians concluded that *Time On the Cross* had demonstrated the limits, rather than the possibilities, of the new economic history. Nevertheless, economic research continued, and Robert W. Fogel later followed *Time On the Cross* with a second wide-ranging economic analysis of plantation slavery. Fogel responded to criticisms of his and Stanley Engerman's work, retreating from some of the more controversial claims made in the earlier book, but not from its central interpretation of the nature of the antebellum South's economy—that southern slavery should be understood as a "flexible, highly developed form of capitalism."[11]

IV

A development of the 1960s that deserves separate mention was the influential scholarship of Eugene D. Genovese. Beginning with a series of articles, brought together with new material in *The Political Economy of Slavery* (1965), Genovese developed a new interpretation of society and culture in the Old South. According to Genovese, slavery in the South was essentially a relationship between classes (rather than races), and this class relationship was the key to understanding southern society and culture. Here Genovese was following the interpretation of historical development laid out by Karl Marx in the nineteenth century.[12] Marx himself thought southern slaveowners had more in common with capitalists than with either ancient slaveowners or feudal lords, but Genovese, taking issue with Marx's analysis of the South, argued that slavery had created a unique, non-bourgeois culture—"a special civilization built on the relationship of master and slave." At the heart of this unique culture lay "paternalism," a worldview that valued personal, family-like relationships over the impersonal workings of the capitalist market. Genovese's willingness to accept slave planters' defense of their world as part of a genuine worldview, rather than mere hypocrisy, even led him to defend some aspects of the almost discredited work of Ulrich B. Phillips.[13] In another long essay, Genovese analyzed the work of pro-slavery writer George Fitzhugh. Fitzhugh had defended slavery by bitterly attacking the injustices of the wage labor system at the heart of modern capitalism. Because Fitzhugh went so far as to imply strongly, without quite explicitly saying so, that white factory workers ought to be reduced to slavery for their own good, most of Fitzhugh's contemporaries had seen him as a somewhat odd extremist. Genovese claimed, however, that Fitzhugh was the best guide to the logic of planter ideology.[14]

Genovese's most influential work was *Roll, Jordan, Roll: The World the Slaves Made* (1974). Here, Genovese drew on a wide range of sources to describe and explain the slaves' side of the master–slave relationship. The result was a complex argument that elaborated the idea of "paternalism" both in theory and in the day-to-day world of slaves. The slaves, he argued, had to a considerable extent accepted the paternalist vision of the planters, seeing the plantation as indeed a kind of family. This partial acceptance was the key to the planters' "cultural hegemony"—their ability to get their natural antagonists to accept some of the basic ideological premises on which slavery rested.[15]

At the same time, Genovese argued that the slaves had turned the premises of paternalism to their own advantage. They had forced masters to agree, if grudgingly, that slaves had certain rights and privileges even under slavery. While adopting Christianity from their masters' culture, the slaves had worked out their own version of a Christian worldview, one that rejected the moral premises on which slaveholders' ideology was based. Thus planter paternalism had not prevented blacks from immediately abandoning the master–slave relationship when the Civil War made this possible.

Roll, Jordan, Roll was controversial, not only because Genovese was a Marxist, but also because he argued that slave masters ruled more through their cultural power than by physical coercion. Nevertheless, the strengths of Genovese's work, and of *Roll, Jordan, Roll* in particular, made him the most important and influential scholar writing on the Old South. *Roll, Jordan, Roll* was based on vast research in a tremendous variety of source material—from the plantation records mined by Phillips to the folklore of slaves. Genovese's attention to comparative material from other slave systems of the western hemisphere and from European history gives his work additional authority, and he has been able to incorporate into his own interpretation much of the best scholarship of others, even those who disagree with his interpretations. Finally, Genovese has created a synthesis that is logical and coherent and which offers solutions to a number of historical questions—for example, why the United States had fewer slave revolts than other slave societies, and why southern planters were willing to fight a civil war to defend their way of life. As historian Drew Faust put it in 1987, Genovese "has been able to construct an explanation of nearly every aspect of the southern way of life [and thereby] set the agenda for much of the research on antebellum southern history undertaken in the past two decades."[16] Since Faust's comment, Eugene Genovese has continued to develop and modify his basic arguments, responding to criticisms and incorporating others' research at times, but never yielding on the essential argument that the Old South was a non-capitalist, paternalist society, not a bourgeois capitalist one. In recent years, most of his scholarly work, often written in collaboration with Elizabeth Fox-Genovese, has focused on the intellectual history of the South, and especially on the pro-slavery theorists and religious thinkers who, he asserts, best represented and articulated "the mind of the master class." The essay included in this volume presents an overview of one part of his work, which has been elaborated at length in a recently published book.[17]

V

Dozens of scholars have continued to follow the lines of inquiry prominent in the 1960s and 1970s, in part responding to Genovese's work, but also opening up new areas to intense study. Several important region-wide studies have appeared, usually focused on a particular institution or aspect of the slaveholding South.[18] Other historians have turned to the study of particular subregions, communities, plantations, or individual planters as a way of approaching the questions raised by the sweeping surveys characteristic of many of the books of the 1970s.[19] Some of these historians have proposed ways to reconcile the apparently conflicting interpretations of the Old South as *either* "capitalist" *or* "paternalist," offering arguments that the South was a kind of hybrid society that embraced elements of both capitalism and paternalism. The essays in this volume by Richard Follett, Mark M. Smith, and Jeffrey R. Young, each in a different way, all make such an argument—with Smith's representative of a region-wide approach, and Follett's and Young's examples of regional and plantation-level research.[20]

Other historians, while still influenced by the old debates, have asked new kinds of questions about the nature of the master–slave relationship. Walter Johnson's essay here examines slavery not on the plantation, but in the courtroom, in a contest over "whiteness" that grew out of the slave trade.[21] Dylan C. Penningroth analyzes the nature of a surprisingly widespread feature of slave life, the ownership of property by slaves.[22] Stephanie Camp, following pioneering work on slave women, argues that secret, after-hours parties were an important site and form of slave resistance.[23] These essays all show the influence of anthropology and cultural theory, and all take issue, explicitly or implicitly, with Genovese's emphasis on the cultural hegemony of the master class in the slave quarters. Another innovative approach can be seen in Kirsten Wood's essay on slaveholding women. If slavery was essentially a patriarchal system, what happened when women came to be the sole masters of slaves, as happened frequently in the case of women whose husbands died?

Wood's essay also illustrates a major stream of recent writing on women in the Old South. Examination of women's lives is particularly relevant to the claim that the Old South was "paternalist," since a paternalist worldview assumes a hierarchy in which women have pre-scribed and subordinate roles. Elizabeth Fox-Genovese published her own, independent analysis of southern women that, while differing in some ways from Eugene Genovese's interpretation, argued that white women in the planter families, at least, accepted and accommodated to their subordinate place within the household.[24] Michael O'Brien, in his essay on the intellectual lives of southern women, and Elizabeth Varon, writing on political behavior, both focus on elite, educated women, but the interpretation of neither is entirely compatible with the idea that the Old South's culture was fundamentally different from that of the north. Two other essays focus on white women whose lives hardly fit contemporary ideas about women's proper place. Michele

Gillespie writes on women from poor white families who worked for wages in Georgia's textile mills, while Laura Edwards writes on women who ended up as defendants in criminal courts. It should be emphasized that these historians do not examine women in isolation. Each can be seen also as an example of recent work in broad patterns of southern history: intellectual life;[25] political culture;[26] and class and economic structure.[27]

VI

As the numerous references to Genovese's work in the notes for these essays illustrate, to some extent it is still true that his interpretation of the Old South as a paternalist society sets the agenda for current scholarship. Several of the essays included here take up the problem of paternalism directly. But this is no longer true to the same extent as it was 20 years ago. Historians often now come to the study of the Old South with problems and questions taken from different sources and different frames of reference. Thus, Dylan C. Penningroth largely sidesteps the problem of the relation of slave and master, preferring to focus instead on what property ownership can tell us about the relationships of slaves with each other. Elizabeth Varon is more interested in questions about the larger American political culture than in the nature of paternalism. These and other essays included here point toward a continuing fertility and creativity in the ongoing scholarly conversation on the society and culture in the slave South.

A NOTE ON EDITORIAL PRACTICE

Cuts in the texts of essays are indicated with ellipses, and when explanatory comments have been added in the text itself, these are enclosed in brackets []. Editor's explanatory notes appear at the bottom of the page. Notes from the original essays appear at the end of each chapter. While few of the authors' original notes have been entirely omitted, many have been cut because of space limitations. In notes, as in the text, omissions are indicated by ellipses.

NOTES

1 This volume is a new edition of an earlier collection; *Society and Culture in the Slave South*, ed. J. William Harris (London and New York, 1992). In keeping with the theme of the series, all the selections here were originally published after the previous edition.
2 Most notably in *American Negro Slavery* (1919, rep. Baton Rouge, 1966); see also his *Life and Labor in the Old South* (Boston, 1929).
3 Phillips, *American Negro Slavery*, 342, 343. On African-American historians,

J. WILLIAM HARRIS

see especially August Meier and Elliott Rudwick, *Black History and the Historical Profession, 1915–1980* (Urbana, Ill., 1986).

4 Kenneth Stampp, *The Peculiar Institution: Slavery in the Antebellum South* (New York, 1956); Stanley Elkins, *Slavery: A Problem in American Institutional and Intellectual Life* (Chicago, 1959).

5 The WPA narratives were published under the editorship of George Rawick: *The American Slave: A Composite Autobiography* (Westport, Conn., 1972).

6 John W. Blassingame, *The Slave Community: Plantation Life in the Antebellum South* (New York, 1972); Lawrence W. Levine, *Black Culture and Black Consciousness: Afro-American Folk Thought from Slavery to Freedom* (New York, 1977); Herbert G. Gutman, *The Black Family in Slavery and Freedom, 1750–1925* (New York, 1976). Other significant books on slave culture published in the decade include Leslie Howard Owens, *This Species of Property: Slave Life and Culture in the Old South* (New York, 1976); Thomas L. Webber, *Deep Like the Rivers: Education in the Slave Community* (New York, 1978); Albert Raboteau, *Slave Religion: The Invisible Institution in the Antebellum South* (New York, 1978).

7 *Journal of Political Economy*, 66 (1958), 95–130.

8 An important collection of these studies was William N. Parker, ed., *The Structure of the Cotton Economy of the Antebellum South* (Berkeley, Cal., 1970).

9 *Time On the Cross: The Economics of American Negro Slavery*, 2 vols. (Boston, 1974).

10 Many of the criticisms were collected in Paul David et al., *Reckoning with Slavery: A Critical Study in the Quantitative History of American Negro Slavery* (New York, 1976).

11 Fogel, *Without Consent or Contract: The Rise and Fall of American Slavery* (New York, 1989), Part I. See also Fogel, *The Slavery Debates, 1952–1990: A Retrospective* (Baton Rouge, 2003).

12 *The Political Economy of Slavery: Studies in the Economy and Society of the Slave South* (New York, 1965). In broad outline, Marx had argued that every society since the earliest era of human history had been driven by struggles between a dominant ruling class and a subordinate exploited class. History had developed through a sequence of stages, each based on a different core conflict: masters against slaves in ancient society; feudal lords against serfs in medieval society, and capitalists (or "bourgeoisie") against workers (or "proletarians") in modern industrial societies such as nineteenth-century England and the United States. The literature on Marx and Marxism is too vast to do more than suggest places for interested students to begin. Marx's most influential single volume was *Capital*, Vol. I (1867). Students who wish for introductions can turn to a sympathetic account by G. A. Cohen, *Karl Marx's Theory of History: A Defense* (New York, 2000); and to a brief critical introduction in Peter Singer, *Marx: A Very Short Introduction* (New York, 2000).

13 Thus, Genovese wrote an introduction, including much praise, for a paperbound reprint of *American Negro Slavery* (Baton Rouge, 1966).

14 "The Logical Outcome of the Slaveholders' Philosophy," in Genovese, *The World the Slaveholders Made: Two Essays in Interpretation* (New York, 1969), 115–244.

15 *Roll, Jordan, Roll: The World the Slaves Made* (New York, 1974), esp. 3–7.

16 Drew Gilpin Faust, "The Peculiar South Revisited: White Society, Culture, and Politics in the Antebellum Period, 1800–1860," in *Interpreting Southern*

8

History: Historiographical Essays in Honor of Sanford W. Higginbotham, ed. John B. Boles and Evelyn Thomas Nolen (Baton Rouge, 1987), 79, 80.

17 Elizabeth Fox-Genovese and Eugene D. Genovese, *The Mind of the Master Class: History and Faith in the Southern Slaveholders' Worldview* (New York, 2006). For their earlier work, see especially Fox-Genovese and Genovese, *The Fruits of Merchant Capital: Slavery and Bourgeois Property in the Rise and Expansion of Capitalism* (New York, 1983).

18 Perhaps the most influential was Bertram Wyatt-Brown, *Southern Honor: Ethics and Behavior in the Old South* (New York, 1982). Wyatt-Brown contended that the Old South's culture was based on a code of "honor" that could be traced far back into early European history. His description of this system of belief was not incompatible with many of Genovese's descriptions of planter mentality, but Wyatt-Brown was little concerned with the economic base for such a culture. Also notable are the first part of Sterling Stuckey, *Slave Culture: Nationalist Theory and the Foundation of Black America* (New York, 1987), and William Kauffman Scarborough, *Masters of the Big House: Elite Slave-Holders of the Mid-19th Century South* (Baton Rouge, 2003). Both Stuckey and Scarborough challenge the paternalist argument, Stuckey by examining the African sources of slave culture, and Scarborough with a careful analysis of the richest of the South's slave masters.

19 Studies of particular plantations and/or owners include William Dusinberre, *Them Dark Days: Slavery in the American Rice Swamps* (New York, 1996); Drew Gilpin Faust, *James Henry Hammond and the Old South: A Design for Mastery* (Baton Rouge, 1982); and Charles B. Dew, *Bond of Iron: Master & Slave at Buffalo Forge* (New York, 1994). Studies of communities and subregions include Wilma Dunaway, *Slavery in the American Mountain South* (New York, 2003); John C. Inscoe, *Mountain Masters, Slavery, and the Sectional Crisis in Western North Carolina* (Knoxville, 1989); Robert C. Kenzer, *Kinship and Neighborhood in a Southern Community: Orange County, North Carolina, 1849–1881* (Knoxville, 1987); Orville Vernon Burton, *In My Father's House Are Many Mansions: Family and Community in Edgefield, South Carolina* (Chapel Hill, 1985); Lacy K. Ford, *The Origins of Southern Radicalism: The South Carolina Upcountry, 1800–1860* (New York, 1988); Stephanie McCurry, *Masters of Small Worlds: Yeoman Households, Gender Relations, and the Political Culture of the Antebellum South Carolina Low Country* (New York, 1995); Charles Joyner, *Down by the Riverside: A South Carolina Slave Community* (Urbana, Ill., 1984); Tom Downey, *Planting a Capitalist South: Masters, Merchants, and Manufacturers in the Southern Interior, 1790–1860* (Baton Rouge, 2006); Joseph Reidy, *Slavery and Agrarian Capitalism in the Cotton Plantation South: Central Georgia, 1800–1880* (Chapel Hill, 1992); J. William Harris, *Plain Folk and Gentry in a Slave Society: White Liberty and Black Slavery in Augusta's Hinterlands* (Middletown, Conn., 1985); Steven Hahn, *The Roots of Southern Populism: Yeoman Farmers and the Transformation of the Georgia Upcountry, 1850–1890* (New York, 1983); Daniel S. Dupre, *Transforming the Cotton Frontier: Madison County, Alabama, 1800–1840* (Baton Rouge, 1997); Michael Wayne, *The Reshaping of Plantation Society: The Natchez District, 1860–1880* (Baton Rouge, 1983); Wayne, *Death of an Overseer: Reopening a Murder Investigation from the Plantation South* (New York, 2001); Don Harrison Doyle, *Faulkner's County: The Historical Roots of Yoknapatawpha* (Chapel Hill, 2001); Christopher Morris, *Becoming Southern: The Evolution of a Way of Life in Warren County and Vicksburg, Mississippi, 1777–1860* (New York, 1995);

Edward E. Baptist, *Creating an Old South: Middle Florida's Plantation Frontier before the Civil War* (Chapel Hill, 2002).

20 For a similar effort on a larger scale, see James Oakes, *Slavery and Freedom: An Interpretation of the Old South* (New York, 1990).

21 Examination of slavery in the courts and the slave market have appeared in a number of books. In 1989, Michael Tadman demonstrated conclusively how widespread the domestic trade was and how often it separated slave families: *Speculators and Slaves: Masters, Traders, and Slaves in the Old South* (Madison, Wisc., 1989). On the trade, see Walter Johnson, *Soul by Soul: Life Inside the Antebellum Slave Market* (Cambridge, Mass., 1999); Walter Johnson, ed., *The Chattel Principle: Internal Slave Trades in the Americas* (New Haven, 2004); and more generally on the westward movement to the west, Joan E. Cashin, *A Family Venture: Men and Women on the Southern Frontier* (New York, 1991); Adam Rothman, *Slave Country: American Expansion and the Origins of the Deep South* (Cambridge, Mass., 2005); and Baptist, *Creating an Old South*; Morris, *Evolution of a Way of Life*; on slavery in the courts, see Ariela J. Gross, *Double Character: Slavery and Mastery in the Antebellum Southern Courtroom* (Princeton, 2000).

22 On slave property, see especially Ira Berlin and Philip D. Morgan, eds., *The Slaves' Economy: Independent Production by Slaves in the Americas* (Portland, 1991); Larry E. Hudson, Jr., ed., *Working Toward Freedom: Slave Society and Domestic Economy in the American South* (Rochester, NY, 1994).

23 The pioneering work on slave women is Deborah Grey White, *Ar'n't I a Woman? Female Slaves in the Plantation South* (New York, 1985). On related topics, see Marie Jenkins Schwartz, *Born in Bondage: Growing Up Enslaved in the Antebellum South* (Cambridge, Mass., 2000); Wilma King, *Stolen Childhood: Slave Youth in Nineteenth-Century America* (Bloomington, Ind., 1995); Ann Patton Malone, *Sweet Chariot: Slave Family and Household Structure in Nineteenth-Century Louisiana* (Chapel Hill, 1992); John Hope Franklin and Loren Schweninger, *Runaway Slaves: Rebels on the Plantation* (New York, 1999); Norrece T. Jones, Jr., *Born a Child of Freedom, Yet a Slave: Mechanisms of Control and Strategies of Resistance in Antebellum South Carolina* (Middletown, Conn., 1990); Roger D. Abrahams, *Singing the Master: The Emergence of African American Culture in the Plantation South* (New York, 1992).

24 Elizabeth Fox-Genovese, *Within the Plantation Household: Black and White Women of the Old South* (Chapel Hill, 1988). Important works on southern white women and families include Ann Firor Scott, *The Southern Lady: From Pedestal to Politics, 1830–1930* (2nd ed., Charlottesville, 1995); Catherine Clinton, *The Plantation Mistress: Woman's World in the Old South* (New York, 1982); Suzanne Lebsock, *The Free Women of Petersburg: Status and Culture in a Southern Town, 1784–1860*; Jane Turner Censer, *North Carolina Planters and their Children* (Baton Rouge, 1984); Marli Weiner, *Mistresses and Slaves: Plantation Women in South Carolina, 1830–1880* (Urbana, Ill., 1998).

25 For an introduction, see Michael O'Brien and David Moltke-Hansen, *Intellectual Life in Antebellum Charleston* (Knoxville, 1986).

26 Many of the community studies cited in note 19 examine political culture; among many general and state studies are William W. Freehling, *The Road to Disunion: Secessionists at Bay, 1776–1854* (New York, 1990), and Freehling, *The Road to Disunion: Secessionists Triumphant* (New York, 2007); William J. Cooper, *Liberty and Slavery: Southern Politics to 1860* (Columbia, SC, 2000); William G. Shade, *Democratizing the Old Dominion: Virginia and the Second Party System, 1824–1861* (Charlottesville, 1996); Christopher J. Olsen,

Political Culture and Secession in Mississippi: Masculinity, Honor, and the Anti-party Tradition, 1830–1860 (New York, 2000).

27 See, for example, Michele Gillespie, *Free Labor in an Unfree World: White Artisans in Slaveholding Georgia, 1789–1860* (Athens, Ga., 2000); Charles C. Bolton, *Poor Whites of the Antebellum South: Tenants and Laborers in Central North Carolina and Northeast Mississippi* (Durham, NC, 1994); Jonathon Daniel Wells, *The Origins of the Southern Middle Class, 1800–1861* (Chapel Hill, 2004); Victoria E. Bynum, *Unruly Women: The Politics of Social and Sexual Control in the Old South* (Chapel Hill, 1992).

1

THE DILEMMA

Eugene D. Genovese

In the following essay, Eugene Genovese examines southern intellectuals' ideas about freedom and progress. Secular and religious thinkers celebrated material progress, even though they also feared the disorder and immorality that, in their eyes, accompanied material progress in the North and Europe. Genovese concedes that these writers shared many ideas and values with "conservative-bourgeois" writers on both sides of the Atlantic, but he insists that they broke decisively with other conservatives because they "explicitly identified the free-labor system itself as the source of the moral evils" of the modern world. Freedom for some was necessary for progress, but only in a society based on "organic social relations." They argued that some form of servitude for the laboring class, under the guidance of a Christian ruling class, would allow for both material and moral progress. The South's slave system thus offered the world an "alternate route to modernity." Genovese's claim that southern intellectuals collectively articulated "the worldview of the slaveholding class" as they struggled to reconcile the claims of freedom and the legitimacy of slavery is consistent with his earlier work, which depicted the Old South as a distinct, non-capitalist society.

* * *

The mainstream of modern Western thought has cast slavery and progress as irreconcilable opposites, insisting that slavery impeded progress by restricting the freedom of every individual to contribute to society through the pursuit of self interest. Slavery, if we are to credit its adversaries, threatened the very identity of the American republic, corroding its virtue and retarding its development. Even the growing demand for rapid economic development through a program of free soil, free labor, and free men elided moral and material progress, tying the fate of the one to the unfolding of the other. The War for Southern Independence appeared to confirm this reading and to embody the triumph of moral and material progress over the forces of stagnation and reaction.

The war, in sealing the triumph of the North over the South, also sealed the triumph of the association of freedom and progress over an alternate reading. If the seeds of the irreconcilable opposition between slavery and progress, like the seeds of the unquestioning association of progress with freedom, were sown in the American, French, and Haitian Revolutions, their blossoming was not immediately assured. The slaveholding intellectuals, clerical and lay, took radically different ground, arguing for an understanding of freedom and progress as grounded in—not opposed to—slavery as a social system.

Edmund Morgan has demonstrated that the slaveholders of colonial Virginia espoused slavery as the necessary foundation of individual freedom and republican virtue and saw themselves as the principal champions of both. David Brion Davis has demonstrated that important strands of Euro-American thought came to challenge the prevalent notion that slavery impeded progress and to conclude that, under certain conditions, slavery in fact generated progress. Despite the inestimable contributions of these and other learned historians, the southern slaveholders' discrete understanding of the precise interrelation of slavery, freedom, and progress remains to be explored.[1]

The southern intellectuals devoted a large number of books, pamphlets, and articles in lay and religious journals to these subjects. The answer they offered, notwithstanding variations of considerable political importance, contained a big surprise. For they viewed freedom, not slavery, as the driving force in human progress, moral and material. They based their defense of slavery on a prior defense of freedom, which they identified as the dynamic in a world progress the cause of which they claimed as their own. Freedom, in their view, could not be extended to all, but it could be extended to increasing numbers and could be expected to result in a better life for those who remained subservient. They thereby invoked slavery as a positive force that grounded the social order required to support the freedom necessary for progress. The slaveholders presented themselves to themselves and to the world as the most reliable carriers of the cause of progress in Western civilization, and they presented their social system as the surest and safest model for a worldwide Christendom that sought to continue its forward march.

The slaveholders had no greater success than others, before or since, in defining "progress," but they settled, as most others have, for a common-sense notion of a steady and irreversible advance in the material conditions of life for the masses as well as for the elites. However qualified their recognition of moral progress, the slaveholders displayed deep ambivalence toward that material progress which the overwhelming majority of them saw as inevitable: Literally, they loved and hated it. They embraced it on balance partly because they did see

it as inevitable, and partly because they welcomed the leisure, knowledge, and comfort it brought. Like most traditionalist conservatives in
Europe, they wanted to guide and temper social change, to slow it
down so as to avoid destructive effects. Unlike the traditionalist conservatives in Europe, they thought they had found the means in the
organization of social relations on a slaveholding basis.

In the eyes of foreign critics, by no means all or even most of whom
were abolitionists, the slaveholders of the Old South qualified as
reactionaries who were desperately clinging to a retrogressive social
system in an age of accelerating economic, social, and intellectual
development. Northerners, Britons, continental Europeans, and Latin
Americans shook their heads at the existence of a backward yet politically powerful regional regime embedded in an economically dynamic,
politically radical—by the standards of the day—republic poised to
challenge for world power. The long list of such critics included not
only radicals, democrats, and liberals of all stripes, but many high
Tories, high churchmen, and other conservatives who shared the slaveholders' grave reservations about the vast changes that were occurring
in the wake of the industrial and French revolutions.[2]

Many of these conservatives, to one extent or another, carried into the
nineteenth century the attitudes associated with, say, Samuel Johnson
during the eighteenth. Even most of those who expressed sympathy
for the Confederacy did so because they hated the bourgeois radicalism of the North, valued the conservatism and aristocratic tone of the
South, and considered the race question intractable, not because they
supported slavery in principle. More often than not—the Vatican may
serve as an example—they hoped that the South would find a way to
shed slavery and thereby rid itself of a moral incubus and the principal
encumbrance to the material wellbeing required to sustain national
independence.

The slaveholders saw themselves differently. Southern intellectuals,
political leaders, and ordinary slaveholders, as their numerous diaries
and personal papers attest, regarded themselves as progressive men
and as active participants in the material and moral march of history.
They saw themselves as men who sought an alternate route to modernity.[3] An occasional George Fitzhugh could pronounce himself a
reactionary and proclaim, "We want no new world." But then, in our
own century, from Allen Tate to M. E. Bradford, the best minds who
have contributed to an intellectually powerful southern conservative
tradition have teasingly also pronounced themselves reactionaries and
yet honestly denied any wish to restore some ancient or medieval
regime.[4] It should be enough to recall the significant contributions of
Tate, John Crowe Ransom, and their fellow Agrarians to the modernist
movement in literary criticism. These modern southern conservatives,

like Fitzhugh and the intellectuals of the Old South, have repudiated neither "progress," nor "science," nor "modernity." They have repudiated the cult of progress, scientism, and the moral and political decadence of a modernity run wild.

The dilemma inherent in the slaveholders' contradictory ideas of progress, freedom, and slavery emerges most clearly in the work of Thomas Roderick Dew of Virginia (1802–1846), whose remarkable literary output ranged well beyond his famous review of the debates in the Virginia legislature over emancipation. As president of the College of William and Mary and a professor of history, political economy, moral philosophy, and other subjects, he devoted much of his career to an interpretation of the development of Western civilization. In 1852 a superb exposition of his thought appeared posthumously as *A Digest of the Laws, Customs, Manners and Institutions of the Ancient and Modern Nations*, which even today deserves careful study for its intrinsic value and not merely as a document of southern intellectual history. It may be doubted that his review of the Virginia debates, which constituted a turning point in the proslavery debate, could be fully understood outside the context of the *Digest*, which itself needs to be supplemented by his *Lectures on the Restrictive System* (1829), an able exposition of classical political economy, and his essays on women in history, usury laws, ancient and modern eloquence, and sundry other subjects.[5]

And let it be noted that the *Digest* and the *Restrictive System* consisted, no doubt with some elaboration, of the lectures he delivered to southern youth many of whom went on to positions of leadership in their society. Indeed, some of the most important books of the day grew out of college lectures that had an inestimable influence on the minds of those who would lead southern slave society: Nathaniel Beverley Tucker on political science; George Tucker on political economy; St. George Tucker and Henry St. George Tucker on constitutional law; R. H. Rivers and William A. Smith on moral philosophy; Samuel Henry Dickson on medicine; James Henley Thornwell on theology, ecclesiology, and social theory. That most of these and other authors of college texts expounded a coherent and distinctly proslavery worldview reveals much about the intellectual formation of the youth of the southern elite.[6]

Dew embraced "progress" with as much enthusiasm as any man of his day. If anything, his enthusiasm far exceeded that of other southern writers. Those who rose to prominence after his death especially displayed an ambivalence Dew largely had avoided. He reveled in the advances in learning, economic production, transportation, communications, even in morals, and he recognized the self-generating power of science and technology. Simply put, life was becoming qualitatively better for an ever-increasing number of men and women, and the root of this welcome progress lay in the expansion of individual freedom. Man, released from servitude and superstition, promoted enterprise, innovation, cultural improvement—in a word, progress. Western civilization stood alone among the great civilizations of the world in having found a way to break the cycle of flowering, stagnation, and decay by liberating the individual to pursue his own destiny within a Christian culture that provided a bulwark against the moral degeneration that marked previous epochs. The *Digest* might better have been entitled, in the manner of the English translation of Benedetto Croce's *Storia di libertà*, as *History as the Story of Liberty*. And who knows? Had it been, it might have sold a few more copies and might even be in print today.

For Dew, God provided harmony in nature and gave man the freedom of will to follow its laws. The sinful aspect of man's nature remained a serious impediment, but by devising free institutions he could promote the appropriate ways and means. His progress depended upon his socially secured freedom to pursue his own happiness in tandem with that of others. The necessary social security depended upon property rights, which had to be guaranteed by a state that protects the individual's right to dispose of his own property with as few restrictions as possible. To meet this responsibility the state must be firmly governed by propertied individuals under a constitution that restrains them from using their power at the expense of other propertied individuals; that is, it must be republican, democratic, and egalitarian.

Dew recognized democracy and egalitarianism only in the limited sense that applied to propertied individuals. He had no patience with the sweeping Jeffersonian formulations of the Declaration of Independence. He recognized neither the equality of races nor of individuals beyond that appropriate to the political life of those who owned property or, at least, respected its claims. Moral, intellectual, and material progress depended upon the special talents of superior individuals whose contributions depended on their release from drudgery. The progress of Western civilization has been spurred by the expansion of a freedom made possible by a class stratification that released some men to cultivate their talents. The expansion of the realm of freedom has generated economic and technological progress that has permitted the further expansion of freedom by reducing the amount of labor time necessary for the production of leisure. Freedom has become available to increasing numbers of men, whose combined efforts have resulted in an ever-quickening of progress. The course of progress and of freedom has remained upward and onward.

But could it continue? The laws of political economy, which Dew carefully studied and taught, pointed toward an unfolding tragedy. Dew pondered the ramifications of the Ricardian theories of rent, diminishing returns to agriculture, and the falling rate of profit, and he accepted Malthus's grim law of population. He concluded, as George Tucker did, that sooner or later, probably sooner, the cost of free labor would fall below that of slave labor and thereby inspire a widespread emancipation of slaves, as it had inspired the emancipation of the European serfs at the end of the Middle Ages. In short, the logic of Dew's political economy pointed toward the end of slavery.

George Tucker, unlike Dew, felt no trepidations. He concluded that slavery had no future and counseled the North to end its agitation and let the laws of political economy do their work. Tucker, arguably the ablest political economist in the United States and a man of generally humane temperament, easily swallowed the implications of the scenario: Slavery would disappear because the cost of free labor would fall and the living standards of laborers would sink to a subsistence level under a system that offered little or no protection during the periodic plunges well beneath that level. The great mass of mankind would have to live not only with poverty and brutal exploitation but with the threat of starvation.

Dew gagged. He regarded the outcome as morally unacceptable, as did the proslavery divines, who bemoaned it regularly in sermons, publications, and lectures to the academy and college courses many of them taught.[7] No Christian should be asked to live with it. Perhaps worse, the outcome was politically an invitation to catastrophe. Dew did not believe that the laboring classes would submit. He took the measure of the French Revolution and the even greater radicalism that it opened the floodgates to. His extraordinary chapter on the French Revolution in the *Digest* reads like a prophesy of the working-class rising of June, 1848, in Paris, which he did not live to see. Dew filled the *Digest*, from its opening discussions of ancient history to its closing comparison of the English and French revolutions, with analyses of the social movements he saw as a constant counterpoint to his principal theme of progress through freedom.

Erudite, deeply thoughtful, and temperamentally optimistic, if cautiously so, Dew delineated the dilemma. The very political and intellectual freedom that lay at the heart of all freedom produced and could only be sustained by economic freedom. Dew, who supported laissez-faire and denounced state interference in the market, recognized economic freedom as the special dynamic of material progress. But he feared that the story would end badly wherever the laws of the market were permitted to apply to labor-power wherever free labor prevailed.

At the risk of distorting Dew's subtle and elegantly crafted analysis, we may reduce it to a few propositions. Freedom generated progress, which permitted a vast expansion of freedom. The extension of freedom to the economy, upon which all material progress has rested, meant submission to laws of economic development that condemned the laboring classes to unprecedented exploitation, immiseration, and periodic starvation. At the same time the historical unfolding of those laws required the extension of republican liberties that could not wholly, if at all, be denied to the laborers who had been removed from the security of their servile status and declared free men. Faced with unbearable privations, they would rise, were already rising, in insurrection. Worse, the intellectual freedom essential to all progress, including economic progress, was inexorably extruding every possible kind of utopian and demagogic scheme, which the revolution in communications was carrying to the desperate masses.

Like every other slaveholding intellectual, Dew denied that the laboring classes could consolidate a revolution and maintain power. They could, however, provoke anarchy and deprive the propertied classes of their power to rule. In the event, the capitalists, in particular, would turn to military despots, who would offer a minimum cradle-to-grave security to the laboring masses while protecting the propertied classes. But in so doing, the despots would have to destroy much of the intellectual, political, and economic freedom of the propertied classes. They would therefore undermine progress.

Dew ended by holding up the social system of the South as a model for a future world order. Only slavery or personal servitude in some form could guarantee republican liberties for the propertied, security for the propertyless, and stability for the state and society. Hence Dew faced a two-pronged dilemma, the ramifications of which he did not live to explore fully: Steady progress remained his great ideal; progress depended upon a regime of self-expanding freedom; a regime of self-expanding freedom provoked social conflicts that undermined it; and only the worldwide restoration of slavery could restore social stability and civilized order. What then of the self-generating progress that constituted the glory of Western civilization? The free market, once extended to labor-power, must end in perpetual civil war or the installation of despotism, but progress depended upon the extension of that very free market. Dew believed that the West faced a stark choice: It could continue a headlong progress that threatened to end in social catastrophe; or, it could effect a worldwide restoration of a servitude that threatened the end of civilization's progressive momentum. With a heavy heart he chose slavery, order, and stability.

His optimistic nature may well have led him to hope that material progress would continue, if at a much slower pace—that slavery, which he saw as the surest social foundation of republican liberty, would leave enough room for freedom of thought to do its work. After all, did not the South have a society free enough to participate in the progress of civilization? The problem nonetheless remained: Virtually all the great achievements associated with the extraordinary progress of the modern world had sprung from the free-labor economies, and it did so for reasons he elaborated as well as anyone in his work on political economy.

The dilemma had a second prong. The slave system of the South faced a relentless foe, determined to settle accounts with it. If Dew read the course of Western Europe accurately, the bourgeois countries would soon have to reinstitute their own forms of slavery and thereby end their criticism of the South. But what of the North? Dew saw the North on the same road that Britain and Europe were treading. But its great territorial expansion and peculiarly favorable social conditions promised to forestall the dreaded outcome for centuries. Dew recognized the increasing hostility to slavery in the North and feared a confrontation. If the North, with its dynamic economy and potentially greater military might, forced the issue, the South faced poor prospects. Besides, even if the South did secede successfully, two hostile regimes would face each other across a gun-bristling border. How could republican freedom on either side survive under such conditions?

Dew took unionist ground and counseled the South to resist provocations and eschew rash moves. His argument had many echoes among the unionists of the South. But again, the problem remained. If the North had centuries before it had to face its own social question and reassess its attitude toward southern slavery, it might very well become —indeed was rapidly becoming—more belligerent and determined to force a showdown. How could the South prepare itself economically and militarily without destroying the very fabric of its social system? Military might depended upon that vaunted economic progress which the free-labor system excelled in generating. Dew had an elegant formula: progress through a widening freedom based upon slavery. But as he well knew, if war came, formulaic elegance would not likely prove a match for the big battalions, and, as he himself showed in fleshing out the formula, the big battalions were likely to be on the side of the enemy.

In making the relation of progress to freedom and slavery the centerpiece of his life's work, Dew was focusing on the problem that increasingly was engaging the attention of thoughtful southerners. With few exceptions the lay and clerical intellectuals, in tandem with their fellow slaveholders, accepted both moral and material progress as the primary tendency in human history and as the unfolding of God's providence. But with varying degrees of emphasis they also recognized human conflict as inherent in that tendency, identifying the innate needs and egocentric practices of individuals as simultaneously its source and its social manifestation. In their own way they interpreted social conflict in the manner of a distinguished French historian who identified the cause of seventeenth-century peasant revolts as original sin and man's inability to live according to the laws of God.[8]

At this level of abstraction the slaveholders' view of progress could be accommodated, albeit with some tension, within the mainstream of modern liberal thought and its bourgeois-conservative variant. Even the special attention to racial stratification and the presumed right of a superior race to enslave an inferior offered nothing new or startling. So long as the slaveholders restricted their defense of social stratification, including slavery, to scriptural justification, legal sanction, historical ubiquity, and economic imperatives, they did not break decisively with the mainstream of transatlantic thought, and especially did not break with its bourgeois-conservative right flank. True, by the nineteenth century liberal thought generally condemned slavery on moral as well as economic grounds, but much bourgeois-conservative thought either did not or so qualified the moral condemnation as to draw its political teeth.

The dizzying outcome of the Mexican War, with its enormous territorial annexations, the projection of American power into the Pacific, and the discovery of gold in California, deepened the sense of progress, indeed of rapid progress, as the controlling law of modern civilization. Military considerations emerged as critical. In a world of aggressive nation-states and rival social and political systems, each participant had to keep abreast of the spiraling revolution in technology and economic performance or risk its life. One event after another taught the same lesson. The fate of Russia in the Crimean War, declared Thomas L. Clingman, the powerful politician from North Carolina, teaches the need for railroads and economic development as a matter of military survival.[9] Even the most "reactionary" of southerners—even George Fitzhugh—had to agree. Material progress would continue, whatever the wishes of those who lamented its pernicious effects. For slaveholders, as for the rest of humanity, the message was clear: Keep pace or die.

From self-proclaimed reactionaries like George Fitzhugh to such self-proclaimed progressives of Young America as Edwin DeLeon, proslavery southerners of every ideological hue invoked the rhetoric of human progress, sometimes with excruciating pomposity. Georgia and the South, exclaimed Whig and proslavery militant John M. Berrien in 1838, must progress under the banner "Onward! Onward!" The no less militantly proslavery Joseph A. Lumpkin, Chief Justice of the Supreme Court of Georgia, concurred, insisting that "the standstill doctrine must be forsaken, and forward, forward, be henceforth the watchword." The course of industrial progress cannot be arrested, he argued, and the slave system of the South must accommodate itself or disappear. "My motto," preached the Reverend Abednego Stephens of Nashville, "is—Upward—Onward!"[10]

Only a bit less flamboyantly, the famed oceanographer Matthew F. Maury of Virginia wrote Senator W. A. Graham of North Carolina in 1850, "Improvement and decay are alternatives. Nothing in the physical world is permitted to be in a state of rest and preservation too. When progress ceases, ruin follows. The moral world is governed by the same iron rule. Upward and onward, or downward and backward are the conditions which it imposes upon all individuals, societies, and institutions." Maury agreed with those who, like Rep. John H. Savage of Tennessee, viewed slavery as an essential element in the progress not only of the South but of the United States and the world. "With the possession of slaves," Savage told the House of Representatives in 1850, "the progress of this country has been onward and upward, with a power so mighty and a flight so rapid as to leave no doubt upon my mind but that the approving smiles of Providence have rested upon us." Calls to bold action normally invoked such language. Thus Francis W. Pickens, the wartime governor of South Carolina, exhorted in 1860: "You are obliged to go forward. You must increase, and the moment you stand still, it will be the law of your destiny to decay and die."[11]

More soberly, Frederick Adolphus Porcher took up the cudgels for a substantial number of southern intellectuals when he argued the modernist side of the regional version of The Battle of the Books. Writing in *Southern Quarterly Review* in 1852, Porcher, a prominent low-country planter who taught Belles Lettres at the College of Charleston, denounced those who wallowed in the glories of antiquity and eschewed those of the modern age. He expressed disgust at Hiram Powers's much admired statue of Calhoun in a Roman toga: "We asked for our statesman, and have received a Roman Senator. We asked for the citizen of the nineteenth century, and have received a specimen of the antique. We asked for our Calhoun, the Carolina Planter, and have received an elaborately carved stone." True conservatives, he insisted, want to guide change, not stifle it. "The great men of this world are they who live in advance of their age, and impress their mighty spirit upon that which succeeds them."[12]

Those who have read the slaveholders' voluminous diaries, letters, and personal papers must surely be struck by their celebration of the southern people as modern, forward-looking men and women, but also by their alarm at a world that was changing too fast and not entirely for the better. The alarm even carried into the pages of *DeBow's Review*, the leading organ of the celebrants of progress, whose upward-and-onward rhetoric could not disguise the deep uneasiness that pervaded all ranks of society. In particular, a belief in God and the deep piety that characterized many of the slaveholders—that "older religiousness of the South," as Richard Weaver called it—made them simultaneously hopeful, skeptical, and fearful that the modern world would suffer the fate of Sodom at the hands of the God of Wrath.[13]

The musings of Everard Green Baker, a planter of Panola, Mississippi, had parallels across the South. An admirer of Dr. Johnson, as many southerners were, he approvingly quoted a letter to Mrs. Thrale from the Hebrides, dutifully citing the appropriate passage in Boswell's *Life*. "Life," Dr. Johnson had written, "to be worthy of a rational being, must be always in progression, we must purpose to do more or better than in times past." Some months later Baker formulated his own view on the sinful nature of man: "strong & aspiring seeking to rise above the terrestrial greatness of all former beings like itself, & striving with that subtle intellect to peer into things which the wisdom of the great Creator has seen fit to shut out from mortals. . . ."[14]

Nothing in Baker's papers suggests that he saw a contradiction between the two thoughts he entered in his diary or that he fretted over the tension. His Christianity, as expounded by the southern divines and integrated into the worldview of his community, taught him that the tension would prove creative so long as southern society adhered to the laws of God. The enemy was not progress, which was God's gift to his beloved children, but the cult of progress, which, as Baker observed, strove to project man to the center of the universe and to make man, not God, the measure of all things. Baker would surely have understood the message intended by the Maryland Institute in 1857, when it opened a series of lectures with the theme, "Slowness as a Law of Progress."[15] . . .

Even George Fitzhugh agreed that the last two thousand years had exhibited "an aggregate of improvement." He hailed the slave South as a "bulwark against innovation and revolution"—"the sheet anchor of our institutions, which the restless and dissatisfied North would soon overturn, if left to govern alone." Yet in the very same article he complained, "Tide-water old fogyism retains its dogged do-nothing spirit." The conservative Virginia tidewater, he observed, opposed "railroads, canals, daily mails, and other modern innovations."[16] Fitzhugh especially admired Governor Henry Wise for his progressive spirit and dedicated *Cannibals All!* to him.

As J. D. B. DeBow and others complained, Fitzhugh loved paradoxes, loved to shock, loved to put-on-the-dog. But he also took himself seriously and meant to instruct. The intrinsically paradoxical nature of progress constituted his subject. "All civilization," he wrote, "consists in the successful pursuits of the mechanic arts. The country is most civilized which most excels in them." None of which prevented Fitzhugh from warning that the extension of railroads and other such wonders would reduce Virginia to the status of Ireland or the

West Indies unless subjected to a wise, conservative regulation that controlled them in the interests of the prevailing slave society.[17]

For Fitzhugh, as for Everard Green Baker, material progress carried the promise of a better life, and, besides, it was inevitable. At issue was its rate and especially its specific content, for the dizzying rate made possible by the self-revolutionizing social and economic system of the transatlantic world threatened to unravel the fabric of civilization. Hence Fitzhugh's infuriatingly paradoxical rhetoric: "Slavery has truly become aggressive, ingressive, and progressive. It is the most distinguishing phenomenon of the reactionary conservative movement of our day." And again: "Let us show to the world that we, slaveholders, are the only conservatives; ready to lead a salutary reaction in morals, religion, and government; that we propose not to govern society less, but to govern it more."[18]

Few in the South could accept Fitzhugh's demand for increased state power, although many more might have if they had had the patience to follow his dialectics and smile at his irony. But then, sophisticated intellectuals and the less reflective country folk may well have intuitively espied Fitzhugh's backing-and-filling. Most southerners seem to have taken for granted that progress depended precisely on the individual freedom they claimed for themselves and agreed that only slavery could discipline individual freedom and thereby render progress morally wholesome and socially safe. But at that very moment transatlantic society, by dispensing with slavery and extending freedom to the laboring classes, was achieving unprecedented progress without the moral and social safeguards. Could, in fact, a modern slave society compete with such a rival in the all-out struggle that increasing numbers saw as just beyond the horizon?

As slave society slowly evolved from its origins in the seventeenth century to its flowering in the nineteenth, its statesmen, politicians, educators, jurists, ministers, and men of letters—in short, its political class and intelligentsia—increasingly recognized the challenge and continued to hope that it could meet the expected test of strength. Articulating the world view of the slaveholding class and, if more problematically, of the yeomanry and the middle classes of the towns, this impressive intelligentsia struggled to reconcile the claims of freedom and the legitimacy of slavery, and to find in their organic social relations a blueprint for ordered progress. On the relation of slavery to individual freedom and to moral and material progress, as on other matters of capital importance, a consensus emerged, notwithstanding its being wracked by the tensions, ambiguities, and quarrels that mark every worldview and social consensus.

In this case the tensions, ambiguities, and quarrels had a special root and quality that derived from a need to reconcile slavery with both freedom and progress. Ultimately, that reconciliation proved impossible, and much of the intellectual, ideological, and political warfare that constantly threatened to disrupt the consensus and unravel the worldview stemmed directly from its impossibility. At the heart of the boldest and most widely embraced of the projected solutions lay explosive contradictions that at last exposed a political dilemma and provoked a headlong plunge into uncharted and forbidding waters.

The contradictions especially signaled the southern intellectuals' determination to claim the Western tradition while criticizing the direction it was taking in Europe and the North, and while advancing their own vision of a healthy modernity. Every talented southern thinker proposed his own solution. The nature of moral progress and of the moral dimension of material progress—distinct if related issues— loomed large at the outset. Virtually all insisted that freedom and moral progress had to be understood not simply as the product of recent political developments, but as rooted in Christianity. The advent of Christianity had propelled the moral progress of mankind, and the spirit and doctrines of Christianity could be read backward in time to demonstrate moral tendencies in pre-Christian civilizations, most notably the Greek. The erudite even saw God's providence in such non-Western and non-Christian civilizations as those of China and India. How else, after all, should Protestants interpret the advent and spread of Christianity, the Reformation, and the missionary work that was going forward in Asia and Africa?

In this perspective, recent material progress was spreading moral progress, or so they interpreted the growth of the Christian missions to heathen lands. The wonders of the industrial revolution were having an especially powerful effect in the innovations in transportation and communications, which were carrying the Word of God to the four corners of the earth. In the words of the Reverend David F. Bittle of St. Michael's Lutheran Church in Rockingham County, Virginia, during the 1830s, and later president of Roanoke College, "As the sciences advance, literature becomes universal, governments become more tolerant and improvements in the arts are continually making—is it not reasonable to suppose the facilities for propagating the cause of the redeemer will be increased and [that] new measures will hence constantly arise?"[19] Southerners, like northerners, generally identified the United States as the modern age's divinely favored nation and saw its rapid rise toward world power as evidence of its Christian mission. That rise revealed God's anointing of a chosen and Christian people. The freedom of the individual, the preachers cried out in unison, was Christ's gift to mankind. The doctrine of the immortality of the soul in the light of the Atonement made man a responsible moral agent and released his energies to perfect his being.[20]

The concept of moral progress nonetheless remained troubling. "The progress of Christianity," Albert Taylor Bledsoe reiterated after the war, "is the progress of man."[21] But if sin and depravity plagued mankind, as Bledsoe believed, then men might not progress to the point at which most, much less all, would be saved. The predestinarian Calvinists hardly expected any such progress, and even the Arminians entertained only the fragile hope that most would heed the call of Jesus. Together, Calvinists and Arminians, surveying the direction of events in the tumultuous nineteenth century, viewed the course of Western civilization with concern.[22]

The Rev. Dr. James Henley Thornwell, the most intellectually powerful of the southern divines, spoke for those of all denominations when he addressed the churches of the world in the wake of secession. The history of society, he wrote, serves as "the moral school of humanity," for God is in history and assigns each man his place.[23] In 1858, his fellow Presbyterian, the Reverend George D. Armstrong, pastor at Norfolk, Virginia, had struck a more somber note, but, then, he did not, at that moment, have to undertake the delicate political responsibility that fell to Thornwell under gathering war clouds. Reflecting on the consequences of original sin and the "sickness" of man, Armstrong wrote in *The Theology of Christian Experience*, "History, is to a very large extent, but a record of human crime." History reveals human nature as wracked by sin and beyond reformation through any philosophy: "Even where we have a record of civil or political reform, it usually presents itself baptized in blood."[24] Yet Armstrong wrote his book, as he wrote *The Christian Doctrine of Slavery*, to uplift humanity, not to denigrate it. The salvation of souls signaled by the spread of Christianity alone measured moral progress. Thornwell would not have disagreed. Armstrong never denied the fact, indeed the inevitability, of material progress, but, like Thornwell, he noted that it always and everywhere depended upon the servile labor of the great mass of mankind.

William F. Hutson of South Carolina expressed the ambivalence toward moral progress as well as anyone. As revolution was setting Europe afire in 1848, he wrote: "The history of the last seventy years has been a series of startling changes, and at the same time, of precocious and hot house growth, in art, science and politics—Europe, for the most part, has been a battle field; revolution has followed revolution so fast, that steam presses can hardly chronicle the shifting lines of states." Art and science, he continued, have rendered space "a mere mathematical term," and civilization has almost reached the refinements of ancient Rome. But toward what end? "What is the advantage we possess over the past? To the rich, have been added comforts, and appliances unknown to our fathers; but are the mass better fed?—better clothed?—happier?—more contented?—even freer?" Hutson saw an unfolding social crisis in Europe, which the United States could not long avoid. As for the qualitative dimension of moral progress, he summed up the dominant southern attitude: "In religion and morals, we doubt all improvements, not known to certain fishermen who lived eighteen hundred years ago."[25] Henry William Ravenel of South Carolina, a respected botanist and unionist, offered reflections upon the secessionist hysteria of 1861 that, ironically, a host of secessionists might easily have agreed with while drawing opposite political conclusions:

> What a commentary does this spectacle afford upon the boasted civilization of the nineteenth century! It is too sad proof that with all the progress made in the *Arts* and *Sciences*—with all the writings of learned men upon *Civil Liberty*, and *Political Rights*—upon *Moral and Intellectual Philosophy*—with all the great *improvements* in *manufactures* and *material prosperity*, mankind are no better now than at any previous time—the evil passions of our fallen state are just as prominent and as easily brought into exercise as in those earlier times that we, in our self-sufficiency have called the *dark ages*. Nations like individuals become arrogant with power, and Might becomes Right. Egypt, Babylon, Ninevah, Persia, Rome have all learned the lesson, but we cannot profit by their example. We are working out our destiny. Deo duce.[26]

For Ravenel, as for Hutson, any rash assumptions about moral progress would have to contend with the inescapable evidence of the society about them: If the quality of moral life was the standard, then progress was hard to find. The southern divines, who did their best to discourage the hubris that claimed qualitative moral progress, evinced a strong, if little noticed, millennialism, although a millennialism largely shorn of the tendency to engage the church in campaigns for social reform. Methodists joined their Calvinist brethren in a literal reading of *The Revelation of St. John the Divine* and foresaw a Second Coming accompanied by social cataclysm and a battle of Armageddon. The southern divines' interpretations of the future varied, but they largely shared a sense of God's imminent intervention to purify a sinful world.[27]

The revolutionary upheavals in Europe, which began with the great revolution of 1789 and surged in 1830 and especially 1848, seized their imaginations. Individual divines differed as to which of the seals of *Revelation* was being opened, but they agreed that the Terror of 1793 and the June Days of 1848 marked the early stages of the prophesied cataclysm. In the wake of the working-class rising in Paris in 1848 and the radical turn in the European revolutions, the sober and politically sensitive Thornwell went scurrying back to *Revelation*, convinced that he was seeing the unfolding of its great prophecy.[28] In 1850 the *Tennessee Baptist* proclaimed that the European revolutions had ushered in the prophesied final battle of the nations. The Methodist Samuel Davies Baldwin, in his popular books *Armageddon* and *Dominion* and in extensive lecture tours with his colleague F. E. Pitt, interpreted the revolutions of 1848 as the "great earthquake" (*Revelation*, 16:18) that would usher in the final struggle. He predicted that the imminent battle of Armageddon would take place in the Mississippi Valley, not the Middle East, and related the expected triumph of American armies over European to the Second Coming of Christ.[29]

Not much imagination was required to translate this thinking into an interpretation of the slaveholders' confrontation with abolitionism as a war of Christ against Antichrist. Especially after the Mexican War, Thornwell and the most learned, temperate, and unionist of the southern divines, as well as the country preachers, repeatedly proclaimed the confrontation with abolitionism as one between a Christian people and the Antichrist. Yet before the War southern millennialism evinced a pronounced cheerfulness that would be replaced after Appomattox by the desperate hope that God would yet deliver his chosen southern people in a worldwide catastrophe. So long as the power of the Christian slaveholders waxed and especially as the prospects of a great new Christian southern nation loomed, the divines could see God's goodness manifested in the material and moral progress of Western civilization.

In that cheerful spirit the Reverend Benjamin Morgan Palmer of Charleston, uncle of a more eminent namesake, cried out in 1816, in a sermon aptly entitled "The Signs of the Times": "It seems as if everything [is] conspiring together in the moral and religious world and a multitude of things in the political world to introduce a new and better state."[30] In subsequent years the principal spokesmen of all the denominations read the signs of the times as a process of moral regeneration and material advancement that would hasten the millennium.

The study of history reinforced the prophecies of Scripture. Southern colleges encouraged the reading of d'Aubigné's history of the Reformation, which enjoyed wide circulation among the slaveholders and often turned up in their private libraries and accounts of the books they were reading. They read it as evidence of the progress of both Christianity and of social and political order.[31] Even the great history of the fall of the Roman Empire by the religious skeptic Edward Gibbon became popular in the South, where it was read for moral instruction despite its denigration of Christianity. For did not the barbarian invasions and the rise of Islam reveal the opening of the Seven Seals?[32]

Here too, the slaveholders' ambivalence toward material progress and the political dilemma it implied became apparent. As Christians, they saw moral progress in history in the wake of the "good news" of Jesus, however much one generation of divines after another stressed the inherent sinfulness of men, warned against backsliding, and thundered about God's wrath against a world too much of which resisted the message. And never had the good news spread so rapidly as at that very moment, carried by missionaries on the wings of a breathtaking revolution in transportation and communications and backed up by unprecedented military might. Yet that very industrial revolution was encouraging, with a no less unprecedented ferocity, a cult of scientism and an accompanying infidelity. New doctrines dared to raise man to the place reserved for God and thereby threatened moral decay and assaulted church and state, divinely ordained family and social relations, and God Himself.

Caveats notwithstanding, the slaveholders did place great weight on the quantitative progress of morality and did see material progress as its handmaiden. They thus linked Protestant Christianity to economic liberalism and political republicanism, much as a host of bourgeois liberals did. But in the slaveholders' perspective, slavery or, more precisely, the several forms of personal servitude, provided the necessary foundation for a society that could sustain a Christian social order and guarantee individual freedom for those who deserved and were competent to wield it.[33] They acknowledged that the greater the extent to which the individual found himself free to pursue his own destiny, the greater his contribution to the economic progress on which the pace, although not the content, of moral progress depended. And in this spirit they joined their liberal adversaries at home and abroad in embracing the claims of freedom as developed in classical political economy as well as in the emerging arguments for freedom of thought.

The southerners' warm praise of the benefits of freedom and progress have led many able historians, reviewing these and other matters, to attribute to the slaveholders a basically bourgeois worldview to which they merely tacked on an opportunistic defense of slave property and racial stratification. These historians have found irresistible the invitation to conflate the slaveholders' searing ambivalence with the kind of moral objections to the social devastation attendant upon unregulated capitalist development that were being heard in London, Paris, New York, and Boston, as well as in Charlottesville and Williamsburg, Columbia and Charleston, Huntsville and Mobile. They err, for the slaveholders, unlike conservatives in the North and abroad, explicitly identified the free-labor system itself as the source of the moral evils and forged a critique that struck at its heart.[34] With varying degrees of boldness, one after another came to view the freedom of labor as a brutal fiction that undermined the propertied classes' sense of responsibility for the moral and material welfare of society.

Despite similarities, only some of the important features of the reigning sensibility and worldview of the Old South may be assimilated to the broad current of conservatism that acted as a counterpoint to the increasingly dominant liberalism of the transatlantic world. In the North, in Britain, and most strikingly on the Continent, conservatives reacted forcefully against the high social costs of the industrial revolution, against radical-democratic and egalitarian social and political creeds, against secularization and the no less dangerous emergence of liberal theologies, and against the insidious pressures toward repudiation of church and family, authority and hierarchy, order and tradition. But for most, even their harshest critiques of the consequences of progress and individual freedom remained grounded in a fundamental acceptance of the reigning capitalist socioeconomic system. Some European and northern conservatives did assail capitalism itself, but they did so as isolated intellectuals who had been stripped of the social base on which the slaveholders stood.

The great divergence of southern thought from northern and transatlantic bourgeois thought, including its bourgeois-conservative variant, appeared in the confrontation with the specific nature of freedom and its implications for the present and future, most significantly the condition of laborers. Even the advocates of the extreme proslavery argument—of slavery as the natural and proper condition of all labor, regardless of race—understood freedom to entail a good deal more than their own claims to freedom as a privileged and preferred status. They acknowledged individual freedom as the motor force of a providential and potentially good historical progress. They simultaneously insisted that slavery afforded the best foundation for a free society.

The slaveholders' reaction against the ravaging consequences of bourgeois social relations had its counterparts in the radical-democratic and socialist onslaught of the Left and the nostalgia, lament, and harsh political response of the traditionalist Right, both of which condemned the moral irresponsibility and political corruption of the bourgeoisie. Unlike the radical democrats and socialists but very much like both traditionalist and bourgeois conservatives, the slaveholders feared the intrusion of the lower classes into politics and loathed the egalitarian doctrines that made it possible. Even when the slaveholders themselves invoked egalitarian rhetoric, as they loved to do at every Fourth of July barbecue, they implicitly, and often explicitly, suggested that equality and democracy could not be sustained outside a class-stratified system or its functional racial equivalent.

Thus at a first but deceptive glance, every southern denunciation of political radicalism, infidelity, and moral decay had its northern equivalent. To settle for a single illustration, the staunchly conservative Old School Presbyterian divines of both North and South, most notably Charles Hodge of Princeton, New Jersey, and James Henley Thornwell of Columbia, South Carolina, agreed on many of the important political and social, as well as theological and ecclesiastical, issues of the day. Yet, as the fierce battles between Hodge and Thornwell over church polity suggest, the issues on which they finally fell out exposed a widening and unbridgeable chasm in theology, worldview, and ultimately in sectional politics.

The break of southern conservativism away from northern in theology and ecclesiology accompanied the break in political theory. Partly as a reflection of a growing theological and ecclesiastical rift, the social conservatism of the southern divines diverged sharply from that of the northern divines. The theological, ecclesiastical, and sociopolitical conservatives of the North were steadily retreating in the face of the rise of Unitarianism in New England and of assorted forms of liberalism in the principal denominations. Meanwhile, orthodoxy continued to hold sway in the South.

The southern churches slowly drifted apart from the northern over theology and ecclesiology and by no means only over slavery, for the northern churches were moving, if haltingly and in intense internal struggle, toward more liberal positions on original sin, human depravity, and the role of the laity. For immediate purposes, that larger sectional cleavage, notwithstanding its enormous importance, may be left aside. More directly relevant and illuminating was the growing estrangement of the theologically orthodox and socially conservative southerners from those northern conservatives who were trying to arrest the liberal trend in their own churches. The fierce polemics that pit James Henley Thornwell, "the Calhoun of the Church," as he was called, against Charles Hodge, doyen of the Old School conservative Presbyterians of the North, may be taken as paradigmatic of the sectionally based antagonisms that were developing within the orthodox and conservative wings of most denominations.[35]

The issues concerned theology and ecclesiology first and foremost and cannot be reduced to a projected ideological reflex of sociopolitical differences. Nor was the slavery question, in its direct political manifestation, the problem, for the northern conservatives condemned the abolitionists, opposed intervention in southern affairs, defended southern state rights, and, in general, resolutely insisted that the church must render unto Caesar that which is Caesar's. Theologically, they conceded the main southern argument that the Bible sanctioned slavery, which therefore could not be condemned as sinful, as *malum in se*. Slavery, in their view, was strictly a civil, a political, question on which the church could take no position.

In broader perspective, the slavery question did lie at the root of the growing sectional antagonism within the conservative clerical fold. Hodge provides a quintessential example. He denied the sinfulness of slavery and defended southern rights so staunchly that E. N. Elliott published his views in *Cotton Is King and Pro-Slavery Arguments*, alongside those of Bledsoe, Harper, Hammond, and other southern luminaries.[36] The conservative divines, North and South, agreed that infidelity and social and political radicalism were on the ascendant that the barbarians were at the gates. They agreed that abolitionism was a Trojan horse for all other detestable isms. They agreed that the fate of slavery should be left to the discretion of the white people of the South. They agreed on more. But they disagreed radically on the nature of a proper Christian social order and of the place of slavery within it.

The argument of the southern divines against the northern conservative divines took many forms, with variations and nuances, and it exhibited different degrees of political tartness. In the end it reduced to one point that brooked no compromise. And that point was made by the outstanding figures in all denominations: by Thornwell, Palmer, Adger, Armstrong, Dabney, Lyon, Ross, among the Presbyterians; by Smith, Brownlow, Pierce, Longstreet, Rivers, among the Methodists; by Stringfellow, Warren, Furman, among the Baptists; by others in virtually every denomination, including Unitarians like Theodore Clapp.

The point came to this: You northern conservatives share our revulsion against growing infidelity and secularism, against the rapid extension of the heresies of liberal theology, against the social and political abominations of egalitarianism and popular democracy, against the mounting assault on the family and upon the very principle of authority. You share our alarm at the growing popularity of the perverse doctrines of Enlightenment radicalism and the French Revolution—the doctrines of Voltaire, Rousseau, Paine. You share our fears for the fate of Western civilization. Yet you fail to identify the root of this massive theological, ecclesiastical, social, and political offensive against Christianity and the social order: the system of free labor that breeds egotism and extols personal license at the expense of all God-ordained authority. You fail to see that only the restoration of some form of personal servitude can arrest the moral decay of society. Indeed, you mindlessly celebrate free labor as a model and urge us to adopt it. In truth, the South stands virtually alone in the transatlantic world as a bastion of Christian social order because it rests upon a Christian social system. If, as you say, the world needs a social and moral order at once progressive yet conservative, dynamic yet regulated, republican yet immune to democratic demagogy, then our system, not yours, must be looked to as a model.

Thus the southern divines masterfully combined theological and socioeconomic arguments. Theologically, Calvinists and Arminians alike took a hard line on original sin and the depravity of man at a time when the mainstream churches of the North were retreating into rosier views of human nature and winning astonishing doctrinal concessions even from most northerners who claimed to be orthodox. The southerners developed an interdenominational social theory that stressed obedience to constituted authority, beginning with that of the male head of family and household, and they especially stressed the ubiquity and necessity of class stratification. At the same time they insisted, in a way completely different from that of northern conservatives, upon the moral duty of Christians to be their brothers' keepers.

Rejecting the kind of social reformism that was becoming popular in the North even among many conservatives, the southern divines insisted upon the solemn duty of the privileged classes to assume direct, personal responsibility for those whose labor supported society. Their rhetoric of family values had its northern equivalent, but with a decisive difference. In southern doctrine the family meant the extended household, defined to include "servants"—dependent laborers. The familiar expression, "my family, white and black," far from being a propagandistic ploy, expressed the essence of a worldview. For good reason Abraham loomed as the principal Old Testament figure among the slaveholders, much as Moses did among the slaves. Abraham was, in their oft-expressed view, simultaneously a great slaveholder and God's favored patriarch of a household that included his many slaves.[37]

From theology the southern divines frequently passed to political economy, which they readily invoked in their books and sermons and in their lectures to the college classes in Moral Philosophy. And with a handful of exceptions, the divines taught the generally required courses in Moral Philosophy. They accepted the principles of classical political economy, much as their northern counterparts did, but they broke decisively in their attitude toward the free-labor system itself. They refused to accept the outcome of Ricardian theories of rent, profit, wages and capital accumulation and Malthusian theory of population, which separately and together predicted the steady immiseration of the laboring classes. They were as ready as the northerners to accept the "laws" of political economy as operative in the market, but, an occasional George Tucker notwithstanding, they did not agree that immiseration exceeded the control of man. Jesus had said that the poor we would always have with us; he did not say that we ought to tolerate starvation and brutality. The system itself, after all, could be changed.

The southern divines' understanding of Christianity forbade a fatalistic capitulation to such monstrous laws and instead pointed them toward an alternate social system that functioned with more humane laws of its own. Sounding like Dew but with a greater sense of urgency,

Thornwell and Armstrong, among others, insisted that the very horror of the laws of political economy could only end in proletarian revolution, anarchy, and a collapse into despotism unless the bourgeois societies assumed responsibility for their laborers through some form of "Christian slavery."

Joseph LeConte, one of the South's most distinguished scientists, summed up the argument in a lecture to the senior class of South Carolina College. A devout Presbyterian, he spoke primarily in secular accents, but the publication of his lecture in the prestigious *Southern Presbyterian Review* should occasion no surprise. By the 1850s such articles by both divines and laymen were readily receiving sanction in the leading religious journals. LeConte argued that sociology must be made scientific through the study of the natural sciences and the use of the comparative method in the study of human institutions. And he concluded:

> No one, I think, who has thoroughly grasped the great laws of development, or practised the method of comparison, will find any difficulty in perceiving that free competition in labor is necessarily a transition state; that, as a permanent condition, it is necessarily a failure; and that the alternative must eventually be between slavery and some form of organized labor, circumstances, perhaps beyond our control, determining which of these will prevail in different countries.[38]

The arguments were often ingenious and the presentations masterly, but the dilemma constantly resurfaced. Notwithstanding all caveats, qualifications, and ambivalence, the slaveholders, lay and clerical, sophisticated and simple, did want to preserve freedom, conventionally if ambiguously defined, and they did want to see progress continue. They extolled freedom as the source of progress. Thus, the Reverend William A. Scott of New Orleans wrote in 1851, "The history of Liberty—the history of the origin, rise, progress, conflicts, triumph and destiny of liberty—the history of men who have acquired their freedom—the history of those great movements in the world by which Liberty has been established, diffused, and perpetuated, is yet to be written."[39] Yet they insisted upon slavery as the only safe, secure, indeed Christian foundation for freedom, while they could not deny that the material progress they celebrated flowed from the performance of the societies that were not merely expanding freedom but eradicating slavery. Since those societies, in the view of American slaveholders as well as of European socialists, were failing and doomed to extinction; since for the slaveholders socialism was neither desirable nor possible; since some form of personal slavery would soon be the order of the day in

Europe—how could progress be sustained? And more ominously, how could the slave South, notwithstanding its claims to moral superiority, stand against an aggressive North that had all the material advantages made possible by an unbridled free economy?

NOTES

1 Edmund Morgan, *American Slavery, American Freedom: The Ordeal of Colonial Virginia* (New York, 1975); David Brion Davis, *Slavery and Human Progress* (New York, 1984). . . .

2 For the slaveholders' view of the French revolution, compared with the view of northern and British conservatives, see Elizabeth Fox-Genovese and Eugene D. Genovese, "Political Virtue and the Lesson of the French Revolution: The View from the Slaveholding South," in Ronald Matthews, ed., *Virtue, Commerce and Corruption* (Lehigh, Penn., 1992).

3 Michael O'Brien has been exploring this theme in his several works. See esp. his remarks in the introduction to O'Brien, ed., *All Clever Men, Who Make Their Way: Critical Discourse in the Old South* (Fayetteville, Ark., 1982), 24–25.

4 Consider such titles as Allen Tate, *Reactionary Essays on Poetry and Ideas* (New York, 1936); and M. E. Bradford, *The Reactionary Imperative: Essays Literary & Political* (Peru, Ill., 1990).

5 For an elaboration of the following discussion and the appropriate references see Eugene D. Genovese, *Western Civilization through Slaveholding Eyes: The Social and Historical Thought of Thomas Roderick Dew* (New Orleans, 1986). . . .

6 Nathaniel Beverley Tucker, *A Series of Lectures on the Science of Government* . . . (Philadelphia, 1845); St. George Tucker, *Blackstone's Commentaries, With Notes of Reference* . . . (5 vols.; Philadelphia, 1803); Henry St. George Tucker, *Blackstone's Commentaries for the Use of Students* (Winchester, Va., 1826); *Commentaries on the Laws of Virginia* . . . (Winchester, Va., 1831); *A Few Lectures on Natural Law* (Charlottesville, Va., 1844); *Lectures on Government* (Charlottesville. Va., 1844); *Lectures on Constitutional Law* . . . (Richmond, 1843); R. H. Rivers, *Elements of Moral Philosophy* (Nashville, Tenn., 1859); William A. Smith, *Lectures on the Philosophy and Practice of Slavery* . . . (Nashville, Tenn., 1856); James H. Thornwell, *Discourses on Truth* . . . (New York, 1855).

7 Eugene D. Genovese and Elizabeth Fox-Genovese, "The Social Thought of the Antebellum Southern Divines," in Winifred B. Moore, Jr., and Joseph F. Tripp, eds., *Looking South: Chapters in the History of an American Region* (New York, 1989), 31–40; and "The Divine Sanction of Social Order: Religious Foundations of the Southern Slaveholders' World View, *Journal of the American Academy of Religion*, 55 (1987), 211–233. . . .

8 Roland Mousnier, *Peasant Uprisings in Seventeenth-Century France, Russia, and China* (New York, 1970), 306.

9 Thomas L. Clingman, *Selections from the Speeches ad Writings of Hon. Thomas Clingman* . . . (Raleigh, 1877), 369.

10 John M. Berrien quoted in Stephen F. Miller, *The Bench and Bar Georgia: Memoirs and Sketches* (2 vols.; Philadelphia, 1858), I, 54; Joseph H. Lumpkin, "Industrial Regeneration of the South," *DeBow's Review*, n.s., 5 (1852), 43; Rev. A. Stephens, *Address before the Academic Society of Nashville University* . . . (Nashville, Tenn., 1938), 25.

11 Matthew F. Maury to W. A. Graham, Oct. 7, 1850, in J. G. deRoulhac Hamilton

and Max R. Williams, Jr., eds., *The Papers of William Alexander Graham* (7 vols.; Raleigh. N.C., 1957–1984); III, 409; Savage quoted in Arthur Alphonse Ekirch, *The Idea of Progress in America, 1815–1860* (New York, 1944), 236; Pickens quoted in William W. Freehling, *The Road to Disunion: Secessionists at Bay, 1776–1854* (New York, 1990), 461.

12 Frederick Adolphus Porcher, "Modern Art," in O'Brien, ed., *All Clever Men*, 312–336.

13 Richard M. Weaver, "The Older Religiousness of the South," in George M. Curtus III and James J. Thompson, Jr., eds., *The Southern Essays of Richard M. Weaver* (Indianapolis, 1987), 14–27. See also Eugene D. Genovese and Elizabeth Fox-Genovese, "The Religious Foundations of Southern Slave Society," in Numan V. Bartley, ed., *The Evolution of Southern Culture* (Athens, Ga., 1988), 14–27.

14 Everard Green Baker Diary, July 22, 1858, and March 13, 1859, in the Southern Historical Collection of the University of North Carolina [SHC].

15 Patricia C. Click, *The Spirit of the Times: Amusements in Nineteenth-Century Baltimore, Norfolk, and Richmond* (Charlottesville, 1989), 30.

16 George Fitzhugh, "The Valleys of Virginia—the Rappahannock," *DeBow's Review*, 26 (March 1819), 275.

17 Fitzhugh, "Make Home Attractive," *DeBow's Review*, 28 (June 1860), 625.

18 Fitzhugh, "Slavery Aggressions," *DeBow's Review*, 28 (Feb. 1860), 133, 138.

19 Quoted in Robert M. Calhoon, *Evangelicals and Conservatives in the Early South, 1740–1861* (Columbia, 1988).

20 Stephen Elliott, the eminent bishop of the Protestant Episcopal Church of Georgia, expressed these ideas and tensions as well as anyone. See *Sermons by the Right Reverend Stephen Elliott* . . . (New York, 1867), xii, 1–10, 44, 47, 76–80, 117–127.

21 Quoted in John Joyce Bennett, "Albert Taylor Bledsoe: Social and Religious Controversialist of the Old South" (Ph.D. diss., Duke University, 1972), 49.

22 . . . even the orthodox Calvinists of the Presbyterian Old School interpreted the doctrines of atonement, sanctification, and justification in a manner consistent with the specifically political reading under discussion.

23 John B. Adger and John L. Girardeau, eds., *The Collected Writings of James Henry Thornwell* (4 vols.; Richmond, Va., 1871–1873), IV, 461.

24 George D. Armstrong, *The Theology of Christian Experience* . . . (New York, 1858), 161–162. . . .

25 William F. Hutson, "The History of the Girondists, or Personal Memoirs of the Patriots of the French Revolution," *Southern Presbyterian Review*, 2 (1848), 398; "Fictitious Literature," ibid., 1 (1847), 78.

26 Arney Robinson Chiles, ed., *The Private Journal of Henry William Ravenel, 1859–1887* (Columbia, 1947), 67.

27 On southern millennialism see esp. Jack P. Maddex, Jr. "Proslavery Millennialism: Social Eschatology in Antebellum Southern Calvinism," *American Quarterly*, 3 1 (1979), 46–68; . . . Pamela Elwyn Thomas Colbenson, "Millennial Thought among Southern Evangelicals, 1830–1860" (Ph.D. diss., Georgia State University, 1980), esp. 49, 70–71.

28 Thornwell to Matthew J. Williams, July 17, 1848, in B[enjamin] M. Palmer, *The Life and Letters of James Henry Thornwell* (Richmond, 1875), 309–311.

29 Samuel Davies Baldwin, *Ameggedon; or, The United States in Prophesy* (Nashville, Tenn., 1845); *Dominion; Or, the Unity and Trinity of the Human Race* . . . (Nashville, 1858); Colbenson, "Millennial Thought," esp. 1, 12–14, 28, 49, 70–75, and 137 for the quotation from the *Tennessee Baptist*.

30 Quoted in Colbenson, "Millennial Thought," 1.
31 D'Aubigné was taught in southern seminaries and was introduced to students in the colleges. References turn up in the private papers of slaveholders across the South. . . .
32 For a striking illustration see Bishop Elliott's sermon [in] Elliott, *Sermons*, 44.
33 For elaborations see Eugene D. Genovese, *"Slavery Ordained of God": The Southern Slaveholders' View of Biblical History and Modern Politics* (Gettysburg, Pa., 1985); Genovese and Fox-Genovese, "Social Thought of the Antebellum Southern Divines."
34 Elaboration and extensive documentation will appear in Fox-Genovese and Genovese, *The Mind of the Master Class*. . . .
35 See Adger and Girardeau, eds., *Writings of Thornwell*, IV, which includes essays by Charles Hodge and Thomas Smyth. . . .
36 E. N. Elliott, ed., *Cotton Is King and Pro-Slavery Arguments* (New York, 1969 [1860]). Hodge's contribution, "The Bible Argument on Slavery," is on 841–877.
37 For an elaboration see Genovese, " 'Our Family, White and Black': Family and Household in the Southern Slaveholders' World View," in Carol Bleser, ed., *In Joy and in Sorrow: Women, Family, and Marriage in the Victorian South, 1830–1900* (New York, 1991), 69–87; for the specific nature of the southern household and its ideological ramifications see Fox- Genovese, *Within the Plantation Household: Black and White Women of the Old South* (Chapel Hill, 1988), esp. ch. 1.
38 Joseph LeConte, "The Relation of Organic Science to Sociology," *Southern Presbyterian Review*, 13 (1860), 59. . . .
39 William A. Scott, "The Progress of Civil Liberty," in Robert Gibbes Barnwell, ed., *The New-Orleans Book* (New Orleans: n.p., 1851), 48.

2

SLAVERY AND PLANTATION CAPITALISM IN LOUISIANA'S SUGAR COUNTRY

Richard Follett

In the following essay, Richard Follett addresses the central question raised by Eugene Genovese—how did slaveholders reconcile slavery with progress and modernity?—by an examination not of intellectuals but of slaveholding planters in Louisiana's sugar country. Sugar plantations were capital-intensive operations and planters readily adopted technological improvements that sharply increased productivity, but they also fully embraced slavery. As Follett puts it, they "embraced the capitalist ideology of the burgeoning market revolution, yet simultaneously retained a commitment to the organic ties of paternalism." He argues, though, that the tensions between capitalist and "pre-capitalist social relations of production" were resolved successfully as "planters forged a novel route to modernity where slavery and capitalism progressed in concert"; planters did not "seriously question the intercompatibility of slavery, modernization, and labor stability." Success in sugar planting required close coordination of labor efforts, especially at the crucial harvest time. Follett, much like Genovese did in Roll, Jordan, Roll, *argues that slaves recognized their "seminal position in sugar production" and used it "to manipulate the master–slave relationship and generate further autonomy and signal prerogatives from the masters."*

* * *

With Union and Confederate troops massing in northern Virginia, William Howard Russell hurried upstream after his sojourn in New Orleans. Anxious to visit the plantations of the Louisiana sugar country, Russell promptly arrived at John Burnside's expansive sugar holdings some 30 miles south of the state capital, Baton Rouge. Climbing the bell tower of the plantation house, Russell's eyes cast over a vast agricultural kingdom:

The view from the belvedere . . . was one of the most striking of

37

its kind in the world. If an English agriculturist could see six thousand acres of the finest land in one field, unbroken by hedge or boundary, and covered with the most magnificent crops of . . . sprouting sugarcane . . . he would surely doubt his senses. But there is literally such a sight—six thousand acres, better tilled than the finest patch in all the Lothians, green as Meath pastures, which can be turned up for a hundred years to come.[1]

Like Russell, those who visited south Louisiana left the region impressed by the superior slave workmanship, advanced horticulture and industrial productivity of the late antebellum sugar estates. His fellow Briton, James Robertson, similarly marvelled at the "enterprise and energy" with which Louisianans committed themselves to improved methods of sugar production, while a travelling planter from the French cane island of Guadeloupe lauded the superior "intelligence and skill manifested in the cultivation and manufacturing of sugar."[2] International praise found its domestic reflection in Frederick Law Olmsted, who noted upon visiting the sugar country "that intelligence, study, and enterprise had seldom better claims to award."[3] Echoing these accolades, Louisianans proudly charged that "there are but few estates either in Mexico, Cuba, or any of the West India Islands which equal . . . the average plantations in Louisiana."[4] These enthusiastic and ambitious declarations of economic modernity, however, masked profound incongruities as planters and slaveholders eagerly embraced the market revolution while simultaneously rejecting the liberal and democratic overtones of nineteenth-century progress.

Preaching the doctrine of economic evolution, the sugar masters exhibited a marked discrepancy as they vigorously advocated modernity while simultaneously conserving an archaic form of social organization that suppressed the emergence of an integrated capitalist society in the sugar country. Responding to Mark Smith's recent injunction that future research in slave studies should tease out "the dialectical relationship between the doses of capitalism and pre-capitalism in southern society," this study establishes that sugar planters embraced the capitalist ideology of the burgeoning market revolution, yet simultaneously retained a commitment to the organic ties of paternalism.[5] Recasting the master–slave relationship to ensure optimal productivity, the sugar masters discovered that capitalist economic predilections coexisted quite harmoniously with pre-capitalist social relations of production. While previous historians found these tensions irreconcilable, this analysis interrogates the dynamic interplay between capitalism and archaic social values to illustrate the evolution of plantation capitalism and the articulation of an economic culture that broached modernity while remaining anchored within arcane modes of societal construction. By rendering alternative matrices for the study of slave-based capitalism, this chapter builds upon the seminal work of Eugene Genovese and James Oakes to suggest that modernizing tendencies and patriarchal paternalism pulsed through the rhythms of southern society as planters forged a novel route to modernity where slavery and capitalism progressed in concert.[6]

In Louisiana, as in Italy, the road to modernization did not guarantee comprehensive development as planters assimilated aspects of individualistic, capitalist and market-oriented thought into a political economy and holistic social ethic that emphasized primordial concepts of reciprocal and mutual equality, personal integrity, social standing, human mastery and autonomous self-definition. Originating in the societal and economic values of the slave plantation complex, southern planter-politicians utilized an ideological vocabulary where capitalist modernity fused with paternalism and a regional commitment to the preservation of liberty, slavery, independence and virtue. Drawing on aspects of the liberal and republican traditions, antebellum southerners defined a singular economic culture that condoned market and entrepreneurial behavior while concurrently depicting regional development through the prism of non-capitalist social relations. The alluvial sugar lords of south Louisiana exhibited these internal dualities, for although they spoke a *lingua franca* of rationality and modernization, their discourse remained wedded to a pre-modern labor structure, an antiquated form of societal construction, and an ideology that remained bound by the organic ties of paternalism and honor. Neither capitalist nor pre-capitalist, ancient nor modern, the antebellum sugar masters bisected categorization and collapsed historical definitions on the nature of southern society. The emerging matrix of economic and social identity provides an opportunity to probe the articulation of the slaveholder's twin commitment to chattel bondage and modern economic and managerial values. The resulting admixture indicates that slaveholding sugar planters embraced truncated concepts of nineteenth-century modernity, for while they managed their estates acquisitively, rationally and efficiently, they found little that was contradictory in slavery and modernization. Indeed, as they strove toward the creation of industrialized vertically integrated plantation units, the sugar masters encountered few incongruities in the use of bonded labor for profit and productivity maximization. Culturally distinct, yet sharing an economic universe with their free labor brethren in the North, the antebellum sugar masters stood at the edge of modernity where the market and its related *laissez-faire* order beckoned the slaveholder.

The emergence of a discrete sectional culture did not operate in polar opposition to the development of a national economic ideology, as southerners enveloped interregional notions of economic progress and embraced the cross-fertilization of mercantile thought. Deconstructing classical and Smithian critiques of slavery, the plantation elite resolved the modernist-traditionalist tension by forging models of development where slavery meshed with modernization and economic development. Amongst the myriad of southern planters, Louisianans considered themselves and their industry as exemplary models of southern economic progress. Ever eager to praise, the prominent New Orleans journalist and publisher, James DeBow, announced in an early edition of his *Commercial Review* that "we congratulate our country on the spirit of enterprise which prevails. The competition evinced in the improvement of the manufacture of sugar shows energetic feelings amongst our planters."[7]

These claims carried more than the hollow ring of antebellum boosterism, for the Louisiana sugar industry underwent a profound transformation in the early nineteenth century. Following the successful production of sugar in 1795, the nascent Louisiana industry spread swiftly from its original core in New Orleans and, by 1810, sugar occupied a premier position amongst agriculturalists on the lower reaches of the Mississippi river. Secure behind the lofty walls of federal tariff protection, the gilt-edged appeal of sugar farming drew successive waves of Anglo-American settlers who extended sugar cultivation beyond the Mississippi and on to the alluvial rich soils of central and western Louisiana. Conspicuous geographical expansion paralleled climbing productivity as masters and slaves "converted waste lands into verdant fields and reaped . . . stores of gold and silver from the glebe they turned up."[8] Clearing land, draining swamps and erecting plantation complexes, the sugar masters oversaw a flourishing trade where both the scale and scope of production advanced briskly. Less than a decade after DeBow's celebrated realization of Louisiana sugar, 70 estates pioneered a small but dynamic industry where the locus of success lay in the lucrative combination of land, capital and slavery.[9] Stimulated by federal tariffs and depressed cotton prices, production expanded keenly as the number of estates increased more than three-fold from 193 in 1824 to 691 in 1830.[10] Remaining relatively constant during the Jacksonian era, production increased significantly in the 1840s when Whig tariff support and lean cotton prices stimulated new sugar concerns from the Gulf Coast to central Louisiana. While the industry qualitatively increased from 1245 sugar houses in 1845 to over 1500 in 1849, Louisiana's nascent sugar interest experienced quantitative gains in productivity despite a comprehensive decline in the total number of sugar plantations in the 1850s.[11]

The economic success of the cane industry rested primarily on the swift expansion of the internal slave trade and on the mass importation

of African-American bondspeople to Louisiana.[12] Astutely characterized as "sugar machines" and "the engines of wealth," the slave population on the sugar estates grew briskly and, by 1830, over 36,000
slaves labored on the cane fields.[13] By mid-century, the slave population had almost quadrupled as 125,000 men and women toiled in the
oppressive heat of Louisiana's sugar bowl.[14] The evolution of slave
labor in the sugar industry underpinned agricultural expansion as
farm output similarly multiplied from a mean of 108 hogsheads in
1830, to 269 hogsheads in 1844, and 310 hogsheads during the bumper
crop of 1853. Production furthermore experienced a comparable expansion as the number of acres cultivated per hand rose from approximately 2 acres in 1802 to 3.5 in 1822. This figure climbed to 5 acres by
the latter years of the ante-bellum era and, on the largest estates,
planters confidently expected their slaves to cultivate 6.6 acres of sugar
per hand.[15] While man–land ratios rose, so did individual productivity
as estate managers measured appreciable increases in plantation efficiency from the 1830s to the Civil War. In 1831, efficient sugar masters
cultivated and manufactured approximately 2.5 hogsheads per slave
or 4 per plantation worker.[16] Sixteen years later, planter Valcour Aime
estimated that the average yield of sugar per hand in the late 1840s
varied between 5 and 8 hogsheads of sugar. Edward Forstall concurred,
noting that on favorably managed estates, sugar producers could
manufacture 7 hogsheads of sugar per slave whilst their competitors in
Cuba struggled to cultivate 5 hogsheads per hand.[17]

Despite these indices of economic progress, the plantation elite
encountered a series of overlapping dilemmas that imposed rigid labor
and production criteria upon slaves and planters alike. In resolving
these difficulties, the sugar masters fused slavery and plantation capitalism and underscored the immediate association between chattel bondage and modernization in the cane country. Of principal concern to
Louisiana's farming community was the region's sporadically icy climate that delimited the agricultural calendar and threatened destructive frost damage. Following an extensive eight-month growing season
during which the slaves tended the crop, planters entered the annual
harvest in a frenetic rush to cut, strip and grind the cane before the first
killing frosts descended in early December.[18] While frost damage, followed swiftly by a warming front, irreversibly diminished the plant's
commercial value, estate managers encountered additional ecological
pressures as they proved understandably reluctant to order the harvest
while the sucrose content swiftly increased in the growing canes.
Botanical obstacles further impelled plantation urgency, for once the
cane was cut, crop deterioration quickly advanced to the detriment of
the sucrose-rich juice. Under these climatically and agronomically trying conditions, sugar planters embarked upon a six-week long grinding

season where speed and labor stability were held at a premium. Telescoping the experience of the sugar masters illustrates that in resolving these production difficulties, Louisiana's slaveholding elite modernized their estates while concurrently yielding to the bondspeoples' desire for greater personal autonomy and financial independence. Reweaving the paternalist web, masters and slaves fashioned a mutual set of reciprocal obligations that accommodated the machine age, ensured labor stability and transformed the dynamics of agro-industrial slavery in the sugar country.

Beyond the crop and climate specific difficulties of sugar production in Louisiana, domestic and global economic forces stimulated the planters to transform the manufacturing stage of their industry from its reliance on primitive horse-drawn sugar mills to costly steam-powered equipment that increased both the scale and scope of industrial sugar production.[19] As Peter Coclanis observes, the key to economic growth lies in rising aggregate demand and the internal capacity of a regional economy to supply that market.[20] In antebellum America, the growth of personal income, combined with declining real and relative costs of sugar, profoundly altered the position of sucrose within the U.S. diet.[21] Consumer demand, in turn, rose keenly from 161 million pounds in 1837 to almost 900 million pounds of sugar in 1854.[22] Per capita consumption paralleled broader national developments as sugar emerged as a widely purchased and income-elastic condiment that found a vigorous market niche as antebellum wages gradually rose. In 1831, for instance, every American consumed 13 pounds of sugar every year, yet by mid-century, US consumption multiplied three-fold as per capita consumption surpassed 30 pounds of sugar annually.[23] With a burgeoning market available for those who sought to tap the nation's savory appetite, Louisiana planters intensified cultivation, enlarged production facilities, and modernized their grinding equipment to maximize yields. Responding to shifting domestic demand, the sugar planting elite increased production ten-fold and, by 1853, Louisiana produced a quarter of the world's sugar. Enthusiastically fanning regional pride, Representative Miles Taylor announced that such progress "is without parallel in the United States, or indeed in the world in any branch of industry."[24] While Taylor's exhortations carried the familiar ring of antebellum boosterism, agrarian commentators lauded the plantation elite as expanding yields matched Louisiana's improved status as the nation's principal sugar supplier.

Technological innovation and economic evolution emerged at the vanguard of a commercial transformation that guaranteed regional primacy in the prosperous market for crystalline sucrose. The rapid introduction of steam-powered technology further boosted the productive capacity of the mills and ensured that planters could expand cultivation, confident that their machinery would grind the crop before the first hard freeze struck. With 80 per cent of the sugar estates utilizing steam power by 1860, cane farmers resolved the combined exigencies of speed and productivity while concurrently minimizing the risk of crop deterioration and cane oxidization. Breaking the technological bottleneck to advanced production and unlocking the potential for economies of scale and speed, steam power resolved diverse climate and crop specific production problems while equipping the Louisiana sugar masters with superior facilities to those utilized in the Caribbean. The urgency to compete with foreign competition appears contradictory given federal protection of domestic sugar, but throughout the antebellum era, Louisianans vied for control of the US sugar market against a technologically inferior yet agriculturally superior industry in the West Indies. Cuban sugar, in particular, challenged Louisiana's privileged position within the domestic market, for although the Washington administration retained a high tariff upon refined sugar, Cuban planters exported raw and unprocessed sugar that refiners subsequently purified in the Northeast for domestic consumption. Trapped within a limited geographic area with scarce room for significant expansion, the Louisiana sugar lords had little choice other than to intensify their operations and bring science to the art of agronomy, and the tools of capitalist industrialization to antebellum labor management.

While regional and international pressures account for the modernization of the Louisiana sugar industry, the introduction of novel technology modified work patterns and recast the matrix of entrepreneurial management in the sugar country. As William Dusinberre, Shearer Davis Bowman, Carville Earle and others have suggested, slavery and entrepreneurial capitalism advanced in tandem as planters fashioned agricultural enterprises that approached the organizational complexity of modern factories.[25] To this extent the sugar masters proved similarly entrepreneurial, yet, as Eugene Genovese suggests, their truncated notions of modernization encompassed diverse concepts emblematic of traditionalism: slavery, honor, an aversion to centralized authority, and profound misgivings over the democratic countenance of liberal capitalism.[26] In Louisiana, however, the slaveholders resolved this paradox by advocating qualitative economic growth and by synthesizing aspects of slave and wage labor to develop productive work crews for the grinding season. Interlacing the disparate and frequently discordant threads of the master–slave relationship, the sugar masters proved singularly effective in merging their pre-modern labor system into a commercial network of plantation economies.

Progress in the nineteenth-century sugar country fused colossal investment in land, labor and machinery. To ensure maximum productivity, the labor lords financed a tri-partite division of capital where investment in the primary factors of production dwarfed those of the cotton South.[27] Funnelling assets into a capitalized labor system that transformed the productive capacity of the Louisiana swamps, the sugar masters sponsored a technological revolution which bore profitable fruit in higher yields and enhanced sugar quality. Charles Fleischmann, for instance, concluded before the US Commissioner of Patents that "there is no sugar growing country, where all the modern improvements have been more fairly tested in Louisiana." Attributing their success to "enterprise and high intelligence," Fleischmann, like other contemporary agronomists, warmly praised the sugar masters for "fulfilling all the conditions . . . for obtaining a pure and perfect crystalline sugar."[28] Effusive in commendation but representative in their findings, editorialists and visiting commentators endorsed Louisiana's technical primacy, noting that the state appeared "far superior to most sugar growing regions . . . in the intelligence and skill manifested in both the cultivation and manufacturing of sugar."[29] Suitably equipped with the latest steam-powered production facilities, one correspondent concluded that the planter "will reap his harvest in half the time, and with half the labor and expense" than he had previously achieved with primitive agronomy and animal-powered mills.[30] Benefiting from time- and labor-saving techniques, steam power emerged as a technical panacea to the sugar planters' harvest difficulties and as an integral means for boosting production standards. Those planters who sought to tap the growing demand for white sugar, and circumvent refining costs, additionally invested in costly vacuum pans and clarification facilities that produced "large and brilliant crystals . . . [of] any size required by the caprice of the customer."[31] While the Rillieux apparatus and allied vacuum evaporators proved too expensive for most planters, over 65 prominent sugar cultivators pioneered these new technologies and produced, on average, 475 hogsheads of crystalline and snowy sugar that Princeton chemist R. S. McCulloh praised as "equal to those of the best double-refined sugar of our northern refineries."[32] Frederick Olmsted echoed Professor McCulloh's enthusiastic endorsement, applauding the sugar planters as "among the most intelligent, enterprising, and wealthy men of business in the United States."[33]

While the introduction of expensive steam-powered machinery in the 1840s dramatically increased the pace, capacity and cane-crushing efficiency of the sugar mills, escalating costs forced the smaller and less competitive out of the burgeoning sugar industry.[34] Those who remained, however, found that steam power established an exacting mechanical rhythm that transformed labor relations on the plantations. Frequently equipped with constantly moving conveyor belts that slaves fed with a constant supply of cane, the late antebellum sugar estate established an early form of assembly line production where the industrial sugar mill imposed an inflexible, persistent and unforgiving labor discipline on the slaves. Striving towards operational efficiency and productivity maximization, the assembly line inaugurated new management practices where each operative, Thorstein Veblen notes, keeps "pace with the machine process . . . and adapts his movements with mechanical accuracy to its requirements."[35] In their quest to establish a disciplined work force that would labor at the measured cadence of the steam age, overseers and owners sub-divided their laborers' tasks, instituted systematized shift work and imposed the regimented order of the mechanical clock. Partisan in both content and readership, the *Planter's Banner* echoed the view that regional economic success rested upon "good management on the improved principle adopted in Louisiana."[36] Correspondent Edward Forstall similarly observed that on favorably managed estates where the slaves' tasks "are made to harmonise so as to assure rapidity and constant working," planters virtually doubled their production of sugar.[37] In the wake of the Civil War, Louisiana's regimented plantation order received further attention when Andrew McCollam joined fellow sugar master James L. Bowman on a tour of Brazilian sugar lands near Rio de Janeiro. Examining the lands and cane operations with the intention of commercially speculating in pro-slave Brazil, McCollam's shrewd business eye quickly focused on the deficiencies of Brazilian land and slave management. After a visit to Julian Rebeiro de Castro's plantation, McCollarn noted in his travel diary that "everything is going to decay," but significantly added that he could "do more work with the same number of hands than was being done" on his Brazilian competitor's estate.[38]

Relying on methodical and structured order, the sugar masters enforced a work discipline and managerial style that visitors to the sugar country frequently described as militaristic in organization. Timothy Flint observed the imposition of formalized work rules, noting that "there is in a large plantation as much precision in the rules, as much exactness in the times of going to labor, as in a gamson under military discipline or in a ship of war." Extending his comment further, Flint recorded that systems dictated plantation management and that "there is no pulling down to-day the scheme of yesterday, and the whole amount of force is directed by the teaching of experience to the best result."[39] Moses Liddell mirrored these observations when he counseled his son that sugar planting requires "energy, activity, and ingeniousness." Success, Liddell confirmed, rests on "strength and capital [combined] with remarkable energy and unbounded perseverance to succeed well." Such qualities Liddell's son-in-law, John Hampden Randolph, surely possessed in great quantities, but even the master of the giant Nottoway Plantation realized that the true key to prosperity in the sugar bowl lay with "perseverance" and above all "good management."[40] Former slave Charles Stewart mused on the African-American position when he recalled that his master "wouldn't stand for no foolin' neither . . . it was jes' stiddy management."[41]

Combining elements of factory and farm on one agro-industrial site, the sugar masters methodically routinized labor and transformed the organizational structure of the plantation to optimize productivity, economies of scale and team interdependence. During the grinding season, the exigencies of sugar production further impelled manager-ial reform as planters instituted drilled inter and intra-dependent gang work that supplied the voracious demand of the mechanized sugar mill from morning to night. Consolidating and synchronizing diverse plantation functions, estate managers reconfigured work patterns and managerial practices to weave unfree labor into a fabric of capitalist productivity. As Robert Fogel, Stanley Engerman and others have sug-gested, gang labor emerged as an unmerciful though efficient struc-ture to provide the slaveholding elite with disciplined teams adept at intense work.[42] Through a stringent division of labor, planters could methodically routinize and specialize work while maintaining strict supervision of their slaves as they toiled beneath the overseer's eye in the open field. Louisiana's sugar masters adapted this model and cre-ated interdependent teams that would swiftly plant the crop in the new year and efficiently harvest the canes come November or December. The combination of these agricultural requirements and the pressures of mechanized sugar production necessitated a labor regime that would advance over the cane fields with military regulation and preci-sion. During the frenetic harvest season, planters exploited potential economies of scale by relying on interdependent gang work and assembly line production techniques. As the lead hand in a gang of 50 to 100 slaves, Solomon Northup graphically described the inter-dependence of teamwork and the division of labor among the cane-cutters on Bayou Boeuf. Flanked on either side, the lead hand advanced slightly ahead of his compatriots, who formed the base of a triangle; all three worked wholly in unison and at the pace of their squad leader. Progressing with their razor-sharp knives, the lead hand sheared the cane from the ground, stripped the stalk of its flags, sliced off the top and placed it behind him. Slightly behind their pacesetter, the two other cane-cutters followed suit and laid their stripped canes upon the first, so that the young slave who followed the squad could gather up the bundle and place it in the cart that followed him. Once filled, the cart left for the sugarhouse, though it was quickly replaced by a second wagon, ensuring that the process of cutting, stripping, collecting and loading the cane rarely ceased or slowed.[43] Throughout the grinding season this brutal, yet efficient, field labor regime continued to supply the insatiable demand of the sugar mill from dawn to dusk.

Operating as the first stage in the assembly line production of sugar, the cane-cutters took their place in the vanguard of a plantation order characterized by labor-saving techniques and "production-raising" methods. On leading estates, this included the replacement of mule trains by railroads and human brawn by steam power. At Madewood Plantation, Thomas Pugh brought the freshly cut cane to the mill on a small iron railroad which arrived at sugarhouse door before dropping its load on to the cane carrier. Conveyor belts subsequently transported the cane shoots to the mill for grinding. Keen to utilize the crushed canes as a cheap and alternative fuel supply, Pugh collected the spent canes (or bagasse) as they fell from the mill. Once dry, the bagasse was recycled and used to fire the steam engines. The cane juice, editorialist Solon Robinson observed, "runs to the vats . . . and thence to the kettles; thence to the coolers, and from there the sugar is carried upon railroad cars along lines of rails between the rows of hogsheads to the farther end of the building."[44] Within the mill house and plantation complex, novel management practices additionally extended to sub-dividing production into distinct units while simultaneously integrating grinding operations through modern technology. Although the cane estates never evolved into complex modern multi-department corporations that were both vertically and horizontally integrated, the presence of separate though interdependent branches of production suggests that the antebellum sugar mill stood within a transitional phase of industrial and organizational development that foreshadowed the corporate model of mass production.

While the introduction of advanced machinery imposed the regimented order of the industrial age, technology impelled the further sub-division of labor and established novel patterns of work organization. Compelling their laborers to toil at the methodical pace of the steam engine, sugar planters established that primitive assembly line management guaranteed optimal productivity and the exploitation of economies of speed in the mill house. Cognizant that speed defined the sugar harvest, planters categorized labor, allocated tasks, and defined work patterns to make sure that crew productivity eclipsed "the sum of the marginal products" of the individual team members.[45] After a visit to the sugar country, New Orleans physician Dr Samuel Cartwright observed that "all of the laborers . . . are divided into two portions—one to labor in the field and to supply the mill house with cane; the other to manufacture the juice . . . into molasses and sugar."[46] On Robert Ruffin Barrow's Residence Plantation, overseer Ephraim Knowlton established a classification list that defined the occupational division of labor for the 1857 grinding season. Listing each slave's name below his or her expected task, Knowlton subdivided his labor force into a number of interdependent teams that worked on all tasks from cooking a communal meal to operating the diverse functions of the industrialized sugar mill.[47] Anxious to fit the pace of work to the unbending regimen of the steam age, planters established regular watches which guaranteed that comparatively fresh hands were readily available to staff the machines and to conduct the complex art of sugar making. Cycling slave workers through the cane shed at different points during the day and night, overseers ensured constant sugar production and resolved the imperative to maintain the mills turning. John Hampden Randolph of Nottoway Plantation employed these managerial strategies when he instituted a system of watches for the 1857 grinding season. Dividing his slave force according to task and to watch, Randolph established a revolving labor system where he divided the working day and night into three watches (approximately eight hours long), of which most slaves worked two. Big Alfred, for instance, began his working day as a cart loader who followed the cane cutters through the fields. Presumably, Big Alfred took a rest through the late afternoon and evening, until he entered the mill house in the early morning hours where he stood guard as the steam engine fireman on the second watch. Weary from his night's labor, where he controlled the fire beneath the sugar kettles, Big Alfred returned to the fields as a cart loader with the first morning light.[48] Brutally punishing for the bondsman, this labor regime hinged upon the imposition of a clock-ordered discipline where the working day was punctuated by formalized work rules and a labor regime that marched to the beat of the ticking clock.

Nineteenth-century industrialists shared a commitment to a clock-ordered labor regime where plant managers established iron-clad factory schedules that increasingly focused on optimizing work force productivity through the drill and punctuality of industrial capitalism. With machinery synchronized to operate as part of a larger calibrated system, the sugar masters punished tardiness and codified timed discipline at the work place. Imbibing the precepts of scientific management from a myriad of agricultural publications, planters seemingly fathomed the value of judicious slave management and the centrality of time-saving techniques. In a syndicated article, released at least six times between 1850 and 1855, one planter counselled fellow agrarians to employ a central slave cook to prepare all meals for the bondspeople. Prudent "time-conscious" management of this sort would yield several hours of saved labor time that the planter could expropriate for fieldwork.[49] With broad dissemination, this advice appealed to the sugar masters who, on most plantations during the grinding season, selected one or two cooks to prepare meals for all. Estimating that each slave family probably required one hour to cook and eat their meal, planters realized that by pooling resources during the harvest, a significant saving in labor time might be achievable. On Oaklands Plantation, Samuel McCutchon delegated three rather elderly and sick women to cook for all hands in 1859. Noting that his cooks included Milly, a perennial rheumatic, 58-year-old physically handicapped Beersheba and asthma-suffering Betsey, McCutchon's kitchen staff prepared meals for 107 working adult hands on his Plaquemine Parish estate.[50] By organizing a refectory meal service, McCutchon expropriated the precious working time of healthy strong adults by centralizing food preparation. James P. Bowman similarly consolidated cooking operations prior to the rolling season at Frogmoor Plantation. After discharging his daily duties, Bowman's overseer, George Woodruff, wrote his plantation journal in a copy of Thomas Affleck's *Sugar Plantation Record and Account Book*. Published primarily for the improving planter, Affleck's register advised overseers to provide plenty of "wholesome well cooked food . . . supplied at regular hours." Evidently following this stricture, Woodruff commenced with centralized cooking on Monday 26 October 1857, exactly one day before the start of the grinding season.[51] Clearly understanding the potential gain in time by centralizing operations, Bowman underscored his commitment "to learn as much of planting as possible . . . [so] that here after I may better understand management and all unnecessary mistakes."[52] While thrifty time management cruelly optimized labor, sugar planters further sub-divided tasks and chimed timed and daily instructions to their slaves. On William Minor's plantations, overseers received strict orders to employ bells and established time signals in regimenting the slaves' day.[53] In exhorting plantation profitability, Minor counselled fellow land and labor elites that "labor must be directed with an intelligent eye" and that agrarian success rested on "the proper adaptation of the means to the end."[54]

Although these managerial innovations paralleled those of the industrializing north, the sugar masters retained an ardent commitment to the omnipresent lash and archaic methods of antebellum labor discipline. Hunton Love, a former slave driver on Bayou Lafourche, revealed the axiomatic relationship between force, discipline and economic success when he recalled: "I had to whip 'em, I had to show 'em I was boss, or the plantation would be wrecked."[55] Upon visiting Andre Roman's sugar estate in Ascension Parish, William Howard Russell similarly underscored the symbiosis of force and proficient slave supervision when he remarked: "the anxieties attending the cultivation of sugar are great and so much depends upon the judicious employment of labor, it is scarcely possible to exaggerate the importance of experience in directing it, and of the power to insist on its application."[56] Thomas Hamilton expounded upon the prevalence of repression and intimidation in the slaveholders' armory of control when he observed that during the grinding season "the fatigue is so great that nothing but the severest application of the lash can stimulate the human frame to endure it."[57] As a slave driver on Bayou Salle, Solomon Northup clarified the centrality of the lash and rigorous supervision in facilitating sugar production. Describing the frenetic pace of the harvest, Northup remembered "the whip was given to me with directions to use it upon anyone who was caught standing idle. If I failed to the letter, there was another one for my own back." In the hot and sticky conditions of the industrializing sugar mill, indolence and loafing evidently received swift punishment as Northup's duties extended beyond maintaining work discipline to additionally calling on and off "the different gangs at the proper time."[58] Confident that they possessed the ultimate inducement for hard work, planters and overseers consequently retained and frequently exercised the threat of physical coercion as a primitive, ancient and unmerciful means to compel break-neck speed in the fields and mill house. Ceceil George eloquently articulated the slaves' memory when she pointedly called south Louisiana "de most wicked country God's son ever died for," while former bondsman Jacob Stroyer bitterly recalled that African-Americans considered the region "a place of slaughter."[59]

Spanning the gap between antiquated and modern, the late antebellum sugar estate exhibited an internal duality as entrepreneurial economic progress was tempered by a coerced labor system that evidently practiced non-capitalist relations of production. Few planters, however, found this discrepancy insurmountable, and neither did they seriously question the intercompatibility of slavery, modernization, and labor stability. Indeed, by pursuing prudent slave management and a sagacious division of labor, planters confidently asserted that "free labor cannot compete, in the manufacture of sugar, with better organized slave labor."[60] These sentiments appear valid, as when alternative laborers entered the labor market, the sugar masters soon found them wanting for the specific crop and labor requirements of the sugar country. Recalling the story of one planter who dispensed with slave labor in favor of Irish and German emigrants, Sir Charles Lyell mused on the catastrophic labor crisis the planter faced when his workers struck for double pay in the midst of the harvest season. Gravely taking note, Lyell recorded that with neither additional laborers or slaves to hand, the planter lost his crop, valued at $10,000.[61] With high turnover costs and a thin labor market, sugar planters entrenched, calibrated the slave system to meet their needs, and rented additional workers to provide further stability during the grinding season.

Despite decades of vigorous scholarship, the compatibility of slavery and modernization provokes constructive debate and prompts historiographic revision. The dominant Genovesean paradigm suggests that slaves rejected the bourgeois work ethic, and resisted the method and structure of the industrial revolution by clinging to a pre-modern work order where a traditional mentality prevailed.[62] More recently, Charles Dew highlighted the conservative effect of slavery on economic innovation in the Chesapeake iron industry, while Mark Smith analyzed the linkages between pre-industrial slave culture and the introduction of clock-ordered discipline.[63] These fruitful approaches facilitate an examination on the interconnectivity of slave agency and the emergence of plantation capitalism in the sugar country. Theoretically, the exigencies of sugar cultivation in Louisiana placed the field hand and mill house operative in a potentially unparalleled position of power. As evidenced from Charles Lyell's account, planters could not afford labor instability, sabotage or production slow-downs during the grinding season. Indeed, by the 1840s many sugar planters had specifically introduced technical and managerial innovations to raise efficiency and increase production speed. The success of these programs, however, rested on the compliance and complicity of the slave gangs who utilized their seminal position in sugar production to manipulate the master–slave relationship and generate further autonomy and signal prerogatives from the masters. Fully cognizant that the bondspeople represented the core of prosperity and wealth formation, the sugar masters acquiesced to slave demands but, in turn, they fashioned a mutual overwork system that proved financially profitable to both parties.[64] Reweaving the paternalist web, slaves and masters wrought a labor system that accommodated the bondspeoples' desires for greater autonomy while additionally providing the slaveholders with the labor stability they sought. Adopting novel modes of resistance in the new technologies of the modernizing sugar industry, Louisiana slaves adapted to mechanization: not because they had imbibed the Protestant work ethic and become "metaphorical clock punchers" as Fogel suggests, but rather because the machine and steam age recast labor relations and provided the slaves with new avenues of economic and social space.[65]

Addressing the stark contradiction of the slaves' apparent willingness to work long hours in exhausting conditions, Frederick Law Olmsted proffered an explanation for this paradox when he observed that the slaves "are better paid, they have better and more varied food and more stimulants than usual."[66] While Olmsted misjudged the power of the whip, he accurately portrayed the central role of incentives in antebellum slave management. Beyond payment to skilled slaves, Christmas bonuses, rewards for rapid work, post- and pre-harvest celebrations, and improved accommodation, slaves and slaveholders established over-work systems whereby bondspeople received financial remuneration for chopping wood, growing corn, or trading moss, poultry and livestock.[67] As Dylan Penningroth, Roderick McDonald and others have shown, slaves eagerly embraced the overwork system and carved out a meaningful orbit of self- and communal identity through the trading of diverse goods. Through independent production, slaves found an avenue for autonomy through which the market emerged as an erratic and conflicted space where wage-earning slaves grasped the essence of liberty while, paradoxically, affirming the sordid economic logic of chattel bondage. In Louisiana's sugar country, slaves swiftly deemed it a customary right to receive payment for their wood and corn just prior to the grinding season, and on most plantations, the slaves entered harvest with their demand for disbursable income at least partially satiated and their fragmentary vision of independence tantalizingly affirmed through the sale of their labor for pecuniary advantage.[68]

Although overwork meshed planter and slave into a grid of mutual duties and obligations, these market relations proved mutually advantageous, for while slaves could sell the product of their labor and materially enrich their lives with goods purchased from the plantation commissary, the slaves' internal economy also fortified the institution of slavery. Not only did overwork seemingly hasten labor stability, but it ensured that the slaves produced key plantation commodities in their own time beyond the margins of the working day. By commodifying labor and purchasing wood or diverse commodities that bondspeople cut or cultivated during the night and on Sundays, planters could wring out the entire "surplus-value" or profit from the slave.[69] A fine line evidently existed in encouraging slaves' market activities, but by exchanging commodities for credit at the plantation store, slaveholders circumscribed the availability of specie, minimized the potential for interaction with free labor and made sure that the fruit of the slaves' overwork seldom exited the confines of the plantation world.

The swift rise of steam power as the primary energy source for the sugar country guaranteed that each estate required at least three to four cords of wood to produce one hogshead of steam milled sugar. Conscious of the time- and labor-consuming nature of timber collection and the voracious appetite of the steam engine for fuel, the sugar masters increasingly relied on the slaves to cut and haul cordage from the back swamp at the cessation of the regular working day. Paying slaves 50 cents a cord to conduct this laborious work in their own time and not in his, a planter could assuage the slaves' pressure for remuneration while simultaneously saving hundreds of hours for alternative duties.[70]

Standing on the hurricane deck of a Mississippi steamboat as it passed through the heart of the sugar country in 1838, Harriet Martineau observed that groups of slaves continued to chop wood under moonlight and "toil along the shore line" even after dusk had turned to nightfall.[71] On the left bank of the river, as Martineau steamed downstream, lay Samuel Fagot's Constancia Plantation, an estate where both master and slave took full advantage of overwork. In preparation for the 1859 harvest, slaves collected and chopped 2,018 cords of wood in their own time, for which they earned $1,077. Aware that he could rely on his slaves' wood to grind the 435 hogsheads that the estate yielded in 1859, Fagot's 130 slaves proved capable woodsmen who produced not only fire wood but additionally over 1,300 hewn boards that Fagot hoped to use as sheeting material. Crediting his slaves at the plantation commissary, Fagot sufficed his cordage requirements for the grinding season while forging an economic link that bound the slave's material well-being to the insatiable demand of the mechanized sugar mill.[72] The same calculating regard for time and profit shaped overwork payments for corn where planters such as Benjamin Tureaud paid his bondspeople to cultivate enough grain in the evenings to meet the plantation's annual dietary requirements. In 1858 alone, Tureaud expended over $1,500 in remunerating slaves for a cereal crop that guaranteed plantation self-sufficiency and secured additional labor time for other tasks.[73] Further, by crediting his slaves just days prior to the rolling season, Tureaud seemingly placated his bondspeople as they entered the most exacting period of the year.

Perennially calculating, John Hampden Randolph additionally fused plantation performance with Christmas bonuses to encourage maximum slave productivity. At Forest Home, Randolph paid the slaves 40 cents a hogshead or $175 as a Christmas bonus in December 1851. One year later, he increased his bonus by $25 and in January 1854, Randolph rewarded his slaves with $300, a significant increase to mark the signal success of the new vacuum pans that produced 680 hogsheads at Forest Home.[74] Randolph's slaves, who controlled the expensive and complex pans with considerable aplomb, found mechanization financially advantageous as each adult slave increased his annual bonus and gained approximately $5 by accepting the new machinery. By scaling the size of the Christmas rewards to the volume of the crop, Randolph quite probably triggered communal pressure in the slave quarters against those who loitered in the sugarhouse. Through overwork and bonuses, the slaveholders surely conceded to their bondsmen's desires for disbursable income, yet by shaping the system to maximize productivity, the slave-holders subtly turned the dynamics of the master–slave relationship to their own profit. Ghastly though it was, slavery had been effectively grafted on to plantation capitalism in the sugar country. Residing on rich sugar land, William Hamilton wrote to his father expressing the quintessential values of the antebellum sugar master. "I am a lover of order and system," Hamilton declared, "to have a certain way of doing everything and a regular time for doing everything."[75] Like Hamilton, those who controlled the sugar plantations of south Louisiana valued industry, discipline and diligence in the management of their estates. Finding little incongruity between their pre-capitalist labor system and the pressures of a capitalist economy, the sugar masters modernized their immense agricultural enterprises while simultaneously embracing both the modern and premodern impulses of southern society. In the cultivation and marketing of sugar on an agro-industrial scale, the sugar masters stood at the vanguard of a booming industry where the dynamics of economic growth lay in the synchronization of agriculture, industry and entrepreneurialism, but above all with the institution of racial slavery.

NOTES

1 W. H. Russell, *My Diary North and South* (New York, 1954), 147.
2 J. Robertson, *A Few Months in America* (London, 1855), 90; *DeBow's Review* 15 (December 1853), 648.
3 F. L. Olmsted, *Journey in the Seaboard Slave States* (New York, 1904), 320.
4 *DeBow's Review* 15 (December 1853), 647–8.
5 M. M. Smith, *Debating Slavery: Economy and Society in the Antebellum South* (Cambridge, 1998), 93.
6 E. D. Genovese, *The Slaveholder's Dilemma: Freedom and Progress in Southern Conservative Thought, 1820–1860* (Columbia, SC, 1992); J. Oakes, *Slavery and Freedom: An Interpretation of the Old South* (New York, 1990).
7 *DeBow's Review* 1 (February 1846), 166.
8 *Planter's Banner* (Franklin), 16 March 1848.
9 B. Duvallon, *Travels in Louisiana* (New York, 1806), 129.
10 *DeBow's Review* 1 (January 1846), 55–6.
11 A. Champomier, *Statement of the Sugar Crop Made in Louisiana in 1845–1846* (New Orleans, LA, 1846), 35; *Statement in 1849–1850*, 51; *Statement in 1859–1860*, 39.
12 R. Follett, "The Sugar Masters: slavery, economic development, and modernization on Louisiana sugar plantations, 1820–1860" (Ph. D. dissertation, Louisiana State University, 1997), 264–314.
13 J. Stirling, *Letters from the Slave States* (London, 1857), 124; T. Nutall, *A Journey of Travels into the Arkansas Territory* (Philadelphia, 1821), 239.
14 R. A. McDonald, *The Economy and Material Culture of Slaves: Goods and Chattels on the Sugar Plantations of Jamaica and Louisiana* (Baton Rouge, 1992), 3.
15 L. C. Gray, *History of Agriculture in the Southern United States to 1860*, 2 vols (Washington, DC, 1933), 11: 750–1; Follett, "Sugar Masters," 222.
16 J. S. Johnston, *Letter of Mr. Johnston of Louisiana* (Washington, DC, 1831), 8.
17 *DeBow's Review* 4 (November 1847), 385–6; E. J. Forstall, *Agricultural Productions of Louisiana* (New Orleans, LA, 1845), 6.
18 F. B. Kniffen, *Louisiana: its Land and People* (Baton Rouge, 1968), 21; W. J. Evans, *The Sugar Planter's Manual* (Philadelphia, PA, 1848).
19 Of 725 sugar estates in 1830, 100 possessed steam engines. By 1841, steam powered 361 of 668 plantations and by 1850, steam engines operated

in over 900 plantations. Johnston, Letter, 9; Forstall, *Agricultural Productions*, 4; Champomier, *Statement in 1856–51*, 43; Champomier, *Statement in 1860–61*, 39.

20 A. Coclanis, The *Shadow of a Dream: Economic Life and Death in the South Carolina Low Country, 1676–1920* (New York, 1989), ch. 3.

21 R. A. Margo, "Wages and prices during the antebellum period," in R. E. Gallman and J. J. Wallis (eds), *American Economic Growth and Standards of Living before the Civil War*, (Chicago, 1992), 173–210; Follett, "Sugar Masters," 133–5; A.H. Cole, *Wholesale Commodity Prices in the United States, 1700–1861* (Cambridge, MA, 1938), 192–357.

22 *Hunt's Merchant Magazine* 27 (December 1852), 681; US Patent Office, *Annual Report of the Commissioner of Patents for the Year 1858* (Washington, DC, 1859), 233.

23 *Hunt's Merchant Magazine* 39 (November 1858), 550; *Farmer's Cabinet and American Herd Book* 2 (October 1837, 78; *Journal of Agriculture* 1 (December 1845), 281.

24 *DeBow's Review* 22 (April 1857), 435.

25 W. Dusinberre, *Them Dark Days: Slavery in the American Rice Swamps* (New York, 1996); C. Earle, "The Price of Precocity: Technical Choice and Ecological Constraints in the Cotton South, 1840–1890," *Agricultural History* 66 (Summer 1988), 25–60; S. D. Bowman, *Masters and Lords: Mid-19th-Century U. S. Planters and Prussian Junkers* (New York, 1993).

26 Genovese, *Slaveholder's Dilemma*, 1–45.

27 Follett, "Sugar Masters," ch. 4.

28 C. L. Fleischmann, "Report on the sugar cane and its culture," US Patent Office, *Annual Report of the Commissioner of Patents for the Year 1848* (Washington, DC, 1849), 275.

29 *DeBow's Review* 15 (December 1853), 648; *DeBow's Review* 1 (February 1846), 166.

30 *Baton Rouge Gazette*, 2 December 1843.

31 J. D. B. DeBow, *The Industrial Resources of the Southern and Western Estates*, 3 vols (New Orleans, LA, 1853), 11: 206.

32 M. Schmitz, "The economic analysis of antebellum sugar plantations in Louisiana" (Ph.D. dissertation, University of North Carolina, 1974), 35; *DeBow's Review* 5 (March 1848), 286; 29th Congress, 2nd Session, Senate Doc. No. 209, "Investigations in Relation to Cane Sugar" (Washington, DC, 1847), 121.

33 Olmsted, *Journey in the Seaboard Slave States*, 671–2.

34 Follett, "Sugar Masters", 90–109.

35 T. Veblen, *The Instinct of Workmanship* (New York, 1914), 306–7.

36 *Planter's Banner* (Franklin), 5 January 1854.

37 Forstall, *Agricultural Productions*, 21.

38 Vol. 1, Brazilian Diary of Andrew McCollam, 1866–1867, 13 July 1866, Andrew McCollam Papers, Southern Historical Collection, University of North Carolina (SHC).

39 T. Flint, *The History and Geography of the Mississippi Valley*, 2 vols. (Cincinnati, 1832), 1: 244–5.

40 Moses Liddell to John R. Liddell, 28 July 1845; Moses Liddell to John R. Liddell, 25 August 1845; John H. Randolph to John R. Liddell, 22 March 1846, Liddell (Moses, St. John R., and Family) Papers, Louisiana and Lower Mississippi Valley Collections, Louisiana State University (LLMVC).

41 C. Stewart, "My Life as a Slave," *Harper's New Monthly Magazine* 69 (October 1884), 738.

42 R. W. Fogel, *Without Consent or Contract: The Rise and Fall of American Slavery* (New York, 1991), 74–9.

43 S. Northup, *Twelve Years a Slave*, edited by S. Eakin and J. Logsdon (Baton Rouge, 1968), 160, 162.

44 H.A. Kellar (ed.), *Solon Robinson: Pioneer and Agriculturalist* (Indianapolis, IN, 1936), 200.

45 J. Metzer, "Rational management, modern business practices, and economies of scale in ante-bellum southern plantations", *Explorations in Economic History* 12 (April 1975), 134.

46 *DeBow's Review* 13 (December 1852), 598.

47 Residence Journal of R. R. Barrow, Thursday, December 3, 1857, Robert Ruffin Barrow Papers, SHC.

48 Slave List, 1857, Randolph (John H.) Papers, LLMVC.

49 "The Management of Negroes," in *Southern Cultivator* 8 (November 1850), pp. 162–4; *Southern Planter* 2 (February 1851), 39–43; *DeBow's Review* 10 (March 1851), 326–8; DeBow, *The Industrial Resources*, 11: 333–6; *DeBow's Review* 19 (September 1855), 358–63; *Southern Cultivator* 13 (June 1855), 171–4.

50 Oaklands Plantation Document 1859, McCutchon (Samuel D.) Papers, LLMVC.

51 Frogmoor Plantation Diary 1857, Turnbull-Bowman-Lyons Family Papers, LLMVC.

52 J. Bowman to Sarah Turnbull, 29 June 1856, Turnbull-Bowman-Lyons Family Papers, LLMVC.

53 "Rules and Regulations on Governing Southdown and Hollywood Plantations," Vol. 34 of "Plantation Diary, 1861–1868," Minor (William J.) and Family Papers, LLMVC.

54 *Southern Planter* 12 (June 1852), 163.

55 Interview with Hunton Love (date unknown), Works Project Administration (WPA) Ex-Slave Narratives, LLMVC.

56 Russell, *Diary*, 180.

57 J. S. Kendall, "New Orleans' Peculiar Institution," *Louisiana Historical Quarterly* 23 (July 1940), 87.

58 Northup, *Twelve Years a Slave*, 148.

59 Interview with Cecil George (15 February 1940), WPA Ex-Slave Narratives, LLMVC; J. Stroyer, *My Life in the South* (Salem, MA, 1885), 423.

60 R. Russell, *North America, its Agriculture and Climate* (Edinburgh, 1857), 249.

61 C. Lyell, *A Second Visit to the United States of North America*, 2 vols (New York, 1849), I: 127.

62 Genovese, *Roll, Jordan, Roll: The World the Slaves Made* (New York, 1974), 286, 309, 312.

63 C. Dew, *Bond of Iron: Master and Slave at Buffalo Forge* (New York, 1994), 333; M. M. Smith, *Mastered by the Clock: Time, Slavery, and Freedom in the American South* (Chapel Hill, NC, 1997), ch. 5.

64 Nutall, *Journey of Travels*, 239.

65 Fogel, *Without Consent*, 162.

66 Olmsted, *Journey in the Seaboard Slave States*, 327.

67 Follett, "Sugar Masters," 391–439.

68 D. Penningroth, "Slavery, freedom, and social claims to property among African-Americans in Liberty County, Georgia, 1850–1880," *Journal of American History* 84 (June 1997), 405–35; McDonald, *Economy and Material Culture*, ch. 2.

69 Marx quoted in R. Ransom and R. Sutch, "Capitalists without capital: the

burden of slavery and the impact of emancipation," *Agricultural History* 62 (Summer 1988), 133.

70 Residence Journal of R. R. Barrow, Tuesday 15 September 1857; Sunday, 18 October 1857, Robert Ruffin Barrow Papers, SHC.

71 H. Martineau, *Retrospect of Western Travel*, 3 vols (London, 1838), 11: 166.

72 Vol. 28, Plantation Journal, 1859–1872, Uncle Sam Plantation Papers, LLMVC.

73 Vol. 46, Plantation Ledger, 1858–1872, Tureaud (Benjamin) Papers, LLMVC.

74 Vol. 5 Expense Book, 1847–1853; Vol. 6, Expense Book, 1853–1863, Randolph (John H.) Papers, LLMVC.

75 William B. Hamilton to William S. Hamilton, 27 September 1858, Hamilton (William S.) Papers, LLMVC.

3

IDEOLOGY AND DEATH ON A SAVANNAH RIVER RICE PLANTATION, 1833–1867

Paternalism amidst "A Good Supply Of Disease And Pain"

Jeffrey R. Young

Jeffrey R. Young's essay examines the question of paternalism through a careful analysis of master–slave relations on a single rice plantation. Rice plantations were largely confined to the coast of South Carolina and Georgia, and they were among the oldest and largest plantations in the South. In the letters of the Manigault family, owners of "Gowrie," Young finds much evidence of sincerely held paternalist values, and he writes that a paternalist ethos "dictated the manner in which lowcountry masters made sense of both their surroundings and themselves." But Young also documents a horrific record of high mortality at Gowrie, largely due to the disease environment of the swamps in which rice grew, as well as continuing resistance from the Gowrie slaves. The Manigaults, convinced of their own good intentions toward their slaves, did not recognize the realities of slavery as the slaves themselves experienced it. Only with the end of slavery during and after the Civil War did the Manigaults come to understand that "their slaves preferred freedom to enslavement by a paternalistic master."

* * *

In recent years, historians have become increasingly aware that North American slavery evolved differently within disparate geographic contexts.[1] In particular, scholars have begun to emphasize the ways that slavery in the Carolina and Georgia lowcountry deviated from the mainstream North American experience of African-American bondage. Unlike the vast majority of nineteenth-century southern masters who planted cotton and resided among their slaves, the tidewater slaveowners planted rice and lived away from their coastal estates for much of the year. Concentrating on this physical separation between master and slave, historians such as Margaret Washington Creel and Charles Joyner have demonstrated that slaves in coastal South Carolina and Georgia enjoyed a relatively large measure of cultural and emotional autonomy from their absentee master.[2] These scholars have done much to illuminate the world of the tidewater slave, but they have not considered the unique lowcountry communities in the wider context of the southern slaveowners' devotion to a shared set of values.

Despite their own regionally distinct brand of slavery, the lowcountry masters committed themselves deeply to a paternalist ethos that could be found all across the nineteenth-century South—an ethos that hinged on the notion of reciprocal responsibilities for master and slave and on the implicit recognition of the slave's humanity. To be sure, this commitment thoroughly contradicted the especially grim conditions that African Americans faced in the coastal swamps.[3] But, as the following examination of one Savannah River rice plantation will reveal, the unhealthful lowcountry environment did not prevent masters from embracing a cohesive set of paternalist values that were, indeed, antithetical to their specific geographic situation. In fact, only by exploring the tension between the slaveowners' paternalism and the physical reality of tidewater slavery can one appreciate the dedication of the master class to an ethos that transcended the tangible boundaries between upcountry cotton and lowcountry rice.

Charles Manigault became a planter in 1825 when his father-in-law presented him with Silk Hope, a Cooper River rice and indigo plantation forty miles above Charleston. At the age of thirty, the prominent descendant of one of South Carolina's wealthiest colonial merchants began planting rice and managing slaves. Like many of the Charleston planters, however, Manigault soon grew frustrated with his upcountry property's marginal soil. In 1833 he turned to the rich tidewater land near the Savannah River and purchased Gowrie plantation for forty thousand dollars.[4]

Continuing to live in and near Charleston for most of the year, Manigault nonetheless took a keen interest in the daily affairs of his Georgia plantation. In numerous letters to his overseers and to his son Louis, who started to manage the property in 1852, Charles Manigault articulated a philosophy of plantation ownership that can only be described as paternalism.[5]

For the Manigaults, slavery necessarily entailed the notion of reciprocal responsibilities. As masters, they expected their slaves to work obediently and efficiently; at the same time, both men explicitly acknowledged their duty to treat their bondservants with compassion. In 1845, for example, Charles Manigault instructed his overseer to "be

Kind in word & deed to all the Negroes for they have always been accustomed to it."[6] Likewise, in 1848, Manigault informed his new overseer that "I expect the kindest treatment of them [the slaves] from you—for this has always been a principal thing with me."[7] By 1853 reference to proper treatment of the slaves had made its way into the contracts that the Manigaults' overseers signed as a prior condition of employment. The overseers agreed that they would "devote all . . . experience and exertions to attend to all Mr. Manigault's interests . . . and to the comfort and welfare of his Negroes . . . treat[ing] them all with kindness and consideration in sickness and in health."[8] And the Manigaults by no means regarded these contracts as empty formalities. On at least one occasion, a potential employee was turned away when he refused to sign one.[9]

Charles Manigault's desire to provide appropriate clothing for his slaves typified his family's paternalism.[10] "My Negroes are very knowing by this time, & will only value what is first Rate," wrote the planter to his supplier in 1847. "I therefore beg your usual care . . . in selecting what you know will give me & them perfect satisfaction. Let the flan-[n]el shirts be . . . of the best quality . . . or they will have to send them back to you—as occurred once before."[11] Moreover, the actual distribution of slave clothing served to reinforce the bond between servant and master. Manigault stressed the importance of personally giving the slaves "their clothes, blankets, etc., *calling each* by *name* and handing it to them." In that moment, the fulfillment of the master's duty toward his slaves brought them face-to-face, in a situation that affirmed the master's self-image as the benevolent patriarch.[12]

Implicit in the Manigaults' attitude toward their slaves was the recognition that blacks were human. By acknowledging that their slaves were people, the Manigaults were conforming to a dominant, nineteenth-century trend among American masters—a trend away from considering African-Americans as savages and toward viewing them as permanently immature but decidedly human beings. "In earlier, harsher times, black slaves had been seen as luckless, unfortunate barbarians," Willie Lee Rose has asserted. "Now they were to be treated as children expected never to grow up."[13] The planters' agricultural journals certainly corroborate this observation. "The master should remember," wrote a Georgia slaveowner in 1851, "that whilst . . . his slaves [are his] . . . property, and as such, owe him proper respect and service . . . they are also persons and have a claim upon his regard and protection." In a similar fashion, a planter reminded the readers of *DeBow's Review* in 1852 that "we should all remember that our slaves are human beings as well as ourselves, and heirs of the same glorious inheritance."[14] And James O. Andrew, a Methodist minister who visited Gowrie in 1857, observed that "the negro is a man, an immortal man, redeemed by Jesus Christ, and cared for by that God who is the universal Father of all men, whatever may be their color."[15] Louis Manigault, for his part, referred to his slaves as "the people" when describing them. "I am now in good trim all day with the people," he wrote his father in 1852, "the only thing I like after all. I sometimes think I could live here with pleasure for six Months without leaving Argyle Island [where the plantation was located]."[16]

Like many other southern planters, the Manigaults did not simply think of their slaves as childlike human beings; rhetorically at least, they regarded their bondservants as their own children, black extensions of the Manigault family. Once again, the Manigaults reflected a larger nineteenth-century southern trend in which slaves were deemed members of their masters' household.[17] Invoking the wisdom of the era, one southern planter asserted that "the first law of slavery is that of kindness from the master to the slave. With that . . . slavery becomes a family relation, next in its attachments to that of parent and child."[18] "Plantation government should be eminently patriarchal, simple, and efficient," maintained a Georgia physician in 1860. The "head of the family, should, in one sense, be the father of the whole concern, negroes and all."[19]

In keeping with this conception of slaves as part of the master's family, Charles Manigault associated his slaves' shortcomings as workers with his own youthful transgressions. "Any accidental stopping [of work] pleases them all I fear," he observed, "just as it used to be with us all at school I suppose. When any thing happened . . . so as to cause a stoppage we subordinates all looked at each other & grinned with delight, &c." Even when he chose to discipline his workers with physical force, Manigault stressed the similarities between such punishment and the floggings his son received from the schoolmaster "Mr. Cotes." Punishment played a role in education and by no means indicated that the recipient was inherently defective. Flogging a particular slave, according to Charles Manigault, did not "take from her value, but only puts you on your guard respecting her, while her good qualities render that a trifle. I did not think it necessary to disclose it to anyone when you used to get so flogged by Mr. Cotes as to leave the black & white marks on your arm & back for some time afterwards."[20] When they "misbehaved," the Manigault slaves were still considered part of the household; when they were whipped, Charles Manigault still associated them with his own son.

Although the Manigaults recognized their slaves' humanity and deemed them members of the household, the owners of Gowrie never assumed that their slaves would work faithfully and efficiently without supervision. As Charles Manigault observed in 1844, his slaves were "cunning enough" to avoid work whenever possible.[21] "Oh! these

Negroes," he would later complain to his son, "when they get out of sight of white control."[22] But, in the Manigaults' opinion, careful management and vigilant protection from the corrupting influence of the outside world would offset the slaves' tendency toward laziness and result in an efficient and happy work force. Like many paternalist masters, the Manigaults sought to isolate their plantation—a measure that would both increase their control over their own household and protect their slaves from outside corruption.[23] "My very quiet & orderly crowd of servants," noted Charles Manigault in 1860, "cannot be trusted with any innovation, strange or unused to them, in their monotonous hum drum routine."[24] Likewise, Charles Manigault informed his overseer in 1848, "I allow no strange Negro to take a wife on my place, & none of [my slaves] to keep a boat," which would have afforded them access to other slave communities.[25] Fearing that even his white overseer could be corrupted by the outside world, Charles instructed Louis to "think twice" before sending the man to Savannah. In order to maximize the attention given to their own affairs, the Manigaults attempted to keep both overseer and slaves "ignorant" of the nearby city.[26] Indeed, Gowrie was to be isolated even when contact with the outside world might have helped the Manigaults control their slaves. For example, Louis Manigault refused to acknowledge the local slave patrol's jurisdiction over the Savannah River estate. Although "true it is that Law & Order should ever reign paramount," he testily informed his neighbor, "still the Master when on his place is the one to examine into his property ... & I Can not allow any new regulations on this place."[27] Insulated within the plantation, the slaves were to be influenced only by their masters' benevolent intentions.[28]

Just like slaveowners all across the South, the Manigaults clearly conceived of themselves as paternalists and acknowledged their duty to treat their slaves in a humane fashion. Yet, simply by virtue of being lowcountry rice planters, they experienced a physical reality that differed greatly from the average southern plantation. Geographically, the crop could be successfully cultivated for profit only on a thin strip of land running down the coast of South Carolina and Georgia.[29] This was the lowcountry, a swampy environment particularly conducive to disease.[30]

Here, the specific labor demands of rice-planting heightened the slaves' risk of becoming ill. Standing knee-deep in the periodically flooded fields, lowcountry rice slaves were directly exposed to a host of water-born infections.[31] The high population density of the rice plantations made the problem more severe. Whereas cotton planters in the mid-nineteenth century owned an average of twenty-four slaves, rice planters employed an average of two hundred and twenty-six.[32] Once contracted, disease could easily pass through the entire plantation population.[33] Because of the crowded and wet environment, slaves toiling on rice plantations experienced far greater mortality than did their counterparts on cotton fields across the South.[34]

Slaves at Gowrie died in appallingly high numbers.[35] The Manigaults' paternalism could not protect their population of workers from the specters of yellow fever, dysentery, pneumonia, and cholera.[36] During the Manigaults' antebellum tenure as owners of Gowrie, the plantation's average crude mortality rate of 97.6 per 1,000 was two-and-one-half times greater than the average annual fertility rate of 37.4 per 1,000; it was also three times greater than the crude mortality rate for North American slaves in the nineteenth century (see Figure 3.1).[37] When cholera decimated two-fifths of the Gowrie slave population in 1834, the plantation's mortality rate approached the level experienced in Europe during the Black Death of the mid-fourteenth century.[38] For a slave like Amey Savage, conditions at Gowrie meant that none of her four children would live through adolescence. For a family of slaves obtained from the Ball plantation in 1854, the Savannah River estate was a death sentence: all six of the newcomers died within a year of their arrival. Old George and his thirteen relatives fared no better. The Manigaults acquired them in 1858 but, as Louis Manigault noted, "Cholera took nearly all off!"[39]

In the face of such mortality, the crude fertility rate for the Manigault slave population remained surprisingly high. New children were born at Gowrie in numbers typical for a noncontraceptive society.[40] The Gowrie slave population was composed of roughly the same number of women and men, an important precondition for a naturally increasing society.[41] And even in the midst of the plantation's high mortality, the slaves formed household relationships conducive to large numbers of children. Nevertheless, had Charles Manigault not periodically augmented the Gowrie population with new purchases and with slaves transferred from his upcountry property, his plantation would have lacked workers. The number of slaves at Gowrie remained approximately the same year after year, despite the Manigaults' purchase of sixteen slaves in 1839, sixty in 1849, and twenty-one more in 1857.[42] By projecting annual population figures for Gowrie slaves as if they were a closed population—in other words, by excluding from yearly totals the slaves brought to Gowrie after 1833 and their offspring—one can see the natural decrease of Gowrie's inhabitants. By 1849 only twenty-nine of the original seventy-two slaves (and their offspring) remained alive. By 1861 the number had fallen to twelve (see Figure 3.2).[43]

Neighboring rice plantations fared no better. In 1834 Savannah River planter John Berkley Grimball stated that "on one plantation *half the workers have died*—on another 40—on another 14—on another 12."[44] Ten years later, Charles Manigault noted that the slave population on a nearby estate had "died off," decreasing from "95 Negroes . . . [to] only 65" in six years. In 1849 the Manigaults' overseer reported that "out of the large number of persons of the [neighboring] Beech Hill & Moorland plantations attacked with Cholera, but one person I am told (& from a reliable source) was saved."[45] According to Langdon Cheves, the lowcountry was "dotted by like misfortunes." Having "placed on this Rice Plantation upwards of 330 negroes & . . . having never sold one," Cheves asserted that "only 230" slaves remained alive.[46]

Such rampant mortality contrasted greatly with the wider North American demographic trend toward a rapidly increasing African-American population. The United States, as Philip D. Curtin has suggested, received only about 5 percent of the approximately 10 million slaves shipped directly from Africa. Yet by 1825, 36 percent of all slaves in the western hemisphere resided on North American soil.[47] Thus, relative to Latin America and the Caribbean, the southern slave population expanded at an astronomical rate. Small wonder, then, that some southern planters believed their slaves "increase[d] like rabbits."[48] Robert William Fogel and Stanley L. Engerman have found that the average southern slave could expect to live thirty-six years from date of birth—a figure that compared favorably with the life expectancy of whites living in contemporary France and Holland.[49] Considered within this context of a relatively healthy North American slave population, the mortality experienced by lowcountry slaves becomes even more dramatic and disturbing. The Manigault slaves could expect to live only nineteen years from their date of birth—seventeen years less than their counterparts across the entire South.[50]

The Manigaults certainly should have realized the risks to which they were subjecting their slaves. Since the colonial era, planters had acknowledged the dangers of the lowcountry. Devastated by disease, early settlers in Georgia quickly discerned the perils of their new environment.[51] By the mid-1700s wealthy tidewater landowners in South Carolina had learned to avoid their plantations in the summer, when sickness was especially prevalent.[52] Planters along the South Carolina and Georgia tidewater continued their pattern of absentee ownership in the nineteenth century. Perceiving that his own coastal property put its occupants at tremendous risk for disease, a Charleston rice planter remarked, "I would as soon stand fifty feet from the best Kentucky rifleman and be shot at by the hour, as to spend a night on my plantation in summer. . . ."[53] Before purchasing property in the Savannah lowcountry, Langdon Cheves was warned that "the mortality on the river is . . . a sad drawback to the otherwise certain profit of our fine and fertile lands."[54] Charleston itself endured its share of disease, earning the epithet "city of disasters." But for the tidewater plantation owners, Charleston proved to be a veritable haven.[55]

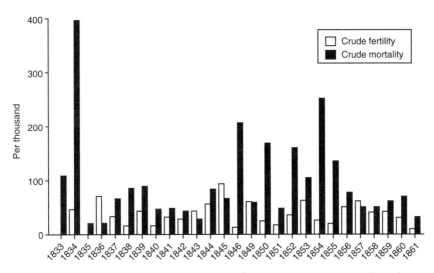

Figure 3.1 Annual crude mortality and fertility rates among the slave population on Gowrie plantation, 1833–1861.

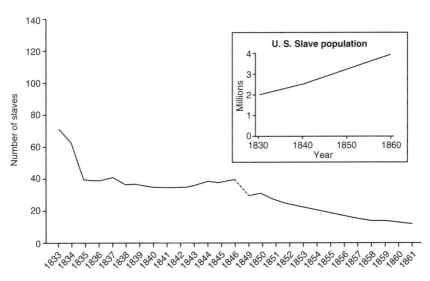

Figure 3.2 Slave population on Gowrie plantation, 1833–1861 (excluding slaves brought onto the plantation after 1833 and their offspring).

Time and time again, both the region's inhabitants and its visitors commented on the poor health of slaves in the lowcountry. One Georgia planter observed that it was common knowledge that "Negroes [i]ncrease on a cotton estate, seldom on a rice estate."[56] Traveling through the lowcountry in 1845, Sir Charles Lyell wrote that "the negroes . . . in the interior, are healthier than those in rice plantations, and multiply faster. . . ."[57] Frederick Law Olmsted noted, as he visited the Carolina coast in 1853, that "the negroes do not enjoy as good health on rice plantations as elsewhere; and the greater difficulty with which their lives are preserved, through infancy especially, shows that the subtle poison of the miasma is not innocuous to them . . ."[58]

Charles Manigault also received regular reports about the suffering on his plantation. K. Washington Skinner, the overseer at Gowrie, notified his employers in 1852 that he had "a good supply of disease and pain among the negroes as usual."[59] A year and a half earlier, Skinner had written that "the woman Jane is yet sick. I fear she will never get well. Hector turned in the Sick House. . . . I have never had such a desperate case of Diarrhrea [sic]. . . . Cudjue died very suddenly [sic] on Tuesday. . . . He lay up one day & died the same night."[60] A few months later, in July 1851, the overseer reported that "the health of the people is not good. I have had a good many cases of fever . . . as well as some of [the] other complaints. On Monday last Cotta and Sarey received a stroke of the sun . . . many of the other negroes staggered about considerably. . . . The children keep unusually healthy—but I fear they will be sick in the Autumn, and many of them sick unto death."[61] In 1855 the overseer, Stephen F. Clark, told Louis Manigault that "the woman Ph[i]llis who cooked for me is dead. . . . Mingos Phillis is dead too. I have lost Charle's Child Ralph and one of Die's Twins and now have 2 very sick at the pine Land. . . ."[62]

In addition, the slaves themselves sent the Manigaults a clear message about Gowrie's dangers. In March 1854 Charles Manigault informed his son that five newly purchased slaves "r[a]n away from Silk Hope" because "they were afraid of going to Savannah River."[63] And Louis Manigault could not help but notice "Able, who has lost nearly all his family, and who himself has been very sick . . . rolling on the ground almost like a Crazy person & Calling his Father & Mother. . . ."[64]

Despite such powerful and abundant evidence, the Manigaults never acknowledged that they were killing their slaves by forcing them to labor in the swamp. Like many other nineteenth-century Americans, both northern and southern, the owners of Gowrie believed that victims of disease were somehow responsible for their own illness—that the morally and physically irresponsible brought sickness upon themselves.[65] Certain that such dangerous behavior was alien to their own communities, the tidewater planters learned to blame outsiders for disease. In 1856, for example, Charles Manigault asserted that the yellow fever in Charleston was "still confined to strangers, or nearly so, & to those amongst them of bad habits, &c. We in our family do not think any thing of it, & hope with Confidence for the best."[66] Prominent lowcountry physicians arrived at similar conclusions. In 1826 Savannah physician William Coffee Daniell attributed a yellow fever epidemic to an influx of Irish families, whose "crowded" households "greatly increased" the city's "filth."[67] Also writing from Savannah, Dr. Richard D. Arnold argued in 1837 that "the deaths that do occur are mostly among the Non-Residents, foreigners, who are victims of intemperance more than climate. . . ."[68]

Having reduced the pathological threat to a question of "habits," the tidewater property owners convinced themselves that proper hygiene would prevent disease. In contrast to the dirty and unhealthy outsiders, lowcountry slaves were expected to adhere to their masters' standards of cleanliness.[69] A. R. Bagshaw, the Manigaults' overseer in 1844, sought to "add to the health" of the plantation by having "the negroe houses all white washed outside and in. . . ."[70] Five years later, another Gowrie overseer assured his employers that he was "using every means in [his] power to ensure cleanliness & health."[71] Of course, mortality at Gowrie could always be blamed on the slaves' inability to internalize the principles of hygiene. Writing to his father in 1854, Louis Manigault explained that "we have had so much sickness" because "the Negroes . . . put all sorts of nasty things in the ditches & then dip up (I am Confident) the same water to drink."[72] By attributing poor health to the slaves' behavior, the Manigaults maintained their faith that disease could be eliminated from the lowcountry environment—a faith shared by doctors in nearby Savannah. "It will be obvious at once," wrote Daniell, "that there is not in the character of our soil, nor in our situation, any thing to preclude us from the enjoyment of health; and, that whatever causes of disease may exist, are within our own control."[73]

Although preventative measures involving hygiene afforded scant defense against sickness, slaveowners like the Manigaults remained undaunted. Armed with a variety of medical cures, they confronted plantation health problems with unbridled and unjustified optimism.[74] In 1854, for example, Louis Manigault told his father "not [to] feel uneasy" about pneumonia at Gowrie. Having already obtained a "recipe" for curing the disease, the younger Manigault confidently asserted that he was "bound to get [the slaves] as well."[75] Ironically, those slaves suffering from the most dangerous afflictions reinforced rather than undermined their masters' paternalism. For when they confronted "serious" cases of disease, the Manigaults willingly incurred the expense of professional medical care—a financial sacrifice that enhanced their sense of moral superiority.[76] In this respect, the lowcountry epidemics enabled the planters to distance themselves from northern manufactures, who, as Richard Arnold observed, could "easily fi[ll] the place of [a] dead operative" and therefore made no effort to protect their employees. Strangely enough, plantation disease allowed the tidewater masters to argue that only in slavery did "Interest & Humanity go hand in hand together."[77]

Filtering their perceptions about sickness through their own self-image of benevolence, the Manigaults never grappled with the harsh and obvious truth about Gowrie. Because of his paternalist outlook, Charles Manigault could credit his "own peculiar care & management" for the increase in his slave population during a period of abnormally low mortality.[78] But the slaveowner hardly commented and certainly never blamed himself when deaths outnumbered births (as they did in almost every year for which slave lists were kept). Louis, for his part, could discuss the slaves' fear of their lowcountry environment without consciously considering the fact that their anxiety was well founded. "I begin to think that it has a bad effect moving them [the slaves out of Gowrie to recuperate]," wrote the younger master. "It makes them think this is a very unhealthy place."[79] Even when composing a list of dead slaves in 1854, Louis Manigault looked to the future with hope. He could "begin now a new [plantation record] book trusting its pages w[ould] not be stained [with the names of the deceased] . . . for years at least to come."[80] Thus, as their own bondservants perished, the Manigaults continued to believe that African-American slaves were thriving under the benevolent guardianship of concerned lowcountry masters.

Clearly, there existed a tremendous disparity between the tidewater slaveholders' perceptions of their environment and the actual conditions on their estates. Troubled by this apparent contradiction, some historians have questioned whether these slaveowners considered themselves paternalists.[81] The Manigaults' experience, however, demonstrates that the paternalist ethos dictated the manner in which lowcountry masters made sense of both their surroundings and themselves. Like other rice planters, the Manigaults first internalized the ideology in Charleston, where the notion of noblesse oblige reigned supreme.[82]

In this urban environment, tidewater slaveowners were born and bred to play the role of gentleman-planter. For even as they extolled the virtues of pastoral life, lowcountry masters made their real home in Charleston.[83] In the summer, they came to avoid exposure to the risks of disease on their lowcountry estates. In the winter, they came for the concerts, the plays, and the horse races.[84] But as the planters watched the musicians, the actors, and the thoroughbreds, they took part in their own social drama. Though they fiercely resented any perceived intrusion of their cherished independence, the planters constantly needed to have their standing in the community affirmed by their peers.[85] Having the right name—Allston, Heyward, Middleton, Manigault— was a matter of tremendous importance, but it was never enough.[86] No matter how respected their fathers and grandfathers may have been, planters still concerned themselves with maintaining the appearance of gentility.[87] The lapse of any individual member put his entire family's reputation at risk. Charles Manigault, for his part, understood that the family's good name depended on the proper image. "If you go wrong *Now* they will say its my fault should either of you on any occasion not shew yourselves well informed well bred Gentlemen," wrote Manigault to Louis and his brother Charles. "So look out sharp," he continued, "lest you Cast any slur on any of us."[88]

By the 1830s the reputation of southern "well-bred Gentlemen" had become inextricably linked to the concept of duty. In planting, in family, and in politics, Charleston's gentry sought to maintain an appearance of noblesse oblige. Resting on the notion of reciprocal obligations, paternalism had become the standard by which statesmen, fathers, and masters were to be judged.[89] Ideally, politicians placed the needs of their constituents before partisan or personal desires, and blood relations gave and received the love that they were obligated to exchange.[90] The standard for planters was, perhaps, the most clearly defined. Defending slavery against increasingly harsh criticism from the outside world, lowcountry masters insisted that the peculiar institution was a noble enterprise—one that required great sacrifice on the part of the planters and caused great improvement on the part of the slaves.[91] Small wonder that Charles Lyell came away with the impression that planters often "retain[ed] possession of inherited estates, which it would be most desirable to sell, and which the owners can not part with, because they feel it would be wrong to abandon the slaves to an unknown purchaser."[92]

Since rice could not be grown for profit without transforming the land itself, tidewater planters struggled to improve their fields as well as their slaves. In order to reclaim the swamps—a process that one lowcountry master remembered as "a great undertaking"—the planters had to control the water level on their land.[93] They therefore constructed an elaborate and expensive network of floodgates, which served to divide the land into neat grids of irrigated soil.[94] Order replaced the chaos of the swamps—a reassuring thought to the lowcountry planters who sensed that their world was being threatened. As these elite southerners were attacked by proponents of free labor and threatened by democratization in the Age of Jackson, their rice plantations reassured them that their social order remained intact.[95] To a low-country planter, the rice estate symbolized the master's ability to control the environment, to mold the physical world until it conformed to the paternalist ethos. As was the case for the manager of one Georgia Sea Island plantation, the rice planter felt pride when "astonished" visitors commented favorably on the "order and regularity" of "such an Establishment in this wild country."[96]

Ironically, the lowcountry masters projected images of control onto a working environment that actually afforded the slaves a great deal of autonomy. Unlike most southern slaves who labored in gangs under the master or overseer's immediate supervision, lowcountry slaves worked individually to finish the tasks allocated to them each morning. Upon completion of their assignments, tidewater slaves were usually permitted to spend the rest of the day on their own activities. The task system allowed slaves who worked quickly (and who were allotted reasonable tasks) to enjoy a few free hours for relaxation; it also fostered an illicit economy that enabled slaves to trade for profit the goods produced on their own time.[97] Yet, as far as the masters were concerned, the task system increased their control over the slaves. Whereas slaves toiling in gangs could surreptitiously work at less than full speed, the task laborer was accountable if the assigned work was not completed by the end of the day. The bottom line, from the master's perspective, was greater efficiency.[98] As absentee slaveowners, the lowcountry planters were unable in any event to supervise their slaves directly. The task system returned to them a measure of control, while simultaneously appealing to their paternalist sensibilities by encouraging a contented work force. "Experience has proven that whenever work . . . can be properly parceled out into tasks, it is much better to do so," wrote a Georgia planter. "If the overseer has judgement, he will get more work, and the negro will be better satisfied . . ."[99] Echoing this conclusion, the *Southern Agriculturist* noted that since "the task of each [slave] is separate, imperfect work can readily be traced to the neglectful worker."[100]

Seeking total power over their slaves, planters like the Manigaults mistakenly imagined that their mastery was complete. In fact, the realities of the environment and the slaves' burning desire for freedom made the slaveowners' vision of the lowcountry a fantasy. To protect their own feelings of self-worth—feelings that hinged on their role as paternalist planters—the Manigaults clung to the notion that their slaves were obedient extensions of a well-maintained household. The perseverance of this belief, even while unfortunate African Americans suffered and died in large numbers, demonstrates the intensity of the lowcountry masters' paternalist convictions—not their insincerity.

Despite the dangers of their environment and the oppressive ideology of their masters, the Manigault slaves continually struggled against the plantation order. Forced to toil in the swamp, they found ways to make their displeasure known. Jack Savage, for example, worked slowly and complained frequently. "I found it absolutely necessary to take hold of Carpenter Jack and learn him how to progress more rapidly with his work, as he did but little, and would always be ready to say that 'him one had all the work to do,' " recounted the Gowrie overseer in 1852.[101] Other slaves displayed their displeasure in more dramatic and direct fashion. Tired of their work, some simply departed until they were in the mood to return. "Judy has walked off," wrote the overseer in 1855, "but I hope that she will feel rested and walk back in a few days as G. Jack did."[102] London, on the other hand, committed suicide rather than endure the continued trauma of life at Gowrie. Hoping to avoid a flogging, he fled to the river, where the driver pleaded with him to return. "His ans[wer]," as Charles Manigault was informed by William Capers, "was he would drown himself before he would and he sank soon after. . . ."[103]

Lowcountry slaves also demonstrated the capacity to resist en masse. Rather than resorting to direct force, which would have been quickly self-defeating, the slaves took advantage of the inherent tensions in the absentee master–overseer relationship. Masters, as a rule, were dissatisfied with the performance of their supervisors, fearing that they were either neglecting the slaves or slighting the crops. Realizing that their owners would often take their word against that of a temporary employee, the slaves understood that an organized protest could change the plantation status quo.[104] James Haynes, the Manigaults' overseer in 1847, certainly discovered that such widespread insubordination could occur. He was dismissed from his position on a neighboring plantation after thirteen slaves "ran off . . . with tales" of his wrongdoing. Haynes blamed the incident on "a fabrication of falsehoods hatched by the negroes and told to [his employer]."[105] Ten years earlier, according to Charles Manigault, "almost every grown Negro [at Gowrie had] . . . pushed off in a body & [gone] to Savannah with serious Charges against" the overseer.[106]

Even as they undermined the plantation household, the slaves at Gowrie were establishing their own network of relatively stable family relationships. Although Charles Manigault sometimes sold slaves as punishment "for their misconduct," very few of them actually departed under these circumstances.[107] When the Manigaults did threaten to separate parent and child, the Gowrie slaves fought to protect their families. "Jenny is confined," wrote the Manigaults' overseer on one such occasion. "I think you will have trouble with her if the Child is taken from her[.] I have been informed she says she [will] run away before she will leave her Child. . . ."[108] Most of the slaves' domestic arrangements, however, endured until death or until the maturation of children changed the household composition. The slaves' naming patterns demonstrated the strength of these relationships. Offspring were named after grandparents, uncles, and aunts. And when parents died, members of the community demonstrated their willingness to welcome the orphaned children into their own households. For example, when Susey died in 1848, her daughter Mary was adopted by Matilda.

Likewise, Betsy welcomed the two-year-old Cato into her household when the boy's mother, Crecia, died in 1855.[109]

Much to Charles Manigault's displeasure, this community had its own semiautonomous economy. Slaves traded among themselves and even sold their clothing, which Manigault viewed as a symbol of his benevolent control over Gowrie. "For they are (some of them) so apt to swap & sell," wrote Manigault, "that I have been several times provoked at hearing that some of the large thick Jackets which cost me so much trouble & money to get made up in Charleston for them have been seen on the backs of my neighbour's Negroes."[110] The Manigault slaves extended their trade to Savannah as well as to nearby plantations. Bob, for example, was apprehended in town with "8 or 9 bushels of Rough Rice" and one of the Manigaults' boats.[111]

The slaves' resistance against the plantation order, however, did not force Charles or Louis Manigault to reconsider their paternalism. At times, they placed their ideals ahead of skepticism and simply believed their slaves when they promised to behave. Bob, for his part, avoided severe punishment for absconding with the Manigaults' boat and rice merely by telling the overseer that he would not repeat the incident.[112] In other cases the Manigaults tried to correct their slaves' behavior with discipline—but only in ways that reinforced the Manigaults' self-image as paternalists. In 1846 Charles Manigault sold the "small Rice"—the inferior portion of his crop—instead of giving it to his workforce, because he was frustrated with their "groundless complaints." The following year, he instructed his overseer to "tell them that tho I can sell it & with half the money buy Corn instead, & put thereby half the money in my pocket, that you wrote to me stating their good Conduct, & that I have decided to let them now have all the small Rice again—on trial; & it depends entirely on them whether they shall have it in future or not."[113] Manigault clearly wanted his slaves to reaffirm his self-image of benevolence; he wanted them to appreciate the sacrifices he made for them, and, paradoxically, he was willing to punish them until they did so.

Only as heightening sectional tension undermined their control did the Manigaults understand that their slaves preferred freedom to enslavement by a paternalistic master. Even then, even as large numbers of the slaves openly defied their authority, the realization came slowly. In August 1860 a slave named Hector liberated himself from the Manigaults. Forsaking the runaway's customary refuge in the swamp, Hector defied his legal owners on their own property. The Manigaults' distraught overseer, William Capers, informed them that the rebel, armed with "a pr. of Pistols & Sword," had "been on the Plantation since he left and . . . [would] not be taken."[114] At the same time Hector left, the Manigaults also learned that "Daniel ran off" after "breaking up" a buggy and turning loose the mule. Several months later, Capers informed the slaveowners that "Big Hector & Carp[enter] George left the Plantation . . . without one word being said to them."[115] In January 1861 Louis Manigault's brother Gabriel suggested that "the only [thing] . . . to do now is to hunt [the runaway slaves] with dogs. . . . It is absolutely necessary to go armed with a double barrelled gun . . . with the intention of shooting . . . any negro who attempts to resist. . . ."[116] The advice did not stop the runaways, and the new year brought continued unrest at Gowrie. The masters were told, for example, that "Big George" had "attempted to run off in presents of the entire force" and in plain sight of the overseer.[117] Capers wrote to Charles Manigault that Jack Savage had "resisted the Driver" who "caught [him] in [the] Back River" attempting to escape. In a letter to his father a few weeks later, Louis Manigault described Savage as "the worst Negro I have ever Known. I have for two years past looked upon him as one Capable of Committing murder or burning down this dwelling, or doing any act."[118]

Their world was crumbling, but the Manigaults proved reluctant to alter their attitudes toward the men and women they held in bondage—attitudes that reflected their firm belief that they understood their slaves and acted always in the slaves' best interest.[119] Thus, Louis Manigault earnestly maintained that his slave Ishmael had "completely changed" for the better, despite having been caught in 1861 stockpiling ammunition to take to the Yankees.[120] The Manigaults even believed that Jack Savage and Big George could be redeemed once they had been properly disciplined. Charles informed his son in 1862 that the two "have been well punished, & profess great Penitence & now see clearly how easy it is to fix a bad Negro."[121]

Indeed, the Manigaults' conviction that they could salvage their relationships with their slaves contrasted greatly with their reaction to white employees who were also beginning to question their authority. Louis Manigault erupted in anger when he learned that Saly, a white dressmaker, had written an "insulting note" to his wife. Manigault characterized the woman as an "ungrateful upstart, whose true character is now at last developing itself. . . . Indeed, God has punished the little Animal, the bright page in her history is ended, & her 1st chapter of Misery, toil, & ruin is at hand." By contrast, the young planter maintained his faith in Captain, even when the slave resisted his wife's authority. "Now I think if you lock him up in one of those upper rooms for 24 hours he will come to his senses," wrote Manigault. If not, he continued, the unruly slave should be sent "to wait on me . . . [after which] Captain will return to you a Changed Negro."[122]

But as the war progressed, the Manigaults finally perceived that the master–slave relationship could not be salvaged. Realizing that their chances for freedom were improving, the slaves no longer gave the impression that they could be easily corrected through physical pun-ishment. William Capers informed his employers that he "had an occasion to whip [Rose, an eighteen-year-old slave] & she refused to be tied & fought me until she had not a rag of clothes on."[123] The masters of Gowrie soon discovered that the most trusted slaves would escape as soon as they were confident of success. When the house slave Dolly ran off in 1863, Louis Manigault did not believe that she had delib-erately rejected her favored position in his household. He surmised that she had "been enticed off by some White Man...."[124] Yet, after investigating the matter, Louis Manigault discovered that Dolly had actually run away on her own volition with a slave that had been "courting" her.[125] Likewise, the young master of Gowrie realized that Hector—a slave who had been "kindly treated ... upon numerous occasions" and who had been "esteemed highly" by the Manigaults— "was the very first to murmur, and would have hastened to the embrace of his Northern Brethren, could he have foreseen the least prospect of a successful escape."[126] The Manigaults' assumptions that they knew their slaves and that their slaves were in a sense their chil-dren steadily evaporated. The young master who had once lovingly called his slaves "the people" now referred to "that stupid dirty Negro Joe" with "his big Cat-fish mouth...."[127] Such hostility intensified as the last of the Manigault slaves emancipated themselves. Having finally been deserted by every one of his house slaves, Charles Manigault "resolved never to have a Negro in our house again."[128]

Encouraged by the success of the Union forces, the slaves at Gowrie and Silk Hope did more than flee. "They broke into our well furnished residences on each plantation," recounted a bitter Charles Manigault, "and stole or destroyed everything therein." And in a scene of tremen-dous poetic justice, the slaves attacked the visible manifestations of the Manigaults' self-image—their portraits, which had been commissioned from leading Charleston painters. Taken by the newly free African Americans, these images were "hung up in their Negro houses, while some of the family portraits (as if to turn them into ridicule) they left out, night and day, exposed to the open air."[129]

Humbled by the war, the Manigaults struggled to survive. "We are certainly experiencing the most trying times.... The future looks gloomy enough ...," wrote Louis Manigault in 1865.[130] To support his wife and children, he began to work as a clerk in a counting house. Desperate for cash, he suffered the indignity of pawning a writing desk—which his father had purchased in 1833, the same year that he had acquired Gowrie—for an extra twelve dollars in spending money.[131] Although his family retained ownership of Gowrie, Louis Manigault rented out the property because he could no longer afford to cultivate a crop.[132]

In this context the previously proud master returned to his plantation in 1867. Walking the banks of the Savannah River for the first time
in two years, he was struck by "the cruel hand of War" and by "the
change on every side. . . ." Seeking out the men and women that he
used to own, a surprised Louis Manigault "beh[e]ld young Women
to whom I had most frequently presented Ear-Rings, Shoes, Calicos,
Kerchiefs &c. &c.—formerly pleased to meet me, but now not even
lifting the head as I passed." Meanwhile, Jack Savage—the slave that
Manigault had feared and despised the most—unexpectedly greeted
his former master. Here was final evidence that the planters had
known "nothing of the Negro Character." Amid the ruins of Gowrie,
Manigault finally appreciated that "that former mutual & pleasing
feeling of Master towards Slave and vice versa is now as a dream of the
past."[133]

Like the Union shell that shattered Louis Manigault's bedroom in
Charleston, the African-Americans' campaign for freedom wreaked
havoc on the Manigaults' conception of a well-maintained household.
The slaveowners now acknowledged the impossibility of harmonious
race relations characterized by reciprocal responsibilities. But just as
the Union shell had left "the Body of the[ir] House untouched," the
Manigaults' new vision of their former slaves did not force them to
abandon paternalism's central premise.[134]

Despite the slaves' emphatic rejection of their owners' authority and
despite the vast disparity between the Manigaults' ideology and the
reality at Gowrie, the Manigaults continued to insist that their mastery
had been benevolent. Reflecting on the former institution of African-
American bondage, Charles Manigault distinguished between slavery
in the South and slavery in the West Indies. Foreshadowing the analysis of modern scholars, the planter asserted that "in the West India
Colonies, their loss of slaves, [was continuous . . . all those Estates . . .
belonged to] slave owners, [who] were generally absentees. . . ." But
southern slaveowners, observed Manigault, were "surrounded by
our Negroes [and] attend[ed] personally to their comforts. . . . We saw,
that they ever received good, wholesome food & the sick & aged
attended to . . . All this, naturally resulted, in mutual family interests &
kind personal feelings so generally prevailing (until recently) between
Masters & their slaves amongst us." Proof that southern "slaves were
not in [a] state of discomfort, & oppression," insisted Manigault, could
be found in their population's "wonderful Increase."[135] Clinging to
his own paternalist assumptions about slavery, the master of Gowrie
perceived no boundary between the Savannah River rice estates and
more healthful upcountry properties. After three decades of devastat-
ing plantation mortality, Manigault still believed that the Gowrie
slaves had flourished under his rule. Had it been otherwise, had the

Manigaults and other tidewater masters acknowledged the grimly unique circumstances on their own coastal estates, they might have agonized over the human suffering they had caused. Instead, they remained confident in the righteousness of their mastery. In this sense, despite all that separated them from their upcountry counterparts, the lowcountry slaveowners truly were members of a distinctly southern master class.

NOTES

1 See, for example, Ira Berlin, "Time, Space, and the Evolution of Afro-American Society on British Mainland North America," *American Historical Review*, LXXXV (February 1980), 44–78. . . .
2 Margaret Washington Creel, *"A Peculiar People"*: *Slave Religion and Community-Culture among the Gullahs* (New York and London, 1988); Charles Joyner, *Down by the Riverside: A South Carolina Slave Community* (Urbana, Ill., 1984). . . .
3 Of course, the paternalist ideology always contradicted the reality of African-American bondage. As [Eugene] Genovese has observed, "the problems inherent in the contradiction in the slave's legal existence as man and thing constantly emerged." Genovese, *Roll, Jordan, Roll: The World the Slaves Made* (New York, 1974), 88.
4 Maurice Alfred Crouse, "The Manigault Family of South Carolina, 1685–1783" (Ph. D. diss., Northwestern University, 1964); James M. Clifton, "A Half-Century of a Georgia Rice Plantation," *North Carolina Historical Review*, XLVII (October 1970), 392–95; and Clifton, ed., *Life and Labor on Argyle Island: Letters and Documents of a Savannah River Rice Plantation, 1833–1867* (Savannah, 1978), xvii–xx.
5 Indeed, the Manigaults make numerous appearances in Genovese's examination of the paternalist ethos. See *Roll, Jordan, Roll*, 15, 19, 100–102, 112, 386–87, and 555; . . . .
6 "Instructions for Sub-overseer," prepared by Charles Manigault for Mr. Papot, 1845, in Clifton, ed., *Life and Labor*, 23.
7 Charles Manigault to Jesse T. Cooper, January 10, 1848, in Clifton, ed., *Life and Labor*,. 61. . . .
8 Overseer Contract between Charles Manigault and Stephen F. Clark, 1853, in Clifton, ed., *Life and Labor*, 135. . . .
9 See four letters from Charles Manigault to Louis Manigault, December 28, 1858, and January 10 and 14 and March 27, 1859, all in Clifton, ed., *Life and Labor*, 267, 270–71, 272–73, and 283–85 respectively. . . .
10 Clifton, ed., *Life and Labor*, xxxii–xxxiii.
11 Charles Manigault to Mathiessen and Co., September 1, 1847, in Clifton, ed., *Life and Labor*, 58. . . .
12 Quoted in Genovese . . . *Roll, Jordan, Roll*, 555. . . .
13 Willie Lee Rose, *Slavery and Freedom*, ed. by William W. Freehling (New York, 1982), 25. . . . George M. Fredrickson has argued that the image of blacks as savages retained its currency. Fredrickson, *The Black Image in the White Mind: The Debate on Afro-American Character and Destiny, 1817–1914* (New York and other cities, 1971), Chap. 2. . . .
14 Nathan Bass, "Essay on the Treatment and Management of Slaves," . . . in James O. Breeden, ed., *Advice among Masters: The Ideal in Slave Management*

in the Old South (Westport, Conn., 1980), 12; "Management of Slaves," *DeBow's Review*, XIII (August 1852), 193–94, in Breeden, ed., *Advice among Masters*, 45.

15 James O. Andrew, "Our People of Color", in Charles F. Deems, ed., *Annals of Southern Methodism for 1857* (Nashville, 1858), 310. . . .

16 Louis Manigault to Charles Manigault, December 31, 1852, in Clifton, ed., *Life and Labor*, 135; .. . . .

17 In particular, see Elizabeth Fox-Genovese, *Within the Plantation Household: Black and White Women of the Old South* (Chapel Hill, 1988), 24–30; and Genovese, " 'Our Family, White and Black': Family and Household in the Southern Slaveholders' World View," in Carol Bleser, ed., *The Joy and the Sorrow: Women, Family, and Marriage in the Victorian South, 1830–1900* (New York, 1991), 69–87.

18 J.B. O'Neall (1852), 278, quoted in Phillips, *American Negro Slavery*, 513.

19 "The Peculiarities & Diseases of Negroes" (1860), quoted in Breeden, ed., *Advice Among Masters*, 59.

20 Charles Manigault to Louis Manigault, October 18, 1856, and January 26, 1860, in Clifton, ed., *Life and Labor*, 230, 292.

21 Plantation Journal of Charles Manigault, [May 5], 1844, ibid., 8.

22 Charles Manigault to Louis Manigault, February 20, 1853, ibid., 138.

23 Traveling through the southern states in 1853, Frederick Law Olmsted observed that most slaveholders discouraged "intercourse" between their own slaves and "those of other plantations." Olmsted, *A Journey in the Seaboard Slave States* . . . (New York, 1963), 448. . . .

24 Charles Manigault to Louis Manigault, March 16, 1860, in Clifton, ed., *Life and Labor*, 293. . . .

25 Charles Manigault to Jesse T. Cooper, January 10, 1848, ibid., 62.

26 Charles Manigault to Louis Mauigault, February 21, 1856, ibid., 210.

27 Louis Manigault to C. W. Jones, December 17, 1855, in Clifton, ed., *Life and Labor*, 202. . . .

28 . . . By the nineteenth century the Gullah dialects of the sea island slaves varied by location, suggesting that the masters had effectively sealed their plantations off from outside linguistic influences. See Peter H. Wood, *Black Majority: Negroes in Colonial South Carolina from 1670 through the Stono Rebellion* (New York, 1974), 190.

29 By the mid-eighteenth century rice growers had begun to take advantage of tidewater planting, in which the flow of water from coastal rivers was controlled by an elaborate system of floodgates . . . [see for example] Joyce E. Chaplin, "Tidal Rice Cultivation and the Problem of Slavery in South Carolina and Georgia, 1760–1815," *William and Mary Quarterly*, 3d Ser., XLIX (January 1992), 29–61.

30 Low summer water levels resulted in pools of standing water, the perfect breeding ground for amoebic parasites and disease-carrying mosquitoes. See Mart A. Stewart, "Land Use and Landscapes: Environment and Social Change in Coastal Georgia, 1680–1880" (Ph.D. diss., Emory University, 1988), 134. As Kenneth Kiple and Virginia King observed in their study of cholera among southern blacks, those living along the rivers were hardest hit by disease. Kenneth F. Kiple and Virginia H. King, *Another Dimension to the Black Diaspora: Diet, Disease, and Racism* (Cambridge, Eng., 1981), 152–54.

31 See Leslie Howard Owens, *This Species of Property: Slave Life and Culture in the Old South* (New York, 1976), 21; and Kiple and King, *Another Dimension to the Black Diaspora*, 156.

32 Smith, *Slavery and Rice Culture*, 9. . . . In keeping with economy of scale, the largest rice plantations were the most profitable. See Dale Evans Swan, *The Structure and Profitability of the Antebellum Rice Industry: 1859* (New York, 1975), 104–12. . . .

33 In her study of South Carolina rice plantations owned by the Ball family, Cheryll Ann Cody asserted that population density might have been a key variable in slave mortality. See Cody, "Slave Demography and Family Formation: A Community Study of the Ball Family Plantations, 1720–1896" (Ph.D. dissertation, University of Minnesota, 1982), 221. . . . Also see Richard H. Steckel, "A Dreadful Childhood: The Excess Mortality of American Slaves", in Kenneth F. Kiple, ed., *The African Exchange: Toward a Biological History of Black People* (Durham, N. C., 1987), 200–201. . . .

34 For the higher rate of mortality on rice plantations, see Robert William Fogel, *Without Consent or Contract: The Rise and Fall of American Slavery* (New York, 1989), 127. . . .

35 I computed mortality and fertility rates from reconstructed biographical data on 337 Manigault slaves. The data was drawn from correspondence and slave lists produced by the Manigaults between 1833 and 1867. . . .

36 Scholars continue to debate whether the genesis of paternalism resulted in a higher rate of increase for slave populations. Some historians have argued that as the slaveowners changed their attitudes about their bondservants, the slave populations experienced a higher rate of natural increase. See J. Harry Bennett, Jr., "The Problem of Slave Labor Supply at the Codrington Plantations," *Journal of Negro History*, XXXVII (April 1952), 137; Daniel C. Littlefield, "Plantations, Paternalism, and Profitability: Factors Affecting African Demography in the Old British Empire," *Journal of Southern History*, XLVII (May 1981), 167–82; . . . . On the other hand, a number of scholars have convincingly argued that planters' attitudes were not a key variable in the slaves' rate of increase. See Herbert G. Gutman, *The Black Family in Slavery and Freedom, 1750–1925* (New York, 1976), 310; Fogel, *Without Consent or Contract*, 123–29; Herbert S. Klein and Stanley L. Engerman, "Fertility Differentials between Slaves in the United States and the British West Indies: A Note on Lactation Practices and Their Possible Implications," *William and Mary Quarterly*, 3d Ser., XXXV (April 1978), 357–74; and Kenneth F. Kiple and Virginia H. Kiple, "Slave Child Mortality: Some Nutritional Answers to a Perennial Puzzle," *Journal of Social History*, X (March 1977), 309 n11.

37 James M. Clifton observed, in passing, that deaths outnumbered births at Gowrie. See *Life and Labor*, xxxiv. Also see Edmund L. Drago's review of *Life and Labor*, in the *South Carolina Historical Magazine*, LXXXII (October 1981), 368. . . .

38 See Philip Ziegler, *The Black Death* (New York, 1969). . . .

39 Information about the births and deaths of Alney Savage's children was drawn from the reconstructed biographical information on the Manigault slaves. See note 35 above.

40 For example, my calculated figure for the average crude fertility at Gowrie, 37.4 per 1,000, fits within the range established for England's population from the mid-sixteenth to the early nineteenth century. See E. A. Wrigley and R. S. Schofield, *The Population History of England, 1541–1871: A Reconstruction* (Cambridge, Mass., 1981), 531–35. . . . Factoring in a conservative estimate for infant slave mortality on antebellum rice plantations (300 per 1,000), the crude fertility rate at Gowrie approaches 46 per 1,000, a figure closer to the southern average. . . .

41 1n 1833 men composed 47 percent of the Gowrie slave population; in 1849, 52 percent; and in 1855, 47 percent. . . .

42 For the purchase of these new slaves for Gowrie, consult the slave lists dated February 1839 and April 30, 1857, Manigault Family Papers, Southern Historical Collection, University of North Carolina (SHC); and the list dated April 1849, Louis Manigault Papers, Duke University (DU). [Figure 2 in the original has been omitted—ed.]

43 My projections for the Gowrie slaves as a closed population were drawn from my demographic reconstruction.

44 John Berkley Grimball Diary, September 18, 1834, series 2, folder 18, Grimball Papers (typewritten transcripts, SHC).

45 Plantation Journal of Charles Manigault, [December 5], 1844, in Clifton, ed., *Life and Labor*, 11; Jesse T. Cooper to Charles Manigault, July 24, 1849, ibid., 68.

46 Langdon Cheves to T. P. Huger, December 30, 1846, Langdon Cheves Papers (typewritten transcripts in the Georgia Historical Society [GHS], Savannah). . . .

47 Philip D. Curtin, *The Atlantic Slave Trade: A Census* (Madison, Wisc., 1969), 88–89. . . .

48 John B. Lamar to Howell Cobb, May 16, 1847, in Ulrich B. Phillips *et al.*, eds., *A Documentary History of American Industrial Society*, Vol. 1 (Cleveland, 1910), 179.

49 Fogel and Engerman, *Time On the Cross*, 125. . . .

50 Before calculating the life expectancy from birth for the Gowrie slaves, I increased the cohort of life spans lasting less than one year until crude infant mortality of approximately 300 per 1,000 was reflected. I did this to compensate for the infant deaths that surely were not reflected in the annually updated Gowrie slave lists.

51 Stewart, "Land Use and Landscapes," 133–36; and H. Roy Merrens and George D. Terry, "Dying in Paradise: Malaria, Mortality, and the Perceptual Environment in Colonial South Carolina," *Journal of Southern History*, 50 (Nov. 1984), 533–50.

52 Wood, *Black Majority*, 73.

53 "Mr. X", quoted in Olmsted, *Journey in the Seaboard Slave States*, 419.

54 James Hamilton, Jr., to Cheves, April 14, 1830, quoted in Archie Vernon Huff, Jr., *Langdon Cheves of South Carolina* (Columbia 1977), 17, 1–72.

55 For Charleston's problems with recurrent epidemics and fires, see Walter J. Fraser, Jr., *Charleston! Charleston!: The History of a Southern City* (Columbia, 1989), 189–217 (quotation 217). . . .

56 Pierce Butler quoted in Stewart, "Land Use and Landscapes," 326.

57 Sir Charles Lyell, *A Second Visit to the United States*, Vol. I (New York, 1849), 249.

58 Olmsted, *Journey to the Seaboard Slave States*, 418. . . .

59 K. Washington Skinner to Charles Manigault, October 13, 1852, in Clifton, ed., *Life and Labor*, 123.

60 K. Washington Skinner to Charles Manigault, May 30, 1851, ibid., 80.

61 K. Washington Skinner to Charles Manigault, July 12, 1851, ibid., 83.

62 Stephen F. Clark to Louis Manigault, August 10, 1855, ibid., 196.

63 Charles Manigault to Louis Manigault, March 3, 1854, ibid., 175; Charles Manigault to Louis Manigault, March 6, 1854, ibid., 177. . . .

64 Louis Manigault to Charles Manigault, December 26, 1854, in Clifton, ed., *Life and Labor*, 190–91.

65 Charles E. Rosenberg, *The Cholera Years: The United States in 1832, 1849, and 1866* (Chicago, 1962), 1–64.

66 Charles Manigault to Louis Manigault, October 11, 1856, in Clifton, ed., *Life and Labor*, 228.

67 W. C. Daniell, *Observations upon the Autumnal Fevers of Savannah* (Savannah, 1826), 23.

68 Richard H. Shryock, ed., *Letters of Richard D. Arnold, M.D., 1808–1876* ... (Papers of the Trinity College Historical Society, Double Series XVIII–XIX, [Durham, N. C.], 1929), 14.

69 For example, "Hygiene in Savannah," *Savannah Journal of Medicine*, I (January 1859), 354–59.

70 A. R. Bagshaw to Charles Manigault, July 20, 1844, in Clifton, ed., *Life and Labor*, 14. ...

71 Jesse T. Cooper to Charles Manigault, August 24, 1849, in Clifton, ed., *Life and Labor*, 72.

72 Manigault to Charles Manigault, December 26, 1854, ibid., 191.

73 Daniell, *Observations upon the Autumnal Fevers*, 20. ...

74 By the late antebellum period, planters could obtain "recipes" for cures from a variety of sources. For professional medical reference books, see Daniell, *Observations upon the Autumnal Fevers*; .. ..

75 Two letters from Louis Manigault to Charles Manigault, both dated February 25, 1854, in Clifton, ed., *Life and Labor*, 171–72.

76 James Haynes to Charles Manigault, June 1, 1846, ibid., 35.

77 Arnold to Mr. McCall, August 29, 1849, in Shryock, ed., *Letters of Richard D. Arnold*, 33–34.

78 Charles Manigault to Alfred Huger, April 1, 1847, in Clifton, ed., *Life and Labor*, 52–53. ...

79 Louis Manigault to Charles Manigault, April 19, 1853, in Clifton, ed., *Life and Labor*, 155.

80 Gowrie Slave List, April 23, 1854, ibid., 184.

81 See George M. Fredrickson, "Masters and Mudsills: The Role of Race in the Planter Ideology of South Carolina", in Fredrickson, *The Arrogance of Race: Historical Perspectives on Slavery, Racism, and Social Inequality* (Middletown, Conn., 1988), 15–27; Creel, *Peculiar People*, 120, 188, 243, and 393 n64; Michael Mullin, ed., *American Negro Slavery: A Documentary History* (New York, 1976), 8–29; Freehling, *The Road to Disunion*, I, 229–30; Kenneth M. Stampp, *The Peculiar Institution: Slavery in the Ante-Bellum South* (New York, 1956), 325; and Randall M. Miller, "The Golden Isles: Rice and Slaves Along the Georgia Coast," *Georgia Historical Quarterly*, LXX (Spring 1986), 90–91.

82 Historians continue to disagree about the circumstances in which planter paternalism originated. Eugene Genovese and Willie Lee Rose have depicted the paternalist ethos as essentially a nineteenth-century phenomenon. James Oakes, on the other hand, has suggested that the ideology flowered in the eighteenth century and declined thereafter. Consult *The Ruling Race: A History of American Slaveholders* (New York, 1982), 196. ...

83 Indeed, Charles Manigault would eventually chastise Louis for spending too much time away from Charleston. ...

84 "William H. Pease and Jane H. Pease, *The Web of Progress: Private Values and Public Styles in Boston and Charleston, 1828–1843* (New York, 1985), 138–42; and Fraser, *Charleston! Charleston!*, 195.

85 Michael P. Johnson, "Planters and Patriarchy: Charleston, 1800–1860," *Journal of Southern History*, XLVI (February 1980). 45–72; and Bertram Wyatt-Brown, *Southern Honor: Ethics and Behavior in the Old South* (New York and Oxford, 1982), 114.

86 A rhyme captured the significance of family names in antebellum Charleston: "I thank thee Lord on bended knee I'm half Porcher and half Huger. . . . For other blessings thank thee too- My grandpa was a Petigru" Quoted in Fraser, *Charleston! Charleston!*, 196. . . .

87 Bertram Wyatt-Brown has discussed the ways in which honor was indistinguishable from reputation in the antebellum South. See *Southern Honor*, 14–15. . . .

88 Charles Manigault to Louis Manigault, November 15, 1846, quoted in Johnson, "Planters and Patriarchy," 49. . . .

89 For a discussion of the evolution of planters' defenses of slavery—defenses that hinged on the assumptions of paternalism—into a coherent ideology, see Drew Gilpin Faust, ed., *The Ideology of Slavery: Proslavery Thought in the Antebellum South, 1830–1860* (Baton Rouge, 1981), 1–20 . . . Larry E. Tise, *Proslavery: A History of the Defense of Slavery in America, 1701–1840* (Athens, Ga., 1987). . . .

90 Kenneth S. Greenberg, *Masters and Statesmen: The Political Culture of American Slavery* (Baltimore, 1985), 18; and Stowe, *Intimacy and Power in the Old South*, 191.

91 On the eve of the Civil War a number of aristocratic Charleston planters articulated their paternalist conception of the proper relationship between whites and blacks. Decrying proposed legislation that would have prevented the city's free black craftsmen from practicing their trades, these planters characterized blacks as "a class of our inhabitants who ought to be objects of our care and protection." "Let us not begin now for the first time in our history," they insisted, "to subject ourselves to the charge of oppressing the weak and unresisting." See undated petition 0010–003-ND-2801–01, Petitions to the General Assembly (South Carolina Department of Archives and History, Columbia). . . .

92 Lyell, *Second Visit to the United States*, I, 210. . . .

93 Duncan Clinch Heyward, *Seed from Madagascar* (Chapel Hill, 1937), 18.

94 Stewart, "Land Use and Landscapes," 251–55. . . .

95 For a discussion of nineteenth-century lowcountry planters' sense that their world was being threatened, see David Moltke-Hansen, "Expansion of Intellectual Life: A Prospectus," in Michael O'Brien and Moltke-Hansen, eds., *Intellectual Life in Antebellum Charleston* (Knoxville, 1986), 37; George C. Rogers, Jr., *Charleston in the Age of the Pinckneys* (Norman, Okla., 1969), 156; Rogers, *Evolution of a Federalist: William Loughton Smith of Charleston (1758–1812)* (Columbia, 1962), 387–88. . . .

96 Roswell King, Jr., quoted in Stewart, "Land Use and Landscapes," 331–32. . . .

97 Morgan, "Work and Culture"; Morgan, "The Ownership of Property by Slaves"; and Berlin and Morgan's introduction to "The Slaves' Economy: Independent Production by Slaves in the Americas," *Slavery & Abolition*, XII (May 1991), 1–27.

98 See Olmsted, *Journey in the Seaboard Slave States*, 434–36 and 478–79; and Frances Anne Kemble, *Journal of a Residence on a Georgia Plantation, 1838–1839* (New York, 1863).

99 Robert Collins, "Essay on the Treatment and Management of Slaves," in Breeden, ed., *Advice Among Masters*, 21.

100 Quoted by Stampp, *Peculiar Institution*, 55.

101 K. Washington Skinner to Charles Manigault, October 9, 1852, in Clifton, ed., *Life and Labor*, 121–22.

102 Stephen F. Clark to Charles Manigault, September 25, 1855, ibid., 198.

103 William Capers to Charles Manigault, June 13, 1860, in Rose, ed., *Documentary History of Slavery*, 284–85 (quotation on p. 285). . . .
104 See Genovese, *Roll, Jordan, Roll*, 382 and 656. . . .
105 James Haynes to Charles Manigault, January 6, 1847, in Clifton, ed., *Life and Labor*, 46; and James Haynes to Charles Manigault, April 22, 1847, ibid., 54.
106 Charles Manigault to James Haynes, March 1, 1847, ibid., 49.
107 Ibid., 50. Over a thirty-year period, Manigault recorded selling only ten slaves. . . .
108 William Capers to Louis Manigault, August 20, 1863, Louis Manigault Papers (DU).
109 Household and naming data were drawn from the reconstructed biographical information on the Manigault slaves. . . .
110 Charles Manigault to James Haynes, August 15, 1846, in Clifton, ed., *Life and Labor*, 38.
111 K. Washington Skinner to Charles Manigault, June 6, 1852, ibid., 99.
112 Ibid.
113 Charles Manigault to James Haynes, January 1, 1847, ibid., 45. . . .
114 William Capers, Sr., to Louis Manigault, November 3, 1860, ibid., 310 (quotations); and Capers to Louis Manigault, August 19, 1860, ibid., 305. . . .
115 Capers to Louis Manigault, August 19, 1860, ibid., 305; and Capers to Louis Manigault, October 31, 1860, ibid., 309.
116 Gabriel E. Manigault to Louis Manigault, January 21, 1861, ibid., 314.
117 Capers to Charles Manigault, November 14, 1861, ibid., 325. . . .
118 Ibid.; and Louis Manigault to Charles Manigault, December 5, 1861, ibid., 331.
119 For extended discussion of slaveowners clinging tenaciously to their values during the Civil War, even as events proved those values to untenable, see Roark, *Masters without Slaves: Southern Planters in the Civil War and Reconstruction* (New York, 1977); Leon F. Litwack, *Been in the Storm so Long: The Aftermath of Slavery* (New York, 1979). . . .
120 Louis Manigault, Plantation Journal, May 1861 to May 1862, in Clifton, ed., *Life and Labor*, 320.
121 Charles Manigault to Louis Manigault, January 20, 1862, ibid., 337.
122 Louis Manigault to Fannie Habersham Manigault, December 14 and December 15, 1861, both in the Louis Manigault Papers (DU). . . .
123 Capers to Louis Manigault, August 14, 1863, Louis Manigault Papers (DU).
124 "Slave Runaway Notice," Louis Manigault, April 10, 1863, Manigault Papers (microfiche, South Caroliniana Library, University of South Carolina).
125 William Capers, Sr., to Louis Manigault, April 9 and 13, June 17, and July 2, 1863, all in Louis Manigault Papers (DU).
126 Louis Manigault, Plantation Journal, May 1861 to May 1862, in Clifton, ed., *Life and Labor*, 320–21.
127 Louis Manigault to Fannie Habersham Manigault, November 11, 1861, in Clifton, ed., *Life and Labor*, 324.
128 Charles Manigault to Louis Manigault, April 30, 1865, ibid., 353. . . .
129 Quoted in Eric Foner, *Reconstruction: America's Unfinished Revolution, 1863–1877* (Cambridge and other cities, 1988), 72. . . .
130 Louis Manigault Letterbook, March 26, 1865, Manigault Papers (microfilm, SHC).

131 Louis Manigault, Plantation Journal describing December 1864, in Clifton, ed., *Life and Labor*, 350.

132 Numerous other southern plantation owners were also forced to lease out their property. See Michael Wayne, *The Reshaping of Plantation Society: The Natchez District, 1860–1880* (Baton Rouge, 1979), 62.

133 Louis Manigault, "Visit to 'Gowrie' and 'East Hermitage' Plantations, Savannah River, 22d March 1867," in Clifton, ed., *Life and Labor*, 354–64 (quotations 356, 361). . . .

134 For Charles Manigault's description of the Union shell and the damage to their Charleston residence, see Charles Manigault to Louis Manigault, April 10, 1865, in Clifton, ed., *Life and Labor*, 352.

135 Charles Manigault, "The Close of the War—The Negro, &c," ca. 1868 (p. 8), Manigault Family Papers (SHC). . . .

4

OLD SOUTH TIME IN
COMPARATIVE PERSPECTIVE

Mark M. Smith

Mark M. Smith's analysis of the use of clocks and watches offers a new angle for investigating the nature of the Old South's economy and society. Since the publication of an influential essay by E. P. Thompson on the changes in time-consciousness brought about during Britain's industrial revolution, historians have often seen such time-consciousness as an essential aspect of modern capitalism. Comparing time-consciousness in the slave South to that in industrialized Britain and New England, Smith finds many similarities. Influenced by merchants, by the arrival of railroads, and by the example of industrialists themselves, slaveowners used clocks and watches to measure labor time for their slaves much as factory owners did for their operatives, even though they rejected "traditional capitalist wage–labor relations." (Richard Follett found a similar use of time pieces on Louisiana's sugar plantations.) Indeed, Smith suggests that the adoption of modern clock-time consciousness was one of the ways slaveholders responded to the "dilemma" of reconciling modernity and slavery, as outlined by Eugene Genovese's essay in this volume: "the clock could be recruited to help create a modern, efficient, and disciplined slaveholders' regime. . . . In a society that coveted profit and enslavement, efficiency and order, clock time—owned and controlled exclusively by masters—proved irresistibly alluring."

* * *

The ages of revolution and capital wrought some critical and lasting changes in the way people perceived and used time. The eighteenth century animated a latent, originally medieval concern about time with its rationalization, saving, and ordering. This appreciation of time, wrapped in the swaddling of the Protestant work ethic, proved an ideal inheritance for nineteenth-century capitalists, who reconstituted it by equating time with labor.[1] These agents of a modern, capitalist time consciousness were also successful in transmitting their valuation of time when venturing abroad. From Australia to Natal to the American North, eighteenth- and nineteenth-century urban industrial workers

found their assumptions about the nature of time challenged and ultimately displaced by a protestant-inspired and capital-consolidated
consciousness of the clock. By the turn of the twentieth century, few
workers and still fewer managers could be found operating exclusively on naturally defined or task-oriented time. In a very real sense,
then, the spread of a rationalized and commodified time consciousness
had witnessed and simultaneously helped promote the modernization
of Western capitalism and the proletarianization of its worker.[2]

For a variety of reasons, but mainly because they have seldom considered the question of time consciousness, historians of the American
slave South have suggested that antebellum masters and bondpeople,
caught as they were in the webs of seasonal agriculture and non-wage
economic and social relations, were necessarily peripheral to the
emergence of clock time.[3] But viewed and evaluated in comparative
perspective, it seems that rather than constituting a place on the edge
of modern time consciousness, the post-1830 slave South was very
much in and of it. In fact, the Old South, though a society nurtured in
nature's womb, was possibly more clock conscious than many
nineteenth-century free wage labor industrial societies. This possibility has eluded not only historians of the Old South but also those
committed to the historical study of time generally. With few exceptions, historical analyses of time consciousness have concentrated on
the evolution of clock consciousness and time discipline in wage-
labor, urban-industrial, conventionally capitalist societies. Even on
those occasions when historians of slave societies have ventured to
consider the relationship between clock consciousness and slavery,
they have done so by borrowing a conceptual lens from historians
who have examined the emergence of time discipline under industrial, free wage labor capitalism.[4]

Drawing on a growing and relatively recent historical literature,
this essay questions the importance of free wage labor industrial capitalism in promoting a modern time consciousness. It compares the evolution of clock consciousness in the American antebellum South, a
society that was neither industrial nor capitalist in the free wage labor
sense, to the emergence of time discipline in more typically capitalist
societies, where industrialism and free wage labor particularly are
seen as important agents in inaugurating and cementing a modern
consciousness of the clock. This article argues that southern slaveholders were motivated by forces both similar to and distinct from those
that propelled British, North American, Australian, and South African
capitalist managers toward the use of clock time and suggests that
American slaves, as much as industrial-urban wage laborers, were
forced to acquiesce to clock-regulated plantation labor. These findings
have some important implications not only for our understanding of

the Old South's mode of production but also for a historical appreciation of the relationship between capitalism and time consciousness generally.

As most historians of time consciousness have recognized, the way a society perceives and uses time is mediated both through its dominant cultural values and, simultaneously, the prevailing mode of production.[5] Yet, it seems fair to say, because historians have for the most part examined the emergence of clock consciousness in free wage labor, industrializing societies, they have tended, if only tacitly, to emphasize the importance of the economic and industrial aspects of the capitalist mode of production in shaping and promoting clock consciousness. Theorist Barbara Adam has suggested that a more helpful formulation may be to keep an open mind about the relative influence and function of culture as well as economic imperatives and industrialization in shaping clock consciousness. As Adam has recently reminded us, Max Weber's emphasis on the culture of "time-thrift" as an integral component of the Protestant ethic, on the rationality and efficiency of time's use, may be profitably combined with Karl Marx's views on the commodification of clock time, specifically his belief in the use of the clock as a tool for economic exploitation and the social control of workers, to suggest that temporal constructs find their locus in a variety of economic, social, and cultural relations. Viewed from this perspective, the way that time is used under the capitalist mode of production is not necessarily limited to the strict and necessarily confining notion of time's commodification under free wage labor. Time is a commodity, but capitalism's time may also laud the civic, personal, and essentially cultural virtues of time-thrift, punctuality, and the husbanding of time irrespective of prevailing economic relations, which may or may not be exclusively wage labor.[6]

The success of Western capitalism in transmitting time discipline to its colonial outposts was due to its two-pronged nature: Western capitalism emphasized the intellectual and cultural legitimacy of rational, orderly time and the economic necessity and logic of work time. According to Adam, "all work relations touched by clock time are tied up with hegemony and power." A varied body of work suggests there are times "that are constituted as the shadows of the time economy of employment relations, times not calculable in monetary terms yet evaluated through the mediating filter of both the rationalized time of the Protestant ethic and the commodified time of the market."[7] Non-free labor modes of production and non-wage-based economic and social relations, like those prevailing under antebellum southern slavery, then, could theoretically harbor and promote a modern clock consciousness, without necessarily embracing traditional capitalist wage-labor relations. In other words, a society's cultural evaluation of time may be as important as the economic imperatives of its mode of production in determining how time is to be constructed and used. . . .[8]

Nor should we be misled, as Michael O'Malley has wisely counseled, into thinking that a naturally derived understanding of time (time defined by sun, moon, wind, and a host of other naturally occurring phenomena) necessarily precludes a commitment to clock time. Not only is the dichotomy false, not only is nature itself sometimes as frenetic as the clock (as humans find when planting and harvesting, for instance), but there is evidence suggesting that natural time and clock time are in many respects complementary.[9] Both are largely cyclical in their movements, and the regular, perpetual movements of the clock are to some extent mirrored in the rhythms of the seasons or sun. . . .[10]

By the same token, neither should we assume that the mere appearance of clocks and watches determines a society's entry into clock-conscious modernity.[11] . . . [I]t is the way that clocks are used, the specific economic and social functions that timepieces serve, and the particular class interests they bolster that are signally important. Clocks plainly serve different functions under different modes of production. Under modernity, the clock becomes a fetish. . . . The dictates and needs of the capitalist mode of production ensure that the clock is used to control workers, measure labor, increase efficiency, and heighten personal time discipline in order to coordinate workers and society generally. . . . Conversely, in pre-modern societies, clock time is usually bound to religion and has little secular significance or function. It follows that very few people in these societies felt the need to own mechanical timepieces, which, of course, were rare and expensive even when they did become more available.[12]

By these standards, the clock consciousness of nineteenth-century urban and industrial Britain, Natal, Australia, and the American North was modern. The secondary literature on these regions suggests that the evolution of clock consciousness and the proliferation of clocks and watches were products of, and handmaidens to, the emergence of wage-labor capitalism, industrialism, urbanism, and the work ethic associated with Protestantism.[13] Although it probably entertained a work ethic not appreciably different from the Puritan one, the antebellum South shared few of these structural features, but it nevertheless developed an equally modern clock consciousness. The slave mode of production, in its antebellum southern configuration at least, managed to introduce a refined and potent clock consciousness to its urban and rural environs without embracing wage labor or industrialism. Similarly high levels of timepiece ownership aside, what united antebellum southern slaveowners and nineteenth-century industrial capitalists was a mutual understanding that their particular class and social (hence political) interests were in some way served and bolstered by regulating labor and behavior by the clock. Industrial capitalists needed the clock to coordinate and discipline nascent wage laborers; slaveowners needed the clock to satisfy their own imperatives, which, from the 1830s on, centered on acquiring the title of "modern" while retaining strict control over, and promoting efficient work practices among, a potentially volatile slave labor force. Both classes subscribed to what Gregory Clark has termed the "coercion theory" of factory discipline, in which "[d]iscipline was designed to *coerce* workers into doing more than they would have freely chosen if they had maintained control over their hours of work and work intensity."[14] Working slowly, horseplay, tardiness, and similar behavior deemed inappropriate to either the factory floor or plantation field could be modified by the clock in both instances. In some respects, planters were more effective than some industrial capitalists at imposing clock order on their environment. Surprisingly . . . both used the clock in remarkably similar ways and produced two classes of workers who held much in common in their understanding of, and obedience to, clock time.

Before anyone, whether master, industrialist, or worker, could reduce time to money, however, they had to dilute, or at least modify, age-old Christian imperatives stressing that all time was God's time. According to Jacques Le Goff, this process began in the Middle Ages, when "[a]mong the principal criticisms levelled against the merchants was the charge that their profit implied a mortgage on time, which was supposed to belong to God alone." But God was not the only impediment to secular commercial time. According to Le Goff, "Like the peasant, the merchant was at first subjected by his professional activity to the dominion of meteorological time, to the cycle of seasons and the unpredictability of storms and natural cataclysms.". . . . [15] And it was the dual forces of God's temporal imperatives and merchants' commercial time that provided the historical basis for the rise of clock consciousness among workers and managers in the eighteenth and nineteenth centuries.

It is probably no accident that Britain was both the first country to industrialize and among the first to have its shift from natural to clock time scrutinized by historians. In his pioneering 1967 essay, "Time, Work-Discipline and Industrial Capitalism," E. P. Thompson asked a deceptively simple but incisive question: was the emergence of industrial capitalism in eighteenth and nineteenth-century Britain "related to changes in the inward notation of time" among managers and especially workers? Thompson contrasted pre-industrial Britain, which he considered to be characterized by a basic "disregard for clock time," the structuring of work by task, and an appeal to natural cues as legitimate arbiters of time, with industrial-era time discipline. Although he was aware that naturally derived, task-oriented time "has by no means lost all relevance in rural parts of Britain today," Thompson discerned a protracted but real shift in conceptions of time in industrializing Britain. Increasing ownership of watches by Britain's working classes and the general diffusion of public, aural time through church clocks coincided "at the exact moment when the industrial revolution demanded a greater synchronization of labour." Public clocks and private watches, argued Thompson, were the instruments "which regulated the new rhythms of industrial life" and energized the advance of industrial capitalism. . . .[16]

The efforts of managers to introduce a respect for the clock among their employees were not uncontested. "In the first stage," according to Thompson, "we find simple resistance. But in the next stage, as the new time-discipline is imposed, so the workers begin to fight, not against time, but about it." Thompson made clear that this battle took place in industrial urban environments: "It was exactly in those industries—the textile mills and the engineering workshops where the new time-discipline was most rigorously imposed—that the contest over time became most intense."[17] Mark Harrison has elaborated on Thompson's ideas and suggests that it was not simply industrial but also non-industrial urban environments such as nineteenth-century Bristol that shared a heightened consciousness of time, not least because public time in the form of civic clocks was easily communicable in an urban environment.[18]

Whatever the emphasis, though, it appears that a sharpened clock-based time consciousness evolved, in the British instance, primarily in urban and industrial environments. Thompson concluded that nineteenth-century British factory workers eventually internalized the time discipline demanded by their employers and, in the process, came to legitimize the very notion of clock time as a true measure of work. But . . . Thompson believed that nineteenth-century British agriculture was too contingent on nature for clock time to be of much importance.[19] In all likelihood, the rural church clock did help introduce a sense of mechanical time into the British countryside and the efforts of nineteenth-century agricultural reformers helped make farm laborers more aware of the idea of time-thrift. As was the case for the British rural housewife and urban port worker, however, Thompson argued that naturally defined and task-oriented time were to remain the predominant ways of conceptualizing time and its passage, even as the clock took hold in urban and industrial nineteenth-century Britain.[20]

Historians of the antebellum American North in particular have been indebted to Thompson and have often applied his insights to the northern experience with industrialization. And naturally so perhaps: the rise of the industrial American North was similar, at least in trajectory, to the British experience, since both societies embraced free wage labor and capitalist economic and social relations relatively quickly.[21] .... The patterns of workers' resistance to factory clock time were, apparently, similar. Both British and American workers invoked appeals to natural time and contested the amount of time to be worked in their efforts to combat managers' imposition of time discipline in the factories.[22]

Recent work on the evolution of a modern time consciousness in colonial and antebellum New England, however, suggests that the factory was not solely responsible for the shift to time discipline: Puritanism and urbanization had important roles to play, too. "New Englanders," writes Paul Hensley, "bore the imprint of time long before the emergence of the factory." Yet, it should be pointed out, much of what Hensley argues had been prefigured by Thompson, who was also cognizant of the importance of Puritan culture and urbanization in laying the foundation for industrial time discipline .... [But] Hensley found little evidence to suggest that pre-eighteenth-century rural New Englanders shared the conception of time that was to take over New England's industrial urban centers. As he puts it, "In spite of the important relationship between time and labor in seventeenth-century New England, work was characteristically elastic and relaxed, attributes influenced by seasonal rhythms, the blending of farming and craft activities, and frequent shifts from one task to another." Hensley suggests that the stimuli for New England's time consciousness rested primarily with merchants and townspeople, not with New England farmers.[23]

.... Here, Hensley's essential thesis is clear:

> Long before factory bells began to compete with church and public bells as arbiters of local time, family clocks well placed in hallways augmented communal time.... Having been trained in time discipline within their communities and at home, they now encountered mill owners and managers who were demanding time obedience.

The victory of the New England mill owners seems as complete as that won by their British counterparts, perhaps more so in light of the limited infiltration of clock time into the northern countryside. What New England mill workers lamented most was not the intrusion of clock time itself but rather "their lack of control over their own time." Here, as in Thompson's England, there was resistance not to time as a category of work, as a measurement of labor, but rather to the perceived unfairness of managers' manipulation of workers' time.[24]

Still more recent work, however, has gone beyond the idea that time discipline in the North was predominantly urban or industrial. In a

thoughtful essay, Martin Bruegel argues that antebellum rural northerners, those in New York's Hudson Valley at least, were time-
conscious clock users by the mid-nineteenth century. Bruegel is rightly
skeptical of "general explanations of the development of temporal
consciousness" that stress "urbanization and industrialization and
tacitly assume that rural society suffered, rather than participated in,
its transformation." . . . .

Instead, Bruegel makes a helpful distinction: "Contrary to the urban
experience where the social utility of timepieces in the organization of
work and leisure appeared upon their introduction, the countryside
underwent a two-stage process." He goes on to explain that "[o]nly
when the diffusion of clocks and watches had reached a majority of
rural households in the 1820s did they begin to attract people's attention to their capacity as timekeepers." . . . By the 1840s, when almost
three-quarters of the valley's rural inhabitants owned a clock or watch,
rural time consciousness was becoming more pronounced. . . . Ultimately, when clocks and watches became cheap enough so that a majority of rural and urban dwellers could afford them, "their utility as
timekeepers superseded their role as markers of social hierarchies."
Consequently, Hudson Valley farm laborers began recording the number of hours they worked and calculated how much time the use of
plank roads would save them in transporting their goods to market.[25]
By qualifying Thompson, Gutman, and others, Bruegel argues that
these rural forces provided the basis for the emergence of industrial
time discipline in the American North.

If Bruegel is right in identifying the evolution of a rural time
consciousness in the American North, then, by nineteenth-century
standards at least, the region was quite exceptional. In the similarly sprawling Australian countryside, for example, mechanical time
remained alien and largely irrelevant to its inhabitants. Attempts by
Thompson's eighteenth and nineteenth-century British colonists to
introduce clock time to the bush failed. . . .[26]

Efforts by colonizing and proselytizing European capitalists to inculcate rural [Australian] Aborigines and settlers to the clock notwithstanding, many still operated on natural time in the 1870s: "In the
bush, then, clock-time was largely subordinated to the natural cycles of
the sun, moon and the seasons." Again, the comparison is made with
Britain or, more precisely, Thompson's depiction of the British experience. "The clock-driven routines that officials had attempted to impose
upon the felonry of New South Wales," observes Davison,

> were closely akin to the new systems of factory discipline that
> industrialists were attempting to inculcate among the British
> working class. But the free, capitalist society which began to

emerge on the crumbling foundations of convictism was of a very different character from that of industrial Britain. . . . The bushman rose at the call of the kookaburra—"the settler's clock" as it was known as early as the 1820s—and his labours were regulated more by the weather, the light and the seasons than by the hours of the day or even sometimes by the days of the week.[27]

As long as these natural time cues predominated, as long as rural inhabitants' needs were met by such cues and not subject to particularly coercive and potent external forces, the clock remained largely irrelevant to bush settlers. The absence of industrial wage incentives in the bush (Davison sees them mainly confined to the towns) meant that the clock had little cultural, social, or economic currency in a rural environment that contained its own, relatively punctual, form of time reckoning. "It was only toward the end of the century," notes Davison, "as the railway and the telegraph began to set the standard of time for the whole society, that the time notations in the farmers' journals became more consistently precise. . . ."[28]

So, too, in Natal province, South Africa, nineteenth-century colonizing European capitalists failed to instill their own sense of time discipline among rural Zulus. Keletso Atkins has recently argued, "Like most preindustrial people, the Zulu used the moon and stars to keep track of time."[29] European capitalists found it impossible to impose anything like a modern time consciousness, Weberian or Marxian, on rural Zulu laborers. Efforts to convert rural Natal Africans to Western time amounted to little because, as Atkins explains, they were able to draw on their own, entrenched culture of time, which had long recognized nature as its legitimate arbiter. Yet if nineteenth-century rural Zulus were able to reject Western ideas about time, those who moved to Natal's urban enclaves found their cultural assumptions about time subjected to different and more potent forces. . . . Colonial urban public clocks and the insistence on wage labor had, it seems, the effect of shaping those Zulus who ventured to the province's cities into time-conscious workers, workers not so different from those in industrial-urban Britain, Australia, and the rural and industrial American North. "[A]t least by 1872, and perhaps well before that date," argues Atkins, "segments of the cities' black labouring population were perceiving time in discrete market as well as noneconomic terms—namely, regular work time, overtime, and leisure time."[30]

How, then, did the time consciousness of Australia's rural peoples, British agricultural laborers, and rural Natal Zulus remain relatively independent of colonial Western time discipline? And why, by contrast, did North American rural farmers not escape the strictures of the

Protestant-inspired capitalist clock? It is important to note that neither the Protestant ethic-Weberian emphasis on rational time nor the capitalist/Marxian time-wage equation will be perceived as legitimate in a society where natural temporal cues outweigh mechanical ones, where the dominant discourse and value systems stressing the legitimacy and function of natural time are too ingrained to be influenced by outsiders' appeal to the idea of an abstracted, decontextualized, clock-defined time. Aborigines and white rural settlers in Australia, British agricultural laborers, and rural Natal Zulus were all nominally free laborers, and they were laboring in their own social and economic context, a context too grounded in its geographic, social, and cultural specificity for Protestant ethic industrial-capitalist constructions of time to be of much potence, relevance, or persuasion. . . . Mechal Sobel correctly discerns a pre-industrial British awareness of time melding with a similar, naturally defined African one to produce, for eighteenth-century Virginia at least, a pre-modern time consciousness.[31]

If this transvaluative aspect of time consciousness is borne in mind, a pattern emerges that might explain why some regions and peoples succumbed to clock time while others did not. At the most general level, it seems that where natural and task-oriented time rhythms are strong and rooted in a specific cultural, social, and economic context, they will endure even when attacked from the outside by clock-wielding, Protestant ethic-inspired capitalists. When removed from these contexts, however, as in the case of migration to towns, and when the technological and cultural forces promoting a clock consciousness begin to penetrate the countryside more forcefully and systematically, as was the case with the coming of mechanical timepieces, the railroads, and clock-regulated bells, then clock time will gradually gain cultural and functional currency and begin to supplant a society's commitment to natural time. With the exception of the American North, clock consciousness took root most quickly and thoroughly in urban-industrial, free wage labor societies, where clock culture was peddled vigorously by European capitalists. As long as they remained in the countryside and as long as clock time remained confined to urban-industrial areas, Natal Zulus, Australian Aborigines and settlers, and British agricultural laborers retained their own understanding of time rooted in natural rhythms and less susceptible to the time-thriftiness associated with the capitalist work ethic. But where rural dwellers already shared in this ethic and where the forces of modern clock consciousness penetrated the countryside more readily (in the American North), capitalist managers found they had an easier time converting rural workers to the dictates of industrial-capitalist time. . . .

Two related factors might help to explain why this was the case. First, it could well be that northern industrialists were simply better proselytizing capitalists. Second, they were more successful because northern farmers appear to have shared a post-feudal, Protestant ethic-inspired evaluation of time with colonizing European capitalists. They were, after all, often one and the same. The culture of Bruegel's Hudson Valley farmers, of Hensley's Puritan New Englanders, of Thompson's British factory workers, and of Gutman's northern mill workers was very similar to, with respect to the social value attached to time at least, the managers' culture. What they fought over was less the definition of time than how much of it each party should have. . . .[32]

Collectively, then, this literature on the evolution of time consciousness identifies several broad historical forces promoting a clock consciousness among eighteenth and nineteenth-century rural and, especially, industrial-urban managers and workers. If we accept the basic point that the larger forces of time's religious and economic rationalization and commodification provided the essential impetus behind the rise of time discipline, then the specific historical developments that created a modern time consciousness among workers and managers in the nineteenth century probably consisted of the following: first, the dilution of God's time and its articulation with a mercantile work ethic stressing that time was money and that, as such, it should be saved, not wasted; second, the concomitant rise of urban clocks to regulate and coordinate personal and public temporal activity; third, the increase in the number of clocks and watches in any given population; fourth, the emergence of industrial wage-labor time discipline;[33] and, lastly, the advent of technologies such as the railroads, which disseminated urban and industrial time to the countryside and helped heighten a preexisting idea that punctuality and time-thrift were forms of religious, civic, and personal virtue.[34]

If we agree with Babette M. Levy, Edmund S. Morgan, and Perry Miller that "the Puritan Ethic" embodied "the values that all Americans held," southerners included, and if some of the aforementioned agencies behind the nineteenth century's drive toward clock time can be found in the antebellum South, were these forces in and of themselves sufficient (plainly, they appear to have been necessary) to push the non-wage antebellum slave South toward the adoption of clock time?[35] If not, what was it about slavery that rendered wage-labor industrialism unimportant while nevertheless encouraging planters to adopt clock time?

A brief examination of the activities and attitudes of southern merchants helps answer these questions. Because of their place in the Atlantic marketplace, eighteenth and nineteenth-century southern merchants appear to have developed a keen sense that time was money, that punctuality in business transactions was a virtue and necessity, not only from the requisites of their own trade but from their dealings

with northern and European merchants.[36] Yankee merchants throughout the colonial period, for example, coached their southern counterparts in the need for punctuality in business. As Boston merchant
Jonathan Johnson advised Edward Telfair's Georgia mercantile firm in
1775, "let me however request of you to execute this order with the
utmost punctuality & Expedition."[37] By 1802, however, the situation was
reversed. Charleston merchant Thomas Aiton complained to his firm's
parent company, William Stanley and Company of New York: "Three
mails have arrived since we received yours by Post informing us of
your intention to Send us by next Mail 2,000 dollars. We have neither
received money nor letter." Aiton then warned: "Such Conduct may be
attended with very serious circumstances if repeated. You know as well
as us that the most strict punctuality is necessary in money matters."[38]
Similarly, punctuality with credit payments became a point of pride,
indeed, of virtue, for southern merchants. When Virginian George
Carter failed to pay the credit on a note signed by Landon Carter in
1806, the latter complained that "you [have] done more injury to the
respectability of my punctual habits in Fredericksburg than any I have
ever had before."[39] . . . . Atlantic merchants, in short, bequeathed an
important legacy to the antebellum South as, in fact, they had to the
nineteenth-century Western world.

The most conspicuous source of this mercantile and civic time consciousness in the South was in its urban environs. Eighteenth and
nineteenth-century southern towns constituted the physical space
where secular and sacred time meshed. Although southern industry
was woefully undeveloped in both centuries, its absence does not seem
to have made the region's urban areas any less clock conscious. Few
cities though there were in the South, those that did exist seem to have
embraced and promoted an urban awareness of time that was little
different from northern, British, Natalian, or Australian urban time.[40]
Charleston's St. Michael's clock, installed in the 1760s, for example,
was "a strong 30 Hour Clock, to show the Hour Four Ways, to strike
the Hour on the largest Bell." In the antebellum period, civic author-
ities expanded the function of the church's time: "It will be noticed that
it is 'to show the Hour Four Ways,' and this is all it showed till 1840,
when, with the consent of the vestry, the City Council added minute
hands."[41] . . . .

In trying to evaluate the importance of urban church bells in promoting clock consciousness in the South, let us return to the significance and function of clock time. Certainly, bells had been important
regulators and communicators of time in many societies, modern and
pre-modern. But whereas medieval European monasteries had used
aural time mainly (though not exclusively) for the express purpose of
announcing God's time, clock bells in the eighteenth and nineteenth

centuries were employed for additional, increasingly profane, purposes. The difference, of course, is best measured in degrees, not absolutes. In the urban environs of the American North, Natal, and Australia, particularly in the nineteenth century, aural time was used to announce not just God's time but increasingly to regulate the time of schools, markets, and factories.[42]

The South's use of aural time was no different. In the 1740s, for example, Charleston's church clocks were enlisted to announce and coordinate the city's market times. The aural dimension of this sacred-secular urban time was often recorded by contemporaries. It was said of Charleston's St. Philip's clock and bells in 1828, for example, "truly nothing can be more awe-inspiring than at the silent midnight hour to hear St. Philip's clock with deep funeral knell tolling another day." For this observer, it was the clock that was heard.[43] .... Although never to lose its religious significance completely, aural church clock time, then, helped govern and coordinate the secular activities of the southern city and its inhabitants.[44]

Added to the mercantile and urban forces promoting a clock consciousness in the South was an increasing disposition on the part of white southerners, both rural and urban, slaveholding and non, to own timepieces, especially in the nineteenth century (see table). The increasing availability of clocks and watches, combined with a reduction in their relative costs in the early antebellum period, had an impact on southern rural and urban areas just as it did on northern ones.[45] And the basic reasons for increased watch and clock ownership in the South were the same as elsewhere. If we agree with Martin Bruegel that antebellum northern timepiece ownership was in part a result of heightening personal time discipline, the same was true in the South. By 1851, three entries in one southerner's diary could speak for the South generally: "Am to send for my carriage today at 5 PM ... Mitchell & Allen family arrive from Glenroy a little before 2 PM ... Am to call Board of Medical College to meet on Saturday 1 PM at Courthouse."[46]

Similarly, if the railroads were primarily responsible for the diffusion of the North's urban time consciousness, the same process is in operation in the antebellum South.[47] In 1834, for example, the Charleston & Hamburg railroad in South Carolina, at the time the world's longest railway under single management, achieved "the greatest possible regularity in the time of running Passenger Engines" by placing clocks at six of its stations. The chief engineer stipulated fines for unpunctual drivers: "regulations have been established fixing the hour of departure, ... as well as that of the earliest time, at which they are permitted under a penalty of five dollars, to arrive at the following [station]." .... The net effect of such time-specific forces as the railroad, not to mention the telegraph and mail, was to heighten southerners' awareness of clock time and need for punctuality.[48]

The antebellum South, however, was not like everywhere else in one important respect: the peculiar institution. But rather than a fetter on clock consciousness and time-thrift, slavery proved to be a powerful stimulant in pushing southern planters toward the clock. The South's shift to clock time in the last thirty or so years of the antebellum period was undoubtedly due to railroads, urban time, mercantile time, and the other forces noted above. But there were also forces created by late antebellum slavery that helped master and slave adopt the clock. Whereas early experiments with the timing of hired labor in the rural North and the emergence of free wage industrial-urban labor else-where promoted clock consciousness, southern slaveowners' bid for slave-based modernity provided a similar catalyst. The notion of pre-modern impulses in southern slavery is, thanks to the pioneering work of Eugene D. Genovese, well known and probably true.[49] But when it comes to conceptions of time, it appears that different impulses applied, impulses from both inside and outside the South's putatively non-capitalist slave regime. These forces were equally conducive to the planters' embrace of a time discipline that was not only just as sophis-ticated as the North's but actually more successful in transmitting clock time to the countryside than wage labor and industrialization had proven in Britain, Natal, and Australia.

As I have argued elsewhere, the fundamental push toward time dis-cipline among the South's master class came in the 1830s.[50] With their time consciousness heightened by railroads and the postal service, and drawing on a long familiarity with the imperatives of mercantile and urban time, slaveholders of the 1830s began to push for more efficient agriculture and a better ordering of their slave work force. Surrounded by a world moving toward free wage labor capitalism, slaveholders were at once repulsed by the dangerous rise of a landless and politically volatile proletariat and eager to garb themselves in modern clothes.[51] The answer to this dilemma, or at least one part of it, was in the use of clock time. The nineteenth century's most obvious icon of modernity, the clock and the time it kept, was simultaneously modern but control-ling, at once an engine for economic efficiency and a tool of social dis-cipline. In the context of the late antebellum period, when slaveowners aimed to modernize slavery without threatening its fundamentally con-servative social relations, the clock proved particularly attractive. Not only could clock time be spliced with more traditional forms of social control like the whip and the old, even revered, urban practice of sound-ing time, not only was clock time perceived to be in harmony with that arbiter of southern agriculture, nature, but the clock could be recruited to help create a modern, efficient, and disciplined slaveholders' regime.

Table 4.1 Clock and watch ownership in comparative perspective, Great Britain and the United States.

	Number of inventories sampled	Percentage of inventories with clocks and/or watches
BRITAIN		
Devon and Cornwall (clocks only): 1531–1699	266	3.0
UNITED STATES		
Rural North: Greene County, NY		
1801–10	27	25.9
1811–20	49	40.8
1821–30	46	63.0
1831–40	35	65.7
1841–50	41	73.2
Urban South:		
Charleston District, South Carolina		
1805–10	394	48.0
1839–44	107	51.0
1863–65	56	66.0
Annapolis, Maryland (clocks only)		
1688–1709	17	5.8
1710–32	72	29.1
1733–54	77	41.5
1755–77	89	42.7
Rural South:		
Laurens County, South Carolina		
1805–09	73	14.0
1839–43	121	67.0
1863–65	125	71.0
Anne Arundel County, Maryland (clocks only)		
1688–1709	320	5.0
1710–32	312	9.6
1733–54	384	14.3
1755–77	408	13.2

Sources: Devon and Cornwall figures from Thrift, "Owners' Time and Own Time," 60; Greene County, New York, figures from Bruegel, " 'Time That Can Be Relied Upon'," South Carolina data from Smith, *Mastered by the Clock*; Maryland data adapted from Paul A. Shackel, *Personal Discipline and Material Culture: An Archaeology of Annapolis, Maryland, 1695–1870* (Knoxville, Tenn., 1993), 171, 180.

It would, ideally, be a regime that borrowed the discipline of the factory—a free wage labor clock without importing wage labor's associated, essentially mobocratic, tendencies. In a society that coveted profit and enslavement, efficiency and order, clock time—owned and controlled exclusively by masters—proved irresistibly alluring.[52]

As Bertram Wyatt-Brown has pointed out, in their efforts to "modernize, to improve the 'home system,' so that its foundations were no less secure, no less progressive than those on which free labor rested," masters looked, of all places, to the free but materialist North.[53] Specifically, they turned to northern agricultural societies and scientific journals, they noted Benjamin Franklin's counsel that time is money, and then they reinterpreted this advice in the context of their slave society. A reprint from the *Boston Cultivator* in the *Southern Planter* for January 1850, for example, suggested that all agriculturalists, southern ones included, should allow "twelve working hours to a day," for "he who by rising at eight instead of five O'clock in the morning, thereby loses three hours daily, parts with one-fourth of his means of supporting himself and family: ten years' labor lost on the course of forty years!"[54] The careful harvesting of this time was essential for profit, and the responsibility rested, in the first instance, with the planter. Moreover, efforts to inculcate an internal time discipline among some planters appear to have succeeded. "My plan for working," revealed one small slaveholder in 1836, "was formed by necessity." Owning few slaves, he was obliged to organize his own time efficiently: "As soon as it was light enough to see, I hitched up and drove briskly until breakfast time—took out and fed while I ate, and for which I only allowed forty-five minutes—worked till one o'clock—rested an hour and a half when cool, two hours when warm."[55]

. . . . Those who did follow the Yankee way in their use of time were applauded publicly. One Alabama planter, for instance, was lauded not just because he "enforces a strict discipline among his negroes" but because the principles of progressive farming were "carried out with the most perfect clock-like precision, to the great benefit of master and servant."[56] And one reason why punctuality was considered a good thing in the South was probably the same reason nineteenth-century Americans generally considered it healthy—it was virtuous and essentially republican. If studies stressing the South's commitment to republicanism, civic virtue, and personal honor are correct, then the following exhortation for subscribers to pay the *Southern Cultivator* on time in 1843 makes a good deal of sense: Punctuality gives weight to character: ". . . punctuality . . . like other virtues, it propagates itself. Appointments become debts . . . Punctuality in paying the printer, is a shining virtue, and is one of the requisites to the character of a good member of the community."[57]

Practically, this advice was translated at the plantation level in a variety of ways. In some instances, planters bought time-saving machinery, especially cotton gins, which promised to clean five hundred pounds "in 31 minutes."[58] Equally, planters tried to import factory methods directly to the plantation. Again, the aping of the North was obvious. Lowell mills, for instance, became models of efficiency, and planters were encouraged to emulate the factory's use of clock-regulated labor.

The *Southern Agriculturalist*, for example, published one southerner's account of a visit to Lowell in 1845 and advised "all those who are politically or otherwise unfriendly to the factory system, to read the following article." The visitor, from Kentucky, was impressed by the fact that "[t]he very few persons that were occasionally seen at all, hurried to and fro, as if their time was precious," enthused over "the most perfect order, system, and regularity . . . everywhere exhibited," and praised the factory's use of aural time control: "At 12 o'clock, M., the factory bells chimed merrily, and the whirl of the spindles, the clatter of the looms, and the hum of the drums and wheels all ceased."[59] In their efforts, then, to realize the ideal of time discipline and precise temporal coordination on their plantations, masters turned to the watch and the clock. Plantation clock time often mimicked the southern urban and northern factory form: it was communicated through sound. Bells and bugles, for instance, were rung or blown "at 9 o'clock, P.M.," when "every servant is required to return to his own cabin."[60]

Sometimes, to be sure, nature intruded, but not as much as might be expected. Natural time and clock time did, of course, coexist on plantations; slaveowners' journals are eloquent on this point. . . .

In some respects, in fact, the vagaries of nature and the strictures they placed on planters' time were important for heightening masters' desire to make the most of time. . . . The seasons still, as they always would, dictated planting and harvesting cycles, and planters deemed this proper and correct. But within these larger rhythms, the clock could be recruited, not to supplant nature but rather to complement and exploit its sometimes frenetic rhythms.[61]

For some planters, the rhythm of the agricultural year, with its slack times, harried periods, and seasonal variations, did require a work schedule that was more flexible than that provided by a clock-defined, standard working day. But significantly, when planters most needed efficiency in slaves' labor, they invoked the clock and rendered all time into masters' time. Among the rules and "Priveleges" on Richard Eppes's Hopewell, Virginia, plantation, for example, was the following fiat issued to his bondpeople in 1857: "You will work from sunrise until sunset but when a press longer. Three quarters of an hour will be allowed you to breakfast and one hour and a quarter to dine from the month of October until April. One hour to breakfast and one hour and three quarters to dine from April until October." In other words, during the busiest but hottest seasons, when Eppes needed intensive and efficient labor the most, he seemed to give his slaves more time off, measured to within fifteen minutes. . . . The effect of giving longer, clock-regulated recuperative breaks in the South's sweltering months actually increased slaves' efficiency at precisely the time when masters needed their people to labor most intensively. . . .

The time spent cultivating some crops had to be more carefully monitored than when growing other staples. Tobacco, for instance, "requires a great deal of labor and attention to produce it of a fine quality." And quality tools were essential in the tobacco planter's fight against losing time:

> how much labor is often lost by giving a hand an indifferent axe or worn out hoe, . . . How much time is often lost in sending to a neighbor's to borrow a spade, or to grind axes for want of a grindstone at home. . . .[62]

But whatever the crop, time lost was a pressing worry for masters. While individual planters were certainly free to impose their own temporal parameters and devise their own work regimes to suit their crop and labor force, all shared in an appeal to the clock as an arbiter of plantation order. . . .

If crop cycles could be coordinated by the clock, so could the specific stages and components of agricultural production. Amelia County, Virginia, planter James Powell Cocke, for example, commenced threshing wheat "at 10 OCk" in August 1854, "[f]inished sowing [the winter] wheat about 12 OCk" in November 1854, and in July of 1856 "[b]egan my wheat Harvest at 10 OcK A.M."[63] So, too, with the human cogs of the plantation machine. In published plantation journals, owners reveal how they attempted to cultivate among overseers the habit of making precise, clock-oriented daily journal entries and provided advice on how long slaves should reasonably spend on particular aspects of plantation agriculture. Before the running of the plantation could be rendered orderly, the overseers themselves had to acquire the habit of time discipline: "The operations, events and remarks of each day should be recorded in the evening of the same day, and not put off until forgot, or until necessarily omitted for want of time. Attention to keeping up the Journal will soon become a habit." Once the overseers had acquired this discipline, then so could the laborers, and managers were urged to regulate rising, work times, and breaks by the clock. Time for kindnesses could then be found or created within the clock-defined working day, regardless of crop:

> Notice them, encourage and reward such as best perform their duties. Even a word of kindness, if judiciously used, will effect much. At other times respite from labor for a few hours of any day, or at the end of the week, may be granted, and when such loss of time will not materially affect the plantation operation.[64]

MARK M. SMITH

Within these broad parameters, more minute distinctions were made. Certain workers had their own work time defined for them. Plowmen and their teams, for example, "should never be actually at work over ten hours a day, the balance of the time should be given to rest, feeding, and careful attendance at the stables." The rationale behind this ten-hour limit was again clock defined and inspired by the need to make sure that slaves worked intensively: "As much work can be done in ten hours, if the horses are in order, as in 12 or 14, worked in the ordinary slow and out of heart style." . . . .[65]

The introduction of the clock to the plantation field made temporal coordination and regulation under southern slavery very similar to that being enforced in free wage labor, industrializing societies. Clock-regulated bells and bugles especially were one way to regulate the work times of laborers slave and free. Compare, for example, the following two statements, the first by a southern slaveowner in 1860, the second depicting the regulation of work time in English factories in 1833. The southern slave, apparently, was "not overworked; . . . He goes out when it is light enough to work, at 8 o'clock takes his breakfast, at 12 o'clock his dinner, at 2 o'clock goes to his work again, . . . [at] 9 or 10 o'clock goes to bed." Similarly, child laborers in Leeds "commenced at six o'clock; at nine, half an hour for breakfast; from half past nine till twelve, work. Dinner, one hour; from five till eight, work; rest for half an hour. From half past eight till twelve, (midnight,) work; an hour's rest."[66]

If aural clock time was one weapon in the masters' arsenal to fight for progress, regulated slave behavior, and increased productivity, the watch was another. It was especially suited to gauging the economic productivity of labor. Because antebellum "laborlords," as Gavin Wright has called Old South planters, sought to maximize output per hand rather than yield per acre, the saving and manipulation of slaves' labor time was of great importance.[67] Although, as John F. Olson has pointed out, slaves worked fewer clock-time hours per year than free laborers, North and South, slaves nevertheless "worked more intensively per hour" because their masters were able to regulate their productivity with the watch backed by the whip. According to Olson, "slaves on plantations using the gang system worked 94 per cent more (harder) each hour than did free men." This level of intensity was achieved because slaveholders, like nineteenth-century managers elsewhere, came to recognize that work and leisure regulated by clock time was a means to increase and maintain the productivity of labor. Of course, if slaves did work so much harder per hour than free workers who were similarly regulated by the clock, one must assume that the whip *coupled* with the clock or watch was a better regulator of productivity than the watch and wage incentive. But planters, while undoubtedly

102

linking the two in their discourse, tended to emphasize the role of the clock alone in maintaining productivity. Georgia planter James Thomas, for example, described how he gave his bondpeople a five-minute break every thirty minutes because he found that such respites from labor increased the amount of work performed by his slaves 15 percent.[68] Other planters also devised procedures to "ascertain the actual cost of any specific work," when "the time it occupies being known." Examples were disseminated in southern agricultural journals. "The *daily labor* of *a team*," reported the *Farmers' Register* in 1834, "must necessarily be regulated by the manner in which it is employed, as well as by its strength." "In some southern and midland counties," the writer explained, "the carters who generally sleep in the house, rise at four in the morning, feed, clean, and harness the horses, get breakfast, and are ready to go a-field at six-'clock, or after seven in the winter, when they work till two, thus making at the utmost a yoking of eight hours."[69] Some antebellum plantation journals had sections like "Work Timed by Watch". . . . The avowed ideal that clock-regulated plantations would render the coordination of plantation labor "like clock-work" was more often than not realized.[70]

We need not rely solely on planters' records to verify that clock time was an important arbiter of work and life on antebellum southern plantations. Slaves remembered the clock and watch and testified that they had come to accept, albeit grudgingly, timed agricultural labor under slavery. Although they originally came from societies where natural time was predominant and that same reliance on natural time remained important to them, southern slaves, like nineteenth-century urban-industrial workers, found their reliance on sun and stars as exclusive arbiters of time attacked and, ultimately, undermined.[71]

Whereas rural workers in nineteenth-century Natal, Britain, and Australia were either slow to accept the legitimacy of the clock or able to reject it, American slaves appear to have succumbed more readily to their masters' admonitions concerning clock-regulated plantation labor. On the one hand, this is surprising because, some black slave drivers excepted, very few slaves actually owned a mechanical time-piece, something E. P. Thompson and others believe to have been important for the inculcation of clock consciousness among workers.[72] But, on the other, it is of little surprise, especially when one considers how masters enforced slaves' obedience to the clock and how potent the aural power of time had proven in all societies, the South's included. Masters' two-pronged method to foist time obedience on their bond-people, aurally communicated clock time backed up by the discipline of the whip, suggests that wage incentives, fines for lateness, and indus-trialization were not always necessary for the successful inculcation of clock time.

. . . .

Because of the ubiquity of the clock in plantation affairs, slaves of the antebellum period as well as former slaves interviewed in the 1930s recalled clearly that clocks and watches were used to regulate their labor.[73] Slaves who were timed in the field by their master's watch, for example, remembered the time pressure of work. A fugitive slave of the 1850s, Moses Grandy, acknowledged that on his North Carolina plantation, work and work breaks were watch regulated: "The overseer stood with his watch in hand, to give us just an hour; when he said, 'Rise,' we had to rise and go to work again."[74] Moreover, being hectored by the timepiece in this way seems to have made slaves punctual. If other masters were anything like Lue Bradford's Texas owner, slaves' compulsion was understandable. "They would have to work until the horn sounded before they could stop for noon. In the morning the field boss would have the record book and each person was supposed to report before starting for work and all were punished who were late." The rationale for such a practice was clear to her: "This encouraged punctuality."[75] Others, like John Washington of Virginia, recalled that during the 1850s if he "had any desire to go out again in a reasonable time," the time specified by his master on his "permission" slip enabling him to leave the plantation "must be punctually obeyed." According to Lu Lee of Texas, the slave knew when to return: "[The] nigger would get a pass and come over and stay with he gal and then he would say, 'I am sorry but it is that certain time and I got to go.' "[76]

Born of their own experience with public, urban time, planters realized the power of communicating time through sound and so regulated plantation operations with clock-governed bells and horns. . . . "All the stock men worked in the field also—so many hours," remembered Cora Carroll of Mississippi. She explained: "They had a bell for them to go to work in the morning, a bell for them to get up by, and another one for noon, and another in the evening when they would knock off for dark." And it was through the constant reinforcement of time through sound that planters developed in their slaves a keen understanding of the precise time at which plantation affairs occurred: "[At] half-past eleven they would send the older children with food to the workers in the field," recalled one South Carolina ex-slave.[77]

Slaves' obedience to the sound of plantation time was a product not simply of the imperious quality of the bell; it had just as much to do with the way masters ensured obedience to their sounding of the times. Former slave Bill Colins felt that the "large plantation bell which rang every morning at four o'clock" had a despotic quality, because "[t]he bell called and said, get up I'm coming to get you," and he understood that if slaves "did not answer the call the overseer would whip them. . . ."[78] Indeed, William Brown's 1847 testimony accords with later recollections by ex-slaves. On his tobacco and hemp Missouri plantation, field hands "were summoned to their unrequited toil every morning at four o'clock, by the ringing of a bell, hung on a post near the house of the overseer. . . ." The whip substituted for the free wage labor fine for those who were dilatory: "At half past four, a horn was blown by the overseer, which was the signal to commence work; and every one that was not on the spot at the time, had to receive ten lashes from the negro-whip . . . ." Plantation clock time and physical violence, then, went together.[79]

What differentiated slaves from Thompson's industrial laborers was that bondpeople succumbed more readily to the dictates of clock time. Unlike free laborers, slaves could not engage fully in a debate over the worth and sanctity of their time. Certainly, they resisted masters' efforts to regulate their work by clock and watch. Some ran away, thus depriving masters of their labor time; others, most notably house hands, feigned ignorance of clock time altogether; and many attempted to carve out their own niches of free time. At most, some slaves negotiated with their masters over how much time was theirs to have. But even this kind of negotiation does not appear to have been widespread, and when it did occur it is surely testimony to the fact that slaves, like Thompson's industrial workers, were debating masters on their own terms, that is, negotiating about time as masters defined it.[80] Most slaves' efforts to resist plantation clock time were unsuccessful because the master could always resort to the whip to enforce punctuality to the clock. The slaves' inability to enter the protracted battle over the legitimacy of the clock as an arbiter of work and rest is revealed most graphically in their almost frenetic responses to the sound of the plantation clock. While it is unlikely that this sense of time was ever internalized to the degree that nineteenth-century industrial-urban workers internalized time, it is nevertheless true that slaves' obedience to the clock was remarkably similar to the time discipline of northern, British, Australian, and Natalian urban-industrial workers. . . . In comparative perspective, slaves as clock-conscious workers ranked alongside northern rural farmers and industrial workers rather than with British agricultural laborers, rural South African Zulus, or Australia's rural inhabitants, not least because their masters proved among the most effective, if ruthless, enforcers of clock time in the nineteenth-century world.

There are several ways to interpret the above evidence. First, one might argue that if the South-as-non-capitalist scenario is correct, then the rise of clock time in any historical context is not an accurate indicator of modernity. This I am inclined to reject, not least because I am unwilling to refute Weber and Marx so cavalierly. A second interpretation that is rather more convincing raises some very interesting possibilities. If we agree that an emphasis on clock time, time-thrift, and punctuality is a legitimate and accurate talisman of a modern time consciousness, then we can argue for one or more of several conclusions. First, it seems that antebellum planters were more successful than British, Australian, and Natalian nineteenth-century capitalists in achieving a modern clock consciousness in a rural environment. In the British instance, this is rather hard to swallow, and it may well be that we simply do not yet know enough about the presence of a rural time consciousness in nineteenth-century Britain to say with any real authority that planters and slaves were comparatively more clock conscious than their rural British counterparts. Second, it seems that African-American slave culture was less able to resist the imposition of clock time than was rural Australian or Zulu culture. This interpretation, however, should not be overemphasized, since it is likely that, as recent studies have suggested, southern white culture was not external to African-American culture; rather, the two evolved in a complex, symbiotic relationship, living off of and shaping one another.[81] And yet, with regard to the culture of antebellum time consciousness, this is one area where African-American culture was transformed by Euro-American attitudes toward time. Because colonial planters were themselves just beginning to appreciate the regulatory power of the clock, Euro-American time conceptions had not always prevailed. . . . By the 1830s, however, the situation had changed. Although the slave mode of production was still in place, southern masters were trying to fulfill new cultural and economic imperatives. The specific forces promoting clock consciousness in the antebellum South rendered slaves more American than African and masters more modern than pre-modern. Once planters in their bid for slave-based modernity had embraced the clock, slaves found themselves more susceptible to masters' insistence, backed as it was by the whip and aural time obedience, on the legitimacy of clock time. . . . [I]t was due in larger part to the redoubtable power of the slaveholders' late antebellum regime in forcing the conversion.*

Viewed in comparative perspective, then, the slave South was evidently one of the few rural regions in the nineteenth-century world to be affected by a modern clock consciousness. The reasons for this are twofold. First, the slave South either shared or imported most of the forces that had promoted time discipline in other nineteenth-century societies. Second, what it refused to import, free wage labor in factory

* A section on time consciousness of Native Americans has been omitted—ed.

or agricultural form, mattered less than we have sometimes been led to believe.[82] The slaveholders' drive for a qualified, clock-defined modernity was sufficient to impel both masters and their chattel toward a clock consciousness that was little different from, and in some ways more advanced than, the northern or British form.[83] The whip coupled with the sound of clock time proved as effective in the South as the Protestant work ethic/free wage labor/industrial combination had in the North. Just as the capitalist time consciousness apparent on Martin Bruegel's antebellum northern farms accompanied and in some ways preceded northern industrialism, so the Old South's time-based plantation capitalism foreshadowed the coming of southern nominally free wage labor after the Civil War.[84] Nor should this be considered especially unusual. As a variety of recent studies have demonstrated, modern industry is, after all, simply one of the outcomes of an evolving, often non-industrial capitalism, and the distance between wage and chattel slavery might not be as great as we have sometimes assumed.[85] If the time consciousness of the antebellum South is considered modern, then we may add to these formulations by suggesting that the postbellum South's transition to free wage labor was in some ways prefigured by a clock consciousness both nurtured from without and nourished from within the Old South's slave regime.[86]

NOTES

1 Characteristically, E. P. Thompson put it more elegantly: "Puritanism in its marriage of convenience with industrial capitalism was the agent which converted men to new valuations of time; . . . which saturated men's minds with the equation, time is money." See Thompson, "Time, Work-Discipline and Industrial Capitalism," *Past and Present* 38 (December 1967): 95. . . .

2 See Dan Thu Nguyen, "The Spatialization of Metric Time: The Conquest of Land and Labour in Europe and the United States," *Time and Society* 1 (February 1992): 29–50.

3 For a critique of clock time in southern historiography, see . . . Mark M. Smith, *Mastered by the Clock: Time, Slavery, and Freedom in the American South* (Chapel Hill, 1997). Eugene D. Genovese uses the supposed failure of slaveholders to inculcate a respect for clock time among antebellum slaves to bolster his larger thesis concerning the non-capitalist nature of the region. See Genovese, *Roll, Jordan, Roll: The World the Slaves Made* (1974; New York, 1976), 286, 309. . . .

4 Genovese, *Roll, Jordan, Roll*, . . . examines clock consciousness under slavery but through Thompson's free wage labor lens. . . .

5 See, for example, Thompson, "Time, Work-Discipline," 95;. . . .

6 Barbara Adam, *Timewatch: The Social Analysis of Time* (Cambridge, 1995), 90–91. For an interpretation of Marx's views, see W. J. Booth, "Economies of Time: On the Idea of Time in Marx's Political Economy," *Political Theory* 19 (February 1991): 7–27.

7 Adam, *Timewatch*, 94. . . . Also see Michael O'Malley, *Keeping Watch: A History of American Time* (New York, 1990), 1–54 . . . .

8 As A. J. Gurevich has suggested, time, its perception, construction, and social application, is partly a function of culture and society. See Gurevich, "Time as a Problem of Cultural History," in L. Gardett, *et al.*, eds., *Cultures and Time* (Paris, 1976), esp. 241. . . .
9 O'Malley, *Keeping Watch*, 1–54 . . . . [See also] Dale Tomich, "Small Islands and Huge Comparisons: Caribbean Plantations, Historical Unevenness, and Capitalist Modernity," *Social Science History* 18 (Fall 1994): 345.
10 Clearly, however, to conflate clock and natural time renders any historical analysis of the emergence of a clock-regulated society heuristically flaccid. There must be, in other words, a difference between the two. Part of that difference, I would suggest, lies in the significance attached to the clock, how it is used and for what purposes. As Norbert Elias observed, *"Clocks (and time-meters generally) human-made or not, are simply mechanical movements of a specific type, employed by people for their own ends"* (emphasis his) . . . See Elias, *Time: An Essay*, Edmund Jephcott, trans. (Oxford, 1992), 118. . . .
11 Clocks and other timekeepers may appear in a variety of societies and may be used for many pre-modern purposes. . . . See especially David S. Landes, *Revolution in Time: Clocks and the Making of the Modern World* (Cambridge, Mass., 1983), 55–66. . . .
12 See, for example, Elias, *Time*, 117–22; and the trenchant essay by Nigel Thrift, "Owners' Time and Own Time: The Making of a Capitalist Consciousness, 1300–1800," in Allan Pred, ed., *Space and Time in Geography: Essays Dedicated to Torsten Hagerstrand* (Lund, 1981), 56–84.
13 Here, I have chosen countries and regions that shared in the Western equation of time and, more important, those whose temporal histories have received fairly thorough treatments. . . .
14 Gregory Clark, "Factory Discipline," *Journal of Economic History* 54 (March 1994): 129, emphasis his. . . .
15 Jacques Le Goff, "Merchant's Time and Church's Time in the Middle Ages," in his *Time, Work, and Culture in the Middle Ages*, Arthur Goldhammer, trans. (Chicago, 1980), 29, 34–36, 38. . . .
16 Thompson, "Time, Work-Discipline," 57, 60, 69, 83–84.
17 Ibid., 85.
18 Mark Harrison, "Time, Work and the Occurrence of Crowds 1790–1835," *Past and Present* 110 (February 1986): 134–68. . . .
19 Although some have challenged his larger thesis, surprisingly few historians have questioned Thompson's assumption that rural Britain remained marginal to time discipline. See, though, the critique in Michael O'Malley, "Time, Work and Task-Orientation: A Critique of American Historiography," *Time and Society* 1 (September 1992): 341–58. . . .
20 Thompson, "Time, Work-Discipline," 78–79. Also see Don Parkes and Nigel Thrift, "Putting Time in its Place," in Tommy Carlstein, Don Parkes, and Nigel Thrift, eds., *Making Sense of Time*, 3 vols. (London, 1978), 1: 119–29, 125–26.
21 . . . .See Paul B. Hensley, "Time, Work, and Social Context in New England," *New England Quarterly* 65 (December 1992): 531.
22 See Herbert G. Gutman, "Work, Culture, and Society in Industrializing America, 1815–1919," in his *Work, Culture, and Society in Industrializing America* (Oxford, 1977), 3–78; David Brody, "Time and Work during Early American Industrialism," *Labor History* 30 (Winter 1989) 34 . . . .
23 Hensley, "Time, Work, and Social Context in New England," 542, 545;

Daniel Vickers, "Competency and Competition: Economic Culture in Early America," *William and Mary Quarterly*, 3d ser., 47 (January 1990): 3–29. . . .

24 Hensley, "Time, Work, and Social Context in New England," 554–56, 558. Also see O'Malley, *Keeping Watch*, 54; and Brody, "Time and Work," 22, 38. . . .

25 Bruegel, " 'Time that Can Be Relied Upon,' " 548, 549, 559, 553. . . . Generally, also see Winifred Rothenberg, "The Market and Massachusetts Farmers, 1750–1855," *Journal of Economic History* 41 (June 1981): 283–314.

26 Graeme Davison, *The Unforgiving Minute: How Australians Learned to Tell the Time* (Melbourne, 1993), 8, 9.

27 Davison, *Unforgiving Minute*, 8–9, 25–29, 31, 33–34, 60–65.

28 Ibid., 24–28, 31–32, 60–65. . . .

29 Keletso E. Atkins, *The Moon Is Dead! Give Us Our Money: The Cultural Origins of an African Work Ethic, Natal, South Africa, 1843–1900* (Portsmouth, N.H., 1993), 80. . . .

30 . . . . Atkins, *The Moon Is Dead! Give Us Our* Money, 81, 86, 88–89, 93–94.

31 Mechal Sobel, *The World They Made Together: Black and White Values in Eighteenth-Century Virginia* (Princeton, 1987), 15–70. . . .

32 Generally, see Louis Hartz, *The Liberal Tradition in America: An Interpretation of American Political Thought since the Revolution* (New York, 1955). . . .

33 . . . See Alan Pred, "Production, Family, and Free-Time Projects: A Time-Geographic Perspective on the Individual and Societal Change in Nineteenth-Century U.S. Cities," *Journal of Historical Geography* 7 (1981): 10.

34 In other words, these forces, which may have operated at different times and with differing degrees and potency in each constituency and culture, are similar to the ones David Landes sketched in his explanation behind the emergence of a modern clock consciousness. See Landes, *Revolution in Time*. . . .

35 Edmund S. Morgan, "The Puritan Ethic and the American Revolution," *William and Mary Quarterly*, 3d ser., 24 (January 1967): 4; Babette M. Levy, "Early Puritanism in the Southern and Island Colonies," *Proceedings of the American Antiquarian Society* 70, pt. 1 (April–October 1960): 86, 119, 308; Perry Miller, *Errand into the Wilderness* (Cambridge, Mass., 1956), 108, 138. For a different interpretation, see C. Vann Woodward, "The Southern Ethic in a Puritan World," in his *American Counterpoint: Slavery and Racism in the North–South Dialogue* (Boston, 1971), 13–46. . . .

36 For evidence of a northern mercantile time-thrift, see Toby L. Ditz, "Shipwrecked; or, Masculinity Imperiled: Mercantile Representations of Failure and the Gendered Self in Eighteenth-Century Philadelphia," *Journal of American History* 81 (June 1994): 51–80. . . .

37 Jonathan Johnson, Boston, to [Edward Telfair], October 21, 1774, Edward Telfair Papers, 1764–1831, in Kenneth M. Stampp, ed., *Records of Ante-Bellum Southern Plantations from the Revolution through the Civil War*, microfilm, Duke University Library, Durham, N.C., ser. F, pt. 2, r. 10, fr. 537, p. 2 [RASP]. . . .

38 Thomas Aiton & Co., Charleston, S.C., to William Stanley & Co., N.Y., February 18, 1802, Thomas Aiton & Co., Letterbook, February 18–June 19, 1802. . . . South Caroliniana Library, University of South Carolina [SCL].

39 Landon Carter to George Carter, Oatslands, near Leesburg, Va., September 29, 1806, section 52, Correspondence of George Carter, folder 1, Carter Family Papers, 1651–1861, Virginia Historical Society, Richmond, Va. [VHS].

40 On the South's lack of urbanization and industrialization generally, see

Fred Bateman and Thomas Weiss, *A Deplorable Scarcity: The Failure of Industrialization in the Slave Economy* (Chapel Hill, N.C., 1981); and Eugene D. Genovese, *The Political Economy of Slavery: Studies in the Economy and Society of the Slave South* (New York, 1965).

41 Unidentified newspaper clipping, Series 3.2, Miscellaneous Items, Undated, John Ewing Colhoun Papers, 1774–1961 . . . in Stampp, RASP, ser. J, pt. 3, r. 29, fr. 582. . . .

42 Landes, *Revolution in Time*, 59–66, 77; Brody, "Time and Work"; O'Malley, *Keeping Watch*, 39–40; Davison, *Unforgiving Minute*, 33–35; Atkins, *Moon Is Dead! Give Us Our Money*, 87.

43 "St. Philip's Church," *Southern Literary Gazette* 1 (November 1828): 173; Mark M. Smith, "Time, Slavery and Plantation Capitalism in the Ante-Bellum American South," *Past and Present* 150 (February 1996)," 147 n. 9.

44 . . . .On aural time in the eighteenth-century South, see Sobel, *World They Made Together*, 21. . . .

45 See Mark M. Smith, "Counting Clocks, Owning Time: Detailing and Interpreting Clock and Watch Ownership in the American South, 1739–1865," *Time and Society* 2 (October 1994): 321–39.

46 Mitchell King Diaries, 1845–1861 . . . in Mitchell King Papers, 1801–1876, Southern Historical Collection, in Stampp, RASP . . .; Bruegel, " 'Time that Can Be Relied Upon,' " 553–55. . . .

47 Bruegel, " 'Time that Can Be Relied Upon,' " . . .

48 "Report of the Chief Engineer, Horatio Allen," in Elias Horry, comp., *Annual Report of the Direction of the South Carolina Canal and Rail Road Company* . . . (Charleston, S.C., 1834), 12; [Eli Bowen], "The Post System," *DeBow's Review* 12 (March 1852): 247. . . .

49 Genovese, *Political Economy of Slavery*; Genovese, *Roll, Jordan, Roll*; and with Elizabeth Fox-Genovese, *Fruits of Merchant Capital: Slavery and Bourgeois Property in the Rise and Expansion of Capitalism* (New York, 1983). . . .

50 M. Smith, "Time, Slavery, and Plantation Capitalism."

51 Consult especially the persuasive study by Eugene D. Genovese, *The Slaveholders' Dilemma: Freedom and Progress in Southern Conservative Thought, 1820–1860* (Columbia, S.C., 1992). . . .

52 On the efficiency of antebellum slavery, see the now-classic statement by Robert W. Fogel and Stanley L. Engerman, *Time on the Cross: The Economics of American Negro Slavery*, 2 vols. (Boston, 1976). . . .

53 Bertram Wyatt-Brown, "Modernizing Southern Slavery: The Proslavery Argument Reinterpreted," in J. Morgan Kousser and James M. McPherson, eds., *Region, Race, and Reconstruction: Essays in Honor of C. Vann Woodward* (New York, 1982), 28. Note, too, the excellent study by Laurence Shore, *Southern Capitalists: The Ideological Leadership of an Elite, 1832–1885* (Chapel Hill, N.C., 1986). . . .

54 [*Boston Cultivator*], "Early Rising," *Southern Planter* 11 (January 1851): 21–22. . . .

55 J. L., "Large Products of Small Farming," *Tennessee Farmer* 1 (January 1836): 218–19.

56 "The Bachelor Farmer," *Southern Cultivator* 12 (July 1854): 208.

57 "Punctuality," *Southern Cultivator* 1 (May 10, 1843): 79. . . .

58 See . . . for example, "Improved Cotton Gin," *Southern Agriculturalist*, n.s., 5 (February 1845): 79.

59 T. S. K., "The Factory System," *Southern Agriculturalist*, n.s., 5 (February 1845): 49–51.

60 Foby, "Management of Servants," *Southern Cultivator* 11 (August 1853): 226, 228.

61 For more detail, see M. Smith, *Mastered by the Clock*, chap. 4.

62 A Maryland Planter, "Essay on the Cultivation of Tobacco, and the Management of the Plantation," *Farmers' Register* 9 (March 1841): 184.

63 Emphasis mine. James Powell Cocke, "Woodland" plantation, Diary, 1836, 1851–1857, August 25, 1854, November 1, 1854, July 23, 1856, Cocke Family Papers, 1770–1860, VHS.

64 *Plantation and Farm Instruction . . . for the Use of the Manager on the Estate of Philip St. George Cocke . . .* (Richmond, Va., 1861), 3–4, 5, 6, in Philip St. George Cocke Papers, 1854–1871, VHS.

65 . . . journal entries made in the same plantation manual suggest that the counsel concerning the centrality of the clock was not lost on overseers. . . .

66 [An Alabama Planter], "Plantation Life in the South–A Picture of Comfort," *Southern Cultivator* 18 (June 1860): 183; [*Fraser's Magazine*], "Laborers in English Factories," *Farmers' Register* 1 (August 1833): 188, 189. . . .

67 Gavin Wright, *Old South, New South: Revolutions in the Southern Economy since the Civil War* (New York, 1986), 17–19; *The Political Economy of the Cotton South: Households, Markets, and Wealth in the Nineteenth Century* (New York, 1978), 43–88. . . .

68 John F. Olson, "Clock Time versus Real Time: A Comparison of the Lengths of the Northern and Southern Agricultural Work Years," in Robert W. Fogel and Stanley L. Engerman, eds., *Without Consent or Contract: The Rise and Fall of American Slavery; Technical Papers*, 2 vols. (New York, 1992), 1: 234, 235; James C. Bonner, *A History of Georgia Agriculture 1732–1860* (Athens, Ga., 1964), 201.

69 "Labor," *Farmers' Register* 2 (June 1834): 51.

70 "Work Timed by Watch," August 1843, Anon., Plantation Journal, Barnwell District, S.C.,1838–1844, August 1843, SCL. . . .

71 Secondary works on this subject that note the role of natural rhythms in African time measurement include Thomas C. McCaskie, "Time and the Calendar in Nineteenth-Century Asante: An Exploratory Essay," *History in Africa* 7 (1980): 179–200. . . .

72 Thompson, "Time, Work-Discipline," 56–90; Genovese, *Roll, Jordan, Roll*, 291–92. The majority of slaves did not own clocks or watches, although it is, of course, difficult to say so authoritatively since, as chattel, any possessions slaves might have accumulated were not recorded in probate inventories. . . . Watch ownership might have been more common among South Carolina and Georgia low country slaves because the task system enabled them to accumulate money and hence personal property. For one Georgia slave who claimed ownership of a watch after the war, see Philip D. Morgan, "Work and Culture: The Task System and the World of Lowcountry Blacks, 1700 to 1880," *William and Mary Quarterly*, 3d ser., 39 (October 1982): 588 n. 94. . . . On the whole, however, slaveholders were understandably reluctant to encourage widespread timepiece ownership among slaves. Like the earliest British industrialists, they feared watch-owning bondpeople would quickly become time-negotiating workers, an intolerable prospect on all but the smallest scale. On this, see M. Smith, *Mastered by the Clock*, chaps. 4–5; and Nguyen, "Spatialization of Metric Time," 36.

73 . . . . In this case the contemporary accounts complement the narratives, which suggests that the 1930s testimony is not as flawed as is sometimes assumed.

74 *Narrative of the Life of Moses Grandy, a Slave in the United States of America* (Boston, 1844), 17, in Katz, *Five Slave Narratives*. Also see Rawick, *American Slave*, supp. ser. 1, vol. 12, Oklahoma Narratives, 277. . . .
75 Lue Bradford's testimony cited in John B. Cade, "Out of the Mouths of Ex-Slaves," *Journal of Negro History* 44 (January 1935): 312. . . .
76 Washington, "Memorys of the Past," 55; testimony of Lu Lee in Rawick, *American Slave*, supp. ser. 2, vol. 6, Texas Narratives, pt. 5, 2298. . . .
77 Rawick, *American Slave*, supp. ser. 2, vol. 1 . . . 81; Annie L. Burton, *Memories of Childhood's Slavery Days* (Boston, 1909), 5, in *Six Women's Slave Narratives* (New York, 1988). . . .
78 Rawick, *American Slave*, supp. ser. 2, vol. 3, Texas Narratives, pt. 2, 881; supp. ser. 2, vol. 2, Texas Narratives, pt. 1, 373, 165.
79 *Narrative of William W. Brown* (Boston, 1847), 14–15. . . .
80 M. Smith, "Time, Slavery and Plantation Capitalism," 164–65;. . . .
81 See, for example, the thoughtful essays in Ted Ownby, ed., *Black and White Cultural Interaction in the Antebellum South* (Jackson, Miss., 1993).
82 For a historian who emphasizes the centrality of wage labor in defining a particular mode of production as "capitalist," see Genovese, *Political Economy of Slavery*.
83 Also see James Oakes, *The Ruling Race: A History of American Slaveholders* (New York, 1983).
84 Regarding the North, this is the logical conclusion to be drawn from Bruegel, " 'Time that Can Be Relied Upon.' "
85 See, for example, P. J. Cain and A. G. Hopkins, *British Imperialism: Innovation and Expansion 1688–1914* (London, 1993), 1–52,. . . .
86 For the postbellum South, see M. Smith, *Mastered by the Clock*, chap. 6.

5

SLAVERY, FREEDOM, AND SOCIAL CLAIMS TO PROPERTY AMONG AFRICAN AMERICANS IN LIBERTY COUNTY, GEORGIA, 1850–1880

Dylan C. Penningroth

Dylan C. Penningroth's essay focuses on the fact—surprising to readers unfamiliar with recent work on the "slaves' economy"—that many slaves did own property. Penningroth examines slave property ownership in Liberty County, Georgia. In this lowcountry region (not far from the Gowrie plantation examined by Jeffrey R. Young), slaves accumulated property by working on their own time after completion of required tasks, by commanding the labor of family members, and even, at times, by inheriting it. Both masters and other slaves recognized private property held by slaves, even though it had no basis in law. Going beyond earlier historians who have established the fact of slave ownership, Penningroth explores in detail "how" they owned it—how did they establish rights to property in the absence of any legal right to such ownership? The answer depends partly on the attitudes of slave owners, but more important, Penningroth argues, on the attitudes and values of the slaves themselves. Thus, the study of property ownership "can not only illuminate the power relationships between black people and white people but also reveal how black people negotiated over power and resources among themselves." Penningroth, thus, largely sidesteps questions about resistance and paternalism in this innovative study of the nature of the slave community.

* * *

"My name is Pompey Bacon. I was born in Liberty County, Georgia, I am 70 years of age I am farming and the claimant in this case." With this statement Bacon, a former slave of plantation owner Thomas Mallard, claimed compensation for property he had owned as a slave, property Union soldiers had taken for "forage" on a raid during the Civil War. With him on this late summer day in 1873 were Bacon's wife, Bellu, his older brother, Joseph, and three other freed people from farms near the one he worked; all intended to serve as his witnesses.[1] Except for Mrs. Bacon each had a petition before the Southern Claims Commission.

Under oath, Bacon unfolded his story of the raid in response to a long list of standardized questions read by Virgil Hillyer, a special commissioner of the federal commission. During the siege of Savannah in December 1864, Judson Kilpatrick's cavalry, part of Gen. William T. Sherman's army, was ordered to forage supplies. Most white people had fled from the countryside near Savannah, with Sherman's Westerners hard on their heels. The troops arrived at Thomas Mallard's plantation just after harvest, when mornings turned the earth "white with frost." Liberty County was a rich agricultural area, and 1864 had been a good year for food crops. Hogs were "in good flesh" in December when the business of butchering and salting began in earnest. Pompey Bacon remembered that the marauding Union soldiers "said they never got provision until they got to Liberty Co. among the colored people." Bacon gladly welcomed them; he later told the claims agent that "after the Union Army came into the county I did all I could in the way of cooking and feeding the poor soldiers. One poor fellow came to me almost naked. I gave him my own hat, clothed and fed him." Bacon reported that such generosity "was a common thing at that time for the Colored people to do; we thought of nothing then but our own freedom and those who made us free." Bacon's brother Joseph, who had watched cavalrymen feed his bountiful 1864 crop to their worn-out horses, told Hillyer that "it seemed to us as if the 'Lord has blessed the earth on purpose to help our deliverer'."[2]

But the foraging parties turned deliverance into a plague of confiscation. A claimant recalled that the soldiers descended "like a hungry wolf & thick as sand-flies" on the grand mansions and slave cabins alike. The "poor soldiers" who freed Pompey Bacon also stripped him of nearly everything he owned. "The soldiers did not say anything," Bacon recalled of the men who crowded into his yard in Riceboro, "only [that] they were in need of the property & would have it." They stuffed his corn into sacks made out of his bed sheets and his wife's underclothing. They took his wagon, shot down his hogs in his yard and carried them off slung across his horse. "We all rushed there to see what was done," said another ex-slave who witnessed the raid on the Mallard plantation, "& we were so scared we went in gangs." All across Liberty County black people rushed to and fro watching gangs of soldiers take property from their friends and relatives, then from their own homes. Kilpatrick's men "were all over the plantation," an ex-slave from the nearby Winn plantation concluded; "every niggers house was full of them."[3]

Some slaves found an officer in the crowd and made a futile protest.

" 'Massa' you going to take all, & leave me nothing to live on," pleaded Samuel Elliott. The soldiers replied: "we are obliged to, we come to set you free, & we must have something to eat, but you must go to 'Uncle Sam.' Uncle Sam's pockets drag on the ground." Soldiers told Paris James "that they had the law to take meat & bread &c wherever they saw it." James complained and got a receipt from an officer, but other troopers tore it up in his face and went on taking what they wanted. . . . After three weeks Kilpatrick's cavalry marched away, but then, said Bacon, "the rebels came in and took every little thing the Yankees left." Bacon found himself "naked as a bird" after two huge and barely disciplined armies had rampaged through the plantations and villages of Liberty County. He and many other slaves entered freedom ruined as property owners.[4]

By 1873, when Bacon met Hillyer in Riceboro, ex-slaves had been waiting nine years for the government to award them compensation for the property they had lost. During the raid, many had asked Union officers for vouchers, clearly intending to request reimbursement once they had an opportunity. The opportunity they had waited for came in 1871, when Congress created the Southern Claims Commission under the Treasury Department to hear claims from Unionist southerners who had lost "stores or supplies . . . taken or furnished for the use of the [Union] army" during the Civil War. Virgil Hillyer was one of 106 special commissioners sent to towns across the South to gather information and to hold formal compensation hearings. Between 1873 and 1880 the special commissioners forwarded more than 22,000 claims, testimony from some 220,000 witnesses, and their official recommendations to Washington, D.C., where the three commissioners of claims passed final judgment.[5]

The commission originally sought to compensate white Unionist southerners. President Ulysses S. Grant signed into law the bill establishing the commission amid stormy debate over whether the government should help people whom many northerners saw as rebels. Therefore, nearly half of the "standing interrogatories" posed to each claimant concerned loyalty during the war.[6]

Much confusion stemmed from the assumption, widespread in the North, that slaves knew nothing about property and personal responsibility and that they would have to learn such concepts from northerners. Groups of teachers, missionaries, and energetic capitalists had been coming to the nearby South Carolina Sea Islands since 1863, offering the black residents an odd mixture of schooling, moralistic preachments, and profit-seeking exploitation. They had found, however, that Low Country blacks did not need to be taught to respect and "regard the rights of property among themselves." Among Sea Island blacks, reported one early observer, "If a man has a claim upon a horse or sow he maintains his right and his neighbors recognize it." Those whites who had come to educate and inculcate were pleased but puzzled to find ex-slaves who already exhibited "a passion for ownership," who "delight[ed] in accumulating" property. To most northerners, however, it still seemed obvious that property could not own property; logically, only free people could own things. As a result, neither the commission's founders nor its representatives expected many claims from former slaves.[7]

Yet despite its seeming illogic and its lack of legal standing, property ownership among Low Country slaves had been widespread and stable. Hundreds of ex-slave claimants came forward to testify to that fact, some backed by their former masters. The officers of the Southern Claims Commission struggled to reconcile the traditional northern viewpoint—that slaves had been systematically deprived of all the fruits of their labor—with the reality of slaves who had had their property confiscated by Union soldiers. "I know it is hard for some to realize or imagine how it was possible for slaves to own property," wrote Hillyer to the commissioners after months of hearing testimony. "You would be astonished to get through the external crust of Southern society and see the inside working of the almost entire business of the Southern States." Although some northerners believed that they were giving black people the first "portion of their rightful earnings which had ever been allowed," by the 1870s representatives of the Treasury Department realized that such confident statements belied what they were finding in Low Country Georgia.[8] Although southern laws did not recognize them as owners, slaves had owned property with the tacit consent of masters and other whites. Testimony by ex-slaves about cows, corn, wagons, and other possessions revealed a complicated world of social relationships among slaves, one that overlapped but was largely apart from their relationships with their masters and the formal institutions of the Low Country.

Unlike the claims officials, most historians today would not be surprised to find slaves who owned property. Studies of property ownership by slaves have proliferated in the last fifteen years, documenting its existence across the American South and the Caribbean. . . . These scholars have tried to create an analytical framework that can encompass both slaves' internal economic strategies and slaves' family relationships, culture, and community. Property ownership and the particular labor system that flourished in the Low Country allowed slaves to carve out "a measure of autonomy," as Morgan puts it. Within this semiautonomous internal economy, slaves drew on their family and community relationships for help in accumulating and protecting property. This independent economic activity fostered a sense of pride, "communal solidarity, and personal responsibility" that helped blacks resist the oppression of slavery and foreshadowed their responses to emancipation.[9]

Some scholars, convinced that concepts of ownership were "alien" to African societies, argue that slaves' independent economic activity was also part of the acculturation process by which Africans became African Americans. Slaves came from "societies where everything had been held in common," writes Loren Schweninger, for example. "Nothing in their African heritage prepared them for the New World emphasis on land ownership and economic individualism." Property ownership brought African Americans' values and cultural practices closer to the individualism and nuclear family structure of European Americans. . . . Yet Schweninger's argument rests on four questionable but not uncommon assumptions: that Africans had a clear system of values about property; that this system was "communal" rather than individually oriented; that slaves brought it to the Americas; and that their values shifted, over time, to an ethos of acquisitive individualism. This logic reflects twentieth-century Western thought about Africa, not eighteenth-century African values about work and property. Studies of various parts of Africa from the seventeenth through the twentieth centuries also suggest caution in using a single characterization of property and social organization in Africa as a baseline for sketching changes in cultural values among African Americans. Historical and anthropological work on Africa has argued that descriptions of "communal" property ownership made by European visitors in the eighteenth and nineteenth centuries were inaccurate. Such descriptions must be seen as part of a broad cross-cultural interaction that helped shape Europeans' conceptions of property ownership in both Africa and Europe. Over the last 150 years, people in both Africa and the Americas have made their claims to property and mobilized productive labor through a continuous negotiation of social relationships and have not relied solely, or even primarily, on formal institutions such as laws, courts, or agencies such as the Southern Claims Commission.[10]

If historians now agree *that* some slaves in the American South owned property, it is still not clear *how* slaves owned property. Few studies have departed substantially from two long-standing themes in African American history: the "dialectic" of accommodation and resistance and the debate over cultural "survivals" and acculturation, sometimes fused into a framework of "cultural adaptation and resistance." Neither of those interpretive themes adequately explains the significance that property ownership by slaves had for slaves' interactions with their masters and with non-slave-owning whites. Most important, although studies of economic activity among African Americans emphasize autonomy, solidarity based on family, community, or the common experience of oppression, we do not know how slaves' property-related efforts shaped and were influenced by their relationships with one another. Julie Saville hints at a promising approach when she briefly discusses the deeper implications of "cooperation" within black families in postwar South Carolina, where elderly ex-slaves used their "networks of accountable kin" to command labor from younger freed people. Studying how slaves acquired and held property opens new possibilities for African American history because it can not only illuminate the power relationships between black people and white people but also reveal how black people negotiated over power and resources *among themselves*.[11]

This essay reconstructs the network of social relationships among Liberty County slaves that enabled them to accumulate property. It then moves outward to analyze how those relationships enabled the slaves to assert property claims that even their masters respected. Finally, the essay explores what it meant for these African Americans when they and their property gained legal recognition in the years following emancipation. While federal officials had to evaluate unexpected claims, ex-slaves like Pompey Bacon had to convince the commissioners that, regardless of the law, slaves did own property and that the foraging soldiers had taken property that belonged to the slaves, not their masters. In their testimony, ex-slaves revealed a good deal about how they understood "ownership" and knew who owned what. Since no law protected a slave's property from other slaves or from his or her master, slaves depended on an informal system of display and acknowledgment to mark the boundaries of ownership. Their ability to transform mere possession into ownership depended on their ability to substitute informal public recognition for public law as the anchor of their title. The affirmation of a slave's property was not a single act but a series of demonstrations over time. In the claims process, such demonstrations were recalled by former slaves and became valuable as a way of proving ownership to the commission. Making a claim to the Southern Claims Commission involved reenacting in a formal, legal, institutional setting the slaves' informal system of display and acknowledgment.

Studying negotiations over labor and property among slaves makes possible a richer understanding of slavery, and of the changes that freedom brought. Drawing on concepts advanced in recent scholarship on the Caribbean and Africa, this paper proposes a new framework for analyzing the connection between people's social relationships and their interests in property. Rather than assess American blacks' claims to property as examples of cultural change or of resistance to political and legal institutions, this paper concentrates on those informal understandings and practices themselves: how they were created, how they worked, and how they changed between 1850 and 1880. A whole world of social relationships and negotiations lay behind the fact that slaves owned property. That world begins to come into focus if, instead of asking, "Whose corn was it?," we pose the more fruitful question, "How did people know whose corn it was?"

Liberty County, Georgia, in the Low Country, is a rectangular band of land stretching northwest from the Atlantic seacoast. In 1860 some of the nation's largest plantations were in the Low Country. . . . By 1860 black people outnumbered white people by three to one in Liberty County, and nearly all of them were slaves. They spent most of their lives cultivating rice, the region's reigning cash crop.[12]

Working by tasks defined the everyday life of slaves in Liberty County. Unlike the gang system that prevailed in most other areas of the South, the task system assigned each slave a certain amount of work each day—a quarter acre to hoe, for example, or a hundred wooden rails to split. The system permitted slaves to help one another in their work and allowed them to use as they wished the time left after finishing the task. By working on their own time to raise more than they needed to eat, slaves accumulated property and created traditions of property ownership and trade. Once they had their start, many slaves invested in a succession of animals, beginning with poultry and moving to larger and more valuable hogs, cattle, and, finally, horses. Jacob Quarterman, who claimed livestock, a wagon, corn, and rice, told the claims agent: "I bought mine sir by taking care of what little I could get."[13] This practice of organizing labor by task rather than by time was the taproot of property ownership by Low Country slaves.

Slave-owned property and the arrangements of land and labor from which it came were part of an important regional informal economy within the more formal economies of the plantation and the city. The former slaveowner Edward DeLegal testified:

> I never interfered with my people, they bought & sold these things at there own prices & spent the money as they pleased & this was customary in Liberty County & I suppose it was in other seaboard counties. . . .

Relatively free to trade the property they had, slaves marketed their goods to Liberty County residents as well as to the urban consumers in Savannah, twenty miles away. "I bought poultry to retail in Savannah the place where I always go," testified Jacob Quarterman. "I carried it in my wagon." Another slave raised rice and "shipped it to town by Capt Charley . . . who runs a vessel to Riceboro." Slaves were sufficiently versed in market practices to handle adroitly the currency instability that plagued the region during the war. When Confederate money became, as one witness put it, "no better than a newspaper after it is read," some slaves began to insist when they could on "silver and United States banknotes." Tony Axon and Pompey Bacon accepted payment in salt, another wartime currency substitute. Salt was an essential resource. Slaves on nearby Edisto Island, South Carolina, consumed one pint every two weeks working under the hot sun. It was crucial to the war effort, especially for preserving meat. Salt thus made a solid investment and a stable currency substitute.[14]

The formal economy of the plantation also depended on slaves' ability to earn, own, and trade property. As historians of the Low Country and the Caribbean have argued, production costs fell when planters were able to shift "part or all of the burden of subsisting their slaves onto the slaves themselves." Moreover, planters could discipline slaves into a reliable work force by threatening to take away their access to land or time.[15]

For many slaves, the task system provided relatively easy access to land but not necessarily time to work the land. While in a sense "the slaves' 'time' became sacrosanct" as the task system became "institutionaliz[ed]" during the late eighteenth century, task requirements and the time needed to finish them changed with the rise of new crops and technologies. With each development, masters and slaves fought to redefine the boundary between "the master's time" and "the slaves' time." Relative to these struggles over time, masters and slaves devoted little attention to land. Generally, Low Country slaves "were allowed all the land they could tend without rent," an average of perhaps four to five acres, far more than any one person could tend. Testimony from task system areas across the Caribbean and North America shows that masters restricted slaves' access to time much more than they restricted their access to land.[16]

Within this economy of time, slaves used three avenues to accumulate property. First, by working faster at their tasks, they could save time and use it to earn property. Some claimants testified that they could finish a task by noon or one o'clock or that they could "save . . . a whole day" by doing several tasks in a single day. However, archaeologists report that "even under the task system the work day might be 15 or 16 hours long during the peak of the harvest season." Planting a personal crop meant committing to long hours of work after a hard day's task, "till the fowls crow for day, by moonlight & firelight." Second, for some slaves, a skill was a valuable and portable kind of "property" that could itself generate more property. Of the 91 ex-slave claimants, 12 worked as carpenters or coopers. Field hands who knew cooping could make small wooden pails called "piggins" and sell them to both slave and free. "I don't think any body ought object to a man going into the woods and cutting the wood for pails and tubs and piggins and selling them," testified William McIver. "This was the way I got my start."[17]

Slaves' third option was to find someone else to labor for them. Slaves negotiated for access to others' time through kin and communal relationships, hiring, and plantation privileges. Because drivers had less after-task time than other slaves, masters often granted them the right to have other slaves work their personal plots for them. Of the 17 claims by Liberty County ex-slaves for over $500, ex-drivers filed 5, even though they made up less than 1 percent of the slave population in the cotton belt in 1860. One white overseer complained in 1828 that drivers used the authority bestowed by masters to attach labor to their own crops and that drivers punished more "from private pique than from a neglect of duty." In measuring out tasks the driver could "screen favorites" and "apply their time to his own purposes." Years later, when witnesses stood before the special commissioner, such tactics could make for lukewarm testimony. Drivers were by no means universally respected, much less loved, for earning their property from the sweat of other slaves. "Some big headed drivers were not always Union," grumbled one former field hand in a statement guaranteed to undercut some unlucky ex-driver's claim.[18]

Slaves who had resources but lacked standing in the hierarchy defined by masters could mobilize labor in other ways. Pompey Bacon, whose master allowed him to plant for himself "all the land I could work," said, "I used to hire men to work it for me some time." But more than hiring or plantation prerogative, slaves drew on their social relationships with other slaves. Husbands and wives expected their partners to work and contribute to the family. Special Agent Robert B. Avery wrote that claimant Josephine James had been "unlucky" in her new marriage to a man named Jones, for "the fellow would not work, and she drove him off." Although several claimants said they brought property to their marriages, it is not clear whether property was a prerequisite or even an incentive for marriage. Some slaves may have married with an eye toward gaining property, and property-owning slaves may have had more marriage proposals. Similar dynamics may have influenced childbearing since slaves also used children as a source of labor. Most claimants who mentioned children not old enough to marry said that their children worked right alongside them on after-task work. Toney Elliott "had a son that helped him—worked only for his father & mother" up to the age of fifteen. Children could also help their parents by tending the smaller animals. About her father's claim for 24 chickens, Annetta Stewart testified: "Most of them was mine. I raised them all." Even after they went to work in their masters' fields, young slaves contributed labor to older slaves. Joshua Cassell reported that "there was a fine lot of young people & they were jealous of one another & tried to see which would get their days work done first." Their master, Thomas Mallard, "used to come in the field, & tell the overseer not to balk we, if we got done soon to let us alone & do our own work as we pleased." .... Children thus helped to create family wealth and learned the importance of gathering property. Such arrangements were part of the constant negotiation that had characterized relations between Low Country masters and slaves since the 1710s, and no one underestimated the value of children as workers. Under the task system, more children meant more property. "We could have all the land we could cultivate," remembered George Gould, and lucky was the man who had as large a family as he did. He, his four children, and his wife all worked by the task, and when they finished, they "all worked the rice" in the family plot. His claim totaled a remarkable $580. Slaves were acutely aware of the value they placed on children's labor. "I was 30 years old before I married," testified Henry Stevens, "my children didn't help me much. I did most of it [accumulating property] myself." Some families continued to pool their labor and resources after emancipation. When freedom came, William Cassels said, "I and my wife and 2 boys worked land together."[19]

Not all cooperation occurred within slaves' immediate families. Twenty-three-year-old Benjamin Hines, a brickmason who had lived with his stepgrandfather at the time of the raid ten years before, said he knew exactly how many turkeys, geese, and ducks the older man had owned because "I had the care of these—that was my business." Whether his parents had sent him there or had themselves been sold away, the boy and his stepgrandfather shared obligations much like those binding immediate family members. Another case involved distant cousins. When Nancy Bacon's husband died in 1863, leaving all of their property at his place on another plantation, she enlisted her second cousin, Andrew Stacy, "to go there & bring them home & take care of them" and, it seems, move into her house. When Bacon's master took her to Walthourville, twelve miles away, she left her hogs and cattle again with Stacy.[20] These slaves called on their kin, however distant or indeterminate by blood, for help in caring for their property.

A range of social relationships among people who were not related by blood at all helped slaves overcome the difficulties involved in acquiring and keeping property in the close living arrangements of the quarters. Slaves unrelated by blood frequently provided labor and material aid to those who needed it. Slaves who lost spouses or were disabled by age or disease often got by on the strength of hale, younger arms. "I had a boy to help me," said Eliza James of the crop she made in 1864 after her husband died. . . . Such affective ties could be intense, and slaves often felt them as kinship, but these ties provided economic as well as emotional support. Claimant John Wilson named, in addition to his wife and children, a "Sister Thompson" as one of the people who had seen his property taken. This turned out to be Charlotte Thompson, an elderly resident of Savannah and a former slave. "I have always been intimate with Mr. Wilson as a neighbor & friend," she testified. Prodded to state whether she had any "interest" in Wilson's claim, she went on, "we are no relation, but he often visited the house as a friend until my sister died then he seemed like a brother." Some adults took young children into their care. "She raised me" was the proof one witness gave that he knew the claimant. York Stevens, who received both property and his name from his adoptive grandfather, was so completely integrated into his adoptive family that in their testimony he and other ex-slaves often neglected to mention that he was not related by blood. Confused, the claims agent eventually took the following testimony from the claimant's former master:

> Claimant was the son, or adopted son, of old York Stevens, a faithful old driver, of Capt. Winn, this old driver, owned horses, cattle and hogs; and Witness understood that old York Stevens gave some of his property to claimant—Witness heard Capt. Winn say so.[21]

Slaves who took in children or worked for elderly neighbors were manifesting more than kindness or solidarity based on a common experience of oppression. Kinship and property were interrelated among Liberty County slaves, but property did not merely follow lines of "blood" and marriage. Slaves' efforts to raise and keep property relied largely on their relationships with one another, especially with family members. At the same time, social relationships were flexible and negotiable, influenced by many factors other than kinship, including people's interests in property.

If the labor of children accrued to adults, inheritance represented the other side of this relationship. Inheritance was one of the most important ways slaves got their start as property owners. "When my Father died he had 20 head of cattle," said Samuel Elliott, "about 70 head of hogs. Turkeys Geese Ducks and Chicken a plenty—he was foreman for his master . . . and had been raising such things for years. When he died the property was divided among his children and we continued to raise thing[s] just as he had." Many claimants mentioned inheriting chickens, one or two hogs or cows, or sometimes a horse from their parents. Mothers bequeathed property sometimes, fathers more frequently, to both their boys and their girls. Generally, however, far fewer women than men mentioned inheriting horses or cattle.[22] Inheritance implies rules that were recognized among the slaves. It was the arena in which slaves decided how property should move among family members, and the paths that bequeathed wealth traveled outlined and strengthened the obligations slaves felt toward each other, obligations that stretched across past and future generations. Part of property's value for slaves, apart from its capacity to be used or consumed, lay in the social relationships it embodied, ready to be called into action. By bequeathing property, slaves defined the boundaries of what and who belonged to them.

There were three significant threats to the security of slave-owned property: theft, masters' legal prerogatives, and the persistence of shared property interests among slaves. Slaves certainly stole from one another, and some former slaves continued to do so after emancipation. However, there is little evidence of theft in the claims testimony. The commission asked only about the large-scale theft by Union soldiers. Claimants and witnesses had little reason to volunteer stories of what other people stole, since they might have weakened their cases by giving the impression that property ownership among slaves had been fraught or unstable.[23]

Masters, who maintained legal rights over everything their slaves possessed, posed a more serious threat. Some ex-slaves reported that their former masters would ask before taking anything belonging to a slave. However, no slave could easily refuse such a "request." Behind the veneer of custom and good faith, said former house slave William Gilmore, the masters "were not any of them too good, they would not allow you to talk of your rights." According to one white witness, "every planter had his own rule" regarding slaves' owning property, and a single master could change the rules capriciously. Perhaps in order to protect themselves, many slaves constantly sought "advice" and "would hardly ever do anything" with their property until they had consulted with their masters. Nevertheless, few masters seem to have taken advantage of their legal rights. . . . Joseph Bacon understood that "legally" slaves had no right to property, but he insisted that "a master who would take property from his slaves would have a hard time." His own master, he said, "never interfered with me and my property at all."[24] Why not?

Slaves protected their claims to property by using public occasions and public spaces to display their possessions and to secure acknowledgment from their masters and fellow slaves. The physical arrangement of the plantation was essential to this practice. According to Robert Quarterman Mallard, a son of Thomas Mallard, the slave quarters on his father's plantation stood in "single and double rows of cottages" for easy monitoring by the master. Slaves stored their belongings separately; attached to each cabin were "vegetable gardens, chicken coops, pig pens, rice ricks, and little store houses," under the control of individuals and families. Ex-slaves' testimony substantiates this picture and carefully distinguishes what belonged to whom. Larger animals were particularly easy to recognize since there were few of them relative to smaller stock. Claimants generally described them individually in great detail in their testimony. One woman testified that when the raid came her husband "counted off his cattle from the rest as they went by. From the white people's cattle & the other col'd people's cattle."[25]

Most of the items that ex-slaves claimed—chicken coops, beehives, hogs, small gardens—were stored in their yards, where they were visible to other people. Cabins and storehouses closely adjoined, and, with three or four slaves living in each cabin, people could see from their own yards what their neighbors had. Often the display of property was more intentional. "We staid door to door to each other," testified Clarinda Lowe about her neighbor James Anderson, "& when we got any thing new we always showed one another." It is also likely that slaves gathered in their yards to socialize. If slaves frequently visited one another, the property that was cooped, penned, or stacked there would have been more or less public knowledge. Samson Bacon testified: "I know it was his because every man on one place know every other man's property. . . . he can't help from knowing it. All go in his yard before his door."[26] Although their master designed the slave quarters with his own interests in mind, slaves used the layout to display and distinguish their property.

Slaves also strengthened their possession of property through display in other circumstances. Robert Quarterman Mallard recorded the social importance of certain kinds of property on Sundays in Liberty County. The roads to Midway Church filled with wagons driven by both planters and slaves, all dressed in their Sunday clothes, "those on foot carrying their shoes and stockings in their hands, to be resumed after they shall have washed in the waters at the causeway near the church; for they believe in treading the Lord's courts with clean feet!" Slaves and planters alike, he wrote, were deaf to the familiar lament of the preacher that "on Sunday many *garnish* themselves and go to church for show; they hear but do not attend." Although the practice may have seemed a petty distraction to white preachers, slaves "showed" their property on Sundays for practical, social, and deeply spiritual reasons. For example, Pompey Bacon, who gladly "clothed and fed" the Union soldiers, refused to part with his "nice" overcoat and shirts but later reported that the soldiers "hustled me round till they carried" off even those items. Bacon took especially hard the loss of "some nice linen shirts I used to go to communion in & they took them and I grieved . . . I wanted them to meet the 'Lord'." The spiritual and practical meanings that individual slaves associated with their belongings took on additional, social significance in the context of public worship. Slaves who could afford to do so kept certain possessions apart to use less frequently. They wore their "common everyday coarse clothes" during the week and saved the "finery" they bought in Savannah to wear on Sundays. William Gilmore, who owned a "spring wagon," said that he "only used it to go to Church on Sunday." This practice not only eased wear on less durable possessions but also visibly marked the day as different from the rest of the week. Although neighbors and friends frequently visited one another in their yards, Sunday services were one of the few occasions for slaves to socialize in large groups. As the slaves did so, they brought their best clothes, driving buggies, and quilted leather saddles into public view.[27] Recognition of the Sabbath was intertwined with the informal system of display and acknowledgment that secured slaves' ownership of property.

People in Liberty County interacted socially in their yards, on the roads between plantations, at church services, and at marriage ceremonies. These social interactions did not simply give psychological satisfaction or a sense of community. They also played an important role in securing slaves' ownership of property.

Slaves sought recognition of their claims to property not just from masters nor from the people who gathered on Sundays but also from spouses and kin. Marriage among slaves called for careful attention to the public dimension of personal property ownership because it rearranged the property interests of two people and their families and often split property between two households. According to Robert Quarterman Mallard, Liberty County slaves were allowed "to marry wherever they chose; and their almost universal choice was of husbands and wives at a distance of from one to fifteen miles." But most masters did not let these couples live together. A slave who lived with his or her spouse at another plantation was thought to enjoy "rather an unusual privilege," one that was probably granted most often to male slaves who hired themselves out. Most slaves who married off the plantation were obliged to maintain two households, more or less complete with gardens, utensils, and all the other necessities of life. Property flowed back and forth between the households as spouses, usually husbands, shuttled between them. "Saturday nights," wrote Mallard, "the roads were ... filled with men on their way to 'wife house,' each pedestrian, or horseman, bearing in a bag his soiled clothes and all the good things he could collect during the week, for the delectation of his household." The bulk of a couple's property usually remained at the wife's house. . . . Slaves viewed the wife's house as the husband's primary residence. Eliza James testified that before her husband died in June 1864, "his home was with me on my master's place."[28] In spite of the masters' intentions, the flow of slave-owned property signaled that slave couples considered themselves to have one "home," though they had two residences, with property at each. Faced with these restrictions on their mobility, slaves made the home, that is, the slave cabin, the multifunctional yard, and the garden a locus of authority over property.

Uniting possessions under one roof helped secure them against threats from outside the household, but it also sparked negotiation within the household over who owned those possessions. Spouses contributed jointly the labor needed to earn property and then shared custodial responsibilities. Yet joint effort did not rule out the possibility that in some situations slaves had an interest in asserting individual claims over property. Many of them distinguished items on the basis of who had "made" them, that is, who had contributed the labor that earned those items. However, custody could carry just as much weight in negotiations between husbands and wives who lived apart. Women were not allowed to travel as much as men and could not have controlled property that was stored elsewhere, but a woman may have been able to control and claim her husband's belongings because they were stored at her house. Men, however, could visit their wives frequently and were more familiar with the property stored at the wives' residences and more often proclaimed themselves owners of it. William Cassels walked the half mile to see his wife most nights and "knew as much about my things there as at my own home." The property belonged to them both but under his expansive aegis: "She doesn't claim anything separate from me we are all one." During slavery, the prevalence of split-residence households and the importance of display and acknowledgment meant that custody and knowledge were likely to override other factors in determining which spouse controlled property and in turning control into claims of ownership. After the war, men's tendency to claim household property was aggravated both by the physical consolidation of households and by the Southern Claims Commission's requirement that women prove separate ownership from their husbands. Male claimants faced no such requirement. Thus Prince Stewart testified that, although some of the things he claimed had "belonged to, and were taken from, my wife . . . 'wesm' are all one now so I put them into my claim."[29] Married people's joint efforts to raise property and their common interest in safeguarding household property did not stop their negotiations over the control and ownership of it.

To ensure that the property interests of their children, nieces, and nephews stayed secure after marriage, some slave parents relied on the public character of marriage. Slaves treasured the public rituals surrounding marriage because these rituals legitimized both social and economic connections that the law did not recognize. Giving property as part of the marriage ceremony publicly affirmed the bonds between newlyweds and their relatives. Public giving also permitted the new couple to avoid confusion or hard feelings in the future by spreading knowledge about how each piece of property had come into the marriage. In this way, women may have retained some control over property. Susan Bennett explained that, although she and her late husband had earned some property together, not all of the property she claimed was jointly earned. "We both had pigs when we married," she remembered. . . . Jane Holmes took care to distinguish between her things and those that had belonged to her two husbands: "I did not get any property by either one of my husband's," she testified, "I kept the property my husband had when the raid came for his son to attend to. I had no children by him so when he died his property went to his son."[30] This careful attention to the ways property came into the marriage made each spouse's claim to ownership stronger and, to some extent, offset the tendency men had to claim all household property as their own. Each spouse's relatives retained an interest in the property they gave to the couple. Because slave families provided so much of the labor that raised property, the knowledge that protected it, and the rules of inheritance that passed it down, they were sites of constant negotiation.

In the absence of legal protection, the claim a slave had to property seems to have depended on his or her long association with a thing, an association that had to be visible to as many eyes as possible. Testifying in the case of Prince Stevens, ex-slave Samson Bacon explained that he "never heard [Stevens's] master claim his horse. No sir no such thing as that, he had been riding the horse too long back & forth between there & his master's." What from a legal perspective seem to have been merely rights of use or possession translated over time into real rights over property. As another witness put it, "I know it was his because it was right there under his 'controlment' & no one else claimed it."[31] Much of property's public visibility through the multipurpose slave yards, inheritance practices, transfers at marriage, showy dress and buggies at church performed an important function. In effect, by dragging their personal property into public view, the slaves cemented their claims to own property in a society whose laws did not admit that possibility.

Kilpatrick's raid and the establishment of the Southern Claims Commission meant that ex-slaves would have to extend their claims of ownership beyond their masters, spouses, and kin to agents of the federal government. The law had not recognized property ownership among slaves, but after emancipation institutional protection of property was extended to former slaves only through a complex process of adjustment. It appears unlikely that all or even most of the county's property-owning former slaves came forward to participate in and benefit from that process. The 91 claimants compensated by the commission represented only a tiny segment of the 6,083 slaves living in Liberty County in 1860. Witnesses frequently mentioned in passing that they, too, had lost property but had not reported it. Some of those witnesses said they had not known about the commission until after the deadline for filing. Others simply doubted that anything would come of it. When asked why he had not filed to recover his own property, Tony Law replied, "I have not put in my claim against the Government yet because I haven't seen those who put in get any money. I heard that some in 'Hilton Head' had got some money but I am afraid that there won't any ever come here in my lifetime." The expense of filing probably discouraged some people as well. Both Special Commissioner Hillyer and Raymond Cay Jr., the local lawyer who filed for most of the county's ex-slaves, received fees and percentages that left some successful claimants with as little as $15 of an official award of $130. Cay, the son of a planter who had owned many of the claimants, came under fire from federal officials in both Liberty County and Washington, D.C., for his excessive fees. . . . Some of the exslave claimants, who may have drawn attention to Cay's unscrupulous conduct, induced a local minister to send several letters to Washington on their behalf asking that their payments be sent directly to them rather than in care of their lawyer.[32]

For those ex-slaves who did file claims, success depended on changes in the assumptions that both they and the claims officials brought to the compensation process. Agents, and especially the three commissioners of claims, came to their tasks with highly legalistic conceptions of property and ownership, conceptions that were strikingly different from those held by the former slaves of Liberty County or even by the former masters. Northern officials expected that ownership was consolidated around one person (though it could be delegated), that property's value could be calculated in money, that law validated ownership, and that property could not logically own property. Northern officials were prepared to evaluate the evidence found in contracts, to hear testimony about the clear, disinterested transfer of ownership from one person to the next. Instead, they heard witnesses tell of neighbors who helped one another keep animals and offer as proof of ownership the simple fact that they had seen the claimants use their possessions. Federal agents found such detailed anecdotal testimony useful for investigating claims brought by Unionist whites but problematic for those of former slaves. One agent wrote that he relied heavily on blacks' testimony to corroborate the claims of whites. "I go to negroes because I find I can really get *detailed* information out of them," the agent explained. They always know if a man was *really* loyal, they know if the cribs were full or not, often remember the names of the mules [and] the oxen." By contrast, "the rich white neighbors of the claimants" tended to "assert with a careless generality that 'so and so had between 50 and 100 head of whatnots, and the Federals took'm all sir; they took everything in the county, they robbed me, and broke me up . . . so and so lost ten times what he has charged the government.' "[33] Yet if some agents considered blacks reliable witnesses in proving the property claims of whites, blacks' testimony was immediately suspect when given in defense of claims by ex-slaves, because agents harbored powerful assumptions about the character of property in a slave society. Ex-slave claims posed a problem, not because agents mistrusted ex-slaves' ability to remember, but because claims officials believed that anything a slave may have *possessed* actually *belonged* to his master.

Former slaves, on the other hand, believed that they *had* owned property and that their ownership of property was not merely an extension of their masters' legal title to their bodies. Ex-slaves thought that an object became property not by being removed completely from the public sphere into the private sphere of a single person but by being associated publicly with people. These associations arose through cooperative labor and custody and the ongoing interchange of display and acknowledgment. Each piece of property embodied the interests of several people, including the master. Those multiple interests and associations made it difficult to calculate property's value strictly in individual and monetary terms as the commission required. Claims officials had to evaluate claims without written evidence of ownership in a county where people who transferred property did not necessarily relinquish all interest in that property. Indeed, it was precisely the fact that property was enmeshed in several overlapping, sometimes competing, social relationships that made ownership possible for slaves and that made possessions into property.

Many of the relationships that shaped and marked property also fit poorly with agents' assumptions about family structure, and even less with the rules of the commission, which required that witnesses state clearly what "interest" they had in the claim on which they testified. Ex-slaves who could discount blood family ties as a biasing motive were unusually persuasive witnesses. "I have done what I have out of neighborly kindness," said one, "& because he was a fellow servant in slavery times." Agents usually accepted such statements at face value, perhaps because they did not expect that people who were neither linked by formal business mechanisms of debt and credit nor related by blood might share a "beneficial interest" in property. According to the rules of the Southern Claims Commission, however, the very strength of these social relationships could have undercut the credibility of ex-slaves as witnesses. After all, slaves' claims to property intertwined with their social relationships in ways that belied their statements of disinterestedness. Linda Roberts, for example, was "not related to" William Golding and had "no beneficial interest in his claim," but she had "known him since he was a little boy," had lived in his father's house, and had contributed labor to the accumulation of the livestock, beehives, tea, and other property that Golding listed in his claim. In Roberts's words, Golding "made it there with 'we'."[34] Observing the variety and flexibility of such personal relationships among slaves, with kinship, friendship, and economic connections mutually influencing one another, scholars today might conclude that many ex-slave witnesses did have an interest in the claims on which they testified, but claims agents accepted the avowals of disinterest. The arrival of the commission thus set in motion a complex process of adjustment. Successful claims had to resolve the conflict of expectations between ex-slaves and federal officials.

To a great extent, they did. Of 208 claims filed in Liberty County, the commissioners allowed 91 by ex-slaves (including 12 by women), 2 by free people of color, and 1 by a white man. These claims met the stringent loyalty test, and the claimants received at least partial compensation on at least one item. A claim could be wholly disallowed over questions of loyalty. However, because each item claimed was examined separately, nearly all claims were disallowed at least in part. Claims by Liberty County ex-slaves succeeded at a higher rate (44 percent) than the national average (33 percent). These successful ex-slaves claimed an average of $332 and received an average of $133, about 40 percent of the amount they claimed. By comparison, the top bracket of successful claimants nationwide (those who claimed over $10,000) received an average of 23 percent of the amount they claimed. The highest claim by a Liberty County ex-slave was for $2,290 by William Golding, a former house slave of John B. Mallard, husband of a free black woman, and in 1873 a member of the Georgia legislature. The lowest claim was for $49. The highest and lowest amounts awarded to Liberty County ex-slaves were $450 and $20.[35]

Several factors contributed to the relative success of these ex-slave claimants. Although no nationwide study of ordinary claimants exists, former slaves probably received higher percentages of their claims than successful claimants in general. This occurred in part because they claimed much smaller sums than most whites. They also won more cases because they faced fewer doubts about their loyalty. The government assumed that slaves had been loyal to the Union, whereas it presumed that white southern claimants had been disloyal until they proved otherwise. . . . For their part, the ex-slaves felt that their property and their dangerous wartime loyalty to the Union deserved compensation. "I was on the side of the United States there was no *oder* way for me," replied David Stevens to the standard questions on loyalty.[36]

As they pursued claims, ex-slaves modified their expectations about property and freedom in order to convince the federal agents. Postwar events show that slaves also felt entitled to the land they lived on, but ex-slaves did not list land among their possessions because the commission would compensate only "army supplies" and did not allow claims for things that soldiers could not carry off. The rules also disqualified many items that had been taken—such as buggies, chickens, beehives . . . and tea—but had no legitimate army use. Even when they adhered to the eligible categories, ex-slaves sometimes had to change their conceptions of value. Soldiers confiscated some items that slaves valued primarily for their cultural or religious significance, items that were "owned" but whose worth as property was difficult to translate into dollars. Liberty County claimants understood that the Southern Claims Commission would reject arguments that not only "the product of their taskwork" but also the rations their masters gave them and the land, buildings, and stock of the entire plantation all rightfully belonged to them. They purposefully limited themselves to the definition specified in the commission rules: movable property taken by Union troops for legitimate army use.[37]

Still, even movable property was subject to many different interpretations. When they could, claimants carefully conformed their testimony to the rules of the commission and the expectations of its agents. Some items clearly had been bought, used, and cared for by groups of slaves but were claimed by individuals. Linda Jones claimed a corn mill taken from beside her house that the plantation slaves had bought collectively "for their own use." Other movables had been possessed and used by slaves but had been bought and given to them by masters. Indeed, the issue of rations had the potential to undermine all of the ex-slaves' claims. On this delicate issue, agents and ex-slaves moved carefully. Many claimants referred to storage practices, distinguishing between "my corn-house" and that of the master. Others emphasized function or quality. Sam Harris insisted that he used "his" wagon only for driving to church and for trips with his wife, while "my master's wagon was used for the farm work." Another ex-slave, Jacob Dryer, summarized: "I had a good sum of clothes that master bought for me," including twelve yards of "white cob cloth" used "to dress the family with." He also had a new "suit of black, that I paid ten dollars for in Savannah." In all he owned "five or six suits," but, he added, "all the good ones I bought for myself."[38]

Lawyers representing the ex-slave claimants found themselves in the odd position of arguing that the law was irrelevant to deciding ex-slaves' claims of ownership. "If it was right they should have had these supplies from the hands of their masters," insisted one lawyer, "no one will dispute their right of property & wish to evade responsibility by technical distinctions, arising out of abstruse questions of legal right." Another lawyer chastised the commissioners for their skepticism: "To say that this property belonged to the master & that therefore it should not be paid for does not look very well from the high moral anti-slavery standpoint." Anything the slave possessed, he went on, was "to all intents his property" because "he would have had the profit and enjoyment of it."[39]

For their part, agents and commissioners modified their presumptive logic about slavery and property by drawing a line between "rations" and things that slaves bought or produced on their own. They began to base their awards on "what [slaves] would have on the average at that season of the year, as the product of their task work." Thus, when William Cassels claimed 140 bushels of corn "because it was given to me before my master left . . . to feed my family and the rest of the people on the place," the commissioners compensated him only for the 60 bushels he had grown himself.[40]

In drawing such distinctions, the commission was essentially tracing the genealogy of slaves' possessions back to the last transaction it could recognize as "legitimate." By the standards of the North in the mid-nineteenth century this meant a cash sale from a free white to a slave or, failing that, a transaction between two slaves. In most cases it excluded objects whose last involvement in a transaction had been a nonreciprocal transfer from master to slave. Awards for drivers and plowmen were an exception that proved the rule. The commissioners viewed objects given to these slaves by their masters as a legitimate compensation for not having access to their own after-task labor. Of course, this logic ignored the "reciprocity" involved in all rations for slaves; to recognize it would have undermined the logic of "free labor" that had underpinned the Union's war effort and that now shaped labor and property relations in the South. Nevertheless, this distinction between rations and legitimate property allowed the commissioners to conceive of property ownership among slaves. Whatever their initial assumptions and doubts, by the 1870s officials in Washington were recognizing not merely "possession" but "ownership" of property by slaves in the Low Country.[41]

Yet emancipation had set in motion massive changes in the southern economy, changes that were especially ironic for blacks. Many Low Country slaves had enjoyed relatively easy access to land, making time the central issue in the contest between slaves and masters. Freedom restricted that relative abundance of land and replaced it with a relative abundance of time. Nevertheless, blacks' legal right to their own time did not end their fierce struggles with whites over how that time would be spent. As the great rice and cotton plantations broke up, masters became landlords who collected rents. Union troops guaranteed that ex-slaves owned their laboring time but also required that they contract it out to a landowner. Although some freed people had followed the army to Savannah, most stayed on their plantations. Beginning in 1864 ex-slaves' lack of either land or movable property had forced many, if not most, of Liberty County's ex-slaves to continue working for their former masters, with Union soldiers acting as overseers. "The Negroes were mystified," one former master observed eight months after the raid,

> thunderstruck that they should receive such treatment (and in some cases very severe, even cruel) at the hands of their friends. Very soon they began to whisper that the said Yankees were only Southern men in blue clothes—that the true Yankees had not come yet.

While the grand slave owners and their families complained of great privations, the county's poorer black residents began with less and suffered more. As Prince Maxwell put it, "all I got was my rations," and for him that was "hardly as good" as when they were slaves and had raised property after their tasks.[42]

The raid by Kilpatrick's cavalry dealt a terrible blow to an oppressed population just entering freedom, including propertied slaves. The blow was both material and psychological. William LeCounte lamented, "they took all I had, and I could not do anything for myself for a long time & I haven't got over it." The raid had stripped slaves of their movable property, but a larger economic transition limited their access to land, sharply lowering blacks' average wealth. A sample of successful ex-slave claimants who appeared in the 1870 census shows that five years after emancipation most of them still owned no land and worked as "farm laborers" rather than "farmers." The average value of their movable property dropped from $385.28 in 1864 to $119.23 in 1870, and six of the claimants reported owning nothing at all in 1870. . . . An influx of ex-slaves from inland, attracted by rumors that General Sherman had set aside land on the coast for ex-slaves, added to their difficulties. Top claimant William Golding asserted: "I can swear to it that there was more stock property owned by slaves before the war than are owned now by both white & black people together in this county." Blacks who once prayed for Union victory "so that we could get our own time" found that the relationship between time and their access to land had drastically changed, leaving them temporarily worse off than before.[43]

Still, if some blacks felt their situation was "hardly as good" as it had been under slavery, others felt that gaining control over their time outweighed the loss of access to land. "I am not willing to be a slave again," said Peter Winn, "because now I can stop & rest, & go about & walk some, then, when I was a slave I could not till I got through with my task. No sir, be a slave I am not willing to be that anymore."[44] Despite such differences of opinion among ex-slaves about the arrival of federal power in Liberty County, ex-slaves cooperated when, in the 1870s, their ability to recover lost property depended on it. Blacks' negotiations with white landowners for time would no longer be part of an informal economy, but the arrival of claims agents gathering evidence about the past promised that informal negotiations might still play a role in matters of property.

As it began its work in dozens of towns across the South, the Southern Claims Commission breathed new life into the old system of display and acknowledgment by which slaves had held property, making it relevant once more. In claims filed by ex-slaves the commission relied on witnesses to prove ownership. The detailed knowledge generated by the prewar living conditions and system of display and the intense affective ties created by shared interests in property enabled ex-slaves to marshal large numbers of witnesses to testify about their property in intimate detail. The relative stability of the large Low Country plantations during the antebellum period meant that by 1873 former slaves were able to call as witnesses people they had known for twenty or thirty years, from birth to middle age, from youth to old age, or, as one witness put it, "since I had sense." The layout of plantations permitted even people who belonged to different masters to live "fence to fence," call one another "nigh neighbor," and see one another "every day" or "every night."[45] This was a significant advantage in claims before the commission. Blacks' ability to mobilize fellow ex-slaves as knowledgeable witnesses thus continued to be important despite the massive changes of Civil War, emancipation, and the formal legitimation of blacks' ownership of property.

In other ways, however, the commission's reliance on witnesses hurt ex-slave claimants. By testifying as witnesses for ex-slaves, white planters, at least for a time, revived their role as protectors of black property ownership. However supportive they were of individual ex-slaves before the commission, and however willing they had been to participate in the prewar system of slave-owned property, ex-masters did not value property in the same way that ex-slaves did. Slaves had valued objects not only for their worth in exchange but also because those objects were enmeshed in a network of social relationships that invested them with personal and cultural significance. Ex-slaves' attempts to translate those components of their value system into money splintered on the testimony of ex-masters. One claims agent reported that the former slave owner he interviewed about Pompey Bacon's claim thought that "the bed clothing and house hold effects

[were] valued too high." This white witness admitted that he "could not state what they were worth, but thought as a general thing, the bed clothing, and household effects, of negroes were not worth as much, as claimant claims." Suspicious of fraud, casting about for clues about the validity of slaves' claims, northern agents quickly latched onto the paternalistic language that the "respectable gentlemen" of the county, such as Edward DeLegal, Raymond Cay Sr., and Lazarus Mallard, used in speaking about slave-owned property. Part expert witnesses, part character witnesses, the white "gentlemen" consistently supported the ex-slaves' claims but scoffed at their "greatly overstated" values. Planters' skepticism about the quality of slave-owned property had the same effect as if they had disputed its quantity. In making final judgments, agents and commissioners applied the former masters' evaluations like a formula, reducing the awards of even free blacks according to a set of racial preconceptions about property. "I suppose [it was] one of the finest in the county," the former slave owner William Winn said of a horse claimed by one of his family's former slaves. Then, catching himself, he clarified: "I mean the horse was one of the finest of those owned by the negroes."[46]

Ex-slaves' experience with the commission was part of a larger adjustment in the Low Country to new, more purely capitalistic relations of land, labor, and capital. Ironically, establishing ownership through social claims under slavery proved easier than winning cash recognition from federal officials. Much of property's value for slaves could not be compensated in cash. Although slaves had long participated in a cash economy, they valued property in part for its social and personal significance, "use" values that former masters and federal agents did not understand, and that had no equivalents in the money awards of the commission. The claims process played an important role in deciding the relevance of the social relationships generated under slavery in the new socioeconomic landscape of Reconstruction. Some elements of the old system survived, but the basic economy of land, time, and property had changed, and what survived now meant something different.

Although former masters were willing to testify to help individual blacks regain property they had owned as slaves, changes in the post-war political economy of the South made it likely that such commitment would not last long. White landowners no longer legally owned the possessions of their black workers. Black residents had the backing of law to sustain their claims to property. On the other hand, as employers of free labor, white landowners now had a bigger stake in the formal system of law and contract and less incentive to participate in the old informal system that affirmed blacks' claims to property.

Among African Americans, however, public display and social claims continued to play an important role in transfers of property and regulation of social relationships. Long after emancipation, features of the old system of slave property ownership endured. In South Carolina, freed people insisted on planting patches on "the old home place" even after moving to live elsewhere in the area. How long this pattern persisted is unknown, but even after the 1950s, when black farm operators "nearly disappeared from the southern landscape," claims to land, property, and labor continued to be bound up in ongoing negotiations between neighbors, spouses, and family members. In the 1930s descendants of the people who appeared before Virgil Hillyer in 1873 were still living in the Georgia Low Country, though not necessarily on the same plantations their relatives had worked. By the 1970s these families had resolved themselves into complex networks of kin that were important both in regulating access to land and in enforcing social obligations. South Carolina Sea Islanders refer to "getting sense" as the time they received "their first instruction on the obligations and responsibilities of kinship," echoing words spoken 120 years ago. These attempts to "make identity objective," as Saville puts it, suggest that despite whites' withdrawal, the intense interrelationship of property and social bonds persisted among African Americans.[47]

Slaves owned property in Liberty County, Georgia. This simple fact raises fascinating questions for the study of slavery, southern history, and African American history. Slavery did not mean the total loss of the fruits of one's labor. Slaves participated with white masters and non-slave-owning whites in an informal economy of time, land, and property, one that overlapped and supported the formal economy of the plantation even as it let slaves push back against the oppression of the system. After the Civil War the Southern Claims Commission provided a forum where northern officials and ex-slaves confronted and adjusted to the differences in their conceptions of property. The participation of southern whites and, later, northern whites in an extralegal, noninstitutional system of black property ownership challenges our assumptions about how nineteenth-century Anglo-Americans conceived of both property and slavery. Negotiating access to resources through social claims may not have been peculiar to African Americans; many nineteenth-century rural and urban whites also lacked written records of ownership and relied heavily on social relationships with kin and neighbors in matters of work and property.[48] Finally, what made slaves' possessions into property were complex networks of social relationships, sometimes expressed in an interchange of display and acknowledgment. Raising, trading, storing, and passing down property depended on slaves' ability to call on other slaves as workers, custodians, and witnesses. Many scholars have recognized the centrality of family and community relationships for African Americans, especially in the face of physical and economic oppression by European Americans. But the evidence in the claims suggests that African Americans also negotiated among themselves over economic resources, and that social relationships were integral to such negotiation.

Just as social relationships helped people make claims to property, property ownership shaped and perhaps even created social relationships. In other words, "blood" and a common experience of oppression were not the only ways that African Americans related to one another. Their varied and flexible social relationships and their ongoing negotiations over property and labor mutually influenced each other. By looking more deeply into the experience of oppression we may see how this intertwining of social and economic relationships came to define an important part of life in the nineteenth-century United States.

NOTES

1 Claim of Pompey Bacon, p. 1, LCGSCC, Records of the 3rd Auditor, Allowed Case Files, Records of the U.S. General Accounting Office, RG 217 (National Archives, Washington, D.C.). [LCGSCC]
2 Claim of Prince Maxwell, p. 4, LCGSCC;. . . .
3 Claim of Pompey Bacon, p. 3, LCGSCC; claim of Ned Quarterman, p. 2, LCGSCC;. . . .
4 Claim of Samuel Elliott, p. 3, LCGSCC; testimony of Clarissa Monroe in claim of Samuel Elliott, p. 3, LCGSCC.; claim of Paris James, p. 2, LCGSCC; claim of Pompey Bacon, pp. 1–6, LCGSCC.
5 Ex-slaves also pursued lost property through the Freedmen's Bureau . . . [on the Claims Commission see] Frank W. Klingberg, *The Southern Claims Commission* (Berkeley, 1955), 65–72, 76–84.
6 Klingberg, *Southern Claims Commission*, 50–56.
7 Willie Lee Rose, *Rehearsal for Reconstruction: The Port Royal Experiment* (1964; New York, 1976); testimony of Brig. Gen. Rufus Saxton (1863) and of Henry G. Judd (1863), in Philip D. Morgan, "Work and Culture: The Task System and the World of Lowcountry Blacks, 1700 to 1880," *William and Mary Quarterly*, 39 (Oct. 1982), 593. . . .
8 Virgil Hillyer to J. B. Howell, commissioner of claims, March 22, 1873, Miscellaneous Letters Received (microfilm: reel 3), General Records of the Department of the Treasury, RG56 (National Archives); *First Annual Report of the Boston Educational Commission for Freedmen* (Boston, 1863), 12–13.
9 Morgan, "Work and Culture," 592; Philip D. Morgan, "The Ownership of Property by Slaves in the Mid-Nineteenth-Century Low Country," *Journal of Southern History*, 49 (Aug. 1983), 399–420; Ira Berlin and Philip D. Morgan, "Introduction," in *Cultivation and Culture: Labor and the Shaping of Slave Life in the Americas*, ed. Ira Berlin and Philip D. Morgan (Charlottesville, 1993), 45. . . .
10 Loren Schweninger, *Black Property Owners in the South, 1790–1910* (Urbana, 1990), 9–11, 235–36. Already by 1973, A. G. Hopkins was criticizing misconceptions about African economic activity, misconceptions that he called the "myth of Merrie Africa." G. Hopkins, *An Economic History of West Africa*

(New York, 1973), 9–10. On property in Africa, see Polly Hill, *The Migrant Cocoa-Farmers of Southern Ghana: A Study in Rural Capitalism* (Cambridge, Eng., 1963). . . .

11 Julie Saville, *The Work of Reconstruction: From Slave to Wage Laborer in South Carolina, 1860–1870* (New York, 1994), 53–56, 103–4. For other studies of black resistance to postwar oppression, see Eric Foner, *Nothing but Freedom: Emancipation and Its Legacy* (Baton Rouge, 1983) . . . .; Kenneth Stampp was the first to frame slaves' culture in terms of "resistance," an idea that Eugene Genovese later elaborated and reshaped into a thesis about slavery as a dialectic of accommodation and resistance. See Kenneth Stampp, *The Peculiar Institution: Slavery in the Ante-bellum South* (New York, 1956); and Eugene Genovese, *Roll, Jordan, Roll: The World the Slaves Made* (New York, 1972). . . .

12 United States Census Office, *Population of the United States in 1860.* . . .; United States Census Office, *Agriculture of the United States in 1860.* . . .

13 Morgan, "Work and Culture," 565–71; claim of Jacob Quarterman, p. 1, LCGSCC. . . . For a comparison of the task system with slave labor organ-ization on the Upper Guinea Coast in the eighteenth century, see Judith Carney, "From Hands to Tutors: African Expertise in the South Carolina Rice Economy," *Agricultural History*, 67 (Summer 1993), 26.

14 For discussion of the "informal economy," see Morgan, "Ownership of Property by Slaves in the Mid-Nineteenth-Century Low Country," 414; and Wood, *Women's Work, Men's Work*. Testimony of Edward DeLegal in claim of Tony Axon, p. 7, LCGSCC. . . .

15 On planters' stake in the informal economy, see Berlin and Morgan, "Intro-duction," in *Slaves' Economy*, ed. Berlin and Morgan, 19.

16 Morgan, "Work and Culture," 578–79; Berlin and Morgan, "Introduction," in *Cultivation and Culture*, ed. Berlin and Morgan, 14–16, 41–43; testimony of Richard Cummings in claim of Lafayette DeLegal, in Morgan, "Ownership of Property by Slaves in the Mid-Nineteenth-Century Low Country," 415. . . .

17 Testimony of Richard Cummings (1873) and Scipio King (1873) in Morgan, "Work and Culture," 586. . . .

18 Testimony of William Golding in claim of Linda Roberts, p. 10, Liberty County, Georgia, Case Files . . .; Michael P. Johnson, "Work, Culture, and the Slave Community: Slave Occupations in the Cotton Belt in 1860," *Labor History*, 27 (Summer 1986), 333; Roswell King, "On the Management of the Butler Estate" (1828) quoted in Julia Floyd Smith, *Slavery and Rice Culture in Low Country Georgia, 1710–1860* (Knoxville, 1985), 69; testimony of Simon Harris in claim of Thomas Irving, p. 2. . . .

19 Claim of Pompey Bacon, p. 2, LCGSCC. . . .

20 Testimony of Benjamin Hines in claim of Paris James, p. 9, LCGSCC; testi-mony of Andrew Stacy in claim of Nancy Bacon, pp. 1–2, LCGSCC.

21 Claim of Elita James, p. 2, LCGSCC; testimony of Charlotte Thompson in claim of John Wilson, LCGSCC. . . .

22 Claim of Samuel Elliot, p. 2, LCGSCC. See also claim of William Cassels, p. 2, LCGSCC; claim of Sandy Austin. . . .

23 . . . . Some historians have discussed theft among slaves as part of a "moral economy" that sanctioned stealing from masters but punished stealing from fellow slaves. Such analysis treats theft as a form of resistance, a dif-ferent framework than is emphasized here. See Creel, *Peculiar People*, 181–82, 207, 239; Alex Lichtenstein, " 'That Disposition to Theft, with Which They

Have Been Branded': Moral Economy, Slave Management, and the Law," *Journal of Social History*, 21 (Spring 1988), 413–40; and Genovese, *Roll: Jordan, Roll*: 599–609.

24 Claim of William Gilmore, p. 9, LCGSCC. . . .

25 R. Q. Mallard, *Plantation Life before Emancipation* (Richmond, 1892), 18; claim of Linda Roberts, for estate of Caesar Roberts, deceased. . . .

26 Average for cabin occupancy calculated from entries of 33 identifiable slave owners, Liberty County, Georgia, 1860 Census. . . . Testimony of Clarinda Lowe in claim of James Anderson, p. 6, LCGSCC. . . . See also Richard Noble Westmacott, *African-American Gardens and Yards in the Rural South* (Knoxville, 1992). . . .

27 Mallard, *Plantation Life before Emancipation*, 83, 133; claim of Pompey Bacon, p. 1, LCGSCC. . . .

28 Mallard, *Plantation Life before Emancipation*, 50–51; claim of Samuel Harris, p. 2, LCGSCC. . . .

29 Schweninger, *Black Property Owners in the South*, 51, 84–87; claim of Paris James, pp. 2–3, LCGSCC. . . .

30 Claim of Susan Bennett, p. 2, LCGSCC. . . .

31 Testimony of Samson Bacon in claim of Prince Stevens, p. 11, LCGSCC. . . .

32 Testimony of Tony Law in claim of Linda Roberts, p. 12, LCGSCC. . . . Klingberg notes that attorneys were charging "exorbitant fees," frequently amounting to half the award, all across the South. Klingberg, *Southern Claims Commission*, 88.

33 After the Civil War, northern states enacted laws that enshrined "liberty of contract" between independent agents as the basis for labor negotiation. See Amy Dru Stanley, "Beggars Can't Be Choosers: Compulsion and Contract in Postbellum America," *Journal of American History*, 78 (March 1992), 1265–93. . . .

34 Testimony of Ceasar Jones in claim of Joseph James, p. 11, LCGSCC. . . .

35 Liberty County average calculated from allowed claims, LCGSCC; national average calculated from Klingberg, *Southern Claims Commission*, 175.

36 Klingberg, *Southern Claims Commission*, 89, 100; claim of Pompey Bacon, p. 1, LCGSCC. . . .

37 Morgan, "Ownership of Property by Slaves in the Mid-Nineteenth-Century Low Country," 409–10; Magdol, *Right to the Land*.

38 Testimony of Joseph James in claim of Linda Jones, p. 6, LCGSCC. . . .

39 C. W. Dudley to Commissioners of Claims, June 3, 1874, Miscellaneous Letters Received. . . .

40 Claim of James Mifflin, judgment, LCGSCC. . . .

41 On treatment of drivers, see, for example, claim of John Crawford, judgment, LCGSCC. For a perceptive analysis of the links among law, free-labor ideology, and postwar developments in the South, see Stanley, "Beggars Can't Be Choosers," 1265–93. . . .

42 Eric Foner and Julie Saville have cogently explored the struggles over labor contracts and land ownership that followed emancipation in the Low Country. See Foner, *Nothing but Freedom*; and Saville, *Work of Reconstruction*. . . .

43 Claim of William LeCounte, p. 1, LCGSCC. . . . Average amount claimed as of 1864 for 13 claimants calculated from judgments, LCGSCC . . .; average 1870 property value calculated from 13 identifiable entries in Liberty County, Georgia, 1870 Census. . . .

44 Claim of Peter Winn, p. 1, LCGSCC. . . .

45 Testimony of Phoebe Ann Norman in claim of Lucy McIver, p. 3, LCGSCC; claim of William Cassels, LCGSCC.
46 Special Agent W. W. Paine to Commissioners of Claims, July 18, 1876, in claim of Pompey Bacon, LCGSCC. . . .
47 Saville, *Work of Reconstruction*, 18; Loren Schweninger, "A Vanishing Breed: Black Farm Owners in the South, 1651–1982," *Agricultural History*, 63 (Summer 1989), 41–57; Bamidele Agbasegbe Demerson, "Family Life on Wadmalaw Island," in *Sea Island Roots: African Presence in the Carolinas and Georgia*, ed. Mary A. Twining and Keith E. Baird (Trenton, 1991), 57–87. . . .
48 See Michael Merrill, "Cash Is Good to Eat: Self-Sufficiency and Exchange in the Rural Economy of the United States," *Radical History Review*, 4 (Winter 1977), 42–71; Steven Hahn, *The Roots of Southern Populism: Yeoman Farmers and the Transformation of the Georgia Upcountry, 1850–1890* (New York, 1983); and Christopher Clark, *The Roots of Rural Capitalism: Western Massachusetts, 1780–1860* (Ithaca, 1990).

6

THE PLEASURES OF RESISTANCE

Enslaved women and body politics in the Plantation South, 1830–1861

Stephanie M. H. Camp

Stephanie M. H. Camp's essay on slave women extends our understanding of the slave community with her analysis of the secret parties where slaves danced, sang, and otherwise amused themselves. In his contribution elsewhere in this volume, Mark M. Smith pointed out the ways in which slave masters attempted to control their slaves' time. Here, Camp shows how slaves "stole" their own time in after-hours entertainments. She draws on the historiography of the slave community, and also on the work of anthropologists and feminist theorists who have explored the ways in which bodies can be both the objects of domination and sources of resistance. Slave women used dress and hairstyles, as well as dance and song, as expressive forms of resistance, seeking control over their own bodies outside of the master's gaze; the slave body was thus "an important site not only of suffering but also (and therefore) of resistance, enjoyment, and potentially, transcendence." Her essay also explores how the cultural analysis of amusements can throw light on cooperation and conflicts within the slave community, not just between slave owners and their slaves.

* * *

As a young woman, Nancy Williams joined other enslaved people and "cou'tin' couples" who would "slip 'way" to an "ole cabin" a few miles from the Virginia plantation where she lived. Deep in the woods, away from slaveholding eyes, they held secret parties, where they amused themselves dancing, performing music, drinking alcohol, and courting. A religious woman in her old age, Williams admitted only reluctantly to her interviewer that she had enjoyed the secular pleasures of dressing up and going to these outlaw dances. "Dem de day's when me'n de devil was runnin roun in de depths o' hell. No, don' even wanna talk 'bout it," she said. However, Williams ultimately agreed to discuss the outlaw parties she had attended, reasoning, "Guess I didn'

142

know no better den," and remembering with fondness that, after all, "[d]em dances was somepin."[1]

Musicians played fiddles, tambourines, banjos, and "two sets o' [cow] bones" for the dancers. Williams was a gifted and enthusiastic dancer; she would get "out dere in de middle o' de flo' jes' a-dancin'; me an Jennie, an' de devil. Dancin' wid a glass o' water on my head an' three boys a bettin' on me." Williams often won this contest by dancing the longest while balancing the glass of water on her head without spilling a drop. She "[jes]' danced ole Jennie down." Like the other women in attendance, Williams took pride in her outfits at these illicit parties, and she went to great trouble to make them. She adorned one dress with ruffles and dyed others yellow or red. Her yellow dress even had matching yellow shoes; they were ill-fitting, as many bondpeople's wooden brogans were, and "she' did hurt me," but, animated by her own beautiful self-presentation, "dat ain' stop me f'om dancin'." By illuminating a part of everyday life that bondpeople kept very hidden, Nancy Williams's account of attending outlaw slave parties helps uncover one part of the story of enslaved women's lives: the role that the body played in slaveholders' endeavors to control their labor force and in black resistance to bondage in the nineteenth-century planta-tion South. Despite planters' tremendous effort to prevent such escape, enslaved women and men sporadically "slip[ped] 'way" to take pleas-ure in their own bodies.[2]

At the heart of the process of enslavement was a geographical impulse to locate bondpeople in plantation space. Winthrop D. Jordan found that it was confinement, "[m]ore than any other single quality," that differentiated slavery from servitude in the early years of American slavery's formation. Not only a power or labor relation, "[e]nslavement was captivity." Accordingly, black mobility appears to have been the target of more official and planter regulations than other aspects of slave behavior.[3] Slaveholders strove to create controlled and controlling land-scapes that would determine the uses to which enslaved people put their bodies. But body politics in the Old South were not dictated by a monologue as slaveholders wished. To the contrary, slave owners' attempts to control black movement—and, indeed, most aspects of black bodily experience—created a terrain on which bondpeople would contest slaveholding power.

Bondpeople, who had their own plans for their bodies, violated the boundaries of space and time that were intended to demarcate and con-solidate planters' patriarchal power over plantation households. Their alternative negotiation and mapping of plantation space might best be called, in Anne Godlewska and Neil Smith's phrase, a "rival geog-raphy." Enslaved people's rival geography was not a fixed spatial formation, for it included quarters, outbuildings, woods, swamps, and neighboring farms as opportunity granted them. Where slaveholders' mapping of the plantation was defined by rigid places for its residents, the rival geography was characterized by motion: the secret movement of bodies, objects, and information within and around plantation space. Together, but differently, women and men took flight to the very woods and swamps that planters intended to be the borders of the plantation's "geography of containment."[4] There they held clandestine and illegal parties. These parties were sporadic affairs, contingent as they were upon opportunity (itself informed by the season), availability of resources, and no doubt on the emotional climate within local black communities and between enslaved people and their owners. This article studies the personal and political meanings of bodily pleasure made and experienced at these parties, focusing on the activities of women, for whom dress was an especially important dimension of their enjoyment of slave communities' secret and secular institution.

No mere safety valve, bondpeople's rival geography demands to be understood in multiple ways. To a degree, black mappings and uses of southern space were the result and expression of the dialogic of power relations between owner and owned—part of day-to-day plantation relations characterized by a paternalistic combination of hegemonic cultural control and violent discipline. To a larger extent, however, the paternalist framework fails to sufficiently explain everyday slave resistance. The paternalist model offers an apt theory of plantation management but a fundamentally incomplete perspective on plantation, and particularly black, life. Viewing resistance other than rebellion or running away as only partial or even as cooptative distracts us from interesting and important possibilities for understanding black politics during slavery, such as the hidden, everyday acts that help to form overt resistance. The tendency to draw a sharp line between material and political issues on the one hand and aesthetic, spiritual, and intimate (emotionally and physically) issues on the other also limits our understanding of human lives in the past, especially women's lives.[5]

Evidence is spare, but it comes to us consistently from the upper South and the lower South in slaveholders' diaries and journals, in state legislative records, in nineteenth-century autobiographies, and in twentieth-century interviews of the formerly enslaved.[6] Many recent studies on American slavery focus on a subregion, a crop, or a county. This trend has deepened our understanding of the variations of work and culture in American slavery, has furthered our sense of important differences among enslaved people, and has added texture and detail to our picture of day-to-day life in bondage. At the same time, studying slavery as a regional system . . . remains a valuable practice, as recent innovative and informative works on the slave past have also demonstrated.[7] Throughout the antebellum period and across the plantation

South, enslaved people took flight to nearby woods and swamps for the secret parties they occasionally held at night for themselves.[8]

This article pieces together the story and politics of these illicit parties, arguing that these celebrations and the bodily pleasures that accompanied them occupied the wide terrain of political struggle between consent and open, organized rebellion.[9] The bondpeople who participated in activities in the rival geography expressed, enjoyed, and used their somatic selves in terms other than those of their relationship to their owners. They took pleasure in their bodies, competed with other enslaved people with them, and contested their owners' power over them. Bondpeople's everyday somatic politics had more than symbolic value: they resulted in temporal and material gains for enslaved people and in some loss of labor for slaveholders. If bondpeople's uses of their bodies and their time were contingent upon the season, the ignorance of their owners, and the ability to find a safe location (and they were), these uses nonetheless also undermined slaveholders' claims to their bodies and their time. Everyday resistance to pass-laws and plantation rules was an endemic problem in the rural South, one that had real and subversive effects on slaveholding mastery and on plantation productivity—both of which rested on elite white spatial and temporal control of enslaved bodies.

The body, as French historian Dorinda Outram has written, is at once the most personal, intimate thing that people possess and the most public. The body, then, provides a "basic political resource" in struggles between dominant and subordinate classes. Second-wave feminists put it like this: the personal is political. Earlier, C. L. R. James, Grace C. Lee, and Pierre Chaulieu had already argued that "ordinary . . . people . . . are rebelling every day in ways of their own invention" in order to "regain control over their own conditions of life and their relations with one another"; oftentimes "their struggles are on a small personal scale." Enslaved people's everyday battles for regaining control—albeit temporally limited—took place on this very personal terrain.[10]

Enslaved people possessed multiple social bodies.[11] Inhabitants of a premodern society, they were made to suffer domination largely through the body in the form of exploitation, physical punishment, and captivity. Theorists of colonialism have analyzed the effects of somatic suffering in other, analogous contexts. Describing the consequences of European colonialism on twentieth-century Africans' somatic experiences, Frantz Fanon wrote: "[I]n the white world the man of color encounters difficulties in the development of his bodily schema. Consciousness of the body is solely a negating activity. It is a third-person consciousness. The body is surrounded by an atmosphere of certain uncertainty." Caught in the white gaze, Fanon argued, blacks were "sealed in that crushing objecthood." Under colonialism, experiences of the body were "negating activit[ies]," in which identification with the colonizer resulted in degrees of self-hatred and humiliation. Students of American slavery will find much with which to agree in Fanon's analysis of black bodily experience. Violence, brutal and brutalizing labor, diseased environments (particularly in South Carolina's rice swamps), and the auction block were basic characteristics of life in slavery. Indeed, these characteristics were, in combination with elite white confinement of the black body, the essence of bondage.[12]

However, brutality did not constitute the whole of black bodily experience. For people, like bondpeople and women as a group, who have experienced oppression through the body, the body becomes an important site not only of suffering but also (and therefore) of resistance, enjoyment, and potentially, transcendence. Studying the body through a framework of containment and transgression grants us access to new perspectives on resistance and the workings of gender difference within enslaved plantation communities. Thinking about the black body in space allows us to think about it materially and to watch as the prime implement of labor in the Old South moved in ways inconsistent with the rigors of agricultural production. And attention to the body also facilitates thinking about issues beyond the material, such as the roles of movement and pleasure in the culture of opposition developed by enslaved people. A somatic approach, such as the one employed here, risks objectifying people, but the point is the opposite: to demonstrate how enslaved people claimed, animated, politicized, personalized, and enjoyed their bodies—flesh that was regarded by much of American society as no more than biddable property.

Most of all, attention to uses and experiences of the body is mandatory for those interested in the lives of women in slavery, for it was women's actual and imagined reproductive labor and their unique forms of bodily suffering (notably sexual exploitation) that most distinguished their lives from men's. Feminist scholars have shown that to study women's lives requires posing different questions of our sources, using new methods to interpret them, and fundamentally changing how we think about politics.[13] Historians of enslaved women have revealed the falseness of the dichotomy between the material/political and the personal, in large measure by showing how the body, so deeply personal, is also a political arena. Their work has demonstrated the extent to which women's bodies were unique sites of domination under slavery; yet, this scholarship has also shown that enslaved and formerly enslaved women used their bodies as sites of resistance.[14] Women employed their bodies in a wide variety of ways, from seizing control over the visual representation of their physical selves in narrative and photographic forms (both of which were in enormous demand among nineteenth-century northerners) to abortion.[15] In addition to the body's reproductive and sexual capacities and its representations, however, enslaved women's bodily pleasure was a resource in resistance to slavery. These diverse uses of the body are a fruitful site for investigating the origins of and women's role in bondpeople's political culture.

Recent scholarship has shown that perceptions of the proper uses of the black body, especially the female body, were central, materially and symbolically, to the formation of slaveholding mastery. As the English became entrenched in the slave trade in the second half of the seventeenth century, their preexisting ideas of Africans concretized into constructions of blackness and representations of bodily difference that justified the economically expedient turn to bound black labor. Jennifer L. Morgan has demonstrated that these constructions relied in large part upon sixteenth and seventeenth-century male travelers' representations of African women's bodies as inherently laboring ones—as female drudges that stood in stark distinction to the idealized idle and dependent English woman. Male travelers to Africa in the earliest years of contact remarked on what they saw as African women's sexual deviance: the women lived in "common" (polygamously) with men, and they bared much of their bodies, most remarkably their breasts, with "no shame." Europeans depicted African women's breasts ("dugs") as large and droopy, "like the udder of a goate" as one traveler put it. Animal-like, African women's exposed dugs struck male observers as evidence of Africa's savagery and inferiority. To European eyes African women's reproductive bodies also demonstrated physical strength: they gave birth "withoute payne," suggesting that "the women here [Guinea] are of a cruder nature and stronger posture than the Females in our Lands in Europe." Confirming this conclusion was the fact that African women commonly worked in agriculture. Unencumbered by the delicacy that prevented the ideal English woman from such arduous work, African women were seen as naturally fit for demanding agricultural and reproductive labor.[16]

Englishmen began to encode these ideas of proto-racial difference based on perceptions of African women's laboring bodies into law in Virginia in 1643. Kathleen M. Brown has shown that in that year free African women were declared tithables (meaning their labor could be taxed), along with all free white men and male heads of households. Because white women were viewed as dependents—as "good wives" who performed household, not agricultural, labor—they remained untaxed. The very different treatment of African and English women, based on conceptions of their capacity to work in the fields, articulated very different projections of the roles each would play in the life of the colony. Two years later African men also became tithables and thus fell within the legal construction of African bodies as inherently laboring ones. Buttressed by ideas of Africans as savages, which themselves

relied heavily on representations of African women's sexual and reproductive bodies, English lawmakers could, by 1670, force those servants
who had arrived in Virginia "by shipping" (Africans) to serve lifelong
terms of servitude, while those who had "come by land" (Indians)
served limited terms. This law, combined with an earlier 1667 law ban-
ning the manumission of converted Christians, helped to crystallize
the racial form of the emergent slave economy.[17] In the context of slavery, issues of representation of the black body, especially the female
black body, and material expropriation could not be separated.

Enslaved people, then, possessed at least three bodies. The first
served as a site of domination; it was the body acted upon by slaveholders. Early constructions of African and black women's bodies and
sexuality played a central role in rationalizing the African slave trade
and gave license to sexual violence against enslaved women. Colonial
and antebellum slaveholders believed that strict control of the black
body, in particular its movement in space and time, was key to their
enslavement of black people. By the late antebellum years planters
were working energetically to master such black bodily minutiae as
nourishment, ingestion of alcohol, and even dress, all as part of their
paternalist management strategies. In the Old South the slave body,
most intensely the female body, served as the "bio-text" on which
slaveholders inscribed their authority.[18]

The second body was the subjective experience of this process. It was
the body lived in moments and spaces of control and force, of terror
and suffering. This was the colonized body that, in Fanon's terms, the
person "of color" experienced "in the white world," where "consciousness of the body is solely a negating activity." Within the "white
world"—within planters' controlled and controlling landscapes, vulnerable to sale, sexual and nonsexual violence, disease, and exploitative
labor—enslaved bodies were, surely, "surrounded by an atmosphere
of certain uncertainty."[19]

And yet, within and around the plantation, enslaved people's bodies
were a hotly contested terrain of struggle. Again and again, enslaved
people violated plantation boundaries of space and time; in the spaces
they created, runaway partygoers celebrated their bodies and did
what they could to reclaim them from planter control and view. This
reclaimed body, this outlawed body, was the bondperson's third body:
For enslaved women, whose bodies were so central to the history of
black bondage, the third body was significant in two ways. First, their
third body was a source of pleasure, pride, and self-expression. The
enormous amount of energy, time, and care that some bondwomen
put into such indulgences as making and wearing fancy dresses and
attending illicit parties indicates how important such activities were to
them. Pleasure was its own reward for those experiencing it, and it

must be a part of our understanding of the lives of people in the past, even people who had little of it. Second, bondwomen's third body was a political site: it was an important symbolic and material resource in the plantation South, and its control was fiercely contested between owner and owned. Just as exploitation, containment, and punishment of the body were political acts, so too was enjoyment of the body. Far from accommodating bondage, or acting as a safety valve within it, everyday somatic politics acted in opposition to slavery's symbolic systems and its economic imperatives.

By the nineteenth century the centerpiece of the theory of mastery that elites laid out in law books and in plantation journals was a geography of containment that aimed to control slave mobility in space and in time. In his detailed memoir of life in bondage, Charles Ball summarized what he called the "principles of restraint" that governed black movement. "No slave dare leave" the plantation to which she or he belonged, he said, not even for "a single mile," or a "single hour, by night or by day," except by "exposing himself to the danger of being taken up and flogged."[20] At stake was nothing less than the good functioning of the plantation itself. One slave management manual instructed its readers that "no business of any kind can be successfully conducted without the aid of system and rule." In pursuit of "system and rule," the manual prescribed two core "maxims": first, "that there must be a time for everything and everything done in its time"; and second, that there must be "a rule for everything and everything done according to rule."[21]

Together, lawmakers and planters made up the rules governing spatial and temporal order. Bondpeople everywhere were forbidden by law to leave their owners' property without passes. Responsibility for enforcing the laws was shared unequally by non-elite whites, who most often manned slave patrols to police rural and urban areas, and slaveholders, who also did their best to enforce compliance with the law by insisting that the people they owned leave only with written permission. Even when planters did grant permission to travel off the plantation, they specified the spatial and temporal boundaries of a pass's tenure by writing the bondperson's destination and the pass's expiration date.[22] Enslaved women experienced the limits of the plantation's geography of containment in especially intense ways. Because most of the work that took bondpeople off the plantation was reserved for men, and because slaveholders almost always granted visiting privileges to the husband in an abroad marriage, women left farms and estates much less frequently than men did. Women were thus fixed even more firmly than men within plantation boundaries.[23]

Recognizing the potential for trouble nevertheless, slaveholders focused much of their managerial energy on regulating black movement in the nighttime. Almost all enslaved people were forbidden to leave the plantation at all in the evenings, and some were prohibited from even stirring from their quarters. In December 1846 Mississippi planter William Ethelbert Ervin codified his ideal of slave behavior by setting to paper the rules that were to govern his human property. Total control over his bondpeople's bodies was central to Ervin's conception of the master-slave relationship, as it was for so many other slaveholders; out of the four fundamental rules on Ervin's estate, two sought to control slave mobility. First, he indicated that plantation borders marked not only the edges of his estate but also hemmed in his bondpeople: No one was to "leave the place without leaf of absence." Second, within those spatial borders, he added temporal limits that bound enslaved people's movement even more: "at nine o'clock every night the Horne must be blown Which is the signal for each to retire to his or her house and there to remain until morning." Doing his best to guarantee a rested and orderly workforce, Ervin directed his overseers to check on people in the quarters, and if anyone was found "out of their places," they would be "delt with" "according to discretion." Most often, transgressors of boundaries of space and time were dealt with violently. Only so long as, in the words of one former bondwoman, "slaves stayed in deir places," were they not "whipped or put in chains."[24]

The nineteenth-century plantation system was a symbol for larger social relations, though, and the importance of rules of containment went beyond plantation efficiency and issues of production: the need for rules struck at the core of what it meant to be a master in the antebellum years. Seeking to restrain black bodies even further, some planters used plantation frolics as a paternalist mechanism of social control. Plantation parties, which carefully doled out joy on Saturday nights and on holidays, were intended to seem benevolent and to inspire respect, gratitude, deference, and importantly, obedience. As North Carolinian Midge Burnett noted sardonically, his owner held plantation frolics on holidays and gave bondpeople Christmas trees in December and an Easter egg hunt in the spring-all "ca[u]se Marse William intended ter make us a civilized bunch of blacks."[25]

Most of all, these sponsored frolics were supposed to control black pleasure by giving it periodic, approved release. Paternalist slaveholders accomplished this goal by attending and surveilling the parties. Indeed, the most important component of paternalistic plantation parties was the legitimating presence of the master. It was common for whites to "set around and watch," while bondpeople would "dance and sing."[26] Though sanctioning black pleasure, the slaveholders' gaze oversaw and contained that pleasure, ensuring that it would not become dangerous. For example, to make certain that the alcohol, music, dancing, "sundrie articles," and "treat[s]" he provided his bondpeople at holiday time served the dual purpose of giving limited expression to and restraining their bodily pleasure in time as well as space, John Nevitt made sure to "s[i]t up until 12 oclock in the morning to keep order with them."[27] Both the former slave Henry Bibb and the former slaveholder Robert Criswell remembered the surveillance role that the slaveholders' presence played at plantation frolics, and both illustrated the constrictive effects of that gaze in their memoirs of antebellum plantation life.[28]

Alcohol proved an important lubricant for production at plantation affairs. Neal Upson watched adults set a rhythm for their work of shucking a season's corn harvest by singing. As they sang and shucked, "de little brown jug was passed 'round." The "little brown jug" of alcohol gave the workers just enough liquor to warm their muscles and their spirits to the enterprise at hand: "When it [the jug] had gone de rounds a time or two, it was a sight to see how fast dem Niggers could keep time to dat singin'. Dey could do all sorts of double time den when dey had swigged enough liquor." Similarly, Bill Heard's owner provided "[p]lenty of corn liquor" to his bondpeople at corn shuckings in order to speed up the work. "[Y]ou know dat stuff is sho to make a Nigger hustle," Heard remembered. "Evvy time a red ear of corn was found dat meant a extra drink of liquor for de Nigger dat found it."[29] Even as planters attempted to master black bodily movement and pleasure in these ways, however, some enslaved people were not satisfied with official parties. They sought out secret and secular gatherings of their own making.

Bondwomen and men who worked in the gang system, the predominant form of work organization in the Old South, worked hard all day, almost every day of the year, with breaks only on Sundays and some holidays. "Dey wucks us from daylight till dark, an' sometimes we jist gits one meal a day," Charlie Crump said of his slavery experience.[30] Bondpeople in South Carolina and parts of Georgia who worked under the task system did not necessarily have to wait for the evening to end their toil, but they, like bondpeople employed in gang labor, were prohibited from leaving their home farms without a pass. Even bad weather meant only a change in routine—respite only from field labor but not from plantation maintenance chores. As they worked, bondpeople, in the words of one folk song sung by women textile workers in Virginia, kept their "eye on de sun," watching it cross the sky as the day wore long. Because "trouble don' las' always," they anticipated the end of the work day and on occasion planned illicit parties in the woods.[31]

Speaking for enslaved people everywhere, Charlie Crump recounted that "we ain't 'lowed ter go nowhar at night . . ." "[D]at is," he added, "if dey knowed it." In violation of the planters' boundaries of space and time, Crump and many of the young people he knew who had worked "from daylight till dark" left at night. At the risk of terrible punishment, blacks "from all ober de neighborhood [would] gang up an' have fun anyhow. . . ." Similarly, Midge Burnett and his friends knew that "[d]e patterollers 'ud watch all de paths leadin' frum de plantation" to prevent bondpeople from running away. What the patrollers did not know, however, was that "dar wus a number of little paths what run through de woods dat nobody ain't watched ca[u]se dey ain't knowed dat de paths wus dar." Many partygoers traveled to their covert events through just such paths.[32]

. . . . Since secrecy demanded a high level of planning, the outlaw gatherings were often prepared well in advance. Austin Steward and his neighbors and friends in rural Virginia were well aware of the laws and rules that forbade enslaved people from leaving "the plantation to which they belong, without a written pass." Nonetheless, they occasionally left their plantations to visit family, to worship, and sometimes, to hold parties. One spring the enslaved people on a nearby estate held an Easter frolic with the permission of their owner. But word of this legitimate "grand dance" quickly spread to "a large number of slaves on other plantations" who intended to attend the party whether or not they could obtain official passes.[33]

Meanwhile, the hosts began preparations. Reappropriation was the main way of obtaining the goods they needed. "[T]hey *took*, without saying, 'by your leave, Sir,' " the food and drink they wanted, Steward wrote, "reasoning among themselves, as slaves often do, that it can not be *stealing*, because 'it belongs to massa, and so do *we*, and we only use one part of his property to benefit another.' " The women took the ingredients and moved their owners' culinary property "from one location to another"—a relocation that made an enormous difference in the purposes of both the frolic and the food. With the ingredients in hand, women hid themselves in "valleys," swamps, and other "by-places" in order to cook in secret during the nights. "[N]ight after night" this went on: women prepared dishes late into the night, then "in the morning" headed back to their cabins, "carefully destroy[ing] everything likely to detect them" on their way. At the same time, the "knowing ones" continued to plan the celebration, encouraging each other's high spirits "with many a wink and nod."[34]

Finally, the appointed night arrived. A little after 10 P.M., the music began when an "old fiddler struck up some favorite tune," and people danced until midnight, when it was time to feast. The food was "well cooked," and the wine was "excellent," Steward reported. But he recalled more than the events; he went to the trouble of recording the affect of the moment. Steward had noted that planters believed that enslaved people hobbled through life "with no hope of release this side of the grave, and as far as the cruel oppressor is concerned, shut out from hope beyond it." Yet, despite—or perhaps in part because of—their abject poverty and the humiliations and cruelties of bondage, here at the party, "Every dusky face was lighted up, and every eye sparkled with Joy. However ill fed they might have been, here, for once, there was plenty. Suffering and toil was forgotten, and they all seemed with one accord to give themselves up to the intoxication of pleasurable amusement." In the context of enslavement, such exhilarating pleasure gotten by illicit use of the body must be understood as important and meaningful enjoyment, as personal expression, and as oppositional engagement of the body.[35]

But there were limits to alternative uses of the body for the enslaved. Late in the night the fiddler suddenly stopped playing and adopted "a listening attitude." Everyone became quiet, "listening for the cause of the alarm." The dreaded call came to them when their lookout shouted, "*patrol!*" and perhaps ran away from the party, a common technique to throw off patrols. If the lookout at this party did so, he was unsuccessful, for the slave patrol, whose job it was to ensure that enslaved people (in Steward's words) "know their place" and stay in it, found the party and broke it up. Many people had run away immediately after the call came, but others, including Steward, had only managed to hide themselves and overheard the patrolmen talking.[36]

Two of the patrolmen debated the wisdom of a few white men attempting to disband a meeting of so many bondpeople. One hesitated to push the matter, arguing that they might "resist." After all, "they have been indulging their appetites, and we cannot tell what they may attempt to do." His colleague mocked his apprehension and wondered if he was really "so chicken-hearted as to suppose those d-d cowardly niggers are going to get up an insurrection?" The first patrolman defensively clarified that he only worried the partygoers "may forget themselves at this late hour." This patrolman's concerns were based on the realities at hand. In these woods, on the figurative if not the literal margins of the host plantation, there was a black majority. This particular black majority was made up of those who already had proven their lack of deference to white authority and their willingness to defy rules. While unprepared and perhaps unwilling to "get up an insurrection," they just might have been capable of "forgetting themselves" by challenging white authority to an incalculable extent. Indeed, in a sense they already had forgotten themselves, having abandoned "their place" in the plantation spatial and temporal order—and the "self" they had to be there—in favor of their own space and their own place.[37]

The party that Austin Steward remembered illustrates what was generally true: that the most important part of preparing a night meeting was evading slave patrols. In addition to doing their best to keep their own movements stealthy, bondpeople carefully monitored patrol activity. Inverting the dominant ideal of plantation surveillance, household, skilled, and personal bondpeople watched their surveillants and sometimes learned of a patrol's plan to be in the area. These bondpeople would pass the word along in the code, "dey bugs in de wheat," meaning the scheduled party had been found out. Sometimes the party was canceled; when it was not, some bondpeople would avoid the party completely, while others would attend anyway, alert and ready to leap out of windows and sprint out of sight when the patrol arrived. Revelers also protected their space by constructing borders of their own. They stretched vines across the paths to trip patrolmen and their horses, and they posted lookouts at key locations along the periphery.[38]

Young people also gathered in spaces outside of their owners' view. Very often they met, like Nancy Williams and the people she knew, in unoccupied cabins in the woods. At other times they simply came together in the open. Occasionally, on very large plantations where outbuildings could be quite a distance from the slaveholder's house, they would meet in barns or in the quarters. Male musicians performed for their friends and neighbors, playing fiddles, banjos, and tambourines. They also made their instruments; for instance, the popular "quill" was created in places where sugar was grown from ten or so cane stems cut to different lengths, with a hole drilled in the top of each, bound together to make a flute. Musicians also improvised instruments out of reeds and handsaws to perform the melody and created the percussion with spoons, bones, pans, and buckets to play songs like "Turkey in the Straw" and other popular tunes.[39]

When no musicians were available, and even when they were, outlaw partygoers made music with their voices, singing lyrics sure to amuse. According to Dosia Harris, one went "somepin' lak dis":

> Oh! Miss Liza, Miss Liza Jane!
> Axed Miss Liza to marry me
> Guess what she said?
> She wouldn't marry me,
> If de last Nigger was dead.[40]

Dancers also sang, perhaps gloatingly, of their subterfuge:

> Buffalo gals, can't you come out tonight,
> Come out tonight, an' dance by the light of de moon?[41]

As morning approached, those who had caroused the night away warned each other of the approach of day and the danger of violating that temporal boundary (which located them properly at work): "Run nigger run, pattyrollers ketch you, run nigger run, it's breakin' days."[42] A variant elaborated:

Run nigger run, de patterrollers ketch you-
Run nigger run, fer hits almos' day,
De nigger run; de nigger flew; de nigger los'
His big old shoe.[43]

Dance tunes contained political meanings as well as entertainment value. The self-deprecating song about the rejected lover is one example: Liza Jane, the object of affection, is called by a title, "Miss," a sign of respect that whites denied bondpeople. Other songs were bolder. Mississippian Mollie Williams danced to and sang the following song, which was inflected by the spirit of resistance nurtured at outlaw parties:

Run tell Coleman,
Run tell everbody
Dat de niggers is arisin'![44]

Together, women and men performed a variety of period dances. Many formerly enslaved people described the dances of their youth as proper and respectable (without the "man an woman squeezed up close to one another," as Mrs. Fannie Berry put it). When she was young, Liza Mention danced "de cardrille (quadrille)[,] de Virginia reel, and de 16-hand cortillion." Mention insisted, "Dances in dem days warn't dese here huggin' kind of dances lak dey has now"[45] Instead, bondpeople chose physically expressive, but still respectable, dances like "pigeon wings" (flapping the arms like a bird and wiggling the legs, while "holdin' yo' neck stiff like a bird do"), "gwine to de east, an' gwine to de west" (leaning in to kiss one's dance partner on each cheek but "widout wrappin' no arms roun' like de young folks do today"), "callin' de figgers" (following the fiddler's challenging calls). . . .[46]

Competition was a common form of amusement at outlaw dances, one that sometimes forged camaraderie among equals. To win a dance competition required the combination of expertly executing complex dance moves while maintaining an outward demeanor of "control and coolness," dance historian Katrina Hazzard-Gordon has written. For example, Nancy Williams competed with another woman, Jennie, to see who could dance most deftly and with the most mastery of their bodies. To make the challenge even greater, the two women danced with glasses of water on their heads; the winner was she who maintained her cool, making the performance of the dances look easy. Dance competition allowed some women to demonstrate the strength and agility of their bodies, as compared with men's, whose physical power was usually recognized as greater. Jane Smith Hill Harmon "allus could dance" and enjoyed, even as an old woman, "cut[ting] fancy steps now sometimes when I feels good." Her talent was awe-inspiring, and she regularly competed with men. . . . Dance competition could provide women moments of relief from black gender hierarchies as well as from slaveholding control.[47]

Such an issue as violence between women and men at secret parties is difficult to access in the sources. We know that enslaved families, like free ones, were home to resentment, betrayal, anger, and other disappointments of family life. Brenda E. Stevenson and Christopher Morris have shown that physical and verbal abuse between spouses was a part of life in the quarters in Virginia and in Mississippi.[48] For a single example, James Cornelius, who had been enslaved in Mississippi, openly told his interviewer about the time he hit his wife in the postbellum years. . . . Cornelius learned of his manly prerogative to violently maintain the rules of his marriage from multiple sources, and a major influence on his conception of domestic life must have been his own (enslaved) family.[49] Violence was also a common aspect of drinking culture among both whites and blacks. It is therefore difficult to imagine that violence, as a part of life in the quarters and a part of drinking culture, did not occur between men, between women, and between men and women at outlawed parties. In particular, men's drinking must have created some difficulties for bondwomen. But violence was not solely a male form of expression. . . . Women's competition could turn viciously bitter and have tragic results. For instance, when two women, Rita and Retta, misunderstood "Aunt" Vira's laughter at a party as directed at them, they poisoned both Vira and her infant.[50]

While women and men danced together, outlaw parties were also characterized by gender differences in ideas of pleasure. Women, more than men, reclaimed their bodies through dressing up; and men, more than women, enjoyed drinking alcohol. Dress was a contested terrain: planters attempted to use it for disciplinary purposes, and women utilized it for purposes inconsistent with the social demands and economic imperatives of slave society. Under cover of night, women headed for secret frolics dressed in their best fancy dress, marking on their bodies the difference between the time that belonged to the master and the time that was their own.[51]

While at work, when their bodies were in the service of their owners, bondpeople looked, according to one observer, "very ragged and slovenly." Planters imprinted slave status on black bodies by vesting bondpeople in clothing of the poorest quality, made of fabric reserved for those of their station. In the summer enslaved people wore uncolored

cotton or tow, a material made from rough, unprocessed flax. Ma
women's dresses were straight, shapeless, and stintingly cut, sometin
directly on the body to avoid wasting fabric. Charity McAllister's
clothes were "poor. One-piece dress made o' carpet stuff, part of de
time." Others were cut fuller, tapered at the waist, and most dresses
were long. Almost all bondpeople's clothes were homemade, not store-
bought, and those who wore them appreciated the difference. Fannie
Dunn disagreed with her mother's assessment of conditions under
slavery in North Carolina on the basis of the clothes she was forced to
wear: "My mother said dat we all fared good, but of course we wore
handmade clothes an' wooden bottomed shoes."[52]

Some planters, as part of their system of rule, annually or biannually
distributed clothes with dramatic flair in order to represent themselves
as the benevolent source of care and sustenance and thereby instill
loyalty in their bondpeople. Many other plantations were characterized
more by slaveholder neglect and avarice than by paternalistic management systems; on such farms slave owners gave little thought
to enslaved people's physical conditions. Year after year, for example, Roswell King, Pierce Butler's Georgia overseer, pleaded with
Butler, who lived in Philadelphia, to provide his bondpeople with
clothing. King subscribed to the paternalist school's combination of
cruel violence, stern order, and benevolent encouragement of disciplined behavior, but he could not find an ally in Butler. "Do you recol-
lect," King wrote Butler on one occasion, "that you have not given
your Negroes Summer clothing but twice in fifteen years past[?]" Old,
torn, shredded, and dirty clothing certainly saved costs for slave
owners, but it also had social effects. Poor-quality clothing reflected
and reified slaves' status and played a role in their subjugation. Harriet
Jacobs wrote bitterly in her 1861 narrative of life as a bondwoman that
the "linsey-woolsey dress given me every winter" by her mistress was
"one of the badges of slavery."[53]

Another "badge of slavery" was the mitigation of gender distinctions that some experienced, effected by the grueling work routines
that many women followed during much of their lives. With a mixture
of pride and bitterness, Anne Clark recalled that during her life in
bondage she had worked like a man. She "ploughed, hoed, split rails. I
done the hardest work ever a man ever did." "Women worked in de
field same as de men. Some of dem plowed jes' like de men and boys,"
George Fleming remembered. Fleming claimed that the women he
knew even resembled men in the fields; he "[c]ouldn't tell 'em apart in
de field, as dey wore pantelets or breeches."[54]

Conversely, when bondpeople, especially women, dressed themselves for their own occasions, they went to a great deal of trouble
to create and wear clothes of quality and, importantly, style. When

possible, women exchanged homespun goods, produce from their gardens, and pelts with white itinerant traders for good-quality or decorative cloth, beads, and buttons. In South Carolina the slaves' independent economy enabled women to purchase cloth, clothing, and dye. But even in Virginia, Frederick Law Olmsted noticed that some women were able to "purchase clothing for themselves" and, on their own time, to "look very smart." Enslaved women located near ports or major waterways were probably able to barter with black boat-workers, who carried on a lively trade with the plantation bondpeople they encountered in their travels.[55] Most women, however, procured fancy dress—when they could at all—simply by eking out time at night to make it, from beginning to end: they grew and processed the cotton, cultivated and gathered the roots and berries for the dye, wove the cloth, and sewed textiles into garments.

When they dressed up and when they refused to perform the regular nightly toil demanded of them in order to make fancy dress, enslaved women indicated that some Saturday nights, Sundays, holidays, and occasionally weeknights were their own. Women, whose bodies were subject to sexual exploitation, dangerous and potentially heartbreaking reproductive labor, and physically demanding agricultural labor, tried not to miss the opportunity to reclaim them from the brink of degradation at the hands of their masters. As much as women's bodies were sources of suffering and sites of planter domination, women also worked hard to make their bodies spaces of personal expression, pleasure, and resistance.

Fancy dress offered a challenge to status-enforcing clothing because dressing up was heterodox behavior. Pierre Bourdieu defines *doxa* as the "naturalization" of the social order accomplished through a number of social and symbolic mechanisms, including assumptions by dominant classes about the "uses" and presentation of the body. Within the reigning doxa, the black body was vested in slave dress, dress that enforced and naturalized its status. Enslaved women sporadically engaged in heterodox behavior—behavior that was conscious of the doxa, exposed its arbitrariness, and challenged it. When they adorned their bodies in fancy dress, rather than in the degrading rough and plain clothing, rags, or livery that slaveholders dressed them in, they challenged the axiomatic (doxic) quality of their enslaved status. In particular, women fashioned new identities that highlighted their femininity and creativity.[56]

Finally, women's heterodox style—expressed as they transgressed the plantation's boundaries of space and time—allowed them to take pleasure in their bodies, while simultaneously denying that their bodies had exclusively fiduciary value and that the sole "[use] of the body" was to labor for their owners.[57] Indeed, the very act of slipping out of plantation boundaries to attend parties withheld labor, in that by failing to rest properly for the next day's chores, enslaved people worked less efficiently, much to the outrage of their owners. In the Old South, issues of representation of the black body and material expropriation could not be separated from one another.

When women adorned themselves in fancy dress of their own creation, they distanced themselves from what it felt like to wear slaves' low-status clothing. "Aunt" Adeline was, as her mother had been, an accomplished dyer. On one occasion she wore a dress that she would never forget "as long as I live. It was a hickory stripe dress they made for me, with brass buttons at the wrist bands." She was "so proud of that dress"; with her identity refashioned by it, she "felt so dressed up in it, I just strutted!". . . .[58]

In addition to the symbolic value dress held for plantation blacks and whites, clothing held more tangible meanings as well. The production, distribution, and uses of King Cotton—and cotton products such as clothing—were very material issues in the slave South. . . . While women and men could both quit working for their owners at sunset, many women began a second shift of labor at night, and sometimes on Saturdays or Sundays, working for their families. At these times women performed reproductive labor, such as cooking, cleaning, gardening, washing, and candle and soap-making, in their homes. Henry James Trentham saw women plowing during the day, working hard to "carry dat row an' keep up wid de men," then quit at sunset "an den do dere cookin' at night." Moreover, in their "off" time and during the winters, women were responsible for some to all of the production of textiles for plantation residents, black and white. Only on the very largest plantations was some of this work concentrated in the hands of women specialists.[59]

Most enslaved women, then, worked grueling first and second shifts. Their second shift of labor, however, also presented an opportunity, one they exploited, to devote a bit of their time to heterodox activity. Women spent some of their evenings turning the plain, uncolored tow, denim, hemp, burlap, and cotton they had spun into decorative cloth. . . . Women dyed the coarse material allotted them with colors that they liked. Nancy Williams's dedication to style was unusual, but it remains instructive. "Clo'es chile? I had plenty clo'es dem days," she claimed. "Had dress all colors. How I get 'em? Jes' change dey colors. Took my white dress out to de Polk berry bush an' jes' a-dyed it red, den dyed my shoes red. Took ole barn paint an' paint some mo' shoes yaller to match my yaller dress." Women set the colors fast in their cloth with saline solutions, vinegar and water, or "chamber lye" (urine). They hung the cloth on lines to dry and from there sewed the fabric into garments. Women also traded the products of their nighttime labor . . .

for calico and fine or decorative cloth, as well as for ornamental objects.[60]

Once they had the cloth, enslaved women went to great effort to make themselves something more than the cheap, straight-cut dresses they were rationed. When possible, women cut their "dress-up" dresses generously so as to cover the length of the body and to sweep dramatically and elegantly. Some women accentuated the fullness of their skirts by crisply starching them. Annie Wallace remembered that when her mother went "out at night to a party some of the colored folks was havin'," she would starch her skirts with "hominy water.... They were starched so stiff that every time you stopped they would pop real loud." Wallace's mother instructed her children to listen carefully for her return, in case the party was broken up by the arrival of Virginia's rural patrols. "And when we heared them petticoats apoppin' as she run down the path, we'd open the door wide and she would get away from the patteroll."[61]

Other women liked to draw attention to their skirts with hoops they made from grapevines or tree limbs. Though Salena Taswell's owner "would not let the servants wear hoops," she and the other household bondwomen sometimes swiped "the old ones that they threw away." .... Camilla Jackson told her interviewer that hoopskirts "were the fad in those days" among black as well as white women, one that enabled bondwomen to appropriate a symbol of leisure and femininity (and freedom) and denaturalize their slave status. "In dem days de wimen wore hoops.... De white folks dun it an' so did the slave wimen," Ebenezer Brown said.[62]

Yet black women's style did not simply mimic slaveholding women's fashions. It was enslaved women's use of accessories that most accentuated their originality. Topping off many women's outfits were head wraps or hairstyles done just so. Nineteenth-century bondwomen made the head wrap into a unique expressive form. Some women wore their favorite head wraps to outlaw parties, and many others removed the wrap to display the hairstyles—cornrows, plaits, and straightened hair—they had prepared. Women could straighten or relax their curls by wrapping sections of their hair in string, twine, or bits of cloth, then covering it during the week to hide the wrappings and to keep their hair clean and protected from the sun. On special occasions such women removed the head wrap and the strings, and their hair fell down straightened or in looser curls. Although accessories were more difficult to obtain, they were not overlooked. Some women made straw hats from "wheat straw which was dried out." They also made buttons and ornaments for their clothing out of "li'l round pieces of gourds" covered with cloth and from "cows and rams horns."[63]

Women's creation and appropriation of cloth and clothing helped them to express their personalities and their senses of style, but their uses of clothing also raised material issues. Women's alternative uses of dress laid claim to the product of their labor: they seized the cotton that they had raised and harvested, and they used it for their own purposes. "How I get 'em?" Nancy Williams seemed pleased with her interviewer's question and eager to tell of her ingenuity. Perhaps exaggerating, Williams said she had "plenty" of clothes during her life in bondage, though not due to any generosity from her owner. In addition to dyeing the plain cloth she was allotted, Williams reappropriated what she needed. Williams, for example, "[h]ad done stole de paint" to make yellow shoes to go with a yellow dress she wore to an illicit dance.[64]

Similarly, Mary Wyatt's Virginia owner had a dress that Wyatt adored. "Lawdy, I used to take dat dress when she warn't nowhere roun' an' hole it up against me an' 'magine myself wearin' it." One Christmas season Wyatt decided to wear the dress to a plantation frolic. "[D]e debbil got in me good," she admitted. "Got dat gown out de house 'neath my petticoat tied rounst me an' wore it to de dance." . . . . [In doing so, she] reclaimed the product of her own labor. Women like her had picked the cotton, processed it, and made it into a dress; the institution of slavery made the dress her owner's, but Mary Wyatt made it hers. In Wyatt's case the act of reappropriation was brief. She returned the dress, putting it "back in place de nex' day." But even as the terror that gripped her while she stole and wore the dress indicates the power of her owners, her act also reveals the strength of her commitment to wearing the dress and suggests something of its importance to Wyatt.[65]

Bondwomen took tremendous risks in procuring and wearing fancy dress to plantation frolics and outlawed slave parties, and the potential extent of this personal endangerment is also a measure of the significance of the otherwise seemingly trivial concerns of dress and style. By dressing up to go to outlaw parties, bondwomen flagrantly violated the somatics of plantation social hierarchy as well as plantation boundaries of space and time. Their fancy dress heightened their risk because their conspicuousness exposed all of them (especially household bondwomen) to detection. The degree of danger involved in dressing up and running away for an evening and women's willingness to take the chance suggest just how urgent it was to some to extricate themselves from their proper places. Frances Miller, a slaveholding woman, encountered such determination as she endeavored to impose a "system of management" within her Virginia household. She rose at 4:30 every morning, in advance of her bondpeople, to wake them and prod them to work, not at all shying away from physical violence when their "insubordination" proved too much for her. Miller dedicated herself, in what she described as a "herculean" manner, to "always righting things up." Thanks to the "open rebellion, impudence and unfaithfulness of domestics," things seemed "never righted" in household.[66]

Among the most egregious acts of "unfaithfulness" and "insubordination" that Miller witnessed in her household was the determination of her unruly bondwoman, Rose, to sneak away at night to a party. On her way to bed one night, Miller encountered Rose on her way out of the house, "dressed up as I supposed for a night's jaunt." Caught, Rose thought on her feet and, thrusting the candle that she held to light her passage toward Miller, asked Miller to carry it back for her. Miller had been hardened by Rose's long history of disobedience, however, and was not distracted from the issue at hand. When Miller sarcastically "asked her why she did not do it herself," Rose claimed that "she was going to wash." Rose's explanation for still being awake and heading out, when, according to the late hour, she ought to have been in bed in her room, was not convincing. Miller could tell by the way Rose was "dressed so spry" that she was not at all going to wash and so "did not believe her." Instead, she reminded Rose of her curfew and of where she ought to be, telling her "it was bedtime and she must go directly upstairs." Rose "refused" and remained determined to go out to "wash." Rose's plans were thwarted only after Miller "shut the door and locked it." With no key Rose had no way out. Angered that she would now miss the party, Rose insulted Miller, telling her "that I was the most contrary old thing that she ever saw."[67]

As punishment for attempting to disobey the household's boundaries of space and time, as well as for her effrontery, Miller promised to flog Rose, prompting Rose to assert that she "would not submit to any such thing and that she would go to the woods first." Rose, however, did not carry out her threat. Perhaps because she was so disappointed about having been prevented from going out, Rose "yielded with less difficulty than usual" to the bondman William's "switches." Miller succeeded in stopping Rose from leaving the household, but the whole incident left Miller "sorely grieved—sorely." She was frustrated "that the necessity had existed" to whip Rose. Rose's transgression of place mandated, to Miller's mind, the deployment of violence, which contradicted Miller's ideal of a mastery so effective as not to warrant its explicit use in the first place.[68]

Black women's and men's absentee nightly pleasures, such as sneaking off to parties to stay up late dancing and drinking, compromised slaveholding authority and plantation productivity. Julia Larken noted that her owner "never laked for nobody to be late in de mornin'," presumably because of the disorder and the inefficiency that tardiness caused. Nonetheless, lateness and fatigue were not unusual. When enslaved people stayed up late into the night worshiping, for example, they would be "sho tired" the next day. Charlie Tye Smith recalled that, no matter how late they had been up the night before, bond-people "had better turn out at four o'clock when ole Marse blowed the horn!" They dragged themselves through the motions of their chores all morning and at lunchtime collapsed in the field. Those who had not attended the religious meeting looked upon a field "strowed with Niggers asleep in the cotton rows" until the midday break ended, and they all resumed work.[69]

And so it was after illicit parties. Jefferson Franklin Henry remembered how other bondpeople, but not he, "would go off to dances and stay out all night; it would be wuk time when they got back. . . ." These revelers valiantly "tried to keep right on gwine," but they were worn out; "the Good Lord soon cut 'em down." These mornings-after did not inhibit future parties, however, nor did the Christian objections of other blacks make an impact: "You couldn't talk to folks that tried to git by with things lak that," Henry regretted. "[T]hey warn't gwine to do no diffunt, nohow."[70]

An extraordinary document survives that articulates for us not the "success" of slave resistance using the body but, given the extent to which the body was a point of conflict between slaves and their owners, what meanings the latter group ascribed to that conflict. In the mid-1840s slaveholders in the Edgefield and Barnwell Districts of South Carolina formed the Savannah River Anti-Slave Traffick Association to put a stop to disorderly-house owners' practice of selling alcohol to bondpeople and published their regulations. Slave drinking, and the theft and black marketing that bondpeople engaged in to obtain liquor and other goods from obliging non-elite whites, resulted in what the Savannah River group deemed "very considerable losses." Bond-women and men—like association member James Henry Hammond's own Urana—appropriated property from slave owners by breaking into "dwelling houses, barns, stables, smoke houses, [etc.]" with "false keys which abound among our negroes," or by "pick[ing] with instruments at which they have become very skilful" at crafting and using. Moreover, the neighbors complained that their crops were also vulnerable to appropriation: "Not content with plundering from Barns, our standing crops are beginning to suffer depredation." Thanks to these various activities, the Savannah River neighbors thought they had noticed their profits decline. "Often when a Farmer has expected to sell largely, he finds himself compelled to use the most stringent economy to make his provisions meet his own wants, and sometimes has actually to buy."[71]

Slaves' trading, stealing, and drinking were not the only "evils" worrying these South Carolina planters. Equally vexatious was the practice of "prowling" off to "night meetings." Because of the "too great negligence of slave owners in maintaining wholesome discipline," every night, or so it seemed, bondpeople could be found sneaking "abroad to night meetings." The association claimed that "hundreds of negroes it may be said without exaggeration are every night, and at all hours of the night, prowling about the country," stealing, trading, drinking, and meeting, almost certainly for secular affairs.

The association weighed heavily the financial loss its members believed that they incurred when enslaved people were too hungover and tired to work well. "The negroes themselves are seriously impaired in physical qualities," it noted. The association's regulations further detailed that "their nightly expeditions are followed by days of languor." Seeing their "owners, and especially their overseers, as unjust and unfeeling oppressors," bondpeople, it seemed to these South Carolinians, responded with insubordination and work characterized by "sullenness [and] discontent."

The Savannah River neighbors were mobilized to action by what they saw as a second pernicious effect of black nightly "prowling." In addition to the damage nightly pleasures had on productivity and the theft associated with such parties, association members complained of the resulting corrosion of slaveholding mastery. Black "minds are fatally corrupted" by these nighttime activities, these South Carolinians believed. In the revisionist history that the association wrote, bondpeople were "beginning to" dissent from the paternalist contract that supposedly governed planters' estates. "Formerly Slaves were essentially members of the family to which they belonged, and a reciprocal interest and attachment existing between them, their relations were simple, agreeable, easily maintained, and mutually beneficial," the association contended. It seemed that the freedom bondpeople tasted at night compromised their willingness to be deferential and obedient during the day. The association complained of the "difficulty in managing" the bondpeople since night activity appeared to encourage many bondpeople to see their "Masters" as their "natural enemies." This perspective facilitated more disorderly behavior, and the members of the Savannah River organization were forced to admit to one another that they were having trouble "preserving proper subordination of our slaves."

The apocalyptic end was clear to the Savannah River residents: in alarmist tones they predicted the end of slavery as they knew it if such unruliness continued. Reappropriating the "fruits of their own labors," working only with "sullenness [and] discontent," and skeptical of the authority of their masters, bondpeople in their neighborhood were creating "[s]uch a state of things [that] must speedily put an end to agriculture or to negro slavery." Engaging in these small, outlawed activities, the association argued, the "negro ceases to be a moral being, holding a position in the framework of society, and becomes a serpent gnawing at its vitals or a demon ready with knife and torch to demolish its foundations."

Drinking and dancing at night rather than resting for the next day's work could not and did not bring down the house of slavery. Nonetheless, the histrionics of the Savannah River Anti-Slave Traffick Association are more than amusing; they are revealing. When engaged in these activities, enslaved people ceased, their owners thought, to hold a proper "position in the framework of society" because they disregarded slaveholders' control over their bodies. Stealing time and space for themselves and for members of their communities, those who attended secular parties acted on the assumption that their bodies were more than inherently and solely implements of agricultural production. While many planters desired and struggled for a smooth-running, paternalistic machine, some bondpeople created, among other things, a gendered culture of pleasure that "gnawed" at the fundamentals—the "vitals"—of slaveholding schemes for domination of the black body, a body that slaveholders had (ideally) located in a particular "position in the framework of society."

In a context where control and degradation of the black body were essential to the creation of slave-owning mastery—symbolically, socially, and materially—bondwomen's and men's nighttime pleasures insulted slaveholders' feelings of authority. Mastery demanded respect for spatial and temporal boundaries, but bondpeople sometimes transgressed these borders and forged spaces for themselves. While slaveowners' drive for production required rested slave bodies, bondpeople periodically reserved their energies for the night and exhausted themselves at play. Perhaps most important of all, enslaved women and men struggled against planters' inclination to confine them, in order to create the space and time to celebrate and enjoy their bodies as important personal and political entities in the plantation South.

NOTES

1 Charles L. Perdue Jr., Thomas E. Barden, and Robert K. Phillips, eds, *Weevils in the Wheat: Interviews with Virginia Ex-Slaves* (Charlottesville, 1976), 316. . . .

2 Ibid.

3 Winthrop D. Jordan, *White Over Black: American Attitudes Toward the Negro, 1550–1812* (Chapel Hill, 1968), 55–56 (quotations), 107; Philip J. Schwarz, *Twice Condemned: Slaves and the Criminal Laws of Virginia, 1705–1865* (Baton Rouge, 1988), 22; Ira Berlin, *Many Thousands Gone: The First Two Centuries of Slavery in North America* (Cambridge, Mass., and London, 1998), 113. . . .

4 Anne Godlewska and Neil Smith cited in Matthew Sparke, "Mapped Bodies and Disembodied Maps: (Dis)placing Cartographic Struggle in Colonial Canada," in Heidi J. Nast and Steve Pile, eds., *Places through the Body* (London and New York, 1998), 305. . . . The phrase "geography of containment" is Houston Baker's [in a] seminar at the Center for the Study

of Black Literature and Culture, University of Pennsylvania, March 27, 1997.

5 Ulrich B. Phillips, *American Negro Slavery: A Survey of the Supply, Employment and Control of Negro Labor as Determined by the Plantation Regime* (New York, 1918; Baton Rouge, 1966), 327; Eugene D. Genovese, *Roll, Jordan, Roll: The World the Slaves Made* (New York, 1974), 3–7. Genovese's paternalism thesis has been the subject of intensive debate. . . .

6 All of these sources present difficulties . . . . Because the Works Progress Administration interviews [from the 1930s] refer, mostly, to the last decades of slavery and because black autobiographies proliferated in the same period, this article focuses on the years between 1830 and the beginning of the Civil War.

7 Thomas D. Morris, *Southern Slavery and the Law, 1619–1860* (Chapel Hill, 1996); Christopher Morris, "The Articulation of Two Worlds: The Master–Slave Relationship Reconsidered," *Journal of American History*, 85 (December 1998), 982–1007; Walter Johnson, *Soul by Soul: Life Inside the Antebellum Slave Market* (Cambridge, Mass., 1999).

8 . . . . There would have been differences between the upper South and the lower South, but the scarcity of sources precludes knowing for certain. It is possible to note, however, that while it might appear that illicit movement would have been more common in the upper South because of its proximity to the free North, the evidence does not support this hypothesis. . . .

9 For the theory of everyday forms of resistance that undergirds the approach taken here . . . see James C. Scott, *Weapons of the Weak: Everyday Forms of Peasant Resistance* (New Haven, 1985), esp. xv–xvi, 35–36, 285–303, 317; and Scott, *Domination and the Arts of Resistance: Hidden Transcripts* (New Haven, 1990), esp. 66, 178, 184–88. . . .

10 Dorinda Outram, *The Body and the French Revolution: Sex, Class, and Political Culture* (New Haven, 1989), 1; C. L. R. James, Grace C. Lee, and Pierre Chaulieu, *Facing Reality* (Detroit, Mich., 1974), 5. . . .

11 This discussion is informed by the work of anthropologists and philosophers who have posited the body as an important terrain of conquest and as a site for the reproduction of the social order. They have also detailed what, following Mary Douglas's account of "two bodies," may be called a second body: the social imprint on the body that shapes and limits the experience of the body. See Frantz Fanon, *Black Skin, White Masks*, trans. Charles Lam Markmann (New York, 1967), 109–40; Mary Douglas, *Natural Symbols: Explorations in Cosmology* (New York, 1970), chap. 5; and Michel Foucault, *Discipline and Punish: The Birth of the Prison*, trans. Alan Sheridan (New York, 1977). . . .

12 Fanon, *Black Skin, White Masks*, 110–11. . . .

13 Mary Douglas, *Purity and Danger: An Analysis of Concepts of Pollution and Taboo* (London, 1966); Douglas, *Natural Symbols*; Carolyn Kay Steedman, *Landscape for a Good Woman: A Story of Two Lives* (New Brunswick, N.J., 1987); Joan Wallach Scott, *Gender and the Politics of History* (New York, 1988);. . . . Evelyn Brooks Higginbotham, "African–American Women's History and the Metalanguage of Race," *Signs*, 17 (Winter 1992), 251–74.

14 . . . see Darlene Clark Hine and Kate Wittenstein, "Female Slave Resistance: The Economics of Sex," in Filomena Chioma Steady, ed., *The Black Woman Cross-Culturally* (Cambridge, Mass., 1981); Deborah Gray White, *Ar'n't I a Woman? Female Slaves in the Plantation South* (New York and London, 1985). . . .

15 White abolitionists used graphic representations of the exploited, abused, or degraded enslaved body to gain support for the antislavery cause. See Phillip Lapsansky, "Graphic Discord Abolitionist and Antiabolitionist Images," in Jean Fagan Yellin and John C. Van Home, eds., *The Abolitionist Sisterhood: Women's Political Culture in Antebellum America* (Ithaca, N.Y., and London, 1994), 201–30;. . . .

16 Jennifer L. Morgan, " 'Some Could Suckle Over Their Shoulder': Male Travelers, Female Bodies, and the Gendering of Racial Ideology, 1500–1770," *William and Mary Quarterly*, 3d ser., 54 (January 1997), 167–92 . . .

17 Brown, *Good Wives, Nasty Wenches, and Anxious Patriarchs: Gender Race and Power in Colonial Virginia* (Chapel Hill, 1996), 116–19, 125, 135–36. . . .

18 "Bio-text" is John O'Neill's phrase, from *The Communicative Body: Studies in Communicative Philosophy, Politics, and Sociology* (Evanston, Ill., 1989), 3.

19 Fanon, *Black Skin, White Masks*, 110–11.

20 Charles Ball, *Slavery in the United States: A Narrative of the Life and Adventures of Charles Ball* (1836; rep., Detroit, 1970), 125.

21 . . . . Inside cover of the Richard Eppes diary, 1858, Eppes Family Papers, Virginia Historical Society (VHS). Mark M. Smith demonstrates the increasing importance of time discipline to plantation production in . . . "Old South Time in Comparative Perspective," [in this volume] . . .

22 For a single example, Virginia slaveholder John Bassett wrote a pass for an enslaved person named Edward: "Edward is sent to Rich[mon]d. To remain till Monday next[.] Feby 25th 1826. John Bassett." . . . .

23 White, *Ar'n't I a Woman?* 75;. . . .

24 December 31, 1846, William Ethelbert Ervin Diaries #247-z, Southern Historical Collection, University of North Carolina (SHC); George P. Rawick, ed., *The American Slave: A Composite Autobiography* (19 vols.; Westport, Conn., 1972), XIII, Pt. 3, p. 128.

25 Rawick, ed., *American Slave*, XIV, 157. . . .

26 Rawick, ed., *American Slave*, XVI, 23. . . .

27 December 27, 1828, John Nevitt Diary #543 (SHC).

28 Henry Bibb, *Narrative of the Life and Adventures of Henry Bibb, An American Slave* (New York, 1849), 21; Robert Criswell, *"Uncle Tom's Cabin" Contrasted with Buckingham Hall, the Planter's Home* (New York, 1852), 113 [Illustrations from these publications have been omitted—ed.]

29 Rawick, ed., *American Slave*, XIII, Pt. 4, p. 68 (Neal Upson), and XII, Pt. 2, p. 142 (Bill Heard).

30 Rawick, ed., *American Slave*, XIV, 213.

31 The lyrics, as Bob Ellis remembered them, were, "Keep yo' eye on de sun, / See how she run, / Don't let her catch you with your work undone, / I'm a trouble, I'm a trouble, / Trouble don' las' always." Perdue et al., eds., *Weevils in the Wheat*, 88. . . .

32 Rawick, ed., *American Slave*, XIV, 213 (Charlie Crump), 156 (Midge Burnett).

33 Austin Steward, *Twenty-Two Years a Slave, and Forty Years a Freeman*, intro. by Jane H. Pease and William H. Pease (Reading, Mass, 1969), 19–22.

34 Ibid., 20.

35 Ibid., 15, 21.

36 Ibid., 20–24.

37 Ibid., 23–24.

38 Hadden, *Slave Patrols*, 109; Gladys-Marie Fry, *Nightriders in Black Folk History* (Knoxville, 1975), 93; Perdue et al., *Weevils in the Wheat*, 93, 297 (quotation); Rawick, ed., *American Slave*, XIII, Pt. 4, p. 80, XIV, Pt. 1, p. 213, and XVI [Maryland], 49–50.

39 Perdue et al., eds., *Weevils in the Wheat*, 316; Rawick, ed., *American Slave*, XIII, Pt. 4, 306. . . .

40 Rawick, ed., *American Slave*, XII, Pt. 2, p. 110.

41 Rawick ed., *American Slave*, VII [Mississippi], 161.

42 Ibid., 126.

43 Ibid., 162.

44 Ibid., 161.

45 Perdue et al., eds., *Weevils in the Wheat*, 49–50 (Fannie Berry); Rawick, ed., *American Slave*, XIII, Pt. 3, p. 124 (Liza Mention).

46 [For descriptions see] Perdue et al., eds., *Weevils in the Wheat*, 49–50;. . . .

47 Katrina Nazzard-Gordon, *Jookin': The Rise of Social Dance Formations in African–American Culture* (Philadelphia, 1990), 20; Perdue et al., eds., *Weevils in the Wheat*, 316; Rawick, ed., *American Slave*, XII, Pt. 2, p. 99.

48 Brenda E. Stevenson, *Life in Black and White: Family and Community in the Slave South* (New York, 1996), 23, 255; Christopher Morris, *Becoming Southern: The Evolution of a Way of Life, Warren County and Vicksburg, Mississippi, 1770–1860* (New York, 1995), 63.

49 Rawick, ed., *American Slave*, VII [Mississippi], 30. . . .

50 Rawick. Ed., *American Slave*, XIII, Pt. 4, p. 104.

51 For more on black style under slavery see Patricia K. Hunt, "The Struggle to Achieve Individual Expression Through Clothing and Adornment: African American Women Under and After Slavery," in Patricia Morton, ed., *Discovering the Women in Slavery: Emancipating Perspectives on the American Past* (Athens, Ga., 1996), 227–40. . . .

52 Frederick Law Olmsted, *The Cotton Kingdom: A Traveller's Observations on Cotton and Slavery in the American Slave States . . .*, ed. Arthur M. Schlesinger Sr. (New York, 1984), 82; Rawick, ed., *American Slave*, XII, Pt. 1, p. 4, XV, 62 and XIV, 272.

53 . . . Roswell King to Pierce Butler, December 7, 1812, April 20, 1816, and July 6, 1817 . . . Butler Family Papers, Historical Society of Pennsylvania; Harriet A. Jacobs, *Incidents in the Life of a Slave Girl, Written by Herself*, ed. Jean Fagan Yellin (Cambridge, Mass., 1987), 11.

54 Rawick, ed., *American Slave*, IV, Pt. 1, p. 223 (Anne Clark); Rawick, ed., *American Slave*, supp. ser. 1, XI, 130. . . .

55 . . . . Olmsted, *Cotton Kingdom*, 82; Thomas C. Buchanan, "The Slave Mississippi: African-American Steamboat Workers, Networks of Resistance, and the Commercial World of the Western Rivers, 1811–1880" (Ph.D. diss., Carnegie Mellon University, 1998), 175–84.

56 Pierre Bourdieu, *Outline of a Theory of Practice*, trans. Richard Nice (Cambridge, Eng. 1977), 164–71 . . .

57 Ibid., 165.

58 Rawick, ed., *American Slave*, XLII, Pt. 4, pp. 212. . . .

59 Rawick, ed., *American Slave*, XIII, Pt. 3, p. 72, and XV, 364 (Henry James Trentham).

60 Foster, *"New Raiments of Self,"* 112, 114; Perdue et al., eds., *Weevils in the Wheat*, 316–17. . . .

61 Perdue et al., eds., *Weevils in the Wheat*, 294.

62 Rawick, ed., *American Slave*, XVII, 306 . . . . (Salena Taswell); Rawick, ed., *American Slave*, XII, Pt. 2, p. 297 (Camilla Jackson);. . . .

63 Shane White and Graham White, "Slave Hair and African American Culture in the Eighteenth and Nineteenth Centuries," *Journal of Southern History*, 61 (February 1995), 70–71; Rawick, ed., *American Slave*, supp. ser. 1,

XI, 57 . . .; Foster, *"New Raiments* of *Self,"* 115, 252. [A section on shoes has been omitted—ed.]

64 Perdue et al., eds., *Weevils in the Wheat*, 316. . . .

65 Ibid., 333.

66 Frances (Scott) Miller diary, July 3, 1858 and July 5, 1858 . . . Armistead, Blanton, and Wallace Family Papers (VHS).

67 Ibid., February 7, 1857.

68 Ibid.

69 Rawick, ed., *American Slave*, XIII, Pt. 3, pp. 39, 276.

70 Rawick, ed., *American Slave*, XII, Pt. 2, pp. 188–89. . . .

71 *Preamble and Regulations of the Savannah River Anti-Slave Traffick Association* (November 21, 1846), 3, 4. . . . Kenneth M. Stampp, ed., *Records of Ante-Bellum Southern Plantation from the Revolution through the Civil War*, ser. A. pt. 1, reel 1. [The following paragraphs are based on this same source—ed.]

7

THE MANAGEMENT OF NEGROES

Kirsten E. Wood

Several of the essays in this volume have examined the nature of slave masters' self-conception as paternalists. But what if the masters were not men, but women? Kirsten E. Wood's essay examines the patterns of behavior and thought among women—usually widows—who themselves owned slaves. She finds that in many respects, female masters were indistinguishable: women, like men, pursued profit, punished slaves for disobedience, and saw themselves as benevolent. In certain key areas, though, gender distinguished widows' actions and attitudes. While they paid close attention to profits and losses in the fields, they often measured their personal success or failure more in terms of house slaves' performance. Widows also differed from men in their willingness to assert their power over slaves in raw physical terms. Planter and yeoman widows alike were less likely than men to whip slaves personally, and sexual domination or its threat did not commonly figure in their mastery; such things were "unladylike." As for the slaves, they "typically behaved much as they did in male-headed households"—sometimes running away and refusing obedience, but, overall, "in no position to ratchet up their resistance when a widow took over."

* * *

Thomas Burge died in December 1858 at his plantation in Newton County, Georgia. For the first month after his death, Dolly Burge used her diary to describe his last days and record her thankfulness that she had the "privillage" of serving him "until the very last moment of his life." By the middle of February 1859, however, she began making very different entries, noting the weather and the slaves' preparations for the next growing season, such as "hauling out manure & bedding cotton land."[1] Dolly and her widowed peers might have preferred to do what Savannah planter Martha Richardson recommended to her sister-in-law: sell off the slaves and "be done with the trouble."[2] But most slaveholding widows did not have that option, while those who could have sold off or freed their slaves almost never did. Few white women raised with slaves could imagine a future without them, and

170

for most widows, having slaves meant managing them. Few widows could rely on relatives to manage everything for them, and only the richest could afford to be fully absentee planters. Consequently, new widows had little choice but to attend to slave management, especially the critical matters of labor, provisions, health, and discipline.

Widows like Dolly Burge worked hard at supervising both house and field slaves. In the process, they conformed but sporadically and unevenly to the ideals of charity and kindness that increasingly dominated southern prescriptions for slaveholding women. Even in the antebellum decades, when benevolent ideals had their greatest currency, slaveholding widows routinely pursued their financial interests and personal comforts at the expense of slaves. Most imposed heavy workloads, often while economizing on rations. When slaves failed to live up to their expectations, widows rarely caviled at corporal punishment, and they expected the state and law enforcement to uphold their rights in human property. In all of these ways, slaveholding widows closely resembled their male peers.

Within this basic pattern, how a widow managed slaves varied with the size of her household and her financial condition. Widows with limited means and only a few slaves had a distinctive (if less well documented) experience of slave management. These widows often had to do remunerative work as well as manage slaves. Yet white southern women had few employment choices that were both reasonably profitable and respectable; needlework, teaching, and boardinghouse keeping were among the most important. Some widows made a living by taking over their husbands' businesses, such as a dry goods store, tavern, or millinery shop. The majority of small slaveholding widows, however, had been married to yeomen farmers, and they had great difficulty filling their husbands' shoes. For both sets of widows, slave labor had the potential to make their own work both more ladylike and more lucrative. Planter widows had less physically demanding work than yeoman widows. Whereas yeoman farmers might have to work the fields alongside slaves, planters ordered that fields be plowed and crops planted, hoed, harvested, and sent to market. They decided how and whether to make capital improvements. They also determined whether and how to give slaves incentives for working well. In all of these areas, planter widows focused on moneymaking staple crops, although they did not always allocate labor efficiently, read markets accurately, or invest wisely. Like their male peers, most stuck with farming methods and staples that they knew instead of experimenting with scientific agriculture or new crops.[3]

Despite the many similarities of widows' slave management to men's, gender distinguished widows' actions and attitudes in certain key areas. While widows paid close attention to profits and losses in the fields, they often measured their personal success or failure more in terms of house slaves' performance. Widows also differed from men in their willingness to assert their power over slaves in raw physical terms. Planter and yeoman widows alike were less likely than men to whip slaves themselves, and sexual domination or its threat did not commonly figure in their mastery. Widows' ambivalent relationship to sexual and other violence against slaves might suggest that their slaves experienced a moderate form of slavery and could resist their bondage more openly than those managed by men, but the evidence points in another direction. Rather than benefiting from a widow's management, slaves often fared no better or even worse than before, for three simple reasons. First, estate settlement made slaveholders into misers, because few estates could fully settle debts and satisfy legacies with the cash on hand. Second, the death of a slaveholder increased slaves' risk of losing kin, either through sale or through distribution among heirs. As many fugitive and former slaves testified, separation from family members could hurt more than a whipping. Finally, slaves discovered that even if some widows were inclined to ignore all sorts of truancy, others were not, to say nothing of the state and other whites who assisted widows in policing their slaves. On the whole, therefore, slaves had little reason to look forward to life under a widow's rule. As former slave Nancy Williams remembered, "de real trouble start for us when ole marsa died."[4]

While even small slaveholders were wealthy compared to most widows, they often had serious trouble making their income match their expenses. When a slaveholding husband died, he deprived his household of his labor, a particular problem for those with only a few slaves. His death also meant that his debts had to be repaid. Although yeomen farmers generally avoided the staggering debts that ruined some planters, some debt was almost inevitable, and their widows could rarely settle all such claims out of pocket. Simply sorting out the tangle of indebtedness could take years. In the meantime, widows had to produce the income needed to feed and clothe themselves and often an entire household. They also had to pay taxes, and those who served as executors or administrators had to pay estate debts and fulfill legacies. In many yeoman widows' households, the income for all these purposes came from their own as well as their slaves' labor.[5]

After her husband's unexpected death in November 1835, Virginia-born Lucy Freeman found herself with a household of young children to support. The family's comparative poverty required that she jealously manage the scant resources of their small Tennessee farm. Making matters worse, her husband had died intestate, and she did not qualify as the estate's administrator, in part for want of timely advice from kinsmen in Virginia. When the administrator hired out the estate's slaves to pay her husband's debts, the "boys" hired for sixty dollars apiece for the year, which suggests they were old enough for serious work. Lucy could afford to hire back only "the woman and children," whose price—"their victuals and cloths"—indicates their low value. Lucy thus had several slaves in her house but little useful labor. She could not rely on her own children because they were either too young for hard work or in school, which she saw as essential to their futures. With so many mouths to feed, Freeman likely had to do double duty, working in the fields as well as the house. Among small slaveholders, such a combination was not unusual. . . .[6]

A gender role that allowed widows to do both indoor and outdoor work was a limited advantage. On the one hand, it gave them a certain flexibility in deciding how best to use their own labor. On the other, a widow could not do all her own work and her husband's as well; there simply were not enough hours in the day. Making up the labor deficit proved difficult for rural widows unless they owned or could hire prime field hands. Hiring a cheaper younger slave might fit a yeoman widow's budget, but such a hire would not likely spare her from all heavy outdoor work. In contrast, widowers could more easily make up for the loss of their wives' labor, even though their gender role virtually banned them from housework. Widowers remarried more often than widows, perhaps because marriage threatened neither their legal personhood nor their property, while a remarried widow certainly lost the one and possibly the other. A widower also found it comparatively cheap to replace his wife's labor by hiring a housekeeper or coaxing a single kinswoman to live with him.[7]

Despite the difficulty of running a farm without adequate labor, Lucy Freeman managed. After four years of struggle, she happily reported that "by the present state of crops it will be seen that we never had a more flourishing year so fare." She noted in particular that "I have this year a verry fine crop of weat and corn and some oats," crops she could both sell and feed to her household.[8] Freeman also boasted that "I run two ploughs," which suggests that her field labor force had expanded by one if not two people, even though her children remained in school. . . .[9]

A decade later and hundreds of miles to the south, Caroline Burke struggled to make a living on an Alabama farm. Burke had moved herself, her son, two daughters, and two handfuls of slaves from South Carolina to Alabama in the early 1840s, hoping that her children would enjoy greater health than they had in Charleston. While the Burke children thrived in Alabama, Caroline Burke's slaves did not. Sickness repeatedly left Caroline with "not force enough to work" the farm. By 1854, eight slaves had died, leaving the Burkes with a slave man, a "sickly" woman, and seven children under ten years old, at least four of them orphans. Like Lucy Freeman, the Burkes had more slaves than labor. Caroline Burke took it "very hard" when her slave Isaac died in 1844, because her son John had hoped to plant a "heavy crop" that year. Without Isaac's labor, John Burke had to scale down his plans or see cotton rotting in the fields at harvest. Six years later, the slaves Margaret and Betsey died, "taken in the spring with a cough ... altho constantly attended by two Eminent Doctors." Caroline mourned them as links to her mother, from whom she had inherited them. But she also lamented their loss because of her daughters: as her son observed, "It will be a difficult matter for them to get the education that we once hoped to give them." What Margaret and Betsey had hoped for their now-orphaned children apparently never entered the Burkes' minds.[10]

With a slave force of infants and sickly or dying adults, Caroline Burke had to do a substantial amount of physical work herself. . . . [S]he grew vegetables and raised poultry, work that even planter ladies might do. In these tasks, Caroline likely drew on the labor of the slave children who were too young for serious field work. Gardening and poultry-raising were not simply make-work for ladies and children. Caroline's produce supplemented the diet of corn and pork that her son raised, reducing the need to buy food, and it also brought in cash. . . . The family dearly needed the money by that time since drought, the death of three horses, and renewed sickness among the slaves had blighted the previous year's cotton and corn crops.[11]

Widows who worked for wages faced a different set of challenges. This work could be less strenuous than farming, but underemployment was a constant threat. Caroline Burke's widowed daughter Rebecca Younge did "all that she can to assist herself and child, but it is only at times that she can get any work to do." (Better employment opportunities were yet another incentive for the Burke family to move closer to Selma.) Even educated widows had problems with underemployment. Boardinghouse keepers struggled to find enough lodgers, and teachers enough students.[12] They were able, however, to make good use of the sort of slaves they owned or could hire for reasonable terms: children and women trained in basic domestic work.[13] In a boardinghouse or school, slaves' domestic work was essential to the business. Without reliable laundry, cooking, and cleaning, a widow could not expect paying lodgers. In Catherine Lewis's Raleigh establishment, Martha and Alana did "all my washing and ironing," while Lucy "attend[ed] to the dining room." Their labor freed Lewis to attend to her five young children and her boarders. . . .[14] Domestic slaves also assisted school-teachers, particularly those with boarding students. Susan Hutchison hired female slaves to sweep the schoolroom, wash clothes, "scour the parlor," prepare dinner, and "get tea" for her students, mostly the daughters of wealthy North Carolina slaveholders. . . .[15]

The slaves whom Catherine Lewis owned and whom Susan Hutchison hired were the sort of slaves who kept Lucy Freeman and Caroline Burke struggling to make ends meet: the young, the elderly, and the infirm. In urban settings, even these slaves could help widows to earn their livings, while any slaves able to work helped both rural and urban widows maintain a claim to ladyhood. The presence of slaves gave widows some freedom to choose what they would and would not do. . . . Equally important, slaves' social and legal degradation served to elevate their white owners and hirers by comparison.[16]

Unlike most yeoman widows, planter widows had the means to be ladies in a far fuller sense of the word. Most obviously, planter widows did not do field or wage work. Instead, their efforts were more narrowly managerial, although most remained involved in the domestic production of food and clothes. Planters also had the financial means to pursue a high standard of gentility, domesticity, and benevolence, all of which were key to southern ladyhood after the Revolution.[17] The nineteenth century's proliferating print culture provided lady planters with explicit models to follow. . . . Virginia Cary wrote . . . about the vexations that plantation mistresses often experienced, [and] invented an . . . idealized model for their conduct. Her fictional widow, Emilia, cared for her slaves as she would for her own children, combining salutary firmness with infinite patience and sincere concern. As a result, Emilia owned "the most moral and correct set" of slaves "in the country." Critically important to this ideal lady planter was her utter unconcern with moneymaking. Totally ignoring the role of slaves in the household economy, Cary's epistolary narrator credited Emilia's daughter for relieving her widowed mother's "embarrassed" finances by teaching painting, as if Emilia's slaves did nothing but receive her bounty.[18]

Widowhood gave slaveholding women new opportunities to act on these benevolent ideals, without interference from their husbands. Most continued to act on Emilia-like motivations only sporadically. Natalie Sumter's efforts to catechize her slaves' children and Marion Deveaux's quest to hire a preacher for her plantation, for example, suggest that these South Carolina cotton planters felt a Christian obligation to their slaves. Planter widows also expressed some commitment to the ideal of "Lady Bountiful" when they distributed gifts and privileges. When Georgia widow Mary Downs visited her fields, she brought treats such as gingerbread for the slave children. . . . Natalie Sumter also gave little gifts from time to time. "Old soldier Tom" received some of her husband's old clothes, Old Venus a "new cotton flanel gown," and Priscilla a new frock and black apron. Once Sumter treated the old slaves to a "good dinner" of "soup & meat & baked apples & peaches," and she allowed her favorites to attend weddings on other plantations.[19] Many widowed planters gave some kind of Christmas treat to their slaves: extra food, whiskey, or a holiday from work. . . . Slaves often came to see such treats as rights, not privileges, but planters typically viewed them as testaments to their own enlightened stewardship.[20]

Some favors gave widows a way to micromanage slaves' family lives. Former slave Fannie Berry recalled that, on her Virginia plantation, "if you wanted to marry one on 'nother plantation, Miss Sarah Ann would fust fin' out" whether the other slave "was a good nigger." If so, Abbott "would try to buy him so husband an' wife could be together." While slaves often preferred "abroad" spouses, for those who wanted to live together, Abbott's practice provided a real incentive to get her approval.[21] Other favors, such as permitting slaves to grow and sell garden crops, chickens, and eggs, benefited planters as well as slaves. These schemes reduced slaveholders' expenses and gave slaves a reason to stay put and busy during their few leisure hours. . . .[22] Micromanaging slaves' marriages was one manifestation of widows' paternalism; linking gifts to productivity was another. During the 1851 cotton harvest, Martha Jackson concocted a variety of schemes to motivate her slaves. In one six-day picking "race," every slave who gathered over four hundred pounds received fifteen cents. Slaves who picked eight hundred pounds got forty cents, with additional incentives for picking over one thousand pounds. During this week, most of Jackson's field hands picked over one hundred pounds a day, while three picked well over 1,000 pounds apiece over six days. . . . Overall, Martha Jackson disbursed almost thirty dollars to her cotton pickers. That year, short-staple cotton earned slaveholders on average 9.8 cents per pound, while Jackson's slaves made roughly one-sixth to one-half of a penny for each pound they picked. Several of the slaves put their money toward dresses, which they bought at a local store on Jackson's account. As a result, a few of the slaves became indebted to Jackson, even as the cotton they picked helped pay off her debts.[23]

The irony of slaves' receiving as gifts or prizes what their labor paid for reappears in the theatricality with which some planters distributed provisions. On her plantation near Columbia, South Carolina, Natalie Sumter made a point of handing out provisions in person; she "went to the to see negro children . . . had the allowances given to all the Negros [and] spoke to them."[24] These events encapsulated key themes in the plantation drama as slaveholders saw it: slaves' dependence, owners' caretaking, and the vertical power relations that bound them. . . .[25]

Sumter's provisioning ritual and Jackson's incentive scheme resemble what Jeffrey R. Young calls corporate individualism. By holding each slave accountable for his or her own conduct, Sumter and Jackson implicitly recognized their slaves' moral agency. These planters also acknowledged differences among their slaves when they rewarded and punished according to each individual's merits or faults (real or imputed). At the same time, they measured slaves by a narrow compass, noticing only those acts that affected the welfare of the household (especially its financial welfare), as defined from the top down. In contrast, planters did not generally reward slaves for helping each other, and they punished slaves for fighting among themselves for the harm slaves did, not to each other, but to planters' interests.[26] The self-justifying and racist assumptions embedded in widowed planters' paternalism can be no surprise. Slaveholding wives who bothered with benevolence shared them, and widowhood brought no magical conversion to altruism—quite the contrary. Although money matters played scant role in prescriptions for the planter lady, widowhood implicated female planters in the financial aspects of slave management as profoundly as it did the more needy yeoman women, particularly in terms of weighing what slaves earned against what they cost in provisions and medical care. In most widows' papers, moments of apparent benevolence were rare counterpoints to the steady rhythm of cotton bales harvested, corn milled, payments received, and slaves beaten.[27]

Planter widows had many reasons to think self-interestedly about slaves' labor, provisions, and medical care.[28] Most obviously, they rarely encountered Africans and African Americans except as chattel, and their husbands' deaths only highlighted the slave's degraded status. When a slaveowner died, his slaves were appraised, sold on the block, divided by lot, or bequeathed. The very language of sales and divisions bespoke the fungible nature of human chattel: slaveowners would put slaves in their pockets or "put 'the niggeres in a hat' and draw for them." These sales and divisions privileged heirs' and creditors' interests well above any concern for preserving slaves' families.[29] Even being bequeathed by name to a new owner was a very ambiguous recognition of personhood.[30] None of this encouraged slaveholding widows to empathize with slaves. Finally, even planters' widows often discovered that "economy should now be the order" for their households.[31] With this in mind, widows could be quite aggressive in their efforts to increase profits by improving production, cutting operating expenses, or both. Their economies typically meant hard work and short rations for slaves, especially during the depressions following the Panics of 1819 and 1837.

Like their male counterparts, planter widows knew the importance of personally inspecting outbuildings, fences, and fields. Just two weeks after her husband's death in June 1840, Natalie Sumter toured the fields of his central South Carolina plantation. While there, she closely observed the cotton and corn, noting crop diseases and weather conditions. She also issued "tous les ordres" for the house and the hands, visited the sick and the slave children, and inspected the mill. During the next year, this transplanted French aristocrat[32] made at least thirty separate visits to fields and outbuildings. Most of them occurred during the fall of 1840 when she employed no overseer and needed to secure the cotton harvest. Many years later, former slaves remembered seeing other widows inspecting their fields. . . .[33]

Based on these inspections and on consultations with kinsmen or overseers, slaveholding widows decided where and how to employ their slaves. Most slaves spent most of their working hours in the fields, but planters had to apportion slave labor among cash crops, food crops, capital improvements, and maintenance. In the winter months, when there was little field work to do, planters might make slaves clear timber stands to prepare new fields and provide wood for buildings and fences.[34] Many tasks competed for attention during the busy summer and fall. . . .[35] Weather also forced planters to jigger work assignments. A summer rainstorm prompted Natalie Sumter "to stop the people from working," perhaps fearing they would get chilled or even struck by lightning.[36] When a storm damaged fences and buildings at Martha Jackson's Alabama plantation, she ordered that slaves stop working on her new house and devote their efforts to repairs and the cotton crop.[37]

Unlike the many widows who wanted for laborers, planter widows sometimes had to cope with surplus labor. Unwilling to leave slaves idle for long, these widows hired out, sold, or moved slaves from place to place. In the Upper South after the Revolution, these moves were often local. In 1787, for example, Susannah Wilcox of Buckingham County, Virginia, directed her overseer to reapportion the slaves between her two tobacco farms.[38] As the Upper South's tobacco economy stagnated and its expanding grain economy demanded fewer slaves, many planters sent slaves farther south and west. Virginia widows Jane Cocke and her daughter Mary Archer sent some slaves to Tennessee and Mississippi in the 1810s and 1820s. By the 1850s, North Carolina's Sarah Alston had divided her slaves between her home and her children's plantations in Texas, in part for want of "responsible" local hirers.[39] . . . . In the 1840s and 1850s, meanwhile, the nascent railroad industry provided some planters with an alternative use for their excess slave labor. Natalie Sumter, fellow South Carolinian Marion Deveaux, and Virginia's Sarah Ann Abbott each hired out male slaves to railway construction projects. For these planters, hiring out even a substantial number of their strongest men did not mean abandoning staple-crop agriculture; a year after sending hands to the railroad, for example, Deveaux made a very respectable eighty-plus bale cotton crop.[40]

Despite their willingness to move and hire out slaves, most slaveholding widows did not take the next step: hire out all their slaves and "be done with the trouble."[41] Instead, they focused their efforts on making slaves produce whatever cash crop their subregion supported. In Charleston, Eliza Flinn and her daughter Eliza Wilkins counted bushels of rice; in Virginia, Susannah Wilcox and Ruth Hairston numbered hogsheads of tobacco, while Georgia's Martha Jackson dreamed in bales of cotton. While these staples made many fortunes, a sudden decline in price could spell disaster. The plight of cotton farmers after the Panic of 1837 is a case in point. In 1836, when Henry Jackson bought Coakshay plantation, the average price of short-staple cotton was 16.8 cents. The year he died, it had fallen to just over eight cents, and it continued to drop, exceeding the 1840 price only in 1847. In those years, Martha Jackson's response was invariably to produce more cotton, even when local prices fell to three and four cents, as they did in 1846. Since she could not afford more hands, making more cotton meant working her slaves more intensively. During the 1840 harvest, her overseer advised her to send any "spare hands" in Georgia "to help to save the crop" in Alabama. Having none to spare, Jackson attempted to increase output in another way—changing her overseer's pay from a flat salary of $500 to a per-bale rate, thereby giving him a strong incentive to drive slaves even harder. Not incidentally, under this scheme he could only match his "enormously great" salary if he made the 100 bales of cotton that Jackson thought Cookshay should produce.[42] . . . .

At the same time that Martha Jackson was trying to get more work out of her slaves, she was also attempting to save money on their provisions. Shortly after her husband died, she decided that her overseer, Henry Smith, should butcher some old cows to feed the slaves instead of buying bacon, their usual meat. When Smith dissented, she debated making a slave churn the cows' milk into butter for sale. But because low cotton prices made large harvests seem especially urgent, she would not divert any hand who was "able to work" from the fields, "not even a small one." Jackson concluded that her house slave Patty—who had a "Rheumatic affection" in her shoulder—should add churning to her existing duties. Any remaining milk would go to the slave children, to "save something in meat, by lessening their allowance." Varying this plan slightly, in 1847 Jackson proposed that Fanny and Patty should both churn. By that point, Fanny was fifty-seven and Patty fifty-two, and both were deemed "old" in the estate appraisal of that year. They could churn without interfering with other moneymaking work, and as before, the slave children would consume the sweet milk and buttermilk and receive less meat. . . .[43]

Yet even in good financial times, slaves still suffered ill health and high infant mortality. Most planters had a very imperfect understanding of the relationship of overwork and poor diet to fetal death and infant mortality. In considering slaves' sickness, widows often spent less time thinking about causes than about the impact on the harvest. In a 1789 letter describing Susannah Wilcox's "prasent affares," overseer James Wills reported that while most of the hands had been sick with "this Enfluency coy they were now "all geting wel and fit for Bisness," namely cleaning the wheat crop.[44] Widows complained mightily about lost labor, but in fact they rarely excused the sick from all work. Martha Cocke cheerfully reported that while young Eliza "has been sick almost ever since she came up," she was "notwithstanding very useful for one of her size and I think in time will become very valuable."[45] . . . .*

Financial self-interest played a central role in widows' decisions about slaves, but nearly as important was the power these decisions had to reflect or distort their self-image as benevolent or hardheaded, prudent or venturesome. Widows' concern with these qualities, like their actual decisions, did not categorically distinguish them from male planters. To that extent, their gender roles and their versions of mastery overlapped. In other areas, however, particularly discipline and domestic housekeeping, male and widowed planters' gender roles diverged without making widows into either the idealized ladies or the hapless incompetents that some interpreters imagined any single slaveholding woman must be.

Notions of elite white womanhood encouraged slaveholding widows —especially planters—to invest considerable importance in genteel housekeeping despite the demands of farming. By the same token, they were far less invested than most white women in their ability to dominate their slaves physically. Indeed, most slaveholders would have said it was unseemly for ladies to beat slaves, while sexually coercing a slave—a common but taboo aspect of male slaveholders' domination—was absolutely unspeakable. Yet despite their rhetorical distance from violence, widows remained deeply implicated in the brutality at slavery's core. On the whole, the challenge of combining ladyhood with force constrained but did not eliminate widows' violence, and it certainly did not make their households more peaceable than male-headed households; a range of other people, from overseers to slave patrollers and judges, tended to be especially free with the whip where widows' slaves were concerned. Whatever problems

---

* A brief discussion of slaveowners' use of physicians to treat slaves has been omitted—ed.

combining mastery and ladyhood posed for widows, their bonds-people had little hope of experiencing a less brutal form of slavery.

For women in the masculine-identified work of farming and commerce, dressing tastefully, presiding over a clean and orderly house, and entertaining guests properly were key touchstones of femininity. In each of these areas, slave labor was indispensable, yet house slaves often could not or would not fulfill their owners' desires.[46] Natalie Sumter regularly complained that she could not go to bed when she wanted because "Priscilla was not to be found" or "priscilla kept me waiting." After Sally "forgot to get vegetables," Sumter brooded that "we had a miserable dinner," and she lamented that she did "not know what to do" when Caty reported that she could not cook.[47] Whereas Natalie Sumter admitted only to helplessness, Keziah Brevard acknowledged her anger: "A mess of a dinner this was—every thing had an odd taste—sometimes my anger rises in spite of all I can do—what is the use of so much property when I can't get one thing cooked fit to eat—such a dinner—I am mad when I think how mean my negroes serve me."[48] Brevard's anger owed much to the fact that eight guests had partaken of the ruined meal and witnessed her inability to offer seamless hospitality.

With rather less cause, widows could be equally resentful when a slave's sickness interfered with entertaining guests, visiting, and writing. Natalie Sumter felt flustered when slaves' ill health inconvenienced her guests. "My house is full & servants sick I dont know what to do—it is 12 oclock before they are all fixed for bed," she wrote—rare words of frustration from this usually phlegmatic diarist. Elizabeth Lee begrudged the days she spent nursing a slave with cholera, especially since she knew Marjory had contracted the disease after running away from her hire-master. "I have little patience," Lee sniped, "when I know she brought this trouble & expense on me by bad conduct."[49] . . . .

Being thwarted by slaves in these and other ways often prompted slaveholders to react violently, especially if they suspected slaves were being deliberately slow or infuriating. For slaveholding men, resorting to force seemed natural, routine, even de rigueur. For slaveholding women, violence was significantly more complicated, and widowhood only made it more so. On the one hand, self-interest dictated that widows not maim their valuable, income-producing property, whether they owned it or held it only for life. In addition, antebellum proslavery writers told them that the peculiar institution hinged not on force but on the organic hierarchy that bound master and servant. Equally important, the arbiters of ladyhood rarely approved of female violence. Virginia Cary's *Letters on Female Character*, for instance, told readers to shrink from the sight of a young lady whipping a slave.

On the other hand, as Cary herself admitted, "the trials incident to domestic life" provoked many a woman to violence.[50] Some historians have argued that this tendency to lash out in anger illustrates that slaveholding women could not personally enforce the slaveholding regime. Historian Drew Gilpin Faust reasons that "rationalized, systematic, autonomous, and instrumental use of violence belonged to men."[51] Former slaves often bore out the first part of this analysis; they recalled women attacking domestic slaves and children with pokers, irons, brooms, and whatever else came handy. Also supporting the claim, some slaves described female slaveholders as too compassionate or too weak to beat slaves into submission.[52]

Even though violence played little or no role in their gender prescriptions, slaveholding women inhabited a world rife with violence and acted accordingly. . . . In a world where mothers expected whippings to teach a four-year-old not to cry (and where wives could count themselves lucky if their husbands did not beat them), we should not be surprised that slaveholding widows used force deliberately and instrumentally against slaves. . . . [Catherine Lewis wrote] "I do not think Leah [a slave] improves . . . I have had her to switch twice since I have been here and intend since I have commenced to conquer her.". . . .[53]

Numerous slaveholding widows delegated punishment to others, especially overseers, kinsmen, and agents of the state. Few bothered, however, to record what these agents did on their behalf. In an 1844 letter, Vincent Pierson made a rare reference to force on Martha Jackson's Alabama plantation, writing "Hester is a fine girl for worke I hav not had to strike her a lick this yeare."[54] Hester had presumably been less fortunate in previous years, and slaves at Cookshay plantation likely felt the lash as well. This sort of discipline was so routine that Pierson felt no need to seek Jackson's approval and she no need to inquire. The overseer on Mary Downs's Georgia plantation "sho' was mean to de slaves." According to former slave Dosia Harris, "Sometimes it seemed lak he jus' beat on 'em to hear 'em holler." Downs witnessed this brutality (or its effects) during her daily visits to the plantation, but she did not restrain him. Thanks to this division of labor, the slave children learned to associate the overseer with whippings, and Downs with the treats she brought them, even though she both sponsored and benefited from his violence. . . . While rural planters could turn to overseers for this violence at a remove, urban slaveholders had easier recourse to agents of the state. Charleston's Mary Motte sent "little Philander" to the workhouse in Charleston at least four times between 1838 and 1842. . . . Ex-slaves themselves recalled seeing "plenty" of slaves "whipped over at the jail."[55]

. . . . [W]hile many whites considered violence unfeminine, few proscribed it, and if ex-slaves' memories are any indication, some widows used violence much like men. North Carolinian Clara Cotton McCoy maintained that her widowed owner "handled de niggers same as a man." . . . . Some slaveholding women even wielded the whip despite the presence of white men competent for the work. Jerry Hill recalled a Spartanburg, South Carolina, woman who carried a bullwhip while touring her brother's fields and used it on "any slave she thought needed it." These examples . . . come from the Civil War years, when the extraordinary military mobilization reduced the numbers of white men available for domestic policing. During this period, slaveholding widows had the greatest responsibility for personally maintaining control over slaves by force and the least chance of success. In peacetime, more widows had the luxury of deploying systematic violence at a remove.[56]

Slaveholding widows' efforts to distance themselves from violence reflected their desire to wed ladyhood and mastery. In 1799, Lucy Thornton of Virginia witnessed her drunken overseer brutally beating one of her slaves. The beating horrified Thornton; "Indeed I feared it might be attended with fatal consequences as the Wounds were on his head and the blood gushed out of his eyes, attended with great swelling." Yet as she related the event to a kinswoman, the story shifted from a tale of a slave's near death into one of her own financial loss and outraged sensibilities. Describing the slave's gruesome injuries quickly gave way to the cheerful news that he recovered "with only the loss of three or four days work." Once the slave could work, Thornton apparently could not imagine that he suffered any lingering ill effects. For herself, however, the wounds of witness lingered. "My apprehensions are so great," she wrote, "that my life is a burden to me." . . . . And despite her expressions of fear and powerlessness, Thornton acted very much like a male master in making herself the center of this drama while displacing the moral responsibility for her agent's abuses onto his shoulders.[57]

In a very different time and place, Keziah Brevard similarly danced around her own power over her slaves. In September 1860 she wrote, "I wish to be kind to my negroes—but I receive little but impudence from Rosanna & Sylvia—it is a truth if I am compelled to speak harshly to them—after bearing every thing from them I get impudence—Oh my God give me fortitude to do what is right to these then give me firmness to go no farther."[58] In praying for "fortitude," Brevard sought not the courage to use violence but the "firmness" to control it. Her concern that she might lose control tends to bear out Drew Faust's conclusions about women's tendency toward frenzied rather than instrumental violence. Yet Brevard's musings illustrate that neither piety nor ladyhood barred women from calculating how best to use force. And when calculation gave way to rage, they could pray for more restraint in the future while blaming the objects of their wrath for provoking them in the first place. Whether any slaveholders really tried to moderate their violence or not, their claims of attempting restraint helped preserve the myth of Christian stewardship. When widows deferred violence to men, they also protected their self-image as gentlewomen without, critically, sacrificing violence as a tool of social control. When they delegated to men whom they considered their social inferiors, such as overseers, it worked a deeper magic: reinforcing class distinctions. Just as a widow might take pride in rebuking an overseer for his mingy reluctance to bring in a doctor, delegating whippings to an overseer or jailer confirmed her refinement and his coarseness.

Keziah Brevard's reflections reveal a further factor that diminished the importance of widows' capacity for systematic violence: the possibility of sale. After dwelling on her slaves' misbehavior and its effects on her own temper, she wrote, "At my death it is my solemn desire that Tama-Sylvia-Mack-Maria & Rosanna be sold—I cannot think of imposing such servants on any one of my heirs."[59] Slaveholding widows understood the power of the slave market: it served as a deterrent, and if that failed, it converted slaves into cash and sent a potent lesson to the remaining slaves.[60] In the fall of 1849, for example, Charleston planter Eliza Wilkins resorted to the market to deal with her slave Billy. As her brother observed, "She had borne his insolence and neglect of duty a long time, but at length they became intolerable, and he was sold for $600." This sale's conditions demonstrated that Wilkins intended not only to be quit of Billy but to punish him as well: she "insisted" that the buyer take Billy "out of the State." Following Walter Johnson's analysis of the slave market, we might speculate that Billy had been angling to be sold, but the condition of being taken outside of South Carolina suggests Wilkins had the final word. If nothing else, transportation beyond the state symbolically linked this sale with the punishment commonly meted out to alleged rebels.[61]

While the most important weapons in slaveholding men's arsenal of domination—violence and the marketplace—were more or less compatible with ladyhood, a third, sexual coercion, absolutely was not. Yet this vexed subject did not vanish in widowhood. On the one hand, vengeful widows sometimes seized the opportunity to sell off their husbands' former concubines or rape victims. . . . On the other hand, slave men sometimes became newly vulnerable to sexual predation. While legal proceedings sometimes created highly public knowledge of sexual liaisons between white women and black men, these cases usually involved socially marginal women charged with bastardy and fornication. In contrast, all but total silence greeted elite women's sexual exploitation of black men. Information about the practice is thus fragmentary at best, and it permits only speculative conclusions about patterns of interracial sex among slaveholding widows. Anecdotal testimony gathered by the American Freedmen's Inquiry Commission during the Civil War suggests that some slaveholding women—married, single, and widowed—sexually coerced enslaved men. One former slave related that his owner " 'ordered him to sleep with her . . . regularly' " after she had been widowed for almost a year. Since many slaveholding widows never remarried and spent at least some of their widowhoods in households without other adult whites around, slave men's vulnerability to sexual exploitation likely increased after slaveholding husbands died.[62] With their large households, planter widows had greater opportunities for privacy than yeoman widows, and they were more likely to have male domestics, whose appearance and manners many whites preferred to field hands'. Planters also had the security of knowing their social status afforded some protection against gossip and prosecution, notwithstanding the considerable risk of bearing an illegitimate, mixed-race child.[63] In contrast, while yeoman widows had less privacy and less protection against public outrage, their small households often fostered a certain familiarity between owners and slaves. For the poorest widows, meanwhile, forming a relationship with another owner's slave (or a free black man) could provide labor as well as sexual companionship. Already on the fringes of survival and respectability, these women had relatively little to lose and perhaps a good deal to gain from such a connection.[64] Regardless, if slaveholding widows seized every opportunity for sex with male slaves—and thus did so far more often than the surviving evidence can prove—the practice still meant something rather different from slaveholding men's sex with slave women. Most obviously, slaveholding women could neither boast of their conquests nor view them as rites of passage. For slaveholding men and boys, sex with slaves was simultaneously illicit and accepted; it confirmed essential qualities of white manhood, including physical vigor and patriarchal rights over women. In contrast, both interracial sex and female sexual aggression jarred violently with normative understandings of white womanhood. Even so, however, both found expression during some widowhoods in addition to the more commonplace and—to whites— more acceptable expressions of power inherent in whipping and selling slaves.[65]

Understanding the potential—and pitfalls—of combining ladyhood with mastery involves considering the matter from slaves' point of view. In the eyes of slaves as well as whites, slaveholding widows' authority did not look exactly like white men's, and to the extent that slaves shared the belief in white women's weakness, they likely disrespected widows' orders more than white men's. However, as slaves

185

well knew, their bondage depended not on any individual slaveholder's forcefulness but on the collective power of the state and the white population. Moreover, a slaveholding husband's death often divided slaves' communities and families and subjected them to more work on smaller rations. As a result, while slaves routinely undermined widows' mastery, they typically behaved much as they did in male-headed households, and many found themselves in no position to ratchet up their resistance when a widow took over.

The picture of slaves' conduct on widows' farms and plantations closely resembles that painted by historians of slave resistance throughout the United States. Especially common forms of willful disobedience were stealing and malingering. Natalie Sumter eventually figured out, for example, that her slaves were leaving the cow house open at night "so they could climb in the stable & steal the Horses corn[.]" She also learned "that my house doors were left open every night" so her enslaved domestics could slip out while she slept.[66] Sumter's house slaves Delia and Priscilla were skilled at another form of subversion: working slowly and misunderstanding orders to provide as much annoyance as service. In a classic example, Sumter instructed Delia "not to let Priscilla wake me up and to tell Hampton I would not go out." But Delia said nothing until "the carriage was at the door & Priscilla woke me up—so I could not go to sleep again." . . . .[67]

Another popular but riskier form of protest was running away. When Elizabeth Lee's slave Marjory ran away from her hire-master, she remained at liberty for three weeks, which perhaps made her bout of cholera seem worth the trouble. Sometimes slaves ran not just to escape but to strike back at their owners. When Elizabeth Cromwell's Tom ran away from her North Carolina farm in 1813, he remained in the neighborhood, killing her "cattle, hogs, sheep, &c." Further south, Natalie Sumter's household witnessed a range of runaway attempts. One August night, Sumter reported that "it is 11 o'clock & I cannot go to bed every body is looking for prescilla." Not absent for long, Priscilla disappeared again in mid-September, and again Sumter complained that she "could not get to bed early" because her slave "was not to be found." . . . .[68]

Why slaves ran away is relatively easy to deduce. Slaves ran from widows for the same reasons that they did from men: to avoid work or punishment, visit distant relatives or friends, or, most ambitiously, reach freedom. Whether slaves ran from widows with special frequency is far more difficult to determine . . . .

In addition to protesting and trying to escape bondage, slaves occasionally struck directly at their oppressors. Historian Philip Schwarz argues that widows and single white women looked particularly vulnerable to slaves, yet widows rarely expressed any fear of being attacked. Of course, the rare insurrection or conspiracy scare left them—as well as other whites—feeling panicky, and their level of alarm also increased markedly just before and during the Civil War. In more ordinary times, however, slaveholding widows generally saw unruliness or stupidity rather than vengefulness when they looked at their slaves and thus lived among them with great complacence. And widows had reason to feel safe because the state and the white population at large devoted considerable resources to keeping slaves in check.[69]

During the early nineteenth century, judges, legislators, sheriffs, slave patrols, and militias all worked to hem in slaves. Their control was far from perfect, but they helped give real meaning to the name of slave. In addition to defining slaveholders' legal rights and responsibilities, the state assisted in day-to-day enforcement. Sheriffs and jailors helped discipline slaves, and they also assisted in capturing runaways. When Eliza Ruffin's slave Nelson absconded, the Goochland County, Virginia, sheriff caught, jailed, and then returned him to her plantation.[70] Intervening more decisively in the owner-slave relationship, the state occasionally prosecuted slaves for crimes. As these examples suggest, beyond the household, upholding slavery was largely a white man's job. In most jurisdictions, all owners of "settled plantations"—male and female—had to contribute to the "security of that district where their interests lie," but only men served on the slave patrol and held offices with the responsibility for apprehending and prosecuting slave criminals.[71] The all-male composition of the South's police power reinforced the assumption that women would be lax in enforcing slavery, a logic no less compelling for its circularity. That assumption created an incentive to intervene in widows' slave management, but it also made it easy for widows to rely on the state's coercive power. If widows feared to act firmly, or simply thought it incompatible with their gender role, judges, slave patrollers, sheriffs, and others had every reason to suspect, convict, and harshly punish slaves for them. Such appears to have been the pattern in eighteenth-century Virginia, where slaves owned by women were disproportionately likely to be prosecuted, convicted, and sentenced to death.[72] . . . . Because upholding slavery was a collective as well as an individual duty, being owned or managed by a woman did not mean a less onerous bondage for slaves. Instead, as Nancy Williams recalled, it often brought them "real trouble."[73]

Many factors prevented slaveholding widows from realizing the idealized mastery of novels and advice manuals, and their ability even to approximate it varied over time. At the beginning of widowhood, many women felt unsure of themselves or were simply too grief-stricken to think much about mastery. Some actively denied their authority even as they began to wield it. When widows first took farm and plantation affairs into their own hands, they regularly claimed that they were only acting on their husbands' wishes. In recording one of her first decisions after her husband's death, Natalie Sumter deftly camouflaged her agency. In her diary, she wrote that she demoted Dennis from his position as slave driver because "he desobeyed us having made the Negros work in the Heat of the day though I had told him it was his master's last order's they should not work when it was hot." By writing "us," Sumter suggested that the plantation's management remained essentially unchanged, that there was still a "we" in charge when in fact there was only her. Equally, by defining the slaves' midday rest period as "his master's last order," she elided the fact that the instruction Dennis had ignored actually had come from her mouth.[74]

Over time, widows began taking credit and dispensing blame, punishment, and favors much like any slaveholding man. When several of Natalie Sumter's slaves got into a fight a year after her husband's death, she reacted much like Ada Bacot, who expected to rein in some disobedient slaves "without much trouble." After the fracas, Sumter sent for a doctor to tend to James, who "got his head broke by Anna." She did not, however, send for anyone to discipline the brawlers. She assumed that she "soon could put them to rights," and instead of castigating herself for failing to suppress the fight, she blamed the slaves.[75] Relatedly, experienced widows rarely gave slaves due credit for good outcomes, appropriating their labor verbally as well as materially. When Lucy Freeman bragged that "I run two ploughs," she wasted no ink on the obvious: slaves had done some or more likely all of the work. Dolly Burge similarly elided enslaved workers from her diary: "laid by all of the corn looks very well but had a bad time getting a stand," and, later, "got a bag of cotton out." At one level, this ellipsis was utterly typical: slaveholding men regularly wrote as if they themselves had done the slaves' plowing, planting, and picking, while their wives took credit for slaves' sewing, gardening, and scrubbing. At another level, widows' usage was distinctive; unlike other women, they appropriated both domestic and field labor, expressing a sense of possession over the entire slaveholding household.[76]

However comfortable they became with juggling mastery and ladyhood, widows still struggled with the economics of slavery, sometimes losing from year to year. The problem was particularly acute early in widowhood. . . . These financial shortcomings were not, however, a distinctively feminine failure. Even in flush times, male slaveholders left estates encumbered with debts, and many teetered on the brink of ruin at one point or another. Women widowed during an economic contraction could hardly expect to escape the foreclosures and bankruptcies that snared so many male slaveholders.[77] When not undone by their husbands' debts, the business cycle, and other factors equally beyond their control, determined widows could make their economizing pay. Lucy Freeman's ability to run two plows by no means made her rich, but it represented a step toward financial security and meant she could keep her children in school. At the other end of the scale was South Carolina's Keziah Brevard. In 1850, she managed two farms valued at $22,500 on which 180 slaves produced 190 bales of cotton, as well as substantial amounts of corn, oats, hay, sweet potatoes, and domestic manufactures. . . .[78]

As slave managers, widows were not fully successful masters, but neither were they benevolent ladies or hapless incompetents. Gender did not guarantee that a widow would fail any more than it ensured her kindness. Gender did, however, profoundly shape how widows responded to the endless struggle to master slaves. Widows assessed their mastery in terms of their entire households, but they judged themselves as women through their domestic management. . . . For men, however, their manhood and their mastery were typically one and the same. Drew Faust suggests that South Carolina planter, senator, and governor James Henry Hammond spent his life trying to become the ideal southern master—a man of implacable will who extracted obedience from subordinates and respect from peers. Hammond's ambition exceeded other men's in intensity but not in substance, and it was a specifically male ambition. Despite a lifetime of effort, Hammond himself fell short of his goal, learning instead to cultivate what Faust calls "the art of the possible." Where Hammond failed, no slaveholding woman could reasonably hope to succeed. But then slaveholding women never expected to achieve the autonomy and power that Hammond considered the essence of southern manhood. Raised to place the interests of their families above their own, slaveholding women grew up knowing that they did not determine their own destinies. While they *wanted* to get their way and often acted petulantly, or worse, when they did not, they never expected to dominate their own little corners of the universe.[79] As a result, when slaveholding women added the duties of master to those of mistress, they did not assume the same psychological burdens that white masculinity entailed. They more readily eschewed the impossible goal of perfect mastery for the reachable compromises—the "art of the possible"—of fictive mastery.[80]

NOTES

1 Christine Jacobson Carter, *The Diary of Dolly Lunt Burge*, 1848–1879 (Athens, Ga., 1997), 95–97.

2 Martha Richardson to James Proctor Screven, April 16, 1817, Arnold and Screven Family Papers (ASFP), Southern Historical Collection, University of North Carolina (SHC).

3 The debate over slaveholders' capitalist or paternalist (or feudal), pro-market or antimarket orientation has raged for years. See, for example, Genovese, *Roll, Jordan, Roll: The World the Slaveholders Made* (New York, 1974). . . . Jeffrey Robert Young has recently argued that the two sides merge when we appreciate how deeply market culture shaped the South and, in particular, helped produce paternalistic proslavery in the antebellum South. Young, *Domesticating Slavery: The Master Class in Georgia and South Carolina* (Chapel Hill, 1999), 3–15.

4 Charles Perdue, et al., *Weevils in the Wheat: Interviews with Virginia Ex-Slaves* (Charlottesville, 1976) [hereafter Weevils], 317–18; Betty Wood, *Gender, Race, and Rank in a Revolutionary Age: The Georgia Lowcountry, 1750–1820* (Athens, Ga., 2000), 34–36.

5 Joseph Jackson to Martha Jackson, September 22, 1840; . . . Jackson and Prince Family Papers, SHC (JPFP). I am using "yeoman" to indicate widows who did not have enough to make their own work primarily managerial. . . .

6 Lucy Freeman to Jessie Vaughan, December 26, 1837, Jessie Vaughan Papers, Duke University (DU); Stephanie McCurry, *Masters of Small Worlds: Yeoman Households, Gender Relations, and the Political Culture of the Antebellum South Carolina Low Country* (New York, 1995), 48, 62, 78–85.

7 Felix Gilbert to Sarah Hillhouse, various dates, Alexander Hillhouse Family Papers, SHC (AHFP); Zaccheus Collins to Elizabeth Lee, May 16, 1800, Richard Bland Lee Papers, Virginia Historical Society (VHS). . . .

8 Lucy Freeman to Jessie Vaughan, June 20, 1839, Jessie Vaughan Papers (DU); . . . .

9 Lucy Freeman to Jessie Vaughan, December 26, 1837. . . .

10 Caroline Burke to William Gilliland, February 3, 1843, March 10, 1844, July 15, 1848, February 8, 1854, Rebecca Younge to William Gilliland, January 10, 1848, John Prior Burke to William Gilliland, March 10, 1844, July 29 and November 28, 1850, October 1853, William Gilliland Papers, Duke University (WGP); Jane H. Pease and William Henry Pease, *A Family of Women: The Carolina Petigrus in Peace and War* (Chapel Hill, 1999), 32. . . .

11 Caroline Burke to William Gilliland, March 2, 1854, WGP.

12 Ibid.

13 Domestic slaves were usually girls too young for full-time field work. Unless they were highly skilled, domestics hired at low rates. Marli Frances Weiner, *Mistresses and Slaves: Plantation Women in South Carolina, 1830–80* (Urbana, Ill., 1997), chapter 1.

14 Catherine Lewis to Emma Speight, October 16, 1845, November 24, 1847, John Francis Speight Family Papers, SHC (JFSP).

15 Susan Davis Nye Hutchison Diary, North Carolina Department of Archives and History, [March] 25, July 25, and November 6, 1840. . . .

16 Carole Shammas, "Black Women's Work and the Evolution of a Plantation Society in Virginia," *Labor History* 26 (1985), 5–28; Suzanne Lebsock, *The Free Women of Petersburg: Status and Culture in a Southern Town, 1784–1860* (New York, 1984), 127–29; McCurry, *Masters of Small Worlds*, chapter 2; Kathleen M. Brown, *Good Wives, Nasty Wenches, and Anxious Patriarchs: Gender, Race, and Power in Colonial Virginia* (Chapel Hill, 1996), chapter 4; J. William Harris, *Plain Folk and Gentry in a Slave Society: White Liberty and Black Slavery in*

Augusta's Hinterlands (Middletown, Conn., 1985), 65–66, 75; Walter Johnson, *Soul by Soul: Life Inside the Antebellum Slave Market* (Cambridge, Mass., 1999), 88–92, 101–2.

17 Weiner, *Mistresses and Slaves*, 23–7 I; Cynthia A. Kierner, *Beyond the Household: Women's Place in the Early South, 1700–1835* (Ithaca, NY, 1998), 139–79; Elizabeth Fox-Genovese, *Within the Plantation Household: Black and White Women of the Old South* (Chapel Hill, 1988), 196–97; Anne Firor Scott, *The Southern Lady: From Pedestal to Politics, 1830–1930* (Chicago, 1970), 3–21.

18 .... Cary, *Letters on Female Character, Addressed to a Young Lady, on the Death of Her Mother* (Richmond, 1828), 28–29, 30–33, 79.

19 Natalie DeLage Sumter Diary, SCH (NDSD), July 12, July 22, August 11, October 4, December 19, December 24, and December 26, 1840; John B. Moore to Rev. J. V. Welch, September 16, 1858, RMDP; Rawick, *American Slave*, 12(2):108–9; "Daily Expenditures for 1842," Plantation Accounts, 1841–42, JPFP.

20 Rawick, *American Slave*, 2(1): 190, 12(2):132, 12(1):320; Joseph Jackson to Sarah Jackson, January I, 1847. ...

21 *Weevils*, 40; Vincent Pierson to Martha Jackson, June 7, 1845, JPFP; Ada W. Bacot September 8, 1862, Ada W. Bacot Papers. ...

22 Carter, *Diary of Dolly Lunt Burge*, 99; Plantation Day Book, November 1851, JPFP; Morgan, Slave Counterpoint, 358–65; Leslie A. Schwalm, *A Hard Fight for We: Women's Transition from Slavery to Freedom in South Carolina* (Urbana, 1997), 14, 25, 60–63.

23 Plantation Day Book, September 8 to November 5, 1851, JPFP. ...

24 NDSD, July 4, 1840; Agnes Hairston to Ruth Hairston, February 28, 1844, Wilson and Hairston Family Papers, SHC (WHFP); Sterling Adams to Ruth Hairston, June 9, 1854, WHFP; John Berkeley Grimball Diary, SHC (JBGD), August 17, 1834; Rawick, *American Slave*, 12(1):206, 14: 105.

25 NDSD, Jay 4, 1840; Genovese, *Roll, Jordan, Roll*, 545; Faust, *James Henry Hammond and the Old South: A Design for Mastery* (Baton Rouge, 1982), 99–104. *Roll, Jordan, Roll* has many critics, but it is still a core text on paternalism. For more recent works, see Young, *Domesticating Slavery*; ....

26 Young, *Domesticating Slavery*, 8–11.

27 See, for example, NDSD, July 4, July 10–15, July 18, August 6 ... 1840. ...

28 .... For widows' purchases of provisions and other plantation expenses, see Account of Paulina Legrand with Isaac Read and Co., September 1, 1819, Henry Carrington Papers, VHS. ...

29 *Weevils*, 42; Codicil to the Will of Mary Motte, May 17, 1837, Jacob Rhett Motte Papers. ...

30 Marriage Settlement between Martha J. R. Jackson and Hezekiah Erwin, JPFP; Wills of Tristim Skinner, 1853 and 1857, Skinner Family Papers; Ann Patton Malone, *Sweet Chariot: Slave Family and Household Structure in Nineteenth-Century Louisiana* (Chapel Hill, 1992), 88–89, 211–16; Thomas D. Morris, *Southern Slavery and the Law, 1618–1860* (Chapel Hill, 1996), 99–101.

31 Joseph Jackson to Martha Jackson, September 22, 1840; Henry Rootes Jackson to Sarah Jackson, n.d. (probably 1842), January 7 and June 10, 1842; Joseph Jackson to Martha Jackson, May 6, 1842, JPFP.

32 ... the royalist DeLage family fled during the French Revolution, at which point young Natalie came to the United States, where she met Thomas Sumter.

33 NDSD, July 1–4, July 10–15, July 18, July 25, August 6 ....; Rawick, *American Slave*, 12(2): 108, 15(2):67; Pease and Pease, *Family of Women*, 34.

34 Linnaeus Bolling to William Acres, November 31, 1805, Hubard Family Papers, SCH (HFP).
35 Paulina Legrand to William Huntington, September 19, 1839, William Huntington Papers, VHS (WHP).
36 NDSD, July 6, 1840, February 23, 1841. . . .
37 Vincent Pierson to Martha Jackson, January 21, June 19, August 6, and December 24, 1844, JPFP. . . .
38 James Wills to Susannah Wilcox, December 28, [1787], HFP.
39 Will of Mary Chastain Archer, May 28, 1841, Richard T. Archer to Capt. James Hobson, June 16, 1835, AFP; Archibald Alston to Sarah Alston, June 24, 1853, Will of Sarah Alston, 1858, Archibald Davis Alston Papers.
40 NDSD, August 18, 1840; Abraham Van Buren to Marion Deveaux, January 20, 1856, Account of Ingraham and Webb, March 24, 1857, RMDP; *Weevils*, 37, 42; Rawick, *American Slave*, 15(2):129, 14(1):77–78, 308, 3(4):148, 12(2):107–8;. . . .
41 Martha Richardson to James Proctor Screven, April 16, 1817, ASFP. For an exception, see accounts of slave hire, 1819–1820, William Patterson Smith Papers.
42 JBGD; HFP; WHEP; Henry Smith to Henry Jackson, March 10 and May 3, 1840, Henry Smith to Martha Jackson, August 23, 1840, Martha Jackson to [James Addison Cobb], n.d., Martha Jackson to Sarah Jackson, October 26, 1848, JPFP; William W. Freehling, *Prelude to Civil War: The Nullification Crisis in South Carolina* (New York, 1966), appendix A, table I.
43 Henry Smith to Martha Jackson, July 11, 1840; Martha Jackson to Henry Smith, October 26, 1840; overseer's contract, 1847; and Estate Appraisal, 1847, JPFP.
44 James Wills to Susannah Wilcox, December 22, 1789, Nathan Wells to Susan Hubard, December 16, 1814, HFP; Caroline Burke to William Gilliland, March 10, 1844, WGP; Account Book, 1847–1855, March 21, 1853, Mary G. Franklin Papers.
45 Martha Cocke to Caroline Cocke, November 14, 1813, CFP.
46 For slaveholding women's ideas of domesticity, see Weiner, *Mistresses and Slaves*, chapter 3; Kierner, *Beyond the Household*, chapter 5.
47 NDSD, July 25, August 7, August 17, August 27, September 15, October 6, October 8, November 11, and December 6, 1840, January 23 and February 4, 1841; Moore, *Plantation Mistress*, 41, 75–76, 83, 95.
48 Keziah Goodwyn Hopkins Brevard Diary, March 28, 1861.
49 NDSD, September 7, September 12–13, October 16, November 19, and December 6, 1840, February 4, 1841; Elizabeth Lee to Anna Washington, September 25, [1832 or 1835], Richard Bland Lee Papers.
50 Cary, *Letters on Female Character*, 173; Martha Richardson to James Proctor Screven, February 25, 1821, ASFP.
51 Faust, *Mothers of Invention: Women of the Slaveholding South in the American Civil War* (Chapel Hill, 1996), 63, see also 54, 56, 62–65; Faust, "Trying to Do a Man's Business: Gender, Violence, and Slave Management in Civil War Texas," *Gender History* 4 (Summer 1992), 197–214. Faust argues that James Henry Hammond concluded that violence signified a loss of control. Faust, *James Henry Hammond*, 72–73, 89–91, 99–104. . . .
52 *Weevils*, 16, 194–95, 284, 309–10; Rawick, *American Slave*, 15: 170, 193, 199, 300–1, 2(1):11; Wood, *Gender, Race, and Rank*, 42.
53 Catherine Lewis to Emma Lewis, August 9, 1838, JFSP.
54 Vincent Pierson to Martha Jackson, May 28, 1844, JPFP. Born in 1828, Hester

had her first child in 1847 and her second in 1851. When Henry Jackson's estate was divided among his four heirs in 1847, Hester was assigned to Martha Jackson's elder daughter.

55 Rawick, *American Slave*, 3(4):158, 12(2):108, 15(2):6; *Weevils*, 102; Account Book, 1838–42, Jacob Rhett Motte Papers; Plantation Account Book-Estate of Adam Alexander, AHFP; Samuel Hairston to sheriff, February 7, 1820, W. Beavers to Mrs. R. Wilson [Ruth Hairston], February 26, 1816, WHFP; JBGD, May 6, 1840; Sarah Cobb to Sarah Jackson, May 6, 1847, JPFP; Mary Steele to Mary Ferrand, October 18, 1835, JSP; Payment for jailing and boarding a slave, June 10, 1818, William Patterson Smith Papers; William Akers's receipt, August 14, 1815, HFP.

56 *Weevils*, 16, 190, 73–75; Rawick, *American Slave*, 2(2):290, 15: 67, 169–70, 193, 300, 2(1):157, 12(2):108, 130, 92–93;. . . .

57 Lucy Thornton to [Mrs. Rootes], November 25, 1799, JPFP; Faust, *James Henry Hammond*, 100; Brown, *Good Wives*, 327, 350–61.

58 Keziah Goodwyn Hopkins Brevard Diary, September 18, 1860.

59 Ibid.

60 Holding slaves for life debarred some widows from this form of punishment, but the possibility of hiring out enabled them too to hold the prospect of separation from kin over a slave's head.

61 JBGD, September 9, 1849. Johnson argues that white women did not go the slave pens in New Orleans, for example, to buy and sell slaves, but white women did deal directly with slave traders, buyers, and sellers in other locations. Johnson, *Soul by Soul*, 100, 92–102 passim, 164, 172–88; Rawick, *American Slave*, 12 (2):131.

62 Martha Hodes, *White Women, Black Men: Illicit Sex in the Nineteenth-Century South* (New Haven, 1997); Nell Painter, *Soul Murder and Slavery* (Waco, Tex., 1995) . . . .; Diane Miller Sommerville, "Rape, Race, and Castration in Slave Law in the Colonial and Early South" in *The Devil's Lane: Sex and Race in the Early South*, ed., by Catherine Clinton and Michelle Gillespie (New York, 1998); . . . Faust, *Mothers of Invention*, 56–62; Weiner, *Mistresses and Slaves*, 135–37, 166–70; Joshua D. Rothman, *Notorious in the Neighborhood: Sex and Families across the Color Line in Virginia, 1787–1861* (Chapel Hill, 2003). . . .

63 While early eighteenth-century planters tended to regard all white women as naturally lustful, by the mid-nineteenth century, white southern men usually believed that elite white women were free from improper sexual desire. . . .

64 Victoria E. Bynum, *Unruly Women: The Politics of Social and Sexual Control in the Old South* (Chapel Hill, 1992), 88–93.

65 On quasi-caste differences between domestics and field hands, see, for example, Michael A. Gomez, *Exchanging Our County Marks: The Transformation of African Identity in the Colonial and Antebellum South* (Chapel Hill, 1998), 219–43; Schwalm, *Hard Fight for We*, 31, 34–37.

66 NDSD, September 1, 1840.

67 NDSD, August 7, August 17, October 6 . . .; James C. Scott, *Domination and the Arts of Resistance: Hidden Transcripts* (New Haven, 1990), 133, 187–201.

68 Elizabeth Lee to Anna Washington, September 25, [1833], Richard Bland Lee Papers;. . . .

69 Philip J. Schwarz, *Twice Condemned: Slaves and the Criminal Laws of Virginia, 1705–1865* (Baton Rouge, 1998), 92–114, 160–62, 164, 209–14, 282–83, 291–93, 297; . . . Faust notes that some Confederate women preferred a black man's protection to no male help at all (*Mothers of Invention*, 62).

70 Receipt of payment to William Bolling, January 24, 1830. . . .

71 John Cushing, ed., *The First Laws of the State of South Carolina*, 2 vols. (Wilmington, Del., 1981), 1:205; Cushing, *The First Laws of Georgia*, 2 vols., (Wilmington, Del., 1984), I:119.

72 Brown, *Good Wives*, 290. . . .

73 *Weevils*, 317–18.

74 NDSD, July 1, 1840; Will of John Steele, Book G, Rowan County, NCDAH.

75 NDSD, June 16, 1841; Ada W. Bacot Diary, February 1, 1861, Ada W. Bacot Papers.

76 Lucy Freeman to Jessie Vaughan, June 20, 1839, Jessie Vaughan Papers; Carter, *Diary of Dolly Lunt Burge*, 108, 110; Johnson, *Soul by Soul*, 102. The once-heated debate over how much work slaveholding wives did revolved in part around this verbal appropriation. Few if any historians, however, have doubted the gulf between words and reality in the case of male slaveholders. See, for example, Catherine Clinton, *The Plantation Mistress: Woman's World in the Old South* (New York, 1982), 25–27; Weiner, *Mistresses and Slaves*, chapter 2.

77 Martha Jackson correspondence, 1840–53, JPFP; John Prior and Caroline Burke correspondence, 1848–54, WGP; 1829 and 1830 Tax Receipts for Eliza R. Ruffin, Hanover County, Virginia, Francis Gildart Ruffin Papers;. . . .

78 See note 9 above and John Hammond Moore, ed., *A Plantation Mistress on the Eve of the Civil War: The Diary of Keziah Goodwyn Hopkins Brevard, 1860–1861* (Columbia, SC, 1993), 10; Pease and Pease, *Family of Women*, 32–33, 163.

79 Faust, *James Henry Hammond*, 99, see also 89–90. . . .

80 Ibid.

8

THE SLAVE TRADER, THE WHITE SLAVE, AND THE POLITICS OF RACIAL DETERMINATION IN THE 1850s

Walter Johnson

In this essay, Walter Johnson examines the relationship of master and slave, not on the plantation, but in the courtroom. The case illustrates the ways in which the apparently triumphant ideology of slavery could give way in everyday life to a "babel of confusion" in which racial categories could not hold.

Jane Morrison, purchased in the slave market by James White, sued for her freedom on the grounds that she was white and had been fraudulently enslaved. The case was made possible in part because Morrison had been sold far from the community in which she had grown up, so the evidence about her status at birth was not definitive. Members of the jury—mainly nonslaveholding white men, according to available evidence—were challenged to decide whether a woman could truly be a slave if, in appearance and behavior, she seemed to be as "white" as their own wives and daughters. Southern proslavery ideology largely depended on the idea that "black" men and women were "naturally" slaves, so that slavery and white supremacy were mutually reinforcing. In cases such as this, however, the imagined absolute difference between "black" and "white" could not be sustained, as it was difficult for the man who claimed Morrison as a slave to show that she was "black" at all. The ideology of white supremacy clashed with the property rights of a slaveholder, and the case raised the question: "Was the southern order based on race or on slavery?" In his conclusion, Johnson challenges the argument of Eugene Genovese that slaveowners truly exercised "hegemony" in the slave South.

* * *

In January of 1857 Jane Morrison was sold in the slave market in New Orleans. The man who bought her was James White, a longtime New Orleans slave trader, who had recently sold his slave pen and bought land just up the river from New Orleans, in Jefferson Parish, Louisiana.[1]

Morrison, apparently, was to be one of his last speculations as a trader or one of his first investments as a planter. Sometime shortly after her sale, however, Morrison ran away. By the time White saw her again, in October 1857, they were in a courtroom in Jefferson Parish where Morrison had filed suit against him. Before it was settled, that suit would be considered by three different juries, be put before the Louisiana Supreme Court twice, and leave a lasting record of the complicated politics of race and slavery in the South of the 1850s. The reason for the stir would have been obvious to anyone who saw Morrison sitting in court that day: the fifteen-year-old girl whom White claimed as his slave had blond hair and blue eyes.

Morrison began her petition to the Third District Court by asking that William Dennison, the Jefferson Parish jailer, be appointed her legal representative and that she be sequestered in the parish prison to keep White from seizing and selling her. In her petition, Morrison asked that she be declared legally free and white and added a request that the court award her ten thousand dollars damages for the wrong that White had done her by holding her as a slave. She based her case on the claim that her real name was Alexina, not Jane, that she was from Arkansas, and that she had "been born free and of white parentage," or, as she put it in a later affidavit, "that she is of white blood and free and entitled to her freedom and that *on view this is manifest*." Essentially, Alexina Morrison claimed that she was white because she looked that way.[2]

In his response, White claimed that he had purchased Morrison (he still called her Jane) from a man named J. A. Halliburton, a resident of Arkansas. White exhibited an unnotarized bill of sale for Morrison (which would have been legal proof of title in Arkansas, but was not in Louisiana) and offered an alternative explanation of how the young woman had made her way into the courtroom that day. Morrison, he alleged, was a runaway slave. Indeed, he said, he had it on good authority that Morrison had been "induced" to run away from him by a group of self-styled "philanthropists" who were "in reality acting the part of abolitionists." In particular, White blamed Dennison, whom he accused of having used his position to "incourage" Morrison to run away and of having "afterwards harboured her, well knowing that she was a runaway." White was drawing his terminology from the criminal laws of the state of Louisiana and accusing Dennison and his shadowy "abolitionist" supporters of committing a crime: stealing and harboring his slave.[3]

. . . . As codified in the statutes of the state of Louisiana and generally interpreted by the Louisiana Supreme Court, the legal issues posed by the case were simple enough: If Alexina Morrison could prove she was white, she was entitled to freedom and perhaps to damages; if James

196

White could prove that her mother had been a slave at the time of Morrison's birth or that Morrison herself had been a slave (and had not been emancipated), he was entitled to her service; if she was not proved to be either white or enslaved, her fate would be decided by the court on the basis of a legal presumption of "mulattoes' " freedom under Louisiana law. Captured in the neat hand of the legal clerk who prepared the record of the lower court hearings of the case, however, are circumstances that were apparently considerably more complicated than the ones envisioned by those who had made the laws.[4]

Testimony from the lower court hearings of *Morrison v. White* provides a pathway into the complex history of slavery, class, race, and sexuality in the changing South of the 1850s: particularly into slaveholders' fantasies about their light-skinned and female slaves; the role of performance in the racial identities of both slaves and slaveholders; the ways anxieties about class and capitalist transformation in the South were experienced and expressed as questions about racial identity; the babel of confusion surrounding the racial ideal on which the antebellum social structure was supposedly grounded; the relationship of the law of slavery as made by legislators and appellate judges to its everyday life in the district courtrooms of the antebellum South; and the disruptive effects of one woman's effort to make her way to freedom through the tangle of ideology that enslaved her body. In the South of the 1850s, Alexina Morrison's bid for freedom posed a troubling double question: Could slaves become white? And could white people become slaves?

Whiteness and slavery

By the time *Morrison v. White* went to trial, Alexina Morrison would claim that her whiteness made her free, but when Morrison and White first met, in the slave market, it might simply have made her more valuable. It is well known that slaveholders favored light-skinned women such as Morrison to serve in their houses and that those light-skinned women sold at a price premium. What is less often realized is that in the slave market apparent differences in skin tone were daily formalized into racial categories—the traders were not only marketing race but also making it. In the slave market, the whiteness that Alexina Morrison would eventually try to turn against her slavery was daily measured, packaged, and sold at a very high price.[5]

The alchemy by which skin tone and slavery were synthesized into race and profit happened so quickly that it has often gone unnoticed. When people such as Morrison were sold, they were generally advertised by the slave traders with a racial category. Ninety percent of the slaves sold in the New Orleans market were described on the Acts of Sale that transferred their ownership with a word describing their lineage in terms of an imagined blood quantum—such as "Negro," "Griffe," "Mulatto," or "Quadroon." Those words described pasts that were not visible in the slave pens by referring to parents and grandparents who had been left behind with old owners. In using them, however, the traders depended upon something that was visible in the pens, skin color. When buyers described their slave market choices they often made the same move from the visible to the biological. When, for example, they described slaves as "a griff colored boy," or "not black, nor Mulatto, but what I believe is usually called a griff color, that is a Brownish Black, or a bright Mulatto," buyers were seeing color, but they were looking for lineage.[6] The words the buyers used—*griffe, mulatto, quadroon*—preserved a constantly shifting tension between the "blackness" favored by those who bought slaves to till their fields, harvest their crops, and renew their labor forces and the "whiteness" desired by those who went to the slave market in search of people to serve their meals, mend their clothes, and embody their fantasies. They sectioned the restless hybridity, the infinite variety of skin tone that was visible all over the South, into imagined degrees of black and white that, once measured, could be priced and sold.

These racial imaginings, however, were more than skin deep. Those who bought people to serve them as agricultural slaves focused their attention on vital capacity: they sought the size they associated with resilience and the dark skin they imagined into immunity to disease, they squeezed arms to test their strength, and inspected fingers to estimate their dexterity for picking cotton, they probed bellies and hefted breasts to search out histories of childbearing and the promise of reproduction. By contrast buyers' attention accreted to different parts of slaves' bodies when they described the mixed people whom they bought to serve in their households. Besides offering the seemingly obligatory references to skin color, descriptions of household slaves focused on mouths and teeth rather than hands and arms, on bodily proportion rather than bodily capacity, on acquired skill, personal demeanor, and proven loyalty rather than supposed immunity. The values slave buyers attributed to light-skinned bodies, that is, were proximate to those they claimed for themselves: this was whiteness made salable by the presence of blackness, what I will call hybrid whiteness.[7]

As Monique Guillory has suggested in her work on the New Orleans quadroon balls, the gaze of the consumer projected a fantasy of white masculinity onto the bodies of light-skinned women: the fantasy that other people existed to satisfy white men's desires. Though that fantasy was particularly associated with the notorious "fancy trade" to

New Orleans, the sale of light-skinned women for sex or companionship occurred all over the South. The word "fancy" has come down to us as an adjective modifying the word "girl," a word that refers to appearances perhaps or manners or dress. But the word has another meaning; it designates a desire: he fancies. . . . The slave market usage embarked from this second meaning: "fancy" was a transitive verb made noun, a slaveholder's desire made material in the shape of a woman like the one slave dealer Philip Thomas described seeing in Richmond: "13 years old, Bright Color, nearly a fancy for $1135." An age, a sex, a complexion, and a slaveholder's fantasy. A longer description of Mildred Ann Jackson traced the same lines: "She was about thirty years old. Her color was that of a quadroon; very good figure, she was rather tall and slim. Her general appearance was very good. She wore false teeth and had a mole on her upper lip. Her hair was straight." Jackson's body was admired for its form, for its delicacy, and for its fetishized details. . . . Solomon Northup, a free black who had himself been kidnapped and sold in the New Orleans market, remembered slave dealer Theophilus Freeman's account of the price that light-skinned Emily would bring in New Orleans: "There were heaps and piles of money to be made for such an extra fancy piece as Emily would be. She was a beauty—a picture—a doll—one of your regular bloods—none of your thick-lipped, bullet-headed, cotton [pick]ers."[8]

Freeman made explicit what lay behind the descriptions; according to the ideology of slaveholders' racial economy, which associated blackness and physical bulk with vitality, such bodies were useless for production. Light-skinned and slender, these women were the embodied opposites of those sought as field hands; their whiteness unfitted them for labor. For slave buyers, near-white enslaved women symbolized the luxury of being able to pay for service, often sexual, that had no material utility—they were "fancies," projections of the slaveholders' own imagined identities as white men and slave masters. . . .

And so, at a very high price, whiteness was doubly sold in the slave market. In the first instance the enslaved women's whiteness was packaged by the traders and imagined into meaning by the buyers— into delicacy and modesty, interiority and intelligence, beauty, bearing, and vulnerability. These descriptions of enslaved light-skinned women, however, were projections of slaveholders' dreamy interpretations of the meaning of their own skin color. Indeed, in the second instance it was the buyers' own whiteness that was being bought. The fantasies they projected onto their slaves' bodies served them as public reflections of their own discernment: they were the arbiters of bearing and beauty; their slaves were the showpieces of their pretensions; their own whiteness was made apparent in the bodies of the people they bought. By buying ever-whiter slaves, the prosperous slaveholders of the antebellum South bought themselves access to ever more luminous fantasies of their own distinction.[9]

But slaveholders' performance of their own slaveholding whiteness depended upon their slaves' ability to perform enslaved whiteness. When I say performance I do not mean to suggest there was anything artificial about the way these women acted, though there might have been. I mean that the ideology that associated hybrid white woman-hood with delicacy, gentility, and sexuality could not exist independent of the immediate appearance and daily behavior of the people it described.[10] Slaves had to be made, sometimes violently, to enact the meaning slaveholders assigned to their bodies. Hence the traders' attention to decorating the mixed women they sold for sex and the practice of sending them to sale in gloves or shawls. Hence the careful instructions they gave slaves about how to act in the market. The buyers had to be even more painstaking: more than simply getting slaves to look the part, the buyers had to make sure they would play it. Stubbornness, recalcitrance, or simple inability on the part of their slaves could make a mockery of slaveholders' projected pretensions by revealing how much their own identities depended upon the behavior of their slaves. And so slaveholders were willing to pay a lot of money for the right kind of performance. The better the slaves' performance, the greater the value produced out of the synergetic whiteness of slave and slaveholder.[11]

Ironically, these slave market syntheses of whiteness and slavery, these costly flirtations with hybridity, were underwritten by slaveholders' ideology of absolute racial difference. The saving abstraction "black blood" held the power to distinguish nearly white women from really white ones, to distinguish what was essentially performance from what was the performance of essence—slaveholders generally believed that "black blood," if present, would be apparent in the countenance, conversation, or carriage of the one who bore its taint.[12] When a performance of enslaved whiteness was too good, however, the combination of "white" appearance and behavior could overwhelm the intended distinction; a slave could become "too white to keep," likely to slip aboard a ship or hop onto a train and escape to freedom. A virtuoso performance of whiteness could breach the categories designed to contain and commodify hybridity; a slave could step over the color line and onto the other side. Perhaps the slave trader who sold Morrison to White was thinking of that type of performance when he remembered that she was "too white." And perhaps that is why James White had apparently curled the young woman's hair and dyed it black after he brought her home from the slave market.[13]

Morrison versus white

According to most versions of the southern social order, Alexina Morrison—whether as enslaved white or passing slave—was not supposed to exist at all. But the color-coding, black slaves and white supremacy, that characterized most of the political debate over slavery was unreliable as a description of the institution's everyday life. First, there was racial mixture and sexual predation: throughout the history of American slavery it was not always easy to tell who was "black."[14] Second, there was manumission: just as racial mixture made it harder to tell who was "black," manumission made it harder to tell who was a slave. The ultimate expression of slaveholders' property right—the right to alienate their property however they pleased—increasingly undermined the ability of slaveholders as a class to keep race and slavery coextensive.[15] Finally, there were the slave trade and inter-regional migration: the antebellum South was a rootless society. The broad transition from an upper South tobacco economy to a lower South cotton economy and the domestic slave trade, through which as many as two-thirds of a million people may have passed in the ante-bellum period, had removed hundreds of thousands of people such as Alexina Morrison from the communities in which their identities were rooted. Through acts as small as lying about their past in the slave market or as audacious as running away and claiming to be white, many of the enslaved people forcibly transported by the trade worked their deracination against their slavery.[16]

By 1857, when Alexina Morrison ran away and sued the slave trader, southern lawmakers already had at least two centuries' experience with the ambiguities of a social order in which not all slaves were black and not all nonwhite people were slaves. Throughout the nine-teenth century, southern states passed ever-more-detailed laws defin-ing the acceptable limits of drinking, gambling, and lovemaking along the lines of race and slavery. Those laws attempted to control sites where black and white, slave and free, bargained and socialized freely with one another, places where the white supremacist ideology upon which the defense of slavery increasingly relied was daily undermined in practice. The capstone of the effort to make the categories of race and slavery once again coextensive was the self-enslavement laws passed by many states in the 1850s. Based on the racist premise that enslaved people were better off than free people of color because they had white people (read *owners*) to take care of them, and flirting with the point at which the edifice of proslavery ideology would collapse beneath the weight of its own absurdity, the laws offered free blacks a chance to choose a master and enslave themselves.[17]

The most explicit legislative consideration of race, however, came in the framing of presumptions assigning legal status as slave or free to an otherwise unknown person. Taken together, the presumption laws outlined two ways of thinking about race: South Carolina, Georgia, and Delaware assigned status on the basis of observation and reputation; other slaveholding states, including Louisiana, attempted to establish presumptions of freedom based upon fractions of "black blood": halves, fourths, eighths, sixteenths, and so on down to one drop, which was the standard only in Arkansas during the antebellum period. The first standard emphasized appearance and performance; the second, more popular standard relied on a supposedly scientific estimation of an imagined blood quantum. The presumptions did not mean that the in-between people who came before the courts were free: Other evidence could overcome the legal presumption, most notably historical evidence that the person before the court had been held as a slave or born to an enslaved woman.[18]

Faced with a person of indeterminate identity, then, antebellum legislators and litigators had three conceptually distinct (though often practically interrelated) ways of locating them in the grid of acceptable social identities: personal history, race science based on discerning "black blood," and performance—the amalgam of appearance and reputation, of body, behavior, and scripted social role. And over the course of the nineteenth century, in cases that resulted from the presumption laws, in cases that arose out of disputes over inheritance and other property claims, and in cases where enslaved people such as Morrison claimed they were white, judges throughout the slaveholding South (not just in Louisiana) were asked hundreds of times to stabilize the visible confusion of a hybrid reality into the stable degrees of difference demanded by a ruling class that wanted to see the world in black and white. Thus, when Alexina Morrison sued the slave trader for possession of her whiteness, she was entering a much broader ongoing contest over the tools used to determine the race of indeterminate bodies.[19]

Like many of the other people who came before the courts in cases of disputed racial identity, Alexina Morrison emerged from a shadowy world in which legal and historical categories may have had only episodic relevance to everyday experience. It was not unheard of in the antebellum South for people who were legally enslaved to live as free for many years before being dragged into court as slaves. Nor was it impossible for someone to appear as "black" or, more likely, "mulatto" on one tabulation of the United States census and "white" on another. It sometimes took a long-dormant claim of ownership or an intruding census taker to make people make sense of themselves in the categories that supposedly ordered southern society—black and white, slave and free.[20]

There are only hints of how Alexina Morrison might have made sense of herself before she sued James White. In 1850, when the census takers passed through Matagorda County, Texas, the household of Moses Morrison included himself, three other white men, and, listed separately on the slave schedule, a woman aged thirty and labeled mulatto, five children aged between one and thirteen, also labeled mulatto, and an enslaved man, listed beneath this apparent slave family, aged thirty-eight and labeled black.[21] Of the children, one was a seven-year-old girl, most likely Alexina Morrison. That the children were listed as mulatto like their mother and that the only enslaved man in the household was not suggests that their father was white— perhaps Moses Morrison or one of the men who boarded with him.

There is no way of knowing the internal life hidden behind the census taker's rendering of the Morrison household in Matagorda, of knowing who was treated as a slave in that household and who, perhaps, as a daughter—as one of the witnesses who testified to having later known Morrison in Arkansas put it about her early days in Texas, "I do not know of my own knowledge as to whether the girl was raised, treated, and bred from her birth as a slave or otherwise." Nor is there any way of knowing whether Alexina Morrison was treated as property or company as she subsequently passed through the households of various members of the Morrison family, whether she thought she was being sold or just moving on. Nor is there any way of knowing if Andre Hutt was telling the truth when he testified at the trial that Alexina Morrison had tried to convince his wife to buy her as a slave in Little Rock, Arkansas, before she appeared in the market in New Orleans; nor, finally, of knowing how Morrison was treated in the New Orleans slave pen where she was sold to White, if her performance of hybrid whiteness was enforced by intimidation or simply enhanced by instruction.[22] But two things are as clear as day: By the time she ended up in White's possession Alexina Morrison was a slave, and by the time she escaped she was white.

When Alexina Morrison escaped from James White, her jailer/protector remembered, the first thing she said was that she was white. And when she brought suit against White, she did so by building this assertion into a story: that she was born of white parents and taken away from her home in Arkansas by "gross fraud," that she had been held by force and falsely claimed as a slave. By the time the case came to trial, however, the pieces of that story had been folded back into the initial assertion of whiteness. Morrison's letters to those whom her lawyers termed "her friends and supposed family" in Arkansas and Texas had gone unanswered (intercepted, the lawyers suggested). As fifteen-year-old Alexina Morrison sat in court while her case was tried, she embodied her lawyer's entire case: her whiteness was "on view . . . manifest."[23]

203

Morrison's claim of whiteness drew its power from three sources: her appearance, her behavior, and the idea that "black blood," if present at all, would necessarily be visible. Most simply, her case took the form of outright description. "From his opinion," one witness testified, "the girl is white. Says he judges she is white from her complexion." Or: "Has seen plaintiff and been intimately acquainted with her. From witness' judgment of plaintiff arising from his intimacy she has not the features of the African Race." Other witnesses placed a greater emphasis on behavior when they described what it meant to be white: "Had witness been introduced to the girl without knowing her, he would have taken her for a white girl. . . . Has had opportunity of Judging her, and she conducted herself as a white girl. She is so in her conduct and actions. She has none of the features of an African." If there had been any of "the African race" in Alexina Morrison, they argued, it would have been outwardly and objectively visible in the way she looked and acted, but from the moment she had made her initial claim of whiteness, there had been no outward sign that she was anything but white all the way through. As one witness put it, on the night when Morrison escaped from the trader, "she seemed to be in trouble . . . from her air and her manners." In other words, she seemed like a white woman in distress. Trying to make Alexina Morrison make sense to the court, Morrison's lawyers and witnesses drew on a set of images of feminine whiteness—modest carriage, unimposing gentility, emotional transparency. Indeed, it was Morrison's performance of her womanhood as much as of her whiteness that seems to have transfixed the white men who supported her cause: Alexina Morrison, they were arguing, was white because white womanhood was always as it seemed. By centering their case in the "flaxen haired, blue eyed," and presumably well-behaved young woman in the courtroom, Morrison and her lawyers had drawn on one of the sacred premises of the antebellum social order—the visible, unquestionable, objective character of race—as it was embodied in the most precious fetish of white supremacy, a white woman.[24]

The slave trader's case began with simple negation. Where Morrison's witnesses looked at the young woman and saw white, White's witnesses looked at her and saw black. Immediately after stating that he would not himself have bought Morrison because she was "too white," W. J. Martin, the dealer who brokered the sale of Morrison to White, testified that "from the appearance of the girl" he nevertheless judged "that she has African Blood." Martin's opinion was seconded by J. A. Breaux, who located Morrison's "African Blood" in "the shape of her cheek Bones and the conformation of the lower part of her mouth." The case by negation, however, was itself vulnerable to negation. In cross-examining Breaux, Morrison's lawyers posed alternative interpretations of the shape of the young woman's face: Had Breaux ever traveled among Indians or been to Mexico, the Antilles, or the West Indies? Had he noticed how straight Alexina Morrison's hair was? Had he looked at the color of her skin, at her hands or her feet? Would he describe Mr. Hall, a spectator in the courtroom, as having high cheekbones?[25] By providing alternative explanations for the supposedly nonwhite characteristics that seemed to show through Morrison's white skin, Morrison's lawyers hinted for the first time at the high stakes they were willing to bring to bear in the case. If Alexina Morrison could be judged black, was there any certainty that others might not be so judged: racial others like Indians, extranational others like Mexicans and West Indians, and indeed other white people like Mr. Hall, sitting right there in the courtroom? If Alexina Morrison was black, they hinted, there was no telling who else might be.

The indeterminacy of the visual evidence and the threat that all kinds of difference might be blackened by the slave trader's claim pushed White's lawyers into the awkward posture of trying to convince a jury of southern white men that they could not believe their eyes (an unaccustomed role for a slave trader, who presumably spent most of his time trying to convince people *to* believe their eyes). They did so by drawing on history, by which they hoped to prove that Alexina Morrison was a slave; race science, by which they hoped to undermine the idea that she was white; and, finally, a different set of images of race and gender performance—images that located the young woman's race in allusion to her sexuality rather than her demeanor.

The slave trader's history came from depositions taken in Texas and Arkansas where people remembered the young woman as a slave. Moses Morrison could not remember in whose house she was born, but he remembered buying Alexina, her siblings, and her mother in 1848; he remembered keeping her for four or five years and then taking her to his nephew's house in Little Rock, where she was to learn to sew and do housework. That was the last he had seen of her. She would have, he added, to highlight the importance of personal history and reputation in regulating hybridity, "passed for a white child anywhere if not known." From Arkansas, Morrison's nephew remembered Moses Morrison bringing Alexina out from Texas in 1850 and trying to give her to his (Moses') niece, Ellen. Ellen's father had said that "he did not want so white a Negro about him" and advised Moses Morrison to sell Alexina. Morrison, instead, gave her to his nephew, who remembered entrusting her to a slave trader, who took her to New Orleans at the beginning of 1857 and sold her to James White. From Morrison to his nephew to the trader to White: James White's lawyers tried to locate Alexina Morrison's apparent whiteness in a traceable history of slavery. Step by step, they outlined a story rooted in the moment in 1848 when she was sold with her mother as a slave to Moses Morrison; according to the standards of historical and legal record, that sale made Alexina Morrison a slave.[26]

And yet in a society as rootless as the antebellum South, the seemingly stable category of "slave" was a less certain legal tool than it might seem to a historian bent on figuring out whether or not Alexina Morrison "really" was what she said she was.[27] The history provided by the slave trader, after all, occurred at a distance of time and space that made it untrustworthy; indeed, one of the judges who heard the case as it passed through the court system threw it out on the grounds that the depositions had been improperly taken and could not be relied upon as authentic.[28] The textual rendering of testimony given in Texas and Arkansas was apparently not history enough to convince him that the fate of the blond-haired and blue-eyed young woman who stood before him in the court should be decided by the depositions of distant witnesses testifying about a shadowy past as a slave.

While White's lawyers concentrated on tracing the young woman's history in their own effort to prove that she was a slave (for if they could prove that, it did not legally matter what color she was), the bulk of their cross-examination concentrated on undermining her lawyers' claim that she was white, a claim they clearly feared would influence the jury. In questioning Morrison's witnesses, the slave trader's lawyers asked repeatedly about hybridity, trying to work their way back to essential blackness from apparent whiteness. What were, they asked each of Morrison's witnesses, the distinctive features of the African race when removed to the fourth or fifth degree? Had not the witness seen people removed to the fourth degree with blue eyes before? Did the witness believe in the unity of the races? That slaves as well as slaveholders were descended from Adam and Eve? Was the witness in favor of amalgamation? Did the witness know the differences between the races at all?[29] Faced with the unquestionably blue-eyed and blond Alexina Morrison, the defendant's lawyers tried to resolve the mystery of hybridity back into the constancy of blackness by making the argument that "black blood" could disappear without a trace into apparent whiteness but still be present. Even if Morrison's witnesses were right and White's were wrong, even if the young woman standing in court was free of any visible trace of "the African," they were arguing, she could still be black. This line of questioning revealed how far White's lawyers were willing to go in contesting Morrison's claim to whiteness: To believe that Alexina Morrison was white, they implied, was to ignore one of the major foundations of much white supremacist and proslavery thought, polygenesis—the idea that blacks and whites were created separately and so should ever remain. Indeed, to try to slip an apparently white black slave like Alexina Morrison across the color line was to lend support to the most toxic of abolitionism's many heresies, the claim that the hold of slavery on the southern states might be attenuated through gradual racial "amalgamation."[30]

The plaintiff's witnesses, however, refused to yield the point. G. H. Lyons told the court that he "knew the difference between the Caucasian and African races" and was "opposed to amalgamation," but he still thought that Morrison was white. J. B. Clawson was familiar with all of the difficulties of crosses of the fourth and fifth degrees and conceded that "at the fifth degree a woman cannot tell" white from black, but he was himself certain about Morrison. And S. N. Cannon assured the court that "colored blood will stick out" even in crosses of the fourth or fifth degree. It was in "the shape of the hairs being curled, the white of the eyes . . . in the shape of the nose and lips." But it was, they all agreed, nowhere in Alexina Morrison.[31]

In the end, the slave trader's effort to summon Morrison's evanescent "black blood" to the surface of her skin through a science lesson about crosses of the fourth and fifth degree was sidetracked at every turn by countersciences and slaveholding common sense. As they attempted to make the invisible visible, White's lawyers remained vulnerable to the impervious confidence of men such as P. C. Perret, a self-identified "Creole" who walked into the court and declared that he could tell Alexina Morrison was white because "it is an impulse with him and with the creoles generally" to be able to tell the race of a person. He explained: "it is the same instinct in the same measure as the alligator, he can tell it the same with the alligator, who knows three days in advance that a storm is brewing. In December the weather may be ever so fair but the alligator will be seen to sink and the next day or the day after the storm will be seen to shew itself."[32] No matter the seeming simplicity of the legal presumption that portions of "black blood" could be made manifest and measured, race science in practice was broadly contested.

White's lawyers apparently adjudged a distant history of slavery and a contested lesson about race science too uncertain to prove their case, and so it was with social practice and sexual performance that they concluded their effort. Where did you meet Alexina Morrison, they asked S. N. Cannon, was it at a ball? The witness responded that he had never seen her at a ball, and for the moment the matter ended there. But by the end of the third hearing of the case in the lower courts, the defense was asking the man: "Are you the father of the child of plaintiff?" And when the plaintiff's lawyers objected to that: "Is not the plaintiff in the family way for you now?" Shortly after, the witness was recalled and testified, under cross-examination, that he had been Morrison's jailer for five years, that she had spent nineteen months of those years out of jail, and that she had a child while in jail.[33]

This line of questioning aimed to establish Alexina Morrison's evanescent blackness by slotting her into one of the prefabricated categories that antebellum slaveholders used to mediate between the confusing hybridity they saw all around them and the imagined racial essences on which they grounded their society. By alluding to her public appearance at local balls and her extramarital sexuality, they drew on the racialized and sexualized image of the quadroon mistress to locate Alexina Morrison's origins. As White's lawyers put it about her supporters in a later petition to the court: "they have dressed her up and taken her to public and private balls." Her sexuality, they implied, was proof of an essential blackness that no elegant dress could conceal. The final story they told about Alexina Morrison contested the imagery of transparent white womanhood used by Morrison's own witnesses. If race was evident in gendered versions of deportment, they were arguing, Alexina Morrison was playing a different part outside the courtroom than inside.[34]

There, the defense rested; the judge gave oral instructions (which the court reporter did not record), and the jury retired. When they returned, they reported to the court that there was "no possibility of any agreement upon a verdict." Faced with Alexina Morrison, the twelve white men who made a jury in Jefferson Parish could not decide whether to believe their eyes or the ways of seeing provided by legal practice, medical science, and white supremacist sexual ideology. Through the repeated and contradictory application of the fixed terms of the antebellum conversation about race to the body of the young woman in the courtroom, the witnesses in the Third District courtroom had called into question something that they all professed to believe was common sense: the idea that there were black people and white people. They left the case to be decided upon retrial.

Whiteness versus slavery

The year 1857, when Alexina Morrison ran away and sued the slave trader, was a banner year in the history of American proslavery. For in 1857 the efforts of southern politicians to shore up the positive-good defense of slavery by erasing any evidence that black people could thrive (or even survive) outside slavery and to circumscribe the freedom of the potential free Negro enemy within seemed to take on new importance throughout the South. In 1857 Chief Justice Roger Taney's famous *obiter dictum* in *Dred Scott v. Sandford* abolished the rights of black Americans—not just slaves—to seek redress in the nation's courts. In 1857 there were continued calls for the reopening of the African slave trade to insure that the growing class of nonslaveholding white southerners would have the opportunity to cement their loyalty to slavery by becoming slaveholders themselves. And in 1857 the first rumblings were heard of the "enslavement crisis," a series of calls for the forcible enslavement of free people of color in states from Maryland to Louisiana. In the heat of the ongoing conflict over slavery, southern judges and legislators were, to all appearances, attempting to eliminate the ambiguities of the southern social order in favor of a fixed equivalence of race and status—of blackness with slavery and whiteness with slaveholding.[35]

The debates over the enslavement proposal, however, reveal that the solidifying South was shot through with a tension between the demands of race and those of slavery, or, put another way, between the privileges of whiteness and those of slaveholding. On the side favoring enslavement, the argument often ran along the line proposed by an overheated Maryland lawmaker and quoted by Ira Berlin: "all Negroes [must] be slaves in order that all whites may be free." On the side opposed to enslaving free people of color, the argument could take the shape proposed by the *Charleston Courier* and quoted by Michael P. Johnson and James L. Roark: "The true policy of the state is to foster slave labor. . . . [The free Negro's] right to hold slaves gives him a stake in the institution of slavery, and makes it his interest as well as his duty to uphold it." On one side was a fundamentalist vision of the political economy of whiteness in which any free black was a potential threat to all whites; on the other was a straight-out adherence to the political economy of slavery in which any slaveholder, even a black slaveholder, was a potential ally in the fight against abolition. The poles of the discussion only begin to outline the shifting political terrain, complicated social underpinnings, and rhetorical jockeying for control of the favored terms of proslavery and white supremacy that defined the enslavement crisis. What they do, however, is starkly outline the existence of two—sometimes contending, sometimes overlapping—versions of the southern social order. In the late 1850s sectional tension was giving new urgency to a very old question: Was the southern social order based on race or on slavery?[36]

Like other southern states in the years leading up to 1857, Louisiana had taken legislative and judicial action to clarify the relationship of race and slavery. In the 1850s the legislature and courts of Louisiana tried to curb manumission, eliminate such states of "quasi-slavery" as *in futuro* emancipation, enforce a stricter segregation of social relations between black and white (especially drinking, gambling, and dancing), and regulate the public behavior of free people of color and slaves more vigilantly. By 1859 Louisiana would pass its own self-enslavement law and offer free people of color the chance to choose a master and enslave themselves. Alexina Morrison's case, then, went to the jury at a time when Louisiana was rebalancing the categories of southern social life by gradually abolishing the very liminal spaces from which she seems to have emerged. But Morrison did not claim to be liminal, she claimed to be white, and in Jefferson Parish in the 1850s that seems to have made all the difference in the world.[37]

The jury that heard *Morrison v. White* was chosen the way most antebellum juries were, from among the voters who lived in the court's ambit.[38] What is striking about the Jefferson Parish jurors who heard Alexina Morrison's case is how hard they are to track down. Of the twelve men on the jury, only two appear in the censuses of Jefferson or Orleans Parish for both 1850 and 1860. Three others appear in one or the other of the surveys. They were a steamboat captain from Alabama; a butcher from Germany; a railroad worker from Ireland; and a forty-seven-year-old clerk, New York–born and living with his family in the household of his employer. A Louisiana-born cotton sampler living in the household of an Irish shoemaker was the jury's foreman. Only the steamboat captain and the butcher owned any real estate; only the butcher and the boarding clerk from New York claimed any personal estate. To judge by the census record, the other jurors arrived in Jefferson Parish sometime after the tabulation for 1850 and left before that for 1860.[39] Taken together, however, the known jurors reflect the character of the community they represented: they were men in motion in a town dominated by steamboat and railroad, immigrants and transients in a newly populated parish, agents of change in a state that, even in the nineteenth century, celebrated aristocratic stasis.

And, with the exception of one juror who owned a sixty-year-old man and a fifty-three-year-old woman in 1860, the known jurors were nonslaveholders in a society based on slavery. They were the type of men for whom "the wages of whiteness" held the promise of a daily psychological supplement to the portion they gained from their work, the type of men for whom slavery posed its own double question: Did they share in the society of slaveholders? Or were they in danger of being themselves enslaved?[40]

It is by now a threadbare truth that whiteness gave nonslaveholders a stake in slavery.[41] Nonslaveholding white men were potential slaveholders. More than that, they were shareholders in a society based on racial caste, entitled to public deference from people of color and involved in the daily discipline of slavery through slave catching and patrols. Finally, they were a constituency for the broad proslavery argument that identified the interests of all white people with those of slaveholders: in a slaveholding society, only black people were treated as slaves. Often, as in the famous poem "The Hireling and the Slave," this strain of proslavery took the form of a critical contrast between the living conditions of the white working class and southern slaves, always to the advantage of the latter. Indeed, "Beauties of White Slavery," which sympathetically portrayed the plight of German journeymen tailors in Cincinnati, "The Female Slaves of London," which analyzed the scandalous living conditions of white working people in the metropolis of antislavery, and "Northern White Slavery," which unfavorably contrasted the plight of northern wage workers to that of southern slaves, were articles that appeared in the *New Orleans Daily Crescent* in the week when Alexina Morrison's case was decided by the Jefferson Parish jury. Slave trader White's lawyers appealed to the jury in the reassuring logic of racial resentment. Sitting in court, Morrison may have looked white and acted white—perhaps more so than the jurors themselves. But her essential blackness insured that she would remain forever a slave, just as their whiteness insured that they might one day be slaveholders. This was whiteness in its familiar guise as the ideological underwriter of slavery.[42]

But the imagery of white slavery was dangerously unstable in an economy that was changing as fast as that of the urban South in the 1850s. It was in 1857, after all, that George Fitzhugh finalized his own famous solution to the anomalous presence of a white working class in a society based upon black slavery: Enslave them all. And, indeed, even as prosperous slaveholders were spending thousands of dollars at a time to buy near-white slaves to work in their households, they were employing increasing numbers of whites (and those, like the Irish, who were in the process of becoming white) as wage laborers, tenant farmers, and domestic servants. New Orleans in the 1850s, as the Louisiana physician and racial theorist Samuel Cartwright described it, daily offered more concrete examples of "white slavery" than did distant strikes or living conditions. "Here in New Orleans," Cartwright wrote in *DeBow's Review*, "the larger part of the drudgery-work requiring exposure to the sun, as rail-road making, street-paving, dray-driving, ditching, building, etc. is performed by white people . . . a class of persons who make Negroes of themselves in this hot climate." As Barbara Jeanne Fields has put it, class relations between white people in such southern cities as New Orleans were being "drawn into [racial] terms of reference, as a ray of light is deflected when it passes through a gravitational field." According to Cartwright, the Irish were not becoming white, they were, like the white workingmen with whom they shared their days, turning black.[43]

In the image of a resentful white laborer put out to do the dirty work of capitalist transformation beneath the summer sun—draining swamps and building levees, digging canals and filling railbeds, work regarded as too dangerous for any (valuable) slave to do—we see a less familiar version of the southern political economy. In the urban South of the 1850s, class differences between slaveholder and nonslaveholder were sometimes experienced and expressed in terms of race, and the *Herrenvolk* strain within the ideology of whiteness and daily practice in the slaveholders' economy were increasingly at odds. Doubts about the commitment of the Irish workingmen of New Orleans to slavery, though they often reiterated it, plagued local nativists and slaveholders throughout the 1850s. Indeed, in 1856 both local and national elections in the city had been marked by nativist violence against Irish and German immigrants who tried to vote. As they told the story of a vulnerable white servant sold as a slave, Morrison's lawyers were drawing rhetorical force from the daily experience of the white men who sat on the jury: in the slaveholders' economy, nonslaveholding white people were increasingly being treated like slaves.[44]

Or, even more pointedly, nonslaveholding white women were. One thing that differentiated nonslaveholding white men from slaves in the antebellum South, one dimension of their whiteness, was that they were legally able to protect their dependents from sexual violation, state attachment, and sale. Indeed, as Stephanie M. McCurry has shown, it was by asserting control over their own households that these men could claim, like their slaveholding neighbors, to be "masters"—an equal partnership in patriarchy that underwrote their supposedly equal participation in politics. And yet, as their wives and daughters daily went to work in the homes of their prosperous slaveholding neighbors, the domestic authority of nonslaveholding white men in urban areas such as New Orleans was being eroded in favor of the class privilege of their slaveholding neighbors.[45] It was on the embattled line between the slaveholders' economy and the inner circle of nonslaveholding white patriarchy that Alexina Morrison staked her claim to freedom when she ran away from James White. Morrison's first legal action, remember, was to ask that her jailer be appointed her legal guardian: she gave the jail in which she was being held the legal shape of a household and took for herself the role of white dependent within that household. And in the months between her escape and her trial, she passed through the households of a number of nonslaveholding white men. First the house of her jailer, William Dennison, where she was placed by leave of the district attorney and from which she was seen walking with the jailer's wife, and later the house of J. B. Clawson, a clerk in whose home she was living at the time of the trial.

But Morrison was not just living in Clawson's household, she was working there as a housekeeper.[46] In return for a place within the protective perimeter of this white household, Morrison was providing its members with access to an unfamiliar region of the world of whiteness and distinction. She was, after all, a young woman who had probably been trained in the slave market to embody the gentility and patriarchy of the slaveholding households to which nonslaveholders such

212

as Clawson would have been admitted only as (occasional and awkward) interlopers. By playing the same role for those who protected her as she would have for those who purchased her, she was giving them an experience of whiteness usually reserved for those who owned slaves.

The service she was rendering Clawson suggests that we should not, despite the urging of Morrison's lawyers that her case was being supported by "philanthropists" and the charge of White's lawyers that the young woman's supporters were "abolitionists," misconstrue the relationship between her protectors and Morrison as being merely benign or even wholly centered on her emancipation. Indeed, Alexina Morrison, in her effort to get free, had been forced to accept attention from white men—many of them nonslaveholders—that went well beyond their identification with her plight. "Saw her naked to the waist"—spoken by Morrison's supporters, those words circulate through the trial record like a *leitmotiv*. Indeed, in the weeks after the mistrial, Morrison's half-naked body seems to have been the center of a festival of whiteness in Jefferson Parish. P. C. Perret remembered seeing her "frequently" exhibited at the hotel in Carrollton after the first trial. And listen to L. Castera, testifying on her behalf and under direct examination in the retrial: "Witness saw the girl at the Hotel and someone asked him if he thought the girl has African blood, at first witness answered no, and then made an examination of her nose, eyes, under her arms, between her shoulders, examined her hair and the conformation of her face, her fingers, nails." Or Seaman Hopkins: "examined plaintiff's back in fact he saw her naked to her waist. Examined her closely and found no traces of the African." These witnesses, part of an apparently leering and possibly threatening group of white men, did things to Alexina Morrison that they would never have done to a white woman in public—not to a maid, not to a dancing girl, not to a prostitute.[47]

Publicly exhibited, stripped to the waist, and examined: Alexina Morrison was paying for her freedom with a performance straight out of the slave market. For the men at the hotel in Carrollton, Morrison's liminal body—now protected, now violated; now free, now enslaved; now white, now black; now Mexican, now Indian, now Caribbean—was a symbol of everything whiteness promised them: that they would never themselves be slaves, but that they were entitled to benefit from race as slaveholders did from slavery—through control and sexual access. Alexina Morrison had passed from the property regime of slavery into that of whiteness, from being subject to the prerogatives that defined mastery in the antebellum South to being subjected to those that defined white patriarchy.[48]

Verdict and conclusion

In the aftermath of the mistrial, James White claimed that "a few days before the last trial" when he had ridden out to Carrollton with one of his witnesses to look at Alexina Morrison, he was "surrounded by a lawless mob" that threatened him with "personal violence because he dared to assert his property in his own slave, who said mob declared to be a white person." Faced with the claim of a man who had once made his living selling slaves who might have been as white as themselves, some citizens of Jefferson Parish were apparently willing to risk their lives in defense of Alexina Morrison's claim. The local papers dignified the event with the silence usually reserved for slave rebellions, but the judge in the Third District Court thought it one of the most extraordinary things he had ever heard. Noting that he had never before transferred a case, that Morrison had been "taken in the Society of white persons" and "was even seen dancing at a ball in Carrollton," that he had it on good authority that someone claiming her as his slave was risking his life, and that it would be several sessions of the court before an unprejudiced jury could be impaneled in Jefferson Parish, he sent the case to the Fifth District Court in New Orleans to be retried.[49]

There, in May 1859, both sides called new witnesses and elaborated arguments made in the first trial (most notably the argument by Morrison's lawyers that the strands of the young woman's hair, when cut transversely, revealed themselves to be the "moderate" ovals of a white person rather than "longer" ovals of a black one). The judge in the Fifth District Court excluded both the unnotarized "private act of sale" presented by White's lawyers and the testimony of the slave trader's witnesses from Texas and Arkansas as "not legally authenticated," and he further instructed the jury to decide only the question of whether or not Alexina Morrison was a slave. Without the evidence of sale and the depositions from Texas and Arkansas, there was no proof whatsoever that Morrison was a slave, and so, apparently following the presumption of freedom in favor of mulattoes under Louisiana law, the New Orleans jury declared unanimously for her freedom.[50]

The lawyers for the slave trader appealed to the state supreme court, which declared that the evidence of the sale and the depositions from Texas and Arkansas had been improperly excluded, voided the verdict of the jury, and remanded the case to the Fifth District with the advice that the Supreme Court found "full proof" that Morrison had been born a slave and the order that "the presumption of freedom arising from her color ... must yield to a proof of her servile origin." Going beyond questions of both fact and procedure in the lower court, however, the Supreme Court considered the case as a matter of public policy: "The Legislature has not seen fit to declare that any number of crosses between the Negro and the white shall emancipate the off-spring of the slave, and it does not fall within the province of the judiciary to establish any such rule of property." . . . .[51]

The case was heard in the lower courts for the third time in New Orleans, where, on January 30, 1862, Alexina Morrison was herself "exhibited to the Jury in evidence." Following the instructions of the Supreme Court, the judge admitted the depositions from Arkansas and gave oral instructions to the jury, which were not included in the trial record. After retiring for "some time," the jury sent word that its members were unable to agree upon a verdict and requested that they be allowed to decide by majority. Present in the courtroom, Morrison consented, and the jury returned to announce that it had voted 10 to 2 in her favor. White's lawyers again appealed to the Supreme Court, where the case was delayed during the Civil War occupation of New Orleans, redocketed five days after the assassination of Abraham Lincoln, and continued a few times until 1870, when it was placed on the delay docket where it sits today, apparently awaiting action on Morrison's request for damages.[52]

It is tougher to track Alexina Morrison. On the Jefferson Parish census of 1860 she is listed as a free white woman, living with her little girl in a house next door to that of William Dennison, the man whom she had first met as her jailer. Morrison's daughter, like the little girl who lived in Dennison's house, was called Mary.[53] Perhaps one-year-old Mary represented Morrison's shadowed claim to a place within Dennison's household, perhaps, more simply, her daughter was Morrison's best hope for a legacy of freedom. For, by the third hearing of the case (in 1862), Alexina Morrison was apparently back in jail, coughing blood, and fearful for her life. And there the trail ends: Neither Alexina nor Mary Morrison appears in the 1870 census of Jefferson or Orleans parishes.

Alexina Morrison was a woman who left her fellow slaves behind to make her bid for freedom alone, framed her case in the grammar of white supremacist patriarchy by presenting herself as a white woman in need, ceded the power over her situation to a legal system that supported slavery, delivered her body from the hands of the slaver to that of the jailer and from the property regime of slavery to that of whiteness. The Louisiana Supreme Court remained ever ready to ensure that the local chaos in Jefferson Parish did not interfere with the state's progress toward a more perfect equivalence of blackness and slavery. Morrison herself may have died of the illness she had con-tracted in prison. In the eyes of many, hers would be a story of hegem-ony: of agency without autonomy, opposition without effect, resistance without revolution; of a woman becoming ever more entangled in the logic of slavery as she tried to get free.[54] Judged by the history recorded in law books and legislative records and according to the Louisiana Supreme Court that had ultimate jurisdiction over her fate, Morrison was swimming against the current of history, finally unable, in spite of her extraordinary effort, to escape the inexorable consolidation of slaveholding power in the years before the Civil War.

But if we pay attention to the local as well as the legal importance of the case and the everyday as well as the systemic impact of individual acts of resistance, if we think about what it must have been like to wake up in Jefferson Parish on the morning after the district court had decided Morrison's case and moved on to other business, historical time has a different scale and Alexina Morrison's story offers a different moral. The covering rhetoric of white supremacy may have remained unquestioned and the power of the Supreme Court to dampen subversive appropriations of that rhetoric by refusing the verdicts coming from the lower courts intact. But Alexina Morrison had raised troubling possibilities in a society based on racial slavery: that a slave might perform whiteness so effectively as to become white; that behavior thought to indicate natural difference might, instead, be revealed as the product of education, construction, and, even, commodification; that one could seem white without really being that way; that the whiteness by which the slaveholding social order was justified might one day be turned against it. The problems Morrison posed were particularly acute when addressed to the white workingmen who increasingly inhabited the antebellum South: How could they continue to claim to be their own masters if they or their wives and daughters worked for someone else? Did race really give them a stake in slavery? Would their whiteness really protect them from enslavement? No longer could a Jefferson Parish jury be trusted to try the case of the slave trader and the white slave; no longer could slaveholders be sure that the property claims of slavery would be supported by the logic of whiteness. Indeed, the notions of a supposedly commonsense differentiation between black and white that were broached in the Third District Court were so various and so contradictory that by the end of 1857 it would have been hard for anyone in Jefferson Parish to say for sure what people there meant when they talked about "race." Whether they realized it or not, as they tugged Alexina Morrison back and forth across a color line that they all thought they could plainly see, the white participants in *Morrison v. White* revealed that line as an effect of social convention and power, not nature.

Indeed, the local history of *Morrison v. White* seems to stand in direct contradiction to its legal history; the relation of race and law over time—the legal history of race—was running in one direction if you were sitting in the Third District Court in Jefferson Parish and another if you were sitting a few miles away in the Supreme Court in New

Orleans. Beneath the gathering tide of proslavery in the 1850s, beneath the proslavery crackdown on interracial socializing and the curtailment of manumission laws, beneath *Dred Scott* and the self-enslavement laws, beneath the prognostications of Samuel Cartwright and the pronouncements of George Fitzhugh, beneath legal definitions of race and textbook versions of proper legal practice, ran an undercurrent of discontented whiteness. As if through the upside-down pinhole of a camera obscura, *Morrison v. White*, a suit in which the slave sued the slave trader, illuminates the complexity of the relation between the economic system of slavery and the ideology of white supremacy by which it was increasingly justified. Though they remained wedded in the official rhetoric of the antebellum South—in the courtrooms and congresses—in the changing political economy of the 1850s, white supremacy and slavery were not coextensive paradigms of social order. Standing before the Third District Court, Alexina Morrison embodied the conflicting property claims of whiteness and slavery, claims that by running away and suing the slave trader she had brought into apparently irreconcilable conflict. In Jefferson Parish at least, the historic bargain at the heart of the southern social order—black slavery for white freedom—was less an accomplished fact than an open argument.

Notes

1 The first of the many questions of identity raised by the *Morrison* case concerns the slave trader whom she sued. He was originally identified in the case as John Rucker White, a slave trader from Howard County, Missouri. Testimony and documents introduced in the case, however, prove that he was James White from Georgia, who owned a slave pen in New Orleans in the 1850s. . . .

2 William Dennison later testified that Morrison had been brought to the prison by "the Officer of the Town of Carrollton" to whom she had "given herself up." . . . . Testimony of William Dennison, June 19, 1858, *Morrison v. White*, Louisiana Supreme Court case 442, 16 La. Ann. 100 (1861), Supreme Court of Louisiana Collection (Earl K. Long Library, University of New Orleans, New Orleans, La.). . . .

3 Answer, Nov. 22, 1857, ibid. . . .

4 See Judith Kelleher Schafer, *Slavery, the Civil Law, and the Supreme Court of Louisiana* (Baton Rouge, 1994), 90–95.

5 Laurence Kotlikoff, "The Structure of Slave Prices in New Orleans, 1804–1862," *Economic Inquiry*, 17 (Oct. 1979), 515; Walter Johnson, *Soul by Soul: Life inside the Antebellum Slave Market* (Cambridge, Mass., 1999), 150–56. . . .

6 The figure of 90% is drawn from Robert W. Fogel and Stanley L. Engerman, eds., "The New Orleans Slave Sample," database available from the Inter-University Consortium for Political and Social Research. . . . The word "griff" denoted the offspring of someone labeled "Negro" and someone labeled "Mulatto." . . . .

7 Johnson, *Soul by Soul*, 150–56. For the idea that race mixture should be treated from both sides of the imagined spectrum between white and

black—as a matter of whiteness as well as of blackness—see Werner Sollors, *Neither Black nor White Yet Both: Thematic Explorations of Interracial Literature* (New York, 1997), 3–30.

8 Monique Guillory, "Some Enchanted Evening on the Auction Block: The Cultural Legacy of the New Orleans Quadroon Balls" (Ph.D. diss., New York University, 1999). . . .

9 On racial ideology in the slave market (including notions of "blackness," slaveholders' views of light-skinned men, and white women's views of the "fancy trade"), see Johnson, *Soul by Soul*, 78–116, 135–61.

10 In the nineteenth century Frederick Law Olmsted invoked what I call "performance" as he described how he identified the race of people in the public market in Washington, D.C.: "All the Negro characteristics were more clearly marked in each than they often are in the North. In their dress, language, manner, motions—all were distinguishable almost as much as by their color from the white people who were distributed among them." Frederick Law Olmsted, *Journey in the Seaboard Slave States, with Remarks on Their Economy* (1856; New York, 1968), 12. On the embodiment and performance of socially scripted roles, see Norbert Elias, *The Civilizing Process*, vol. I: *The History of Manners*, trans. Edmund Jephcott (New York, 1978); Paul Connerton, *How Societies Remember* (Cambridge, Eng., 1989); Candace West and Don H. Zimmerman, "Doing Gender," in *The Social Construction of Gender*, ed. Judith Lorber and Susan Farrell (London, 1991), 13–37; and Judith Butler, *Gender Trouble: Feminism and the Subversion of Identity* (London, 1990), 79–149.

11 On slaveholders' dependence on their slaves' performances, see Johnson, *Soul by Soul*, 197–207.

12 See Guillory, "Some Enchanted Evening on the Auction Block," 149–81; and Sollors, *Neither Black nor White Yet Both*, 142–61, 220–45.

13 Olmsted, *Journey in the Seaboard Slave States*, 639–41. . . .

14 Ira Berlin, *Slaves without Masters: The Free Negro in the Antebellum South* (New York, 1974), 365–70; Thomas D. Morris, *Southern Slavery and the Law, 1619–1860* (Chapel Hill, 1996), 35–36; Ariela J. Gross, "Litigating Whiteness: Trials of Racial Determination in the Nineteenth Century South," *Yale Law Journal*, 108 (Oct. 1998), 109–88.

15 [On curtailing of manumission] see Morris, *Southern Slavery and the Law*, 371–423.

16 On the domestic slave trade, see Bancroft, *Slave Trading in the Old South*; Michael Tadman, *Speculators and Slaves: Masters, Traders, and Slaves in the Old South* (Madison, 1989); Steven H. Deyle, "The Domestic Slave Trade in America" (Ph.D. diss., Columbia University, 1995); and Johnson, *Soul by Soul*.

17 Olmsted, *Journey in the Seaboard Slave States*, 639–41; Morris, *Southern Slavery and the Law*, 31–36; Richard C. Wade, *Slavery in Cities: The South, 1820–1860* (New York, 1964), 80–110; Barbara Jeanne Fields, *Slavery and Freedom on the Middle Ground: Maryland during the Nineteenth Century* (New Haven, 1985), 40–89; Victoria E. Bynum, *Unruly Women: The Politics of Social and Sexual Control in the Old South* (Chapel Hill, 1996), 88–110; Martha Hodes, *White Women, Black Men: Illicit Sex in the Nineteenth-Century South* (New Haven, 1997), 116–22; Morris, *Southern Slavery and the Law*, 17–36; Schafer, *Slavery, the Civil Law, and the Supreme Court of Louisiana*, 179.

18 For the broader legal context of *Morrison v. White*, see Morris, *Southern Slavery and the Law*, 17–36; Schafer, *Slavery, the Civil Law, and the Supreme*

Court of Louisiana, 220–88; Hodes, *White Women, Black Men*, 96–122; Peter Bardaglio, *Reconstructing the Household: Families, Sex, and the Law in the Nineteenth-Century South* (Chapel Hill, 1995); Adrienne D. Davis, "Identity Notes Part One: Playing in the Light," *American University Law Review*, 45 (Feb. 1996), 695–720; and Gross, "Litigating Whiteness," 109–88. . . .

19 For other states, see Morris, *Southern Slavery and the Law*, 17–36; and Gross, "Litigating Whiteness," 109–88.

20 *Eulalie v. Long and Mabry*, case 3979, 11 La. Ann. 463 (1856), Supreme Court of Louisiana Collection; *Euphemie v. Juilet and Jourdan*, case 6740, unreported Louisiana Supreme Court case (1860), ibid. . . .

21 Manuscript Population Schedules, Matagorda County, Texas, Seventh Census of the United States, 1850. . . .

22 Deposition of James C. Anthony, March 1, 1858, *Morrison v. White*; Deposition of Giles, March 1, 1858, ibid.; Deposition of Moses Morrison, July 26, 1858, ibid.; Deposition of Andre Hutt, May 10, 1858, ibid.

23 Plaintiff's Petition, Oct. 19, 1857, *Morrison v. White*; Petitioner's Affidavit, Oct. 19, 1857, ibid.

24 Testimony of J. B. Clawson, June 19, 1858, *Morrison v. White*; Testimony of S. N. Cannon, June 19, 1858, ibid.; Testimony of Kemper, June 19, 1858, ibid.

25 Testimony of Martin, June 19, 1858, *Morrison v. White*; Testimony of J. A. Breaux, June 19, 1858, ibid. Throughout this article, I have reconstructed the questions asked on cross-examination from the answers recorded by the courtroom clerk. . . .

26 Deposition of Morrison, July 26, 1858, *Morrison v. White*; Deposition of Giles, March 1, 1858, ibid.

27 Or even, as I have been asked many times—and this seems to me evidence of the lingering imaginative hold of the quadroon ball fantasy—if she was really beautiful.

28 Defendant's Bill of Exceptions in the Fifth District Court hearing of the case, 1858, *Morrison v. White*.

29 Cross-examination of G. H. Lyons, June 19, 1858, *Morrison v. White*; Cross-examination of Clawson, June 19, 1858, ibid.; Cross-examination of Cannon, June 19, 1858, ibid.

30 On polygenesis (and its opposite, monogenesis), the nineteenth-century debate about them, and the religious and scientific context of the arguments, see William Stanton, *The Leopard's Spots: Scientific Attitudes toward Race in America, 1815–1859* (Chicago, 1960); Thomas Gossett, *Race: The History of an Idea in America* (Dallas, 1963); George M. Fredrickson, *The Black Image in the White Mind: The Debate over Afro-American Character and Destiny, 1817–1914* (New York, 1971); and Reginald Horsman, *Josiah Nott of Mobile: Southerner, Physician, and Racial Theorist* (Baton Rouge, 1987).

31 Cross-examination of Lyons, June 19, 1858, *Morrison v. White*; Cross-examination of Clawson, June 19, 1858, ibid.; Cross-examination of Cannon, June 19, 1858, ibid.

32 Testimony of P. C. Perret, May 18, 1859, *Morrison v. White*.

33 . . . . Testimony of Cannon, June 19, 1858, June 30, 1862, *Morrison v. White*; . . . .

34 Petition for Change of Venue, July 1, 1858, *Morrison v. White*. On the image of the quadroon and octoroon mistresses, see Guillory, "Some Enchanted Evening on the Auction Block"; . . .

35 See Don E. Ferenbacher, *The Dred Scott Case: Its Significance in American Law and Politics* (New York, 1978). For the African slave trade, see John Ashworth, *Slavery, Capitalism, and Politics in the Antebellum Republic*, vol. I:

Commerce and Compromise (Cambridge, Eng., 1995), 268–69. On the "enslavement crisis," see Berlin, *Slaves without Masters*, 369–80;. . . .

36 Berlin, *Slaves without Masters*, 369–70; Johnson and Roark, *Black Masters*, 169; Fields, *Slavery and Freedom on the Middle Ground*, 67–89.

37 Morris, *Southern Slavery and the Law*, 29–36, 371–423; Berlin, *Slaves without Masters*, 318–40; Schafer, *Slavery, the Civil Law, and the Supreme Court of Louisiana*, 179.

38 Ariela Gross, "Pandora's Box: Slavery, Character, and Southern Culture in the Courtroom, 1800–1860" (Ph.D. diss., Stanford University, 1996), 217–21. . . .

39 [Details of sources on jurors' identities have been omitted—ed.]

40 The slaveholder on the jury was J. J. Guttierez, who appears on the Jefferson slave schedule for 1860, but not on the census. Thus, although I can tell that he was a slaveholder, I have no other information about his origins, household, occupation, or property. . . . On the class tensions expressed in southern jury trials, see Bertram Wyatt-Brown, "Community, Class, and Snopesian Crime: Local Justice in the Old South," in *Class, Conflict, and Consensus: Antebellum Southern Community Studies*, ed. Orville Vernon Burton and Robert C. McMath Jr. (Westport, 1982), 173–206. Wyatt-Brown shows that jury trials were an occasion for nonslaveholding white men to exert political power over their social betters, and that southern courts were a place where the values of "the community" could be negotiated between classes. He does not, to my mind, note how class differences between white people in the antebellum South were experienced and expressed in terms of race and slavery. David R. Roediger, *The Wages of Whiteness: Race and the Making of the American Working Class* (London, 1991).

41 Edmund Morgan, *American Slavery, American Freedom: The Ordeal of Colonial Virginia* (New York, 1976). [See also] Kathleen M. Brown, *Good Wives, Nasty Wenches, and Anxious Patriarchs: Gender, Race, and Power in Colonial Virginia* (Chapel Hill, 1996), 137–86, 247–82.

42 On whiteness as entitlement, see Cheryl I. Harris, "Whiteness as Property," *Harvard Law Review*, 106 (June 1993), 1709–91. On nonslaveholders' expressing their property in whiteness through slave patrols and harassment of slaves, see Walter Johnson, "Inconsistency, Contradiction, and Complete Confusion: The Everyday Life of the Law of Slavery," *Law and Social Inquiry*, 22 (Spring 1997), 425–30. On "white slavery" in southern proslavery thought, see Noel Ignatiev, *How the Irish Became White* (London, 1995), 69; and Eugene D. Genovese, *The World the Slaveholders Made: Two Essays in Interpretation* (Middletown, 1969), 208–11. On northern labor, see Roediger, *Wages of Whiteness*, 65–92. . . . William J. Grayson, *The Hireling and the Slave, Chicora, and Other Poems* (Charleston, 1856); *New Orleans Daily Crescent*, June 22, 25, and 28, 1858.

43 George Fitzhugh, *Cannibals All! Or, Slaves Without Masters*, ed. C. Vann Woodward (1857; Cambridge, Mass., 1960). On George Fitzhugh and the white working class, see Genovese, *World the Slaveholders Made*, 208–11; and Ashworth, *Slavery, Capitalism, and Politics in the Antebellum Republic*, I, 228–46 . . .; Samuel Cartwright, "How to Save the Republic, and the Position of the South in the Union," *DeBow's Review*, 11 (no. 1, 1851), 195–96 . . . .; Barbara Jeanne Fields, "Ideology and Race in American History," in *Region, Race, and Reconstruction: Essays in Honor of C. Vann Woodward*, ed. James M. McPherson and J. Morgan Kousser (New York, 1982), 162.

44 On the *Herrenvolk* outlook, see Fredrickson, *Black Image in the White Mind*

...; Frederick Law Olmsted, *The Cotton Kingdom, A Traveler's Observations on Cotton and Slavery in the American Slave States*, ed. Arthur M. Schlesinger (1861; New York, 1962), 232; Ignatiev, *How the Irish Became White*, 19–23; Shugg, *Origins of Class Struggle in Louisiana: A Social History of White Farmers and Laborers during Slavery and After, 1840–1875* (Baton Rouge, 1968), 146–47. . . .

45 Stephanie M. McCurry, *Masters of Small Worlds: Yeoman Households, Gender Relations, and the Political Culture of the Antebellum South Carolina Lowcountry* (New York, 1995), viii, 5–35; Shugg, *Origins of Class Struggle in Louisiana*, 88–94; Burton and McMath, eds., *Class, Conflict, and Consensus*; Wade, *Slavery in Cities*, 274–75. . . .

46 Testimony of Clawson, June 19, 1858, *Morrison v. White.*

47 Testimony of Seaman Hopkins, May 18, 1859, *Morrison v. White*; Testimony of Perret, May 18, 1859, ibid.; Testimony of L. Castera, May 18, 1859, ibid.

48 On the social practice of bodily examination in the slave market, see Johnson, *Soul by Soul*, 135–61. Harris, "Whiteness as Property."

49 Prayer for Change of Venue, July 1, 1858, *Morrison v. White*; Judgment on Prayer for Change of Venue, July 24, 1858, ibid.

50 Reasons for Refusing New Trial, May 30, 1859, *Morrison v. White*; Decree of the Supreme Court, Feb. 4, 1861, ibid.

51 Decree of the Supreme Court, Feb. 4, 1861, *Morrison v. White.*

52 Verdict, Jan. 30, 1862, *Morrison v. White*; Bond of Appeal, Feb. 11, 1862, ibid.; Supreme Court of Louisiana Docket Record, Supreme Court of Louisiana Collection. For post–Civil War action on cases involving slavery, see Schafer, *Slavery, the Civil Law, and the Supreme Court of Louisiana*, 289–304.

53 Manuscript Population Schedules, Jefferson Parish, Eighth Census, 1860, dwellings 1470 and 1471.

54 This is the argument made in Eugene D. Genovese, *Roll, Jordan, Roll: The World the Slaves Made* (New York, 1974), 25–49, 587–98. See also Mindie Lazarus-Black and Susan F. Hirsch, *Contested States: Law, Hegemony, and Resistance* (New York, 1994).

9

TIPPECANOE AND THE LADIES, TOO

White women and party politics in antebellum Virginia

Elizabeth R. Varon

Both those who accept and those who reject the paternalist interpretation of antebellum southern society have usually agreed that women in southern families were, because of the South's more thoroughgoing patriarchal values, far more restricted in their behavior than women in the North. Above all, most have assumed, women were denied all participation in the most public part of the public sphere, partisan politics. Elizabeth R. Varon challenges this understanding with her essay on women's contributions to the Whig party in Virginia in the 1840s and after. Even though the South saw no woman's rights movement, Varon writes that her study shows "that meaningful change can take place for women in an antifeminist atmosphere." Women wrote, rallied, and raised money for Whig candidates and Whig-related causes, she demonstrates, and this the "dichotomous picture of northern women's political activism and southern women's political marginalization needs to be rethought."

* * *

The nineteenth-century ideology of "separate spheres," which prescribed that men occupy the public sphere of business and politics and women the domestic sphere of home and family, has exercised a powerful hold over historians of the antebellum United States. As a result, the fields of antebellum political history and women's history have used separate sources and focused on separate issues. Political historians—relying on sources such as voting records, newspapers, and the writings of politicians—have described the emergence in the 1840s of what the historian Joel H. Silbey has called a new "American political nation." Gone was the political world of the early republic, with its widespread antiparty sentiment, deferential behavior by voters, and political dominance by social elites. In the new order, political parties, led by professional politicians, demanded disciplined partisanship from the electorate. The "electoral universe" was in constant motion. Men participated in a frenzied cycle of party rallies, processions, committee meetings, conventions, caucuses, and elections. What about women? Since they were neither voters nor politicians, women have received only brief mention in the new political history.[1]

Women's historians, for their part, have shown little interest in the subject of party politics. . . . Those few scholars—Paula C. Baker, Mary P. Ryan, and Michael E. McGerr—who have tried to integrate political history and women's history have not challenged the historiographical impression that the realm of antebellum party politics was a male preserve. While these scholars note that women took part in political campaigns, they stress the theme of female exclusion from male political culture. As McGerr has written, women were let into the political sphere only "to cook, sew, and cheer for men and to symbolize virtue and beauty." They were denied "not only the ballot but also the experience of mass mobilization."[2]

The distance between antebellum political history and women's history is perhaps nowhere so great as in the historiography on the Old South. While northern feminist abolitionists who demanded political enfranchisement have begun to receive their due from historians of northern politics, no such radical vanguard existed in the South to command the attention of political historians. Both the major historians of antebellum southern politics and the major practitioners of southern women's history have neglected the subject of female partisanship. The current historiographical consensus holds that southern women, in keeping with the conservatism of their region, by and large eschewed politics even as northern women were fighting for access to the political sphere.[3]

This essay attempts to close the gap between women's history and political history. Focusing on the Commonwealth of Virginia, it argues that historians have underestimated the extent and significance of women's partisanship in the antebellum period. In the presidential election campaigns of the 1840s, Virginia Whigs made a concerted effort to win the allegiance of the commonwealth's women by inviting them to the party's rallies, speeches, and processions. Though the Whigs never carried the state for their presidential candidates, they repeatedly claimed that the majority of women favored their party over the Democrats. Whig campaign rhetoric, as presented by the party's newspapers, and women's private and public expressions of partisanship articulated a new ideal of feminine civic duty, one that I call Whig womanhood. Whig womanhood embodied the notion that women could—and should—make vital contributions to party politics by serving as both partisans and mediators in the public sphere. According to Whig propaganda, women who turned out at the party's rallies gathered information that allowed them to mold partisan families, reminded men of moral values that transcended partisanship, and conferred moral standing on the party.

The Whigs' claim that there was a "gender gap," to use a modern phrase, between them and the Democrats did not go unanswered. During the 1844 campaign, the Virginia Democrats made sporadic appeals to women. A full-scale public debate over women's partisanship erupted in the months after the presidential election of 1844, when the Whig women of Virginia formed the Virginia Association of Ladies for Erecting a Statue to Henry Clay. The Clay Association believed its work was the perfect expression of female patriotism. The Democrats disagreed, branding the association's activities unladylike and even rebellious. The debate fizzled out in a few months, with the Whigs apparent winners. Gradually, Democrats in Virginia adopted Whig tactics for developing female allegiance to their own party. By the mid-1850s the inclusion of women in the rituals of party politics had become commonplace, and the ideology that justified such inclusion had been assimilated by Democrats.

In Virginia, the Whig party's "Tippecanoe and Tyler, Too," campaign of 1840 marks a turning point in women's partisanship. Prior to 1840, women, with a few notable exceptions, were marginal to the public discourse and rituals of political parties in Virginia. To be sure, many women felt partisan allegiances. Evidence of such partisanship can be found primarily in the letters of female relatives of politicians. Such women as Judith Rives, wife of United States senator William Cabell Rives, were trusted advisers to their husbands and frequently expressed partisan opinions in their correspondence with family members. Some women, particularly relatives of officeholders and those who lived near Washington, D. C., or Richmond, attended political speeches and legislative deliberations, but political parties made no systematic efforts to encourage or to publicize women's presence in the galleries.[4]

The rhetoric and symbolism of presidential election campaigns in the 1830s were predominantly masculine and martial. For example, the *Staunton Spectator* of October 20, 1836, featured the following exhortation to the voters of Augusta County: "Let every man then gird on his armour for the contest! Let the beacon FIRES be lighted on every hill, to give warning to all that the enemy is at hand! Let the WAR DRUMS beat a loud REVEILLE!"[5]

The only expression of partisanship by a woman found in the Virginia newspapers from the 1830s sampled for this essay is a poem to Harrison that appeared in the *Staunton Spectator* of September 1, 1836. A "young lady" from Pennsylvania defended Harrison and chided his critics with the words: "Those who would thus *disgrace their land* / Are found in every age; / Not ev'n our Washington could stand / Untouch'd by *Party rage*." The *Spectator's* editors said of the poet, "We are glad she is for Harrison—though we understand most of the Ladies are so."[6]

The *Staunton Spectator* editors were ahead of their time in suggesting that an affinity existed between women and the Whig party; so, too, was Lucy Kenney of Fredericksburg, who made a similar claim. A single woman aspiring to be a professional writer, Kenney published a series of pamphlets in the 1830s, including one in which she proclaimed her support for Democratic president Andrew Jackson and his heir apparent, Van Buren. In 1838 Kenney switched allegiances and became a Whig. A fervent supporter of slavery and states' rights, Kenney believed that the passing of the Democratic torch to northerner Van Buren—who had supported the Missouri Compromise and, so southerners charged, had abolitionist supporters—boded ill for the South. But her defection from the Democrats was not purely ideological. When Kenney had called on Van Buren in 1838, asking that he and his party remunerate her for her efforts on their behalf, the president, much to her disgust, had offered her a mere dollar. Some "honorable Whigs," however, had a different notion of Kenney's worth and offered her one thousand dollars for her services.[7]

Kenney took the Whigs up on their offer, and later that year published a scathing pamphlet, *A Letter Addressed to Martin Van Buren*, in which she predicted that the 1840 election would strip Van Buren of the "usurped power" he had gained by "false pretences." Kenney's attack on the president prompted a response, in pamphlet form, from Van Buren supporter Eliza B. Runnells. According to Runnells, Kenney possessed none of the "elevated tone of feeling and celestial goodness, that has distinguished the female character." Kenney had been enlisted and armed for battle by "Whig magicians" and in the process "transfigured from an angel of peace, to a political bully."[8]

The exchange between Kenney and Runnells prefigures later developments. In 1840, as Whig recruitment of women began on a grand scale, Democratic commentators echoed Runnells's doubts about the propriety of women's partisanship. Stung by their loss in the presidential campaign of 1836, the Whigs in 1840 overhauled both their message and their strategy for taking it to the voters. . . .[9]

The new medium for the message was equally important. The Whigs decided that to win the election, they needed to "agitate the people"— and that the people included women. Leading Whigs around the country called for strong local organization and the use of "every lawful means" to bring men to the polls. Means for influencing the electorate included dinners, barbecues, picnics, and processions, with women as spectators and participants.[10]

Historians generally agree that the Whigs' 1840 campaign marks the first time a political party systematically included women in its public rituals. All around the country, women turned out at Whig rallies; on occasion they even made speeches, conducted political meetings, and wrote pamphlets on behalf of the Whigs. And yet, while many scholarly studies note these developments, none draw out their implications. Historians have relegated women's partisanship to a few pages of description here and there; and they generally present women, not as political actors, but as "audience and symbol." . . . .[11]

The Virginia evidence suggests that to characterize women's partisanship as passive is to obscure the transformation in women's civic roles that the election of 1840 set in motion. Newspapers, pamphlets, and speeches, taken together with women's diaries, letters, and reminiscences, chart that transformation. The function of antebellum newspapers, which were the organs of political parties, was to make partisanship seem essential to men's identities.[12] With the campaign of 1840, Whig newspapers took on the additional task of making partisanship seem essential to women's identities.

Whig newspapers in Virginia, in lockstep with the party's national organ, the *Washington National Intelligencer*, featured invitations to women to attend the speeches and rallies of "Tippecanoe and Tyler, Too," clubs and provided glowing reports of such events. The *Staunton Spectator* noted, for example, that the women of Mt. Solon favored its "Tipp and Ty" club with their attendance and "enjoyed very highly the display of eloquence" by the speakers. Whig rhetoric argued that the presence of women at such events bespoke not only their admiration for Harrison but also their opposition to the policies of the Democrats. . . .[13]

Anecdotes celebrating women's influence began to circulate in the Whig newspapers of Virginia. One such story, "Another Conversion," told the tale of Miss Bond, "a warm Harrison woman," who refused to marry Mr. Provins, her Democratic suitor. After hearing a particularly convincing Harrison speech, Provins finally came around: "*he* declared for Harrison, and *she* declared for PROVINS on the spot." The very fact that the writer referred to Bond as a "warm Harrison woman" reflects the new political climate. Women who felt partisan identities in the 1820s and 1830s were often referred to as "men": in 1827 James McDowell wrote to his wife, Susan, that his sister Sopponisha was an "Adams-man"; in 1834 William Cabell Rives referred to his friend Mrs. James Cocke as a "warm *Jackson-man*." In 1840, and in the presidential campaigns that followed, partisan women were commonly described, and described themselves, as "Whig women" and "Democratic women."[14]

According to the Whig press, women could contribute to the campaign not only by listening to speeches and by exerting influence over men but also by making public presentations. On October 1, 1840, the "Whig Ladies of Alexandria" presented a banner with the motto "Gen. Wm. H. Harrison, the Glory and Hope of our Nation" to the local Tippecanoe club; male delegates of the club carried the banner in a Whig procession that took place four days later in Richmond. Whig newspapers also occasionally published Harrison songs and poems by women. One Virginian wrote a song in honor of her party's candidate that ended with the refrain "Down with the Locos / dark hocus-pocus / The Banner of Liberty floats through the sky."[15]

The single most vocal female contributor to the Tippecanoe campaign was Kenney. She published two pamphlets, *A History of the Present Cabinet* and *An Address to the People of the United States*, in support of Harrison's 1840 campaign. He was an honorable statesman who had earned the "blessings of thousands of women and children" in his career as an Indian fighter. In keeping with a favorite Whig theme, Kenney asserted that Harrison's private character was as unassailable as his public record. . . .[16]

The personal papers of Virginia women confirm that the 1840 campaign was different from its predecessors. "Fashionable topics seem to turn on politics more than anything else at present," Whig Judith Rives wrote her son in February 1840, from the family plantation in Albemarle County. "I never saw anything like the excitement here," Sarah Pendleton Dandridge of Essex County informed her sister; "we hear of nothing but Gen. Harrison." Girls as well as women were caught up in the campaign hoopla. Sara Pryor, who grew up near Richmond, relates in her reminiscences that she knew many a young girl who enjoyed "singing the campaign songs of the hero of the Log Cabin." . . . .[17]

Private residences and businesses became sites for the consumption and production of partisan material culture. Women not only bought a vast array of Whig paraphernalia (such as stationery, songbooks, plates, buttons, glassware, and quilts bearing Harrison's name) but also made their own. In preparation for a Whig procession, Celestia Shakes of Alexandria made a model log cabin, which she placed in the window of her shop where everyone was sure to see it; "the Cabin pleased the Whigs very much [and] they cheered it," she wrote her sister.[18]

In the age of mass politics, even women's housekeeping could serve partisanship. Party conventions, rallies, and processions might bring thousands of visitors who had to be lodged, fed, and cared for. Naturally, women played a key role in providing these services and so facilitated the political process. One such woman, Mary Steger of Richmond, wrote to a friend in September 1840 about her preparations for the upcoming state convention of the Whig party:

every Whig house in the city is to be crammed we expect to
have 10 or 12 sleep here to say nothing of the stragglers in to
dinner &tc you will think perhaps it needs not much preparation but we are all in a bustle. . . . Our Log Cabin is open
almost every few nights (the regular meetings being once a
week) to some speakers from a distance. The Cabin holds 1,500
and it is always full.

In all likelihood, Steger had been to the "Log Cabin" (the Whig campaign headquarters) herself to hear Whig discourses. It was quite
impossible to remain aloof from politics, she told her friend: "I never
took so much interest in politics in my life . . . the fact is you have to
know something about them for nobody here thinks of any else."[19]

For Whig women in Virginia, the crowning event of the 1840 campaign was Whig luminary Daniel Webster's visit to Richmond during
the October convention. Susan Hooper, who achieved some renown as a
writer during the Civil War, was at a reception for Webster on his arrival
in Richmond and later wrote a detailed description of the event. Her
father, a staunch supporter of Webster, "could not permit so golden an
opportunity of his child's seeing his political idol to pass unimproved;
so, girl, almost baby as I was, he hurried me down to the honorable
gentleman's reception . . . that in after years I might boast of having
heard Webster, the immortal."[20]

After giving two speeches to huge crowds of enthusiastic Whig men
and women, Webster yielded to the "particular request of the ladies of
Richmond" and agreed to present a special address on women's political role to them at the Whig campaign headquarters. On October 7,
some twelve hundred women turned out for the event. Webster took
issue with the popular maxim that "there is one morality for politics
and another morality for other things," and he looked forward to the
day when the standards of private life would govern public conduct. It
was women's special duty, he suggested, to bring that day about.[21]

Because their moral perceptions were "both quicker and juster than
those of the other sex," Webster continued, women could infuse society
with the "pure morality" on which sound government depended.
Mothers had to teach their children that

the exercise of the elective franchise is a social duty, of as
solemn a nature as man can be called on to perform; that a man
may not innocently trifle with his vote; that every free elector is
a trustee as well for others as himself, and that every man and
every measure he supports has an important bearing on the
interests of others as well as on his own.[22]

. . . . Webster's views were echoed by two of Virginia's leading Whigs, former governor James Barbour and Richmond lawyer James Lyons, who spoke to the crowd after Webster had finished. They made explicit what Webster had implied: women's civic duty was to create Whig families, and their public participation in Whig events empowered them to fulfill that role. Barbour expressed delight at having seen throngs of women attend Whig rallies throughout "the length and breadth of this land" during the year's canvass. Those women were "animated with the one holy purpose of redeeming from destruction those liberties earned for us by our fathers, which are equally dear to woman as to man, and which she, with us, is equally bound to transmit untarnished to our children for ages to come." . . . . Guarded by the "shield of female purity," Lyons concluded, the Whigs were sure to conquer.[23]

The *National Intelligencer*, which reprinted the speeches in their entirety, praised Webster for celebrating the "vast influence" of women on the well-being of society. The *Richmond Whig* saw the turnout of women as evidence that the "better part of creation were and are, almost unanimously Whig." Women's support for the party "ought to silence Loco Focoism, and sanctify the inevitable Revolution which is about to occur," the editors proclaimed.[24] The "Revolution" the editors had in mind was the victory of Harrison over Van Buren. But they, along with Webster and his colleagues, were helping to actuate another revolution—one in gender conventions.

Webster and his fellow speakers were in effect articulating a new theory of women's civic duty. That theory, Whig womanhood, attempted to reconcile women's partisanship as Whigs with the ideology of domesticity or "true womanhood." The canon of domesticity, like the revolutionary-era theory of republican motherhood, celebrated woman's power and duty to mold the character of her sons, to instill in them civic virtue and a love for the Republic. At the same time, domestic doctrine held that the "true woman" was nonpartisan. Men embodied the "baser instincts"—selfishness, passion, and ambition—which partisanship expressed. By contrast, women were selfless, disinterested, and virtuous. Men pursued their self-interest in the public sphere; women maintained harmony, morality, and discipline in the domestic one.[25]

What was new about Whig womanhood was its equation of female patriotism with partisanship and its assumption that women had the duty to bring their moral beneficence into the public sphere. Whig rhetoric held that women were partisans, who shared with men an intense interest and stake in electoral contests. No longer was patriotism a matter of teaching sons to love the Republic. A patriotic woman would teach her family to love the Whig party; she, after all, understood that the Whigs alone could ensure the health and safety of the Republic.

That very understanding was forged in public. Rather than affirm a cherished tenet of the ideal of domesticity, that women must avoid the contentious political arena in order to safeguard their virtue, Whig speakers argued that by attending campaign events, women could transform the public sphere, fostering "domestic" virtues such as fairness, harmony, and self-control in a larger setting. Women's "countenance" sanctified the Whig cause; their presence bespoke the party's moral rectitude. Not only did women legitimize partisan behavior, they helped set limits on it—they guarded men with a "shield of purity" and made them understand the moral consequences of their actions. In a sense, Whig womanhood was the ultimate testament of faith in true womanhood. Its expositors held that *even* participation in party politics could not corrupt women or erase the fundamental differences between them and men.

How well did Whig rhetoric about women conform to reality? The Whigs' claim that the "ladies are all Whigs" was, of course, a fanciful fabrication. Even though expressions of partisanship by Whig women outnumber those by Democratic women in extant writings from 1840, it seems unlikely that a majority, let alone the entirety, of Virginia women supported the Whigs. Despite Harrison's vigorous campaign, the Democrats still had the support of a majority of voters in Virginia in 1840; women's private papers simply do not bear out the Whig contention that many of these Democratic voters had Whig wives. Since women did not cast ballots, the Whigs' assertion that there was a gender gap in politics cannot be empirically proven or refuted—therein, no doubt, lay some of its viability as propaganda. But the Whig party clearly did much more than its rival to encourage and celebrate female partisanship, and Whig women, most likely as a result, outdid their Democratic counterparts in displays of partisan zeal.

Judging by the campaign reports of Democratic newspapers, the Democrats were deeply ambivalent about women's partisanship. Jackson, the grand old hero of the Democratic party, drew admiring crowds of men and women when he toured the South, but such Democratic newspapers as the party's national organ, the *Washington Globe*, did not make a concerted effort to publicize or encourage women's presence at Democratic rallies.[26]

The leading Democrats in Virginia did little to contest the Whig party's assertion that it alone had the blessing of women. Some Democrats openly expressed their contempt for Whig tactics. The *Richmond Crisis*, a Democratic campaign paper, mockingly suggested to the Whigs that they might increase the "swelling pageant" at their state convention if they ran the following advertisement: "A meeting of the Babies of Richmond, with their Nurses, is respectfully requested this evening, at the Log Cabin, in order to form a Tippecanoe Infant Club."

After Webster's speech to the Whig women of Richmond, a correspondent to the *Richmond Enquirer* lambasted speaker and audience alike, asking "Are the ladies of Virginia so destitute of religious and moral instruction, that they need a thorough politician to enlighten them on the subject of the training of their children?". . . . [27]

Why was the Whig and not the Democratic party the first to seize the opportunity to make, as one Democrat put it, "politicians of their women"? Answers to the question must be speculative, for neither Whig nor Democratic commentators explicitly accounted for this difference in the political tactics of the two parties. Studies of Whig ideology argue that women were central to the Whigs' world view. Although the Democrats sought to maintain a strict boundary between the private and public spheres and resented attempts to politicize domestic life, the Whigs invested the family—and women in particular—with the distinct political function of forming the "stable American character" on which national well-being depended. While the Democrats acknowledged the reality of social conflict, the Whigs preferred speaking of a society in which harmony prevailed; women's "special moral and spiritual qualities," Whigs maintained, fitted them for the task of promoting such harmony. [28]

Historians Joe L. Kincheloe Jr., Ronald P. Formisano, and Richard J. Carwardine suggest that inclusion of women in partisan rituals was a by-product of the Whig party's efforts to blend religion and politics. Many Whig leaders were steeped in evangelical religion and applied what they had learned in the religious sphere to the political one. They practiced "secular revivalism"—the great rallies of the 1840s were, in essence, secular camp meetings. Using the evangelical idiom, Whig orators told crowds of enthusiastic men, women, and children that a presidential campaign was not simply a contest over political principles but a clash between good and evil. [29]

While some Whig men may have conceived of religious revivals as a model for partisan rituals, it is also likely that the connections of Whig leaders to benevolent reform movements predisposed them to recognize the value if women's aid. Scholars have long identified the Whig party with benevolent reform. The Whigs believed, the historians Daniel Howe and Lawrence Kohl have argued, in the malleability of human nature. They championed institutions that could help individuals achieve the "self-mastery" on which social order depended: schools, benevolent societies, reformatories, and asylums. All around the country, Whigs were leaders in reform movements. Henry Clay of Kentucky served as president of the American Colonization Society, and Theodore Frelinghuysen of New Jersey served as president of the American Tract Society and the American Bible Society. In Virginia, too, Whigs championed moral reform. Prominent Whigs such as Governor

Barbour supported a variety of reform causes, from a conviction that public education and benevolent societies were a means to create a more harmonious society.[30]

As many recent studies show, by 1840, women had long been active in the sphere of benevolent reform. They had proved that they were effective organizers, skilled at mobilizing public support for their projects. In Virginia, men had enthusiastically enlisted female support in the temperance and African colonization causes, arguing that the participation of "disinterested" and virtuous females would legitimate those causes. In short, when reform-minded Whig leaders such as Barbour encouraged women to join in the party's glorious crusade, they were not inventing or advancing new arguments to justify public activism by women, but rather recasting old ones, adapting the ideology of benevolent femininity to the new realities of mass party politics.[31]

On balance, Whig propaganda about women more closely resembled the rhetoric of disinterested benevolence than that of religious enthusiasm. Women's roles in the two settings, evangelical revivals and partisan rallies, differed in one essential way. Camp meetings were known for their high emotional pitch. Kincheloe asserts that women who attended them "screamed, participated in the 'exercises,' exhorted, sang, and did anything else that men could do." Women's role at political rallies, by contrast, was more to contain passions than to give in to them. Political passion, according to nineteenth-century rhetoric, was a sort of "blindness"; critiques of "blind party spirit" float through the campaign rhetoric of the 1840s.[32] Whig rhetoric implied that women, by virtue of their moral superiority, could resist this blindness. Whig men occasionally praised female enthusiasm, but they more often stressed Whig women's disinterestedness, dignity, and decorum.

In other words, the participation of women helped to relieve men's anxieties about changes in electoral behavior. Even though men likened partisan competition to warfare, they were intensely concerned with constraining the behavior of partisans. This concern, it might be argued, ran especially high among Whigs in 1840, when they began their appeals to women. The Whigs wanted to have it both ways: to steal the Jacksonians' democratic thunder and to claim that the Whigs were a breed apart from the Democrats—and a superior one at that. The Whigs' 1840 campaign was masterminded by a new cadre of professional politicians who sought to beat the Jacksonians at their own game of rousing the common man. . . . [Yet] in contrast to the Democrats' excessive partisanship and executive corruption, the Whigs, so they claimed, represented disinterested virtue, a love of the Union, and a reverence for the traditions of the Founding Fathers.[33]

If this message seems dissonant, it was. Men such as Webster, Clay, and John Quincy Adams initially resisted the notion that the Whig campaign of 1840 should focus on "style, song and hysteria." When these "old guard" leaders began to taste victory, however, they came around and played the demagogue to crowds of enthusiastic followers in places such as Richmond, telling them what they wanted to hear. The Democrats naturally asserted that the Whigs' efforts to unleash voter enthusiasm were immoral and destructive to the public peace; particularly disturbing, Democrats charged, was the way the dispensing of hard cider by Harrison campaign workers encouraged intemperance.[34] But the Whigs had the perfect counter-argument—the very presence of women at Whig events insured decorum and sobriety. With women on their side, Whigs could lay claim both to popular democracy and to dignity.

The Whig party's victory in the 1840 presidential contest proved to be short-lived. The death of Harrison within a month after his inauguration exposed the fault lines in the Whigs' fragile coalition. Seeking a consensus candidate in 1844, the Whigs chose Clay, whom their northern and southern wings could agree on. Clay, a southerner, opposed the annexation of Texas unless on terms acceptable to the North. And he championed an "American System" of internal development that would bind the country together through commercial ties.[35]

The years between Harrison's victory in 1840 and Clay's campaign in 1844 afforded women and men alike fewer opportunities to display partisanship than the presidential campaign season had. Women did attend political speeches and debates in nonelection years.[36] But they were not generally included in the year-round succession of meetings, held behind closed doors, in which the state business of the Whig party, such as the selection of delegates to state conventions, was conducted. Women's function in partisan life had clear limits: their role was not to choose Whig candidates but to affirm the choices of Whig men, particularly in high-stakes presidential campaigns; to help maintain party discipline; and to bring new members into the Whig fold.

As soon as the presidential canvass of 1844 got underway, the tide of female partisanship rose again, to new heights. The Whig party in Virginia flooded women with a virtual torrent of invitations to Whig events. As in 1840, Whig men thought that the approval of women legitimized the Whig campaign. "If we doubted before," a correspondent wrote after seeing the large number of women at a Whig rally in Goochland County, "now we know the Whigs must be right and will be more than conquerors."[37]

Women's support for the Whigs, Virginia newspapers were at pains to point out, was not restricted to such urban strongholds as Petersburg and Richmond. Women attended Whig events in towns, villages, county courthouses, and rural settings around the state. The presence of 350 women at a Whig rally in Clarksburg, for example, was evidence that "ladies in the remote and retired Mountain districts take the same interest in the success of the Whig cause, which they do everywhere else."[38]

The Whig party's campaign rhetoric conjured up an image of the ideal Whig woman: a chaste, honorable lady who attended political rallies to sanction the party, to dignify its proceedings, to affirm her loyalty, and to gather information that would allow her to transmit Whig culture to her family, friends, and acquaintances. Although often spoken of, Whig women rarely got the chance to speak for themselves before partisan audiences in 1844. On at least one occasion, however, a Virginia woman addressed a Whig crowd through a male proxy. On September 3 the *Richmond Whig* featured "AN EXAMPLE TO THE WHIG LADIES OF RICHMOND!", the story of Miss Martha Peake of Charlottesville. Peake presented a "splendid Banner" to the Clay Club of Charlottesville in September 1844, along with a "chaste and beautiful letter" that one of its male members read aloud. When Clay is elected, she cautioned the Whig voters of the town, "forget not that those whom you have vanquished are your brothers, subjects of the same government, struggling as ardently and as honestly, as you, for what they believe, with mistaken judgment, in my poor opinion, to be the true path to national honor, happiness and glory." Only if the victorious Whigs were able to transcend the fierce emotions of party competition would the nation "bask in the sunshine of moral, social and political purity and peace."[39]

Webster and his fellow Whig luminaries undoubtedly would have approved of Peake's message, for she was imposing her superior moral sensibilities on the conduct of politics and admonishing men of the proper limits of partisanship. Apparently the *Richmond Whig* agreed that Peake successfully harmonized partisanship and true womanhood: she was bound to get married soon, the editors allowed, for her Whig credentials made her "pre-eminently qualified to confer domestic happiness" on some fortunate man.[40]

In 1844, the Whig party's claim that it had the support of the commonwealth's women was most certainly intended, as it had been in 1840, to provoke the Democrats. The *Lexington Gazette* printed a letter to the Whigs of Fishersville by Benjamin Johnson Barbour, in which he taunted the Democrats for alienating the female population. Eve had been deceived "by the prince of the Locofocos, and had ever since eschewed both him and his party"; no Democrat would stand a chance to get married until after the November election.[41]

Virginia women's own accounts of the campaign of 1844 echo the party's rhetoric. Virginian Marion Harland, a nationally famous novelist and author of domestic guidebooks for women in the mid-nineteenth century, asserts in her autobiography that even as a child of thirteen, she was a violent Whig partisan and supporter of Clay. In

1844 the Whigs invited the women of her county to a political rally, the first time such an invitation had been extended to ladies, according to Harland; the innovation "set tongues wagging," she remembers, and "practically guaranteed the county for Clay."[42]

. . . .

In the early stages of the 1844 campaign, Democrats made few overtures to women to join in partisan activities, but by the fall of 1844, the party was actively appealing to women and trying to counter Whig propaganda with its own claims. Hundreds of women attended a Democratic rally in Fairfax in September; twenty-eight young ladies carried flags bearing the "different mottoes of the states." "About 100 ladies favored Mr. L. [Mr. Leake, the speaker at the rally] with their presence, and their approving smiles," wrote the *Richmond Enquirer* of another Democratic meeting, "demonstrating the falsity of the charge that the 'Ladies are all Whigs.' "[43]

These appeals notwithstanding, some Democrats continued to be critical of female mobilization. At a Loudoun County political debate, a Democratic orator "assail[ed] the ladies for attending political meetings" and "for giving their smiles" to the Whigs. Describing a Whig procession in New York, a Democratic correspondent to the *Washington Globe* declared that while the Whigs' "showy pageant" might "amuse the wives, daughters and sisters of our sovereign lord the people . . . it can neither buy, bribe, nor beat the staunch and sterling democracy of New York, when it comes to the matter of MEN." Such skepticism about the propriety and utility of Whig appeals to women was not confined to men. According to Serena Dandridge, a Democrat from Essex County, the reason the Whigs lost the election of 1844 was that they had "too many women & children in their ranks."[44] Ironically, the strongest articulations of Whig womanhood and the most strident attacks on it came after the election of 1844 had been lost. For it was then that Whig women in Virginia tried to snatch a symbolic victory from the jaws of defeat.

On November 19, 1844, the *Richmond Whig* published a seemingly innocuous letter that would touch off months of debate in the Virginia press. The letter, from Lucy Barbour of Barboursville, Orange County, proposed that the "Whig women of Virginia" give some "token of respect" to Clay, who had just lost his third bid for the presidency of the United States. Barbour was a member of Virginia's social elite. Her husband James, who had died in 1842, had been one of the most prominent Whigs in Virginia. He had served as governor of the commonwealth, United States senator, and the secretary of war under John Quincy Adams. The Barbours counted Clay among their close friends.[45]

Barbour anticipated that her call to action would raise eyebrows. "I know our sex are thought by many unstable as water," her letter continued, "but after crowding the Whig festivals, and manifesting so much enthusiasm, few will be found so hollow-hearted as to refuse a small sum to so good—I had almost said, so holy a cause": the tribute to Clay. The editors of the *Richmond Whig* agreed to adopt Barbour's scheme as their own. The editors of the *Richmond Enquirer* wasted no time in ridiculing the plan to honor Clay: "Has it come to this, that the 'gallant Harry' has been turned over to the tender mercies of the ladies . . .?" The *Enquirer* also printed a letter from one "Incognita," who thoroughly disapproved of the notion that Whig women should hold a meeting to decide on a strategy for honoring Clay: "a public meeting of political amazons! . . . Was such an event ever recorded, or before heard of, in the annals of time?"[46]

Barbour vigorously defended her project. In a December 4 letter to the *Richmond Whig*, she stated that women deserved "freedom of thought even on political subjects; and the power of performing an act of justice to an injured statesman; when, doing so, we neglect no duty assigned to us by the most rigid." "We are the nursing mothers of heroes, statesmen, and divines," she continued, "and while we perform a task so important, we mean to be counted something in the muster-roll of mań."[47]

Inspired by Barbour's appeal, a group of Whig women met on December 9 at the First Presbyterian Church in Richmond and formed the Virginia Association of Ladies for Erecting a Statue to Henry Clay; they elected Barbour as president. The statue was to be funded by membership subscriptions, costing no more than one dollar each. Men could make donations but not become members. . . .[48]

Thanks to the survival of a subscription book from around 1845–1846 that lists contributors to the Clay Association by county, we can get a sense of the breadth and nature of the organization. The book lists the names of 2,563 subscribers, covering counties from Accomac on the Eastern Shore to Nelson on the Blue Ridge; at least 2,236 of the subscribers were women. The association, which received national publicity in the *National Intelligencer*, also had auxiliaries in Alexandria (204 subscribers) and in Boston (215 subscribers). Additional contributions came from families in Vermont, Mississippi, and Georgia.[49]

The list of subscribers confirms that there was a strong connection between Whiggery and female benevolence in Virginia. Seventeen of the thirty-six members of the Female Humane Association of Richmond in 1843—an organization that provided food and shelter to destitute girls—subscribed to the Clay Association in 1845. Lucy Otey of Lynchburg and Ann Clagett of Alexandria, directors of orphan asylums in their respective towns, are two more of the many benevolent women who contributed to the Clay project.[50]

. . . . As auxiliaries sprang up around the state, so, too, did debate over the propriety of the association. On December 22, 1844, for example, two days after the Whig women of Lynchburg formed an auxiliary, the editors of the Democratic *Lynchburg Republican* attacked the Clay Association, suggesting with derision that "the name of every lady who mingles in this great work of generosity and patriotism will be handed down to posterity as a *partisan* lady." "Is not this whole movement conceived in a spirit of rebellion?" the editors asked. The Democrats mocked the notion that partisanship was appropriate for women—that partisanship and patriotism were synonymous. The Whiggish *Lynchburg Virginian* defended the Clay Association, commending it for advancing the Whig cause. . . .[51]

A week later, two more male defenders of the association came forward, urging Whig women to stand their ground. A correspondent with the pen name "Peter Caustic" proclaimed, "There is too much firmness of character, and nobleness of soul about Virginia's daughters to suffer themselves to be intimidated by the denunciations of Locofocoism." The second defender agreed, stating that "the Whig ladies of Virginia consider themselves at least as well qualified to judge of their own acts as the Locofoco editor, who has undertaken to lecture them."[52]

Perhaps the most strident defense of the association came from a correspondent of the *Lexington Gazette*, who jumped into the fray after an auxiliary was formed in that town in January 1845. The Democrats, he claimed, were being disingenuous: "The sneering democratic gentry who ridicule the idea of ladies meddling with politics, would not be so bitterly sarcastic if they could have a little of this meddling on their side of the question." "We are willing to avow our own opinion that woman's proper sphere is HOME," the writer continued. But "there are occasions . . . when her domestic duties themselves demand that she should enter the arena which man has considered his exclusive province."[53]

Whig women themselves came forward on their own and Clay's behalf. In December 1844 a female correspondent to the *Richmond Whig* wrote that women had a duty to honor Clay since he had been "shamefully neglected by his countrymen." . . . .[54]

Susan Doswell, president of the Hanover auxiliary, asserted in an address to her colleagues that women "cannot but erect a statue . . . that our children may early learn well to distinguish the true difference between exalted worth and that cringing sycophancy, which, in a Republic, too often usurps its highest honors." A pledge by the women of Lunenburg County also was a clear testament to Clay's worth: "we hereby resolve to contribute our humble mite in conferring honor where honor is due." Sarah French, vice president of the Warrenton auxiliary, wrote to Clay on February 27, 1845, asking him to visit her town (he graciously declined). The association's goal, she stressed, was to teach the young men of Virginia to imitate Clay's "noble deeds."[55]

The women who spoke for the association tapped into two currents in Whig political culture: the party's social elitism and its emphasis on "statesmanship." The Whigs considered themselves the party of "property and talents." One prominent Virginia Whig recorded in his memoirs his belief that the Whigs "represented the culture and the wealth of the State. . . . It had become an old saw that 'Whigs knew each other by the instincts of gentlemen.' " Furthermore, as historian Thomas Brown has pointed out, the Whigs claimed to stand for "statesmanship" over "partisanship." The Whig party carried on the Founding Fathers' tradition of disinterested statesmanship, transcending partisanship and sectionalism in the interests of national unity.[56]

One of the central issues in the 1844 campaign was Clay's stature as a gentleman and statesman. The Democrats assailed Clay's character, charging him with the unchristian practices of dueling, gambling, and womanizing. The Whigs countered that Clay was the epitome of a southern gentleman, a model of gallantry and social grace. Just as women's support had helped Harrison establish a virtuous reputation, so, too, did it help, in Clay's case, to defuse the "character issue." Women around the country flocked to Clay's speeches and showered him with gifts. "If nothing else, Clay had the women's vote," Clay biographer Robert V. Remini asserts, repeating a favorite theme of Whig rhetoric.[57]

According to the Whigs, Clay's public record was as spotless as his character. The man who had steered the Union through the nullification crisis, Clay was known as "the Great Pacificator." In 1844, Clay's reputation as a peacemaker had special meaning, in light of Whig fears that Polk's election would bring a bloody war with Mexico. Clay's antiwar stance, Whigs argued, endeared him to women. An article on the Clay statue that appeared in the *Richmond Whig* in March 1845 suggested that Clay represented the "love of peace which is the sweetest attribute of woman."[58]

The notion that Whig women saw Clay as a guarantor of peace finds support in the correspondence of Ellen Mordecai, a fervent Whig from Richmond. Mordecai believed that Clay's defeat was a horrible omen for the Union. On the subject of Polk's inauguration in March 1845, she wrote: "I don't know that I am feeling too much apprehension for the welfare of my country, yet it appears even to me . . . that dark clouds are gathering, which unless scattered by elements now unseen, will thicken and bursting, overwhelm us in misery."[59]

Even as Mordecai penned her lament, debate over the Clay Association was dying down. Perhaps it had become clear to Whigs and Democrats alike that the Whig women were determined to see their project through. In November 1845, barely a year after Barbour's initial appeal, the association commissioned sculptor Joel Tanner Hart to design and to execute the marble statue; he was to be paid five thousand dollars for the project. Once sufficient money had been raised to pay Hart, the association's only purpose was to encourage him to finish the statue. Finally, in 1859, after a series of delays because of ill health, Hart completed his work.[60]

On April 12, 1860, the eighty-third anniversary of Clay's birth, the Clay statue was inaugurated in Richmond, amid great public celebration. Business in the city had been virtually suspended so that the entire community could participate in the inaugural ceremonies; an estimated twenty thousand spectators witnessed the unveiling. . . .[61]

The 1844–1845 debates over the Clay Association, though short-lived, are significant for revealing the tensions inherent in Whig womanhood, a new variation on the timeworn and resilient doctrine of "indirect influence." This doctrine, which eventually emerged as a key argument against woman suffrage, held that women's civic duty lay, not in casting a ballot, but rather in influencing men's opinions and behavior.[62] The Whig innovation was to suggest that in the era of mass party politics, women could not fulfill this mandate properly unless they were integrated into the culture of political parties. For all its homages to female influence, the concept of Whig womanhood still ultimately vested women's power in male proxies. An unanswered question at the heart of Whig womanhood was implicitly posed by Lucy Barbour. What if men, despite the benign efforts of women, simply failed to do the right thing? What if they elected the wrong man? What were women to do then?

In the wake of Clay's 1844 defeat, Barbour and her supporters offered an answer: women had the duty to restore the reputation of their party's rejected hero. Barbour conceived of women as opinion makers. They were not simply to affirm the choices of men, but to advance their own ideas of what constituted political worth in men—before, during, and after campaign season. In attacking the association, Democrats worried out loud about the potentially radical implications of this view and paid backhanded tribute to women's influence. When Whig men rushed to defend Barbour, they reminded Democrats that Whig women's partisanship came with the full approbation of Whig men; the women of the Clay Association were not challenging the authority of all men, only of Democratic ones. Rather than symbolizing female rebelliousness, the Clay Association came to symbolize the efficacy and propriety of political collaboration between men and women.

By the time the Clay statue was inaugurated in 1860, both Clay and the Whig party were long gone. Clay had died in 1852, the same year that the Whig party—its fragile coalition of supporters torn apart by sectionalism—ran its last presidential campaign. But in at least one respect, Whig political culture, like the Clay statue that symbolized it, proved more enduring than the party itself. For even as the Whigs disintegrated, their policy of making "politicians of their women" became standard practice in Virginia politics.

In the presidential campaigns of 1848, 1852, and 1856, each of the parties competing for voters in Virginia actively appealed to women to join its ranks. . . .

The Democrats seem to have finally come around by the campaigns of 1848, 1852, and 1856. Virginia Democrats nearly matched their opponents' zeal for female support and participation. The rhetoric of Democratic women and men reveals how fully they had appropriated Whig ideas about female partisanship. At a Democratic meeting in Norfolk in September 1852, a certain Miss Bain addressed the crowd, urging men to support Democratic presidential candidate Franklin Pierce with the following words:

> Patriotic sons of Patriotic sires! . . . Oppose with all power of rectitude that odious and destructive policy that would plant the seed of discord within our borders . . . battle with the foes of Pierce and King; use all proper exertions to defeat them. . . . You can inspire others with a love for the pure, uncontaminated tenets of democracy, the only principles which represent the best interests of our beloved Union.[63]

Like Barbour before her, Bain fused partisanship and patriotism, but she associated the Democrats with sectional harmony and the Whigs with "discord."

The Whig argument that women both legitimized and purified partisan activities was now enthusiastically advanced by Democrats. Describing an October rally in Norfolk, a Democratic correspondent wrote: "There was no fuss—no disturbance. The ladies—guardian angels that control our natures—were around us with their illuminating smiles to cheer, and their bright countenances to encourage us on to victory."[64]*

Any scholar engaged in a project such as this—the project of expanding our definition of meaningful political activity—is ultimately confronted with the inevitable question: So what? The partisan women

---

* A section analyzing the novel, *The Life and Death of Sam, in Virginia* (Richmond, 1856), as an example of Democratic acceptance of female participation in politics has been omitted—ed.

described above do not meet the paradigmatic standards of political participation. They did not vote, nor did they agitate to win the suffrage. We cannot measure their impact on the outcome of elections or demonstrate, for that matter, that they had any impact at all. Women were partisans. So what?

I would like to address this question head on. The kind of evidence presented here has far-reaching implications for the fields of political history and women's history. On the one hand, my findings underscore what political historians have been saying for years. Partisanship was indeed a consuming passion and pastime for antebellum Americans. On the other hand, the Virginia evidence calls into question a common assumption in the historiography of antebellum politics: participation in campaign activities was a highly significant form of political expression for men, but not for women. McGerr makes a very convincing case that in the nineteenth century, men "voted twice at an election—once at the polls by casting a ballot, and once in the streets by participating in campaign pageantry." I hope to have demonstrated that voters and potential voters were not the only ones caught up in the "process of communal self-revelation" that campaigns represented; their wives, mothers, daughters, and sisters, too, were an integral part of the new American political culture.[65] . . . .

A recognition of the extent of women's involvement in campaigns may hold the key to understanding another issue of great interest to political historians: political socialization. Party loyalty was notoriously strong during the era of the second party system. Scholars have explored the importance of families and kin groups in transmitting partisan loyalties; Whig discourse, along with women's own testimony, shows that women played a key role in the socialization of young voters.[66]

Not only were women integral to party politics; gender was integral to party ideologies. Two recent studies suggest that Whig womanhood had its roots in Federalist and Adamsite gender ideologies. Rosemarie Zagarri has found that Federalists were more inclined than Democratic-Republicans to acknowledge publicly women's civic contributions as republican mothers. Supporters of John Quincy Adams, according to Norma Basch, espoused "proto-Whig" ideas about women and politics. They offered women a "few rays of autonomy" by arguing that household and polity were intimately linked, and that the moral standards that governed the former should govern the latter; Jacksonians by contrast upheld the notion of a sharp demarcation between the public and private spheres.[67]

The Whigs' innovation in the 1840s was both tactical and ideological. The party is noteworthy for the sheer quantity of invitations and publicity it offered to partisan women. Even more important was the

241

meaning the Whigs attached to women's presence. Whig propagandists vigorously made the case that women's support said something crucial about the party—women's allegiance was proof of the Whigs' moral rectitude. Whigs in effect claimed that a "gender gap" separated them from the Democrats.

Over the course of the 1850s, the Democratic party in Virginia went a long way toward closing that gap, although Democrats never developed the Whiggish penchant for making grand claims (such as "the ladies are Democrats"). . . . A growing body of scholarship suggests that a gender gap between political parties—measurable before woman suffrage in appeals and assertions, not in votes—may be an enduring feature of the American political landscape.

If evidence on antebellum women's partisanship serves both to deepen our understanding of party politics and to suggest avenues for further inquiry, so, too, does it shed light on fundamental issues in women's history. Whig womanhood represents a distinct stage in the historical evolution of women's civic role. Linda K. Kerber's path-breaking study has established that in the early republic, republican motherhood, the notion that women should serve the state by raising civic-minded sons, was the dominant theory of women's civic duty. Numerous studies have shown that in the first three decades of the antebellum period, republican motherhood was transformed into benevolent femininity—the idea that women had the duty to promote virtue not only within their families but also in the surrounding community by supporting benevolent enterprises.[68]

Whig womanhood took the assumption of female moral superiority embedded in these existing concepts of female duty and adapted it to the realities of mass party politics. Women's moral virtue, their influence within the home, and their proven benevolence fitted them, the Whigs held, to play a distinct role in the new political order. They could exert a civilizing influence on partisan competition, even as they fostered partisan loyalties in their families and communities. Whigs wedded the doctrine of indirect influence to the notion of women's incorruptibility—women who assumed a public identity as Whigs did not, so the party asserted, lose their claim to special virtue.

Baker has rightly argued that the "cultural assignment of republican virtues and moral authority to womanhood helped men embrace partisanship" by relieving their anxieties about electoral competition; what she and others have failed to appreciate is the extent to which women themselves embraced partisanship in the antebellum era and were embraced by parties.[69] The testimony of Marion Harland, Lucy Barbour, and others reveals that women understood that their inclusion in mass politics was a profoundly significant development. Through the medium of partisan campaigns, both womanhood as a construct and individual female voices entered the public discourse on politics in a way they had never done before.

The Whigs reconciled female moral superiority and women's partisanship and opened up new opportunities for women in the process. But did Whig womanhood represent a step toward full political enfranchisement for women? Rather than fitting comfortably into a narrative of progress, my findings affirm Suzanne Lebsock's hypothesis that meaningful change can take place for women in an antifeminist atmosphere. Although female partisanship flourished in antebellum Virginia, no woman's rights movement took shape there. The very same Virginia newspapers that encouraged women's partisanship routinely mocked and lambasted the woman's rights movement, likening its supporters to Amazons and "cackling geese."[70]

Lebsock and Anne Firor Scott have effectively challenged the notion that southern women lagged behind northern ones in benevolent activity. Women's partisanship demonstrates, even more dramatically than their work in benevolent societies, that our dichotomous picture of northern women's political activism and southern women's political marginalization needs to be rethought. Southern women were, indeed, much less inclined to embrace woman suffrage than northern ones. But we should not equate their conservatism with uniformity of opinion or with passivity. Women in antebellum Virginia—like conservative women in the modern era—debated each other fiercely over political issues and actively worked on behalf of political causes.[71]

During the 1840s, the principal political fault line in Virginia was the line dividing Democrats and Whigs. Allegiances to party not only bound like-minded women and men together but also linked them to their political counterparts in other states. At its height, the second party system, by pitting two national parties against each other, united northern and southern partisans and thereby minimized the impact of sectional issues.[72] While northern and southern women may have lived in strikingly different settings, those who followed political events and identified themselves as partisans shared the experience of mass mobilization. The advent of Whig womanhood and the story of the Clay Association reveal that partisanship united women, as well as men, across sectional boundaries.

Even in the heyday of mass politics, however, sectional tensions suffused partisan rhetoric. Southern Whig women shared with northern ones the experience of participating in political rallies, but what southern women heard at those rallies was different—sometimes subtly and sometimes dramatically—from what northern women heard. For the southern Whigs and southern Democrats, in contrast to northern ones, claimed their party and theirs alone could simultaneously protect slavery from northern intervention and preserve the Union. In the 1850s, as slavery became the overriding theme in partisan discourse, political parties increasingly promoted rather than restrained sectionalism.[73] The splintering of the second party system along sectional lines culminated in the election of 1860, the first in which regional rather than national parties squared off against each other in the North and South.

Just as the emergence of the second party system is reflected in political discourse by and about women, so, too, is its demise. During the crucial election campaign of 1860 and throughout the Virginia legislature's famous secession debate of 1861, unionists and secessionists called on women to join their ranks and adapted the Whigs' old battle cry to their own purposes. "The ladies are all for *Union*," declared the unionist *Lynchburg Virginian* in September 1860; six months later, a Petersburg correspondent to the pro-secession *Richmond Dispatch* declared that women "have all abandoned the Union and raised the cry of secession."[74]

As the antebellum period drew to its explosive close, Whig womanhood was transmuted in Virginia into Confederate womanhood. Male and female secessionists argued that women should be Confederate partisans and should play a public role in promoting the cause of southern independence. Sectional identities had come to eclipse partisan affiliations: for example, on April 18, the day after Virginia seceded from the Union, a woman from Louisa County submitted a piece entitled "A Woman's Appeal" to the *Richmond Dispatch*. "Farewell to Whigs and Democrats, Secessionists and Submissionists, and political characters of every variety of here heretofore," she wrote. "Farewell, forever! 'Tis now North or South, Liberty or Slavery, Life or Death. . . . Mothers, wives and daughters, buckle on the armor for the loved ones; bid them, with Roman firmness advance, and never return until victory perches on their banners." This "woman's appeal" can and should be read two ways: as a statement inaugurating a new stage in the sectional conflict in Virginia, and as the product of two decades of political activity and discourse by women. In Virginia, and, I venture to suggest, in the South as a whole, the political mobilization of white women that began in 1840 culminated, not in the formation of a woman suffrage movement, but in active support of the Confederacy by most women and active support of the Union by some.[75]

NOTES

1 Women's partisanship occupies two footnotes in . . . Joel H. Silbey, *The American Political Nation, 1838–1893* (Stanford, 1991), 270, 308–9. See also ibid., 46–48. For short discussions of women's partisanship, see Ronald P. Formisano, *The Transformation of Political Culture: Massachusetts Parties,*

1790s–1840s (New York, 1983), 262–67; Harry L. Watson, *Liberty and Power: The Politics of Jacksonian America* (New York, 1990), 22 1–22; and Lawrence Frederick Kohl, *The Politics of Individualism: Parties and the American Character in the Jacksonian Era* (New York, 1989), 72–74.

2 . . . . On women and antebellum party politics, see Paula C. Baker, "The Domestication of Politics: Women and American Political Society, 1780–1920," *American Historical Review*, 89 (June 1984), 627–32; Mary P. Ryan, *Women in Public: Between Banners and Ballots, 1825–1880* (Baltimore, 1990), 135–38; and Michael E. McGerr, "Political Style and Women's Power, 1830–1930," *Journal of American History*, 77 (Dec. 1990), 866–67.

3 On Southern politics, see, for example William J. Cooper Jr., *Liberty and Slavery: Southern Politics to 1860* (New York, 1983); and John McCardell, *The Idea of a Southern Nation: Southern Nationalists and Southern Nationalism, 1830–1860* (New York, 1979). On southern women, see Catherine Clinton, *The Plantation Mistress: Woman's World in the Old South* (New York, 1982), 181–82; Elizabeth Fox-Genovese, *Within the Plantation Household: Black and White Women of the Old South* (Chapel Hill, 1988), 195; and Suzanne Lebsock, *The Free Women of Petersburg: Status and Culture in a Southern Town, 1784–1860* (New York, 1984), 224. The party designations "Whig" and "Democrat" do not even appear in the indexes of these three works.

4 Eugene Genovese, "Toward a Kinder and Gentler America: The Southern Lady in the Greening of the Politics of the Old South," in *In Joy and In Sorrow: Women, Family, and Marriage in the Victorian South, 1830–1900*, ed. Carol Bleser (New York, 1991), 129–33; Judith Rives to William Cabell Rives, Dec. 8, 1838, William Cabell Rives Papers, Manuscript Division, Library of Congress (LC).

5 Staunton Spectator, Oct. 20, 1836.

6 Ibid., Sept. 1, 1836.

7 Lucy Kenney, *Description of a Visit to Washington* (Washington, 1835), 4–12; Lucy Kenney, *A Pamphlet, Showing How Easily the Wand of a Magician May be Broken, and that if Amos Kendall Can Manage the United States Mail Well, a Female of the United States Can Manage Him Better* (Washington, 1838), 2–5, 15. On southern opposition to Van Buren, see William J. Cooper Jr., *The South and the Politics of Slavery, 1828–1856* (Baton Rouge, 1978), 74–75.

8 Lucy Kenney, *A Letter Addressed to Martin Van Buren, President of the United States* . . . (Washington, 1838), 6; E. B. Runnells, *A Reply to a Letter Addressed to Mr. Van Buren* . . . (Washington, 1840), 4–6.

9 . . . . Richard Patrick McCormick, *The Second American Party System: Party Formation in the Jacksonian Era* (Chapel Hill, 1966). 186–98.

10 *Staunton Spectator*, Sept. 10, 1840; *Fredericksburg Political Arena*, March 24, Sept. 22, 1840.

11 Ronald P. Formisano, "The New Political History and the Election of 1840," *Journal of Interdisciplinary History*, 23 (Spring 1993), 681; Watson, *Liberty and Power*, 221; Robert Gray Gunderson, *The Log-Cabin Campaign* (Lexington, Ky., 1957), 4, 7–8, 135–39; Ryan, *Women in Public*, 135–38.

12 Silbey, *American Political Nation*, 54.

13 *Staunton Spectator*, Sept. 10, 1840; . . . .

14 *Richmond Yeoman*, Sept. 10, 1840; James McDowell to Susan McDowell, May 24, 1827, James McDowell Family Papers, Southern Historical Collection, University of North Carolina (SHC); William Cabell Rives to Judith Rives, Sept. 7, 1834, Rives Papers.

15 *Richmond Yeoman*, Oct. 15, 1840; *Fredericksburg Political Arena*, Sept. 1, 1840.

16 Lucy Kenney, *An Address to the People of the United States* (n.p., [1840]), 1, 6, 11. (copy in LC.) Lucy Kenney, *A History of the Present Cabinet* (Washington, D.C., 1840), 6.

17 Judith Rives to Frank Rives, Feb. 29, 1840, Rives Family Papers; Sarah (Pendleton) Dandridge to Martha Taliaferro Hunter, April 18, 1840, Hunter Family Papers, Virginia Historical Society (VHS); Mrs. Roger A. Pryor, *My Day: Reminiscences of a Long Life* (New York, 1909), 47; . . . .

18 Edith P. Mayo, "Campaign Appeals to Women," in *American Material Culture: The Shape of Things around Us*, ed. Edith P. Mayo (Bowling Green, 1984), 128–32, 143; Celestia Shakes, as quoted in T. Michael Miller, " 'If elected . . .'—An Overview of How Alexandrians Voted in Presidential Elections from 1789–1984," *Fireside Sentinel*, 10 (Oct. 1988), 100.

19 Mary Pendleton (Cooke) Steger to Sarah Harriet Apphia Hunter, Sept. 13, 1840, Hunter Family Papers.

20 Mary T. Tardy, ed., *The Living Female Writers of the South* (Philadelphia, 1872), 409–10.

21 *Richmond Whig*, Oct. 9, 1840. References to the *Richmond Whig* for the years 1840–1844 are to the semiweekly run of the paper; references to it for 1845–1860 are to the daily run.

22 Ibid.

23 Ibid.; *Washington National Intelligencer*, Oct. 9, 1840. (References to the daily run of the paper).

24 *Washington National Intelligencer*, Oct. 10, 1840; *Richmond Whig*, Oct. 9, 1840.

25 Linda K. Kerber, *Women of the Republic: Intellect and Ideology in Revolutionary America* (Chapel Hill, 1980); Nancy F. Cott, *The Bonds of Womanhood: "Woman's Sphere" in New England, 1780–1830* (New Haven, 1977), 66–70; Baker, "Domestication of Politics," 629–31.

26 *Washington Globe*, Oct.27, 1840.

27 *Richmond Crisis*, Sept. 16, 1840; *Richmond Enquirer*, Oct. 15, 1840; . . . .

28 Ryan, *Women in Public*, 136; William R. Taylor, *Cavalier & Yankee: The Old South and American National Character* (Cambridge, Mass., 1957), 115–40; Watson, *Liberty and Power*, 2 19–2 1; Kohl, *Politics of Individualism*, 72–73, 108.

29 Joe L. Kincheloe Jr., "Transcending Role Restrictions: Women at Camp Meetings and Political Rallies," *Tennessee Historical Quarterly*, 40 (Summer 1981), 159; Formisano, *Transformation of Political Culture*, 262–64; Richard J. Carwardine, *Evangelicals and Politics in Antebellum America* (New Haven, 1993), 33–34, 53–55, 65.

30 Daniel Walker Howe, *The Political Culture of the American Whigs* (Chicago, 1979), 36, 158; Kohl, *Politics of Individualism*, 72–74; Robert V. Remini, *Henry Clay: Statesman for the Union* (New York, 1991), 179, 664; Charles D. Lowery, *James Barbour, A Jeffersonian Republican* (University, Ala., 1984), 229.

31 Lori D. Ginzberg, *Women and the Work of Benevolence: Morality, Politics, and Class in the Nineteenth-Century United States* (New Haven, 1990); Lebsock, *Free Women of Petersburg*, 195–236; Elizabeth R. Varon, " 'We Mean to be Counted': White Women and Politics in Antebellum Virginia" (Ph.D. diss., Yale University, 1993), 53–62, 102–4.

32 Kincheloe, "Transcending Role Restrictions," 165; Baker, "Domestication of Politics," 630–31.

33 Silbey, *American Political Nation*, 112–17; Kohl, *Politics of Individualism*, 89; Sydney Nathans, *Daniel Webster and Jacksonian Democracy* (Baltimore, 1973), 127–31; William W. Freehling, *The Road to Disunion: Secessionists at Bay, 1776–1854* (New York, 1990), 361.

34 Gunderson, *Log-Cabin Campaign*, 125, 144, 183; Carwardine, *Evangelicals and Politics*, 61.

35 Freehling, *Road to Disunion*, 411–36.

36 For an example of a woman attending a political debate, see Capps Diary, Dec. 15, 1843.

37 *Richmond Whig*, April 26, May 2, 1844.

38 Ibid., Sept. 6, 1844.

39 Ibid., Sept. 3, 1844.

40 Ibid.

41 *Lexington Gazette*, Oct. 31, 1844.

42 Marion Harland, *Marion Harland Autobiography* (New York, 1910), 12, 1, 127–29.

43 *Washington Globe*, Sept. 26, 1844; *Richmond Enquirer*, Oct. 7, 1844.

44 *Richmond Whig*, Aug. 13, 1844; *Washington Globe*, Nov. 1, 1844; Serena Catherine (Pendleton) Dandridge to Mary Evelina (Dandridge) Hunter, Dec. 11, [1844], Hunter Family Papers.

45 *Richmond Whig*, Nov. 19, 1844. See Lucy Barbour's obituary, ibid., Dec. 3, 1860. Lowery, *James Barbour*, 9–16, 39–40, 52–53, 178–79, 196.

46 *Richmond Whig*, Nov. 19, 1844; *Richmond Enquirer*, Nov. 29, Dec. 2, 1844.

47 *Richmond Whig*, Dec. 13, 1844.

48 Letters and articles from December 1844 . . . printed . . . in *Richmond Whig*, April 12, 1860.

49 Virginia Association of Ladies for Erecting a Statue to Henry Clay, Subscription List, c. 1845–1846, VHS. Some subscribers can be identified as men; some signed only their initials. *Washington National Intelligencer*, Nov. 18, 1845; *Staunton Spectator*, Feb. 6, 1845; *Richmond Whig*, March 17, 18, 1845.

50 *Constitution and By-laws of the Female Humane Association of the City of Richmond* (Richmond, 1843), 1; Legislative petitions, Lynchburg, Jan. 2, 1846 (Library of Virginia); *Lynchburg Virginian*, Dec. 22, 1844; Legislative petitions, Alexandria, Feb. 19, 1847 (Library of Virginia).

51 *Lynchburg Republican*, Dec. 22, 1844; *Lynchburg Virginian*, Dec. 26, 1844.

52 *Lynchburg Virginian*, Jan. 2, 1845.

53 *Lexington Gazette*, Jan. 9, 1845.

54 *Richmond Whig*, Dec. 13, 1844.

55 Ibid. Feb. 12, 22, 1845; Sarah S. B. French to Henry Clay, Feb. 27, 1845, in *The Papers of Henry Clay*. vol. 10, ed: Melba Porter Hay (Lexington, Ky., 1991), 203.

56 John Herbert Claiborne, *Seventy-Five Ears in Old Virginia* (New York, 1904), 131; Wilfred Binkley, *American Political Parties: Their Natural History* (New York, 1965), 152; Thomas Brown, *Politics and Statesmanship: Essays on the American Whig Party* (New York, 1985), 154–69.

57 Carwardine, *Evangelicals and Politics*, 72–75; Remini, *Henry Clay*, 539, 544, 578, 613, 633–43, 650–58.

58 Howe, *Political Culture of the American Whigs*, 138; *Richmond Whig*, March 15, 1845.

59 Ellen Mordecai to Peter Mordecai, March 3, 1845, Mordecai Family Papers (SHC).

60 *Richmond Whig*, April 12, 1860; W. Harrison Daniel, "Richmond's Memorial to Henry Clay: The Whig Women of Virginia and the Clay Statue," *Richmond Quarterly*, 8 (Spring 1986), 40; Elizabeth R. Varon, " 'The Ladies Are Whigs': Lucy Barbour, Henry Clay, and Nineteenth-Century Virginia Politics," *Virginia Cavalcade*, 42 (1992), 72–83.

61 .... *Richmond Whig*, April 12, 13, 16, 17, 18, 1860.
62 Sarah Hale, Whiggish editor of *Godey's Lady's Book*, summed up the doctrine of indirect influence perfectly when she stated, "This is the way women should vote, namely, by influencing rightly the votes of men." Sarah Hale, "How American Women Should Vote," *Godey's Lady's Book*, 44 (April 1852), 293.
63 *Norfolk Southern Augur*, Sept. 23, 1852.
64 *Richmond Enquirer*, Oct. 23, 1852.
65 Michael E. McGerr, *The Decline of Popular Politics: The American North, 1865–1928* (New York, 1986), 37.
66 Formisano, "New Political History and the Election of 1840," 674–75; Jean H. Baker, *Affairs of Party: The Political Culture of Northern Democrats in the Mid-Nineteenth Century* (Ithaca, 1983), 45–52.
67 Rosemarie Zagarri, "Gender and the First Party System," in *Federalists Reconsidered*, ed. Doron Ben-Atar and Barbara Oberg (forthcoming); Norma Basch, "Marriage, Morals, and Politics in the Election of 1828," *Journal of American History*, 80 (Dec. 1993), 914–18.
68 Kerber, *Women of the Republic;* Ginzberg, *Women and the Work of Benevolence.*
69 Baker, "Domestication of Politics," 646.
70 Lebsock, *Free Women of Petersburg*, 243; *Alexandria Gazette*, Oct. 20, 1852; *Richmond Dispatch*, Sept. 16, 1852.
71 Lebsock, *Free Women of Petersburg*, 240–44; Anne Firor Scott, *Natural Allies: Women's Associations in American History* (Urbana, 1991), 19–20, 195.
72 Richard P. McCormick, "Political Development and the Second Party System," in *The American Party Systems: Stages of Political Development*, ed. William Nisbet Chambers and Walter Dean Burnham (New York, 1975), 90–116; Daniel W. Crofts, *Reluctant Confederates: Upper South Unionists in the Secession Crisis* (Chapel Hill, 1989), 49–51.
73 Crofts, *Reluctant Confederates*, 51–54.
74 Lynchburg Virginian, Sept. 5, 1860; Richmond Dispatch, March 8, 1861.
75 Drew Gilpin Faust, "Altars of Sacrifice: Confederate Women and the Narratives of War," *Journal of American History*, 76 (March 1990), 1200–28; *Richmond Dispatch*, April 18, 1861; Varon, " 'We Mean to Be Counted,' " 446–67; George C. Rable, *Civil Wars: Women and the Crisis of Southern Nationalism* (Urbana, 1989).

10

THE SEX OF A HUMAN BEING

Michael O'Brien

Michael O'Brien has been in the forefront of new scholarship on intellectual life in the Old South. In the following selection, excerpted from his recent survey of the subject, he examines what southerners thought about women and what southern women thought about themselves. Although the lives of adult women were "greatly restricted" by patriarchal assumptions, southern women from elite families were quite well educated by national standards, and women became novelists and essayists. He focuses in particular on two women, both from South Carolina, who represent "the antipodes of southern female thinking on gender." Sarah Grimké moved to Philadelphia, where she became a well-known abolitionist and pioneer in the first movement for women's rights. Louisa Cheves McCord, by contrast, defended slavery and the subordination of women in public life. Both Eugene Genovese and Elizabeth Fox-Genovese have seen McCord as representative of the "mind of the master class," but O'Brien points out that Grimké, no less than McCord, was shaped by her upbringing in a wealthy and well-known family of South Carolina slaveholders.

* * *

On his travels in Europe, William Campbell Preston was a young man whose thoughts, just sometimes, dwelled on sex. In Edinburgh in 1818, he found the young ladies forward and blunt. They greeted him on the street; he saw them walking about at all hours. The Virginian was disconcerted. "This may be all well enough to the eye of reason—but either my prejudice or my pride makes me like to see woman—with a shyness which requires the first advance and a sense of imbecility which requires to be sustained and protected." He hazarded a climatic explanation, in the spirit of the young Blumenbach and the mature Montesquieu. "As we travel from North to South—we find the space between woman and man gradually widening—from the perfect equality of both sexes in the Lapland fishing boat—until we arrive at the Seraglios of the luxuriant south—where women are trained for the bed as beasts are fatted for the table." On the whole, he preferred what he knew at home, the "weakness not to say helplessness" of Southern ladies. "Such an one is certainly more lovable—with her languishing black eyes and light fragile person—and luxurious indolence and seducing dependance and conquering blushes than these plump active —rosy cheeked—bustling ladies."[1]

Yet when Preston came to marry Louise Penelope Davis, he married a woman with a sharp mind, who wrote well, was a shrewd observer of persons and politics, and was a brisk critic. "Dined en famille at Mr. E. Greenway's," her diary in 1838 noted of a visit to Baltimore. "No one but Mr. Kennedy, author of 'Swallows Barn,' & one or 2 indifferent American Novels, to meet us. The family were as agreeable as folk can be whose idea of worth, power, happiness, all consists in wealth." Such a woman noticed when men condescended to her. "Was amused at the littleness of a great man, as some folk think Mr. [Daniel Webster]," she wrote after another dinner party. "He had commenced to tell me why Cicero and the Romans were more intellectual than the Greeks," when a lady called out to speak about flowers. After this, she "again assumed a listening attitude to Mr. Webster, who somewhat testily remarked, I pray you, madam, not to turn from these pleasantries." She noticed, but she smoothed it over. "However I replied truly I was interested, and must beg to have the rest; when he went on to tell me that Cicero said the Romans called their feasts conviviums, which signified 'Live together,' and the Greeks symposiums, which meant to drink together."[2] It is not impossible that she knew more of the matter than Webster, who knew little enough.

Louise Preston was in a tradition of high-born, intelligent women who had the delicate task of mediating between the lively interests of their intellect and the deadening expectations of their society. Their problem began in childhood with the matter of education. Before the 1820s, girls had tended to be educated episodically at home. Brothers had tutors or were sent to school, while sisters occasionally shared the tutors, sometimes were sent to schools, and often educated themselves with guidance from mothers and, rarely, fathers. Sarah Grimké at the turn of the nineteenth century in Charleston sat in on the lessons being given to her brother Thomas by his tutor; these concerned mathematics, geography, history, Greek, natural science, and botany. This was in addition to the studies thought peculiar to her sex; arithmetic for the household accounts, sketching, needlework, French, piano, and matters of courtesy and etiquette. Louisa McCord, partly because she spent some of her childhood in a North that came to the idea of elementary female education more quickly, fared a little better. When very young, her education had been handled by her mother. In 1819, when she was about ten and her family had removed to Philadelphia, she was sent with her sister Sophia to a school for young ladies run by

William Grimshaw, and to another where she was taught French by the Picots, an emigré French couple. At home, her brothers had tutors, to whom she seems to have been denied access. Being inquisitive, she was said to have sat behind the door and taken notes on the mathematics lessons. Discovered, she was licensed by her father to step inside the school room and "be instructed also in subjects taught more usually to boys."[3]

It was common for households to leave first matters to the mother or her surrogate, a maiden aunt or an elder sister. Augusta Evans, after a brief spell in school terminated by illness, was mostly educated (and well) by her mother. Louisa McCord, in her turn when twenty-four, helped to educate her younger siblings, Charles and Anna, in English, French, writing, and arithmetic. . . . This, indeed, was what Thomas Jefferson in 1818 had thought the education of women was for: "I thought it essential to give them [his daughters] a solid education, which might enable them, when become mothers, to educate their own daughters, and even to direct the course for sons, should their fathers be lost, or incapable, or inattentive."[4] In general, what girls were allowed outside the household depended much upon the whim and finances of patriarchs, for boys had to be educated but for girls such things were optional. In 1835 James Louis Petigru sent his daughter Caroline off to be schooled in New York, and then changed his mind after a year.[5] Sarah Grimké was forbidden Latin by her father, when her brother progressed to it, but Greek seems to have been permissible. . . . A learned woman might frighten off a witless beau, the kind of man who might casually write "commending very highly the waters the donkeys & the women." Yet an intelligent man might temperately "want a wife a clever companionable woman to get through the evening with, and to keep a neat parlor and a choice table for me and my friends."[6] The scope of "clever" was great, from pert, uninstructed wit to erudition intelligently used.

In general, it is more surprising how expansive was the scope of female education in the South than how restricted. Marcus Cicero Stephens from Florida wrote in 1841 to his granddaughter Mary Ann Primrose of New Bern, North Carolina, then in the Burwell School in Hillsboro. . . . He saw a need for much beyond the usual studies such as French and music, urging her to "Study History, Geography and some of the best ethical writers—with care and attention—this will greatly add to your stock of ideas." No doubt, he reasoned thus because he saw women as contributory. Such ideas would "enable you when occasion serves, to take part in a rational conversation, for nothing is so insipid as some ladies I have seen, they have been asked to sing & play on some instrument, or to exhibit their drawings to the visitors after doing which they retire to their seats and sit mumchance, until some dandy of a beau sidles up to them and talks of the weather, the last ball or some such frivolities." Still, he thought that "the women have not been treated with Justice by the male sex." Men hazarded and were destined for "the rougher walks of life" and needed "the knowledge necessary for such purposes," but "if the woman be inferior to the man in bodily strength, her mind is equally vigorous as his, & the records of ancient and modern History set this matter beyond doubt." Indeed, he confessed that "the men have entered into a kind of conspiracy to keep the women in the back ground—a prejudice has been excited against their improvement beyond a certain limit—the women have been cowed if I may so term it for should she in her remarks on any subject of conversation shew any superiority of intellect, she is instantly announced as a bas bleu, or blue stocking, and is avoided in a measure by both men & women." This was ungenerous and he encouraged her to venture herself intellectually. Still, he was a man and a grandfather, and his last words to her were perhaps less liberal, if meant to be kindly. "Learn to play and sing 'Highland Mary[.]' It is the sweetest thing I ever heard and should we ever meet, it will be the first tune I shall call for."[7]

. . . .

Thomas Dew, in his 1835 "Dissertation on the Characteristic Differences between the Sexes, and on the Position and Influence of Woman in Society," was full of advice. Like Stephens, he was not convinced that women were intellectually inferior, or not naturally so, for bodies were not everything: "I am inclined . . . in the belief, that there is *no natural* difference between the intellectual powers of man and woman, and that the differences observable between them in this respect at mature age, are wholly the result of education, physical and moral." In this, doubtless, he was atypical of Southern male opinion, even of Southern female opinion, for the latter had often learned to derogate themselves. "I find La Harpe rather a bore & shall not proceed," Anne Deas observed with self-satisfaction in 1813. "The two volumes I have of him are criticism of the french poets, & it does not interest me at all for I am not a *Literary Lady*." For Dew, as for many Americans, it came to seem that the sexes had their spheres which were founded upon their physical natures, which distributed mixed strengths and weaknesses to both, which in turn occasioned an interdependence rhapsodic in its beauty. Henry Hilliard of Alabama rooted the idea of separate spheres in the premise that, "The very soul of the universe is harmony." For Dew, men were physically strong, adventurous, warlike, courageous, active, candid, but also vain, rude, selfish, misanthropic, dissipated, less religious, sophist, and wanting in stamina when faced with adversity. Women had the obverse of these qualities: passivity against initiative, weakness against strength, morality against degradation, fortitude against the palsied will. While women might not be naturally inferior in mind, education and society made them so, or so Dew believed: "It is now a conceded point, that under the actual constitution of society, and with the superior education of our sex, the intellectual endowments and developments of man are generally found superior to those of woman at the age of maturity." This was so, now and historically, "every where and in every age."[8]

In particular, Dew felt that men, by training, acquired the greater gift for the "higher" powers of mind, by which he meant abstract and synthetic reasoning, the power of generalizing from the particular to the general. "The intellectual eye of woman," by contrast, "is like the pleasing microscope; it detects little objects, and movements, and motives, upon the theatre of life, which wholly escape the duller and more comprehensive vision of our sex." This was partly because boys were taught things women were not, more science and more Latin and Greek, but mostly because they went on to college at the moment that girls were plunged into the maelstrom of society and compelled to learn the arts of womanhood. . . .[9]

Nonetheless, female education grew more expansive. In 1810, the debate hinged on whether a girl needed education at all. By 1830, it had conceded the point but now hovered around what should be taught, for how long, and for what purposes. The consistent answer was to make wives who were ladies. But the notion of what sort of wives and ladies varied. "It has justly been considered . . . that the minds of the gentler sex should be cultivated and enlarged by every practicable means, that the *mothers* of an enlightened nation, should be well prepared to train the mental faculties of their offspring," the *Southern Literary Messenger* observed in 1835. "Much greater attention is now bestowed upon the culture of the female mind than formerly; and parents generally seem more impressed with the propriety of giving to their daughters a solid education." By 1850, matters had progressed to concede the reality, if not the universal necessity, of female higher education. So gradually the number of female schools proliferated, and their curricula went much beyond what the late eighteenth century had offered. . . .[10] Usually, Latin and Greek were not taught, though it was not unknown (the Mordecai family's Warrenton Female Academy did so in 1822) and it seems to have been less taboo than in the North.[11]

By 1839, the Methodists had established in Macon the Georgia Female College, which was not only the South's first college for women, but precedent to anything else in the rest of United States and (it is claimed) western Europe. This began partially to remedy a situation, which in 1831 Henry Nott had lamented with a liberality unusual in his culture. "We have colleges from Maine to Florida for young men," he wrote, "but the talents of an Agnesi, a Montague, a Sévigné or de Stael, have no resource but schools set up on speculation, without libraries, without apparatus of any kind. Our State legislatures meet annually, and take into consideration, with befitting gravity, the important subject of education, leaving out of their deliberation exactly one half of the whole community." By the 1850s, thirty of the thirty-nine female colleges chartered in the United States were in the South, and in some states female colleges outnumbered those for men.[12] From the beginning, they took male education as a standard to be emulated. It was hazarded in 1843 in Macon that "our daughters" ought to have "as good a disciplinary education as was offered by the best colleges for our sons," and in 1856 in Asheville that they should have a mental discipline and knowledge "not inferior to those enjoyed by the other sex in the best American Colleges."[13] This seems not to have been completely accomplished, though many of the female colleges gave a better education than many male ones. Young ladies at the Mansfield Female College in Louisiana were being asked in 1857 to read Vergil, Cicero, Horace, Juvenal, and Livy. . . . Their scientific education was about equivalent, their teaching of modern foreign languages perhaps better, and certainly their attention to the fine arts (painting, music) was superior. Many of the prescribed texts were identical to those used in male colleges. . . .[14] No doubt the intellectual rigor of the teachers was, on average, less high, not because the female professors were inadequate, but because the male ones were often those unable to find a place in the better male colleges.

Missing from female higher education, however, were the clubs and debating societies that trained men for public life, for the bar or the legislative chamber. Women might read Lord Kames and Hugh Blair on rhetoric, but they concentrated on his advice about letter writing rather than the forensic arts. Somewhat more prominent was religion, for female colleges were usually sponsored by religious denominations, while the state universities lived at least fitfully in the shadow of Mr. Jefferson's prescriptions about the separation of church and state. Religion fitted, too easily, into the arts of the private realm, where women were supposed to be confined: conversation, dancing, singing, playing the piano or guitar, even the making of wax flowers.[15] In general, it was presumed that a woman's education was more practical, more vocational, and the vocation was the home or (if a husband was unforthcoming or delayed) the education of other young ladies. In this spirit, compared to the rough spartan quality of male colleges, their female counterparts devoted more attention to comforts, as the foreshadowing of how a home should be arranged. . . . Female college students were often advised to exercise, by walking, riding, or calisthenics. Botany, indeed, was often recommended because it required outdoor rambles. Moreover, "They [the students] will not be crowded together in one, large, ill ventilated building, but placed in groups, according to age, sympathy, class, etc., in separate circles, in each of which the paramount object will be, to continue to them, so far as may be possible, the several advantages of their own homes; the genial relationships and loving cares which make the charm, and are the source, of the refinement, the gentlenesses, and the pure delights of the family circle."[16]

Consistent with this emphasis, Southern society told young women to be very conscious of their bodies. As Sarah Grimké put it in 1838, "We approach each other, and mingle with each other, under the constant pressure of a feeling that we are of different sexes . . . that we must never forget the distinction between male and female. Hence our intercourse, instead of being elevated and refined, is generally calculated to excite and keep alive the lowest propensities of our nature." So, minds and eyes were full of the curve of a neck, the clarity of a complexion, the shape of breasts, the thinness of a waist, the hips to bear children, and many women were, willingly or not, followers of fashions, close and anxious students of what to wear and how to carry themselves. High society licensed an awareness of sexuality and authorized some of its arts, the teasing flirtatiousness of the drawing room. Religious society, however, did not; it kept its women away from balls, playing cards, flounced dresses, and décolleté. Evangelicalism especially denounced the erring woman and seems not to have accepted the premise that women were naturally passive and pious. "The Devil in Petticoat is to me a most dangerous animal," Basil Manly as a young man in Beaufort, South Carolina, once announced. . . .[17]

But even high society was formally puritanical about sexuality itself, which was forbidden beyond marriage and little discussable even within it. Sexual transgression meant social death, if discovered. Madaline Edwards, who was the mistress of a New Orleans businessman in the 1840s, knew herself to be "pollution" and was not surprised, if hurt, when her family turned away from her on the street. William Porcher Miles in the early 1850s had an affair with a woman whose marriage had been contracted for money not love, and the liaison had become known. For Miles, "the full glare of fashionable notoriety" was a mild social impediment. For the woman, it meant immurement, a banishment to "the country to find with God and her children what comfort she might." For her, "no future can compensate her past—for the rest sorrow may sanctify—hope can never brighten it." For Miles, as Trescot explained and the code required, "it is not so."[18] . . . .

On the whole, Southern men feared the dangers posed by women's bodies more than their minds, or rather felt at ease about the minds because the bodies were so imprisoned. In the North, where women's rights had begun to make more headway, female higher education was more constricted, more feared. But it was also the case that the domestic realm was, for a Southern woman who was born or married well, a greater domain, for a plantation was also a business in which wives and mothers participated actively; a certain knowledge and shrewdness was useful. As the Rev. C. W. Howard reminded the graduating class of the Cassville Female College in South Carolina in 1858: "It is a common mistake . . . to represent the life of a southern matron as one of indolence and self-indulgence. But . . . she has the care to provide, in sickness and health, for the numerous laborers under her control; to preside over the system of slavery, which is one, not of oppression, but of protection to the laborer." . . . .[19] Yet this was, though important, a limited power.

The expansion of Southern female education was, potentially, on a collision course with the adult role of women, which was greatly restricted. Charles Fraser, when an old man, observed in 1814 the growth of all these " 'Female Institutes,' and 'Female Collegiate Establishments' " and thought them "unsuitable," for "the object of their instruction ought not to be to make them learned, but it should be directed to the development of the moral and intellectual qualities suitable to the becoming discharge of the peculiar duties designed for them by nature; to their position in society, and their relations in domestic life." Certainly a Southern woman's legal position and prerogatives were drastically constrained. A single woman and a widow controlled her own property (a one-third dower was usual), but a married one conferred all on her husband and lost the power of independent contract, unless an equity court made a special exception. This was somewhat softened in the late antebellum period, especially in the western South, and Louisiana's Napoleonic Code had long given more discretion, but in general the law discouraged female economic independence and action.[20] A woman was denied almost all the public realm, except as an informal adviser: the franchise, officeholding, juries, religious office. Most, too, of the informal realm of public culture was forbidden or inaccessible; most libraries, conversation clubs, all debating societies. No woman was allowed public speech if her body was present (no sermons or orations, except student ones), but was permitted a voice when her body was absent, as in the printed word.

A Southern marriage was a republican purdah, for youth ended very quickly; the average marrying age for elite women was about 19, some five years earlier than their Northern counterparts.[21] (It may be significant that many of the South's female intellectuals tended to marry later than the average.) Jefferson had set the tone even in the 1780s, when he condemned the life of the aristocratic French woman, explicitly for frivolity and license, implicitly for the freedom and mobility with which she dodged "in and out of the doors of her very sincere friends." By contrast, in America "the society of your husband, the fond cares of the children, the arrangements of the house, the improvements of the grounds, fill every moment with a healthy and an useful activity." A fear of intellectual freedom was mated to that of sexual freedom, which the salon had notoriously sanctioned. Alice Izard saw the connection with precision. She advised her daughter to be hospitable, not secluded, but with a propriety that was opposed to "the present riotous, boisterous manners." . . . . Such opinions were not based upon a sense of the impotence of women, but was a back-handed compliment to the power of mothers. "They are the reformers of the World," Alice Izard coolly asserted.[22] "Give me a host of edu-cated, pious mothers and sisters," Thomas Grimké once asserted, "and I will do more to revolutionize a country, in moral and religious taste, in manners and in social virtues and intellectual cultivation, than I can possibly do in double or treble the time, with a similar host of educated men."[23]

This helps to explain why women had a restricted role in Southern intellectual life, as well as the character of their contribution, which was much preoccupied with the matter of sex, that mixed blessing. By contrast, men seldom found the premise of manliness to be problem-atical.[24] (Anxiety about performance was, of course, another matter.) Dew was unusual in finding fault with male characteristics, Trescot more common in casually speaking of "healthy manliness" and pre-suming that masculinity and health were natural companions. . . .[25] But women understood "womanly" as a more complicated thing, being both praiseworthy and suspect. "See our vanity; woman-like," Elizabeth Ruffin once ironically enjoined herself and the readers of her diary.[26]

Southern men felt very little pressure for a readjustment in the civil standing of women. During the Virginia State Convention of 1829, it was idly mentioned that women were often thought to be men's equals and were certainly superior to slaves, Indians, or foreigners. So why should they not have the vote? Samuel Moore had an answer: "It is not because we deny to these an equality of natural rights, or because they are inferior in intelligence, morality, or virtue, to our-selves; for I will be as ready to admit as any gentleman on the opposite side of the question, that in all these particulars they are our equals at least, and in most of them, our superiors." So why? "The women have never claimed the right to participate in the formation of the Government, and that until they do, there can be no necessity for our discussing or deciding upon it." These are burdens they do not want, "are unwilling to bear." Besides, "their interests are so completely identified with our own, that it is impossible that we can make any regulation injuriously affecting their rights, which will not equally injure ourselves." Do they not have "unlimited confidence in our sex"?[27] . . . .

. . . .

In general, the social configurations of the Old South made it extremely difficult for any woman who was not well born to become a writer. This was in some contrast to the experience of men, among whom modest origins were common. Society leaned against the literary woman; so she tended to need affidavits of respectability or the confidence that social standing conferred to hazard her opinions. Hence many female intellectuals were the wives or daughters of notable men, usually of means, if often self-made men; most, too, had children of their own. Louisa McCord was the daughter of Langdon Cheves, who had been Speaker of the House of Representatives and president of the Second Bank of the United States. . . . The sisters Grimké were the daughters of a wealthy judge, and (while Sarah remained single) Angelina became the wife of Theodore Weld, an abolitionist of note and some means. . . . As for the novelists, they offer a slight variation; though often well born and usually married, they were not infrequently harried into print by adverse financial circumstances, the death or incompetence of husbands. . . .[28]

It was very unusual, therefore, for a Southern female writer to break free from matters of gender as saliently understood from within the household (love, courtship, disappointment, marriage, religion, education, and death) and write on the genres of "public" matters (history, politics, economics), except by embedding the latter into the former. Indeed, Louisa McCord is probably the only Southern woman who managed to do so, and even she often turned such essays into a meditation upon the family. Hence, too, their writings provide a very partial understanding of women's understandings in their culture, for many women were poor or unmarried or childless. But, as the writings of Sarah Grimké show, even the unmarried could be drawn to speak of the family as normative and motherhood as the center of a woman's meaning.

To sample the antipodes of Southern female thinking on gender, it will be helpful to look at Sarah Grimké and Louisa McCord. The former stood for turbulent defiance of the old ways expressed in exile, the other for turbulent defense from within slavery's heartland. But both offered a grim assessment of men's ways and power.

The story of the Grimké sisters has often been told, if seldom in books about the South, yet their thought was indelibly formed by their Southern experience and their words often were aimed deliberately at the community of Southern women, whom they were among the first to define as a community. "I stand before you as a southerner, exiled from the land of my birth by the sound of the lash and the piteous cry of the slave," Angelina Grimké told a committee of the Massachusetts state legislature in 1838.[29] For our purposes, Sarah's story is more salient, for she came closest to feminism. While Angelina tended to see the problem of women as subsidiary to that of slavery, Sarah moved beyond that to a fuller sense that women had their own problems, mission, and need for social thought. The latter's story was, in outline, simple enough. She grew up in the prosperous and idiosyncratic household of Judge John Faucherand Grimké in Charleston. She had the usual sort of half-education, went into society as a belle and hated it, partly because she nurtured the impossible ambition of being a lawyer like her father and brother. She became religious under the influence of Henry Kollock, the Presbyterian minister, put away fashionable things, and took to prayer meetings and visits to almshouses. Visiting Philadelphia in 1819 with her terminally ill father, she came to know Quakers. After his death, she returned to stay there for another fifteen years, became a Quaker, refused to marry a widowed Quaker minister with children, and was joined by Angelina in 1829, the sister who being thirteen years her junior was, in many ways, a surrogate child. Angelina had come to antislavery and Quakerism by her own route, more marked by revulsion at slavery's violence and the unsettling experience of being formally tried for religious nonconformity.[30]

From Quakerism, with which they both grew disillusioned for its racial intolerance, Sarah advanced by 1835 to abolitionism, the more so after Angelina married Theodore Weld in 1838 and the sisters continued to share a household. In truth, Sarah's experience of both South and North was disquieting, for in the latter she and her allies were abused and vilified for their advanced opinions, while in the former her antislavery views made it impossible or dangerous for her to visit, the more so as Angelina's *Appeal to the Christian Women of the Southern States* was publicly burned by the Charleston postmaster. After they became abolitionists, neither woman was ever to see Charleston again, for no one was sure that even the Grimké household would be proof against a proslavery, antifeminist mob. As such, Sarah's mature writings sought to learn from but transcend both places. Angelina was, in many ways, the bolder spirit when it came to public performance, but Sarah was the deeper thinker and more adventurous intellectually, though each saw beyond the problem of slavery to that of racial prejudice, which was further than many abolitionists saw.

The vital text is Sarah Grimké's *Letters on the Equality of the Sexes and the Condition of Woman*, first published in 1838. It is a work part theology, part comparative ethnography, part memoir, and all sermon, which above all contemplates "woman as an immortal being, travelling through this world to that city whose builder and maker is God." During its composition, she was still a Quaker and the spirit of that religion much informed the book, for she was anxious to be plain and modest: "To me it appears beneath the dignity of woman to bedeck herself in gewgaws and trinkets, in ribbons and laces, to gratify the eye of man." Consistent with this, she mistrusted sexuality and wanted "our intercourse [to be] purified by the forgetfulness of sex," which might diminish a degrading emphasis upon woman's "animal nature." Her greatest complaint against slavery was its habitual sexual abuse; "the virtue of female slaves is wholly at the mercy of irresponsible tyrants, and women are bought and sold in our slave markets, to gratify the brutal lust of those who bear the name of Christians." So, being religious, she was preoccupied with a quarrel with biblical exegesis, by arguing that Genesis showed God making man and woman equal, that Adam and Eve shared in a fall "from innocence, and consequently from happiness, *but not from equality*," and that the old charge that Eve was delivered into inferiority by her temptation of Adam was unfounded, that man and woman shared equally in sin. So, thereafter, the growth of male dominion grew contingently, but not legitimately. The Fall let men acquire a "lust for dominion . . . and as there was no other intelligent being over whom to exercise it, woman was the first victim of this unhallowed passion." Quickly men's abuses mounted. In the age of ancient Jewish patriarchy, women became property, bedecked as was Rebecca with golden earrings and bracelets, but property nonetheless. Hence there were all the abuses around the world, which Grimké painfully and episodically documented; the sale of women at auction in Babylon, the raffles for them in Hindostan, the hard labor of the Muslim woman whose husband takes his ease, the sufferings of European women from the ancient Greeks onwards, the indignities of the Native American woman.[31]

When she came to speak "On the Condition of Women in the United States," Grimké became reminiscent and scathing. (She was always good at scorn, because sensitive to slights.) "During the early part of my life, my lot was cast among the butterflies of the *fashionable* world," the young women who abjured intellectual acquirements for fear of being shunned by men who wanted only "pretty toys" and "mere instruments of pleasure." Just as bad, she was trained to think of marriage as "a kind of preferment." "To be married is too often held up to the view of girls as the sine qua non of human happiness and human existence." So should one, as an act of freedom, refuse marriage? Here Grimké was old-fashioned, for she did not understand singlehood as a disconnection from marriage, but as an experience implicated in it. After all, she lived her later years in the household of her married sister, which was a common enough accommodation for single women. This was not always easy. Sarah, being older and making large financial contributions to the household, had a way of taking over household duties, even mothering the offspring whom she tellingly called "Theodore's children," not Angelina's. Once, indeed, in 1853–54, Sarah left temporarily because Angelina came to resent this and wrote to her, "It seems unnatural that a wife and Mother should ever thus be willing to share of the affection of her dearest ones with any human being and my heart refuses its assent." But such experiences were foreshadowed in what otherwise might seem a curious passage in the *Letters on the Equality of Sexes*, where Sarah wrote, "I believe that a complete knowledge of household affairs is an indispensable requisite in a woman's education,—that by the mistress of a family, whether married or single, doing her duty thoroughly and *understandingly*, the happiness of the family is increased to an incalculable degree, as well as a vast amount of time and money saved." Nonetheless, though often part of an extended family—even, she seems to suggest by the phrase "mistress," head of one—a single woman might often have to work, so Sarah was sensitive to the problem of economic discrimination, what she called "the disproportionate value set on the time and labor of men and of women," and was even aware of the injustices experienced by lower-class working women, such as seamstresses and launderers. Rather, she seems to have wanted that women effect a balance: they needed to work both outside and inside the home, because exclusively within it they tended to be "supported, in idleness and extravagance, by the industry of their husbands, fathers, or brothers, who are compelled to toil out their existence, at the counting house, or in the printing office," and this was diminishing for the women, who thus missed out on the "strength and dignity" that might attach to useful work. The passage is Janus-faced, looking back to the gilded indolence of Charleston, but forward to the more modest, hard work of her Northern life, where she helped to run a school but also to bake pies with her own hands. In both cases, however, she never quite shed her class origins. "Brute force, the law of violence," she wrote with a lady's shudder, "rules to a great extent in the poor man's domicil; and woman is little more than a drudge. They are less under the supervision of public opinion, less under the restraints of education, and unaided or unbiased by the refinements of polished society." How did she know this? "Duty as well as inclination has led me, for many years, into the abodes of poverty and sorrow."[32]

Hence Grimké's idea of separate spheres was complicated. At one level, she was its fierce critic. She insisted that women ought to have a public role, that history proved (Semiramis, Elizabeth I) their competence in authority. "Intellect is not sexed," she boldly asserted, nor "strength of mind." "Our views about the duties of men and the duties of women, the sphere of man and the sphere of woman, are mere arbitrary opinions, differing in different ages and countries, and dependent solely on the will and judgment of erring mortals." So did this mean, as Margaret Fuller was in her *Woman in the Nineteenth Century* (1845) to assert, that spheres might dissolve, that women might be sea captains, that Grimké would "have every arbitrary barrier thrown down . . . every path laid open to woman as freely as to man"? Grimké was gnomic: "As moral and responsible beings, men and women have the same sphere of action, and the same duties devolve upon both; but no one can doubt that the duties of each vary according to circumstances; that a father and a mother, a husband and a wife, have sacred obligations resting on them, which cannot possibly belong to those who do not sustain these relations. But these duties and responsibilities do not attach to them as men and as women, but as parents, husbands, and wives." She glimpsed possibilities: she praised Harriet Martineau for writing, working to improve lighthouses, and knowing various languages; she trumpeted Madame de Stael as "intellectually the greatest woman that ever lived." She knew the old order was wrong, she deeply resented the scoffing condescensions of men, she detailed with passion all the mortifying legal and financial disabilities of women, but her sense of what the new order would look like was shadowy. Women will be free to choose; "they will regard themselves, as they really are, FREE AGENTS, immortal beings, amenable to no tribunal but that of Jehovah." She wanted them to have the right to be preachers, for example, to reassume their old sacerdotal roles as priestesses.[33]

But, on the whole, she was tentative and vague. "It is not my intention, nor indeed do I think it is in my power, to point out the precise duties of women. . . . There is a vast field of usefulness before them." What was in the field was a matter of some obscurity. In Grimké's *Letters* women seem often to choose something like the old roles, as parents and wives. She has a long and stern defense of marriage, perhaps the sterner because she admitted many would think her "altogether disqualified for the task, because I lack experience."[34] She was very insistent that marriage was one of God's blessed institutions. As one might expect, her vision of marriage was rooted in her theory that God had made men and women equal, and she tried (with a necessary lack of success) to show that the Bible did not sanction patriarchalism and, *inter alia*, she afforded herself the easy luxury of abusing the wretched Saint Paul. Nonetheless, she seemed to oppose divorce, for she wrote that "God established [marriage], and man, except by special permission, has no right to annul it."[35] And in 1838, she was not claiming the suffrage, as she would do later in life, or the right to sit in legislatures, but only (as Angelina asserted elsewhere) the right of petition.[36] What Sarah wanted, above all, was the right to be heard, the freedom to choose, the ability to control her life, but she was too close to the eighteenth century in which she was born to choose anything drastically radical. . . .

The Grimké sisters were formally abolitionists before they were advocates of women's rights; they became "feminists" (to use an anachronistic term) partly because of the hostilities from the Northern public they had encountered as antislavery activists, partly because the abolitionist community liked to restrict them to being Southern women. For talking about slavery bound them, in memory, to the South. It was their utility as testifiers from within the citadel of the Slave Power that made them useful to the abolitionists and, like Frederick Douglass who wanted to be more than a fugitive slave, the Grimkés wanted to be more than just cultural refugees. To be a reasoner upon women, in general, was to become more than a Southern woman, in particular, and the *Letters on the Equality of the Sexes* touch only glancingly upon Southern matters. Nonetheless the Grimkés used their Southern experiences habitually, scathingly, both as women and as ex-slaveholders, and their mature writings can be read as autobiography. Yet they connected the issues of womanhood and slavery differently.

In many ways, Angelina came to women's rights, because she started with a visceral revulsion from slavery: "The investigation of the rights of the slave has led me to a better understanding of my own."[37] Though she claimed otherwise in retrospect, Sarah seems to have felt the constricting bonds of womanhood before she noticed that others were in heavier chains.[38] The earliest memories she recounted concern gender, especially the story of being denied tutors. "The only answer to my earnest pleadings was 'You are a girl—what do you want with Latin and Greek etc.? You can never use them,' accompanied sometimes by a smile, sometimes by a sneer." In both cases, however, this nexus of gender and slavery meant that the Grimkés were especially alert to the role of women in the sustenance of slavery. Their contributions to the chamber of horrors that was Theodore Weld's *American Slavery As It Is: Testimonies of a Thousand Witnesses* (1839) were insistently drawn to the image of the cruel mistress. "A punishment dreaded more by the slaves than whipping, unless it is unusually severe, is one which was invented by a female acquaintance of mine in Charleston," relates the author in one of the earliest incidents in the "Narrative and Testimony of Sarah M. Grimké." "It is standing on one foot and holding the other in the hand. Afterwards it was improved upon, and a strap was contrived to fasten around the ankle and pass around the neck; so that the least weight of the foot resting on the strap would choke the person." This same acquaintance "had the ears of her wait-ing maid *slit* for some petty theft." Another woman "had starved a female slave to death." . . . .[39]

There is only one reference to the Grimkés in the writings of Louisa McCord. In her 1852 essay on the "Enfranchisement of Woman," she speaks of women's rights activists and mentions Angelina Grimké Weld, whom she mocks as "the gentle" and "the fair," someone who would be wise not to contest with the crudity of men in the public arena.[40] Yet they came from the same, small South Carolina and it is improbable that they did not know of each other, since theirs was a world of gossip and the Grimkés, at least, were notorious and McCord was the daughter of fame. They shared much, powerful fathers and troublesome brothers, the discomfort of being awkward belles, the witness and consciousness of men's violence, the meditating upon God and suffering, the idea that slavery offered a key to a woman's self understanding. They agreed, in fact, on much, except the crucial thing of how a woman should respond to the pressure of a harsh world; above all, they disagreed on the cogency of hope.

Most of McCord's published writings on gender were written in response to the ideas of Northern and European theorists. Super-ficially, she did not like them, but as with most conservatives she came to know what she wished to conserve in dialectic with those who wished to reform her world. Indeed, she was among the earliest Amer-icans habitually to use the world "conservative" to describe her ideol-ogy and to say "we, of the conservatives."[41] Most of her response came in a brief burst in 1852, when she reviewed for the *Southern Quarterly Review* and *DeBow's* in swift succession: first, an article by John Stuart Mill and Harriet Taylor (who, being anonymous, she mistook for Harriet Martineau) in the *Westminster Review* on the "Enfranchisement of Women" and the proceedings of the Woman's Rights Convention held in Worcester, Massachusetts, in 1851; then, second, Elizabeth Oakes Smith's book on *Woman and Her Needs*. . . . Much was impelled into clarity by the problem of slavery, for she became engaged by the problem of gender in the same year she read and abused *Uncle Tom's Cabin*.[42]

In general, Louisa McCord had little sympathy with hope and reform. Whilst she conceded that mankind, though not perfectible, was capable of great improvement, little proposed for that amelior-ation (beyond the theories of Adam Smith) met her approval. Scorn was her usual response to the "wild dream of 'fraternity,'" the "extrav-agant madness" of the "right to labor," the futility of "the possibility of forcing brotherly love upon the world." For her, the world was growing dangerous with "free-soilers, barn-burners, antirenters, abol-itionists," who threatened social anarchy. This was the more so, as (she reasoned like a mother) America was young, a "child of wide and expansive mind" easily impressed and led astray. The proponents of women's rights fell easily under this rubric. But her disagreements can be readily misunderstood. In fact, she shared many of their presumptions; it is even possible that her understandings were partly derived from reading them, that McCord was a sort of wayward Grimké. She had the same contempt for "silks or ribands, frippery or flowers,"[43] and for the belle, whom she calls "a flirt, a coquette, a heartless trifler ... [who] forgets duty, conscience and heart, in the love of notoriety."[44] .... She freely conceded that "woman's condition certainly admits of improvement." If anything, her estimate of men was more scathing. "When have the strong forgotten to oppress the weak?" she asked, and knew the answer in woman's case. "Man is corporeally stronger than woman," she observed, "and ... he, in the unjust use of his strength has frequently, habitually ... and even invariably, oppressed and abused woman." She even was willing to own that a majority of women were "out of place, unappreciated, having their talents and powers not only hidden under a bushel, but absolutely thrown away, while she becomes either the slave or the toy of men."[45] .... She even acknowledged, and forcibly, the analogy of woman and slave: "In every government, and under every rule, woman has been placed in a position of slavery—actual, legal slavery." This was not so perfect a slavery as that experienced by "our negroes," but was still "a very decided state of bondage," because it involved the deprivation of rights and being "legally subjected to the supremacy of man." From this came hardship and suffering. "Many a woman of dominant intellect is obliged to submit to the rule of an animal in pantaloons, every way her inferior."

Why then so conservative? It is a mistake to imagine that conservatives have been so because they did not see injustice or approved of it. Often they were so, because they saw no choice. "The individual ... who finds the laws of society irksome to him, has no resource but submission to the discomfort entailed upon him," McCord wrote of men and women alike. She founded much upon her idea of nature, about which she permitted herself an unwonted mysticism. She blamed God for these cold facts of submission. "Go then ... and cavil with God who hath thus dictated it. *He* gave to the man the right, even as He gave him the power. *He* laid upon his strong right arm those folds of muscles by whose might he can rule, must rule—ay, and in all physical right ought to rule—all that God in his wisdom has made weaker. Ought to rule, we say; because whatever God has made ought to be." That is, McCord had no interest in gender as a thing socially constructed. She believed in the reality of sex, because she believed in the compulsion and fate of bodies, both in the case of women and of slaves. She emphasized this even in the case of children, whose bodily weakness might be temporary but was inescapable. "Sex and colour are severally so essential to the being of a woman and a negro," she asserted, "that it is impossible to imagine the existence of either, without these distinctive marks. . . . [T]he sex of a human being was fixed long before its entrance into this world, by rules and causes, which, entirely unknown to man, were equally beyond *his* reach and that of accident."[46]

Much in McCord's criticism of the women's rights advocates rested in her sense that they merely succeeded in becoming a "*third* sex" or "unsexed," unable to be men, ceasing to be women. Women's bodies enforced upon them certain duties, sensibilities, and feelings. Of God's creatures, they were mandated to endure, suffer, love, and nurture. . . .[47]

Women were, in short, charged with Christ's mission, redemption by love. So they had no place in the public sphere, in voting booths, on hustings, or in legislatures. They had no claim upon power or property, in the ordinary sense. "The *world of action* must to her be almost entirely a closed book," she once told William Porcher Miles. Corporeal weakness and nature's bargain meant women needed men's strength for protection, however ugly was that strength. But McCord unquietly expanded this meek sphere. She was adamant that a woman's duties were not confined "to shirt-making, pudding-mixing, and other such household gear, nor yet even to the adornment of her own fair person." She placed intellect within woman's sphere, as well she (the author) might if she was to retain any sense of personal rationale. She insisted that woman was not inferior, merely different, and she flirted with asserting superiority. For she thought that, if mankind was to improve, it was by the intensification of woman's mission to man: "By perfecting herself, she perfects mankind; and hers . . . is the highest mission, because, from her, must the advance towards perfection begin." The millennial ambition McCord mocked in the socialist, she was willing to grant to the woman "in her true place," which was "the quiet, unwearied and unvarying path of duty, the home of the mother, the wife, and the sister, teaching man his destiny." . . . .[48]

Her own history casts a complicated light on all this. She worshipped her father, "my idol through childhood and womanhood," and probably did not have a very happy marriage to David James McCord, a widower of a famously hot temper, the wielder of a cane and a fist, a man gifted in storytelling and known as "Handsome Davy."[49] He is the most likely candidate for the "animal in pantaloons," a man whose funeral she declined to attend. Her references to her own mother are few and matter-of-fact, including the letter in which the latter's death was announced.[50] . . . .

Yet nothing, in her mature life, mattered more to Louisa McCord than being a mother, especially to her son, Langdon Cheves McCord. She wished to be for her woman's sphere what she romantically believed her father was to the public realm, an influence for stability and good in a world full of the less prescient and less competent. But this does not quite capture the complexity of her views. . . . McCord's surviving correspondence shows her tacking between . . . two impulses, the fearsome strength she took as necessity and which others habit-ually discerned in her, and the desire to be protected. "I like a woman who *leans* a little," Dexter Clapp of Savannah once observed, and it will seem odd to observe that McCord could be such a woman, if often against her will. It was her misfortune that, during her life, she needed strength more than she was satisfied in being protected, for after her father the men she knew intimately seemed often to have been violent, weak, or inadequate. Over them she had powers of persuasion, but not power. Power was the mother's prerogative, including the power to protect, just as it was understood to be the prerogative of the slave-holder over the slave. "You believe the negro to be an oppressed race, while we believe him to be a protected one," she once told Henry Carey.[51] Part of McCord's incomprehension of abolitionism was that she did not understand why anyone would wish to forfeit protection for freedom, if freedom meant a reckless danger.

The complexity of her position is most starkly exposed in the story of her father's long dying, which casts a bleak light on what was possible for even the strongest of Southern women in a man's world.

Langdon Cheves grew old and, after a stroke which occasioned par-tial paralysis, his mind started to become "constantly confused, con-stantly restless, constantly changing." So, in the middle of the winter of 1855–56, his daughter took him into her Columbia house and away from his residence in the Sandhills. This was awkward, as it usually is between generations. She was a widow, in possession of her own household, in charge of her children and slaves. He was a patriarch—her patriarch—a man accustomed to command, bringing his own slaves, a man half lost in mind but one whose "firm will is uncontrou-lable." It rapidly became clear that he would not accept living in a house not his own, and talked often of returning to the Sandhills. This action would (as she told her brother) have been "a wretchedness and a shame," which others would not understand: they would conclude that "he who has made us all, is turned out to pine and to suffer." "I do not think it will be possible to keep him here, unless he could get the impression that this house belongs to him," she saw. . . . She threw herself into the task, though, as she said, "I do not know what to do, I am giving up every moment of my time, neglecting business, children and every thing else, but without success." For, as she knew, her father "*needs control*," and would not take it from a woman. "Some form, some apparent transfer must be gone through, before he will submit to be so told. He now gets angry or at least displeased if I say so." She was distraught; "I become almost crazy myself and do not know what to do." This not knowing, for so competent a woman, was terrible, desperate. Her letter of 25 January, 1856 says, "I do not know what to do," three times. Though, in fact, she did know what to do, for she had lived her life around men of her father's kind: "He must own property, he must be told 'this is yours,' wherever he stays." It was just that such men did not listen to a woman, so she needed constantly to inform her brother, ask his advice, seek his consent for legal and financial transactions, while he seems to have been negligent and inattentive to the mounting and debilitating crisis. . . .[52]

. . . . Eventually she was driven to build a second, small house on her town lot, where she could hide herself and her children, to leave him with the belief that he lorded over the main building. She spent her own money to protect Cheves and then had to beg recompense from her brother's stewardship of her father's means: "I am sorry to trouble you now but I really need money." Consistently, she protected her father from bad news, especially that his son Hayne was dying in Florence. She had often to lie, to contrive the "concocted falsehood."[53] She flattered his self-importance, for "he thinks that he has a hundred important communications to make." She dealt with his slaves (who clashed with her own). . . . She came very close to despair: "My position here is so intensely distressing that you must excuse me if I press upon you more urgently than you think right," she told her brother. "I know you have troubles, I know you have cares; perhaps even, you are not well yourself, perhaps I am goading you beyond endurance, but God help me what can I do?"[54] And all this at a time when her eyes were beginning to trouble her, and she feared blindness.

Eventually the crisis eased. The old man grew too weak to express his wayward will, became "helpless almost as an infant," and a woman was permitted to deal authoritatively with infants. . . .[55] He died in June 1857.

All this was, in many ways, a stark commentary on even McCord's version of the separate spheres. It confirmed her hard assessment of woman's difficult lot and man's brute insensibility. But she had liked to think that the boundaries of the spheres were distinct, that everyone knew his or her place. Yet it was not so. Keeping place required effort, a repression: "Although I have been pushed back in every possible way," she told Miles in 1848, "and have myself endeavoured for many a long year to crush my own propensities, there has been a struggling consciousness of something which has goaded me on." Necessity half-dissolved boundaries and compelled different fictions, a blurring of his and hers. "I think he will be much happier when he sees something of a house getting up on my lot and will feel that *this* is *his*," she observed at one point of her father.[56] This was the "concocted falsehood" of the doctrine of separate spheres. Everyone was told what they must be, but it was seldom possible to accomplish this, for reality was too fluid, "constantly confused, constantly restless, constantly changing."

NOTES

1 WCP to Major O'Connor, 4 December 1818, WCP Papers, South Caroliniana Library [SCL].

2 Louise Penelope Davis Preston Diary, 46, 25, Mrs. William Campbell Preston Papers, SCL.

3 Gerda Lerner, *The Grimké Sisters from South Carolina: Pioneers for Woman's Rights and Abolition* (Boston, 1967), 17–18; Richard C. Lounsbury, ed., *Louisa S. McCord: Poems, Drama, Biography, Letters* (Charlottesville, 1996), [PDBL], 425n; Lounsbury, *Louisa S. McCord: Political and Social Essays* (Charlottesville, 1995) [PSE], 13.

4 "A Note on Augusta Jane Evans," in *Beulah*, by Augusta Jane Evans (1857; reprint, Baton Rouge, 1992); Lounsbury, *McCord*: *PSE*, 3; . . . Thomas Jefferson to Nathaniel Burwell, 14 March 1818, in *Thomas Jefferson: Writings*, ed. Merrill D. Peterson (New York, 1984), 1411.

5 Jane H. Pease and William H. Pease, *Ladies, Women, & Wenches: Choice & Constraint in Antebellum Charleston & Boston* (Chapel Hill, 1990), 73–74.

6 Ibid., 73–74; Henry Middleton Jr., to Mary Hering Middleton, 13 July 1836, Hering-Middleton Papers, South Carolina Historical Society [SCHS]; 28 March 1838, Philip Pendelton Kennedy Diary . . . Virginia Historical Society [VSH].

7 Marcus Cicero Stephens to Mary Ann Primrose, 7 November 1841, Marcus Cicero Stephens Papers, Southern Historical Collection, University of North Carolina [SHC].

8 A. I. Deas to MIM, 6 August 1813, Manigault Family Papers, SCL; Henry W. Hilliard, *Speeches and Addresses* (New York, 1855), 477; Thomas R. Dew, "Dissertation on the Characteristic Differences between the Sexes, and on the Position and Influence of Woman in Society," *Southern Literary Messenger* [SLM] I (August 1835): 676.

9 Dew, "Dissertation on the Sexes," 679, 677.

10 "Female Education: Young Ladies Seminary at Prince Edward Court House," *SLM* I (May 1835): 519; . . . .

11 Jane Turner Censer, *North Carolina Planters and Their Children, 1800–1860* (Baton Rouge, 1984), 44, notes that teaching the ancient languages was unusual, but Christie Anne Farnham, *The Education of a Southern Belle: Higher Education and Student Socialization in the Antebellum South* (New York, 1994), 31, cites five schools in various states that did.

12 Henry Junius Nott, "The Life and Times of Daniel De Foe," *Southern Review* [SR] 7 (May 1831): 81; Farnham, *Education of a Southern Belle*, 11, 18. . . .

13 *Circular of the Georgia Female College, 1842–43*, and the 1856 Catalogue of the Holston Conference Female College, quoted in Farnham, *Education of a Southern Belle*, 17.

14 Farnham, *Education of a Southern Belle*, 21–28.

15 Ibid., 76, 86.
16 Quoted in Edgar W. Knight, ed., *A Documentary History* of *Education in the South before 1860*, 5 vols. (Chapel Hill, 1949–53), 5: 438.
17 Sarah Grimké, *Letters on the Equality of the Sexes and Other Essays*, ed. Elizabeth Ann Bartlett (1838; reprint, New Haven, 1988), 41–42; BM to Iveson Brookes, 19 March 1819, Manly Family Papers, University of Alabama [UA].
18 9 February 1845, Madaline Edwards Diary, Charles W. Bradbury Papers, SHC, reprinted in Dell Upton, ed., *Madaline: Love and Survival in Antebellum New Orleans: The Private Writings of a Kept Woman* (Athens, Ga., 1996), 238; William Henry Trescot to Willam Porcher Miles, 13 November 1853, William Porcher Miles Papers, SHC.
19 *Russell's Magazine* 4 (October 1858): 92-91, reprinted in Knight, *Documentary History of Education*, 5:451; . . . .
20 Charles Fraser, *Reminiscences* of *Charleston* (Charleston, 1854), 11–12; Sally G. McMillen, *Southern Women: Black and White in the Old South* (Arlington Heights, 1992), 40–44.
21 McMillen, *Southern Women*, 29.
22 Jefferson, *Writings*, ed. Peterson, 888; ADI to MIM, 31 March 1811, and Henry W. DeSaussure to MIM, 30 November 1818, Manigault Family Papers, SCL.
23 Quoted in Sarah Grimké, *Equality of the Sexes*, 58.
24 For a different view, which suggests a crisis of male confidence caused by the "market revolution," see Christopher Morris, "What's So Funny? Southern Humorists and the Market Revolution," in *Southern Writers and Their Worlds*, ed. Christopher Morris and Steven G. Reinhardt (College Station, 1996), 9–26.
25 William Henry Trescot to JHT, 25 June 1856, JHT Papers, SCL.
26 28 February 1827, Elizabeth Ruffin Diary, SHC.
27 *Proceedings and Debates of the Virginia State Convention, of 1829–30* (Richmond, 1830), 227.
28 Lounsbury, *McCord: PDBL*, 276; Lerner, *Grimké Sisters*, 281.
29 Lerner, *Grimké Sisters*, 8.
30 Lerner, *Grimké Sisters*, 40–41; Sarah Grimké, *Equality of the Sexes*, 15–16.
31 Sarah Grimké, *Equality of the Sexes*, 67, 70, 42, 59, 33, 35.
32 Lerner, *Grimké Sisters*, 323, 324; Sarah Grimké, *Equality of the Sexes*, 57, 59, 61.
33 Margaret Fuller Ossoli, *Woman in the Nineteenth Century* . . ., ed. Arthur B. Fuller (1847; reprint, Boston, 1855), 37; Sarah Grimké, *Equality of the Sexes*, 47–48, 66–67, 99, 85–95.
34 Sarah Grimké, *Equality of the Sexes*, 100, 78.
35 Ibid., 78; Lerner, *Grimké Sisters*, 334, writes that Grimké "never quite could make up her mind to come out in favor of divorce."
36 Angelina Emily Grimké, *Letters to Catherine Beecher* (Boston, 1836), 41.
37 Letter 12, ibid., 114.
38 "It was when my soul was deeply moved at wrongs of the slave that I first perceived distinctly the subject condition of women": "Condition of Women," in Sarah Grimké, *Equality of the Sexes*, 130.
39 Ibid., 114; Theodore Dwight Weld, *American Slavery as It Is* (1839; reprint, New York: 1969), 23, 44, 53.
40 Lounsbury, *McCord: PSE*, 115–16.
41 For example, ibid., 77, 114, 115.
42 She had "lately" read the book in early October 1852: see LSM to Mary Cheves Dulles, 9 October 1852, in Lounsbury, *McCord: PDBL*, 294.

43 Lounsbury, *McCord: PSE*, 109–10.
44 Ibid., 58, 59, 61, 73, 74, 109–10, 132.
45 Lounsbury, *McCord: PSE*, 108, 131.
46 Lounsbury, *McCord: PSE*, 406, 407, 151, 441, 113.
47 Ibid., 109, 110.
48 LSM to William Porcher Miles, 12 June 1848, in Lounsbury, *McCord: PDBL*, 277; Lounsbury, *McCord: PSE*, 108, 119 . . .
49 Susan Smythe Bennett, comp., "The McCords of McCords' Ferry, South Carolina," *South Carolina Historical and Genealogical Magazine* 34 (October 1933): 192.
50 Ibid., 192; LSM to Sophia Cheves Haskell, 8 April 1836, in Lounsbury, *McCord: PDBL*, 268.
51 Dexter Clapp to Henry W. Bellows, 12 January 1844, Henry W. Bellows Papers, Duke University; LSM to Henry Charles Carey, 18 January 1854, in Lounsbury, *McCord: PDBL*, 297.
52 LSM to Langdon Cheves Jr., 18 February, 1 February, 25 January, 7 March, 29 January 1856, in Lounsbury, *McCord: PDBL*, 312, 309, 304–5, 318.
53 LSM to Langdon Cheves Jr., 1 February 1856, ibid., 309.
54 LSM to Langdon Cheves Jr., 29 January, 1 February, 5 May, 13 April, 29 February, 5 March 1856, ibid., 332, 309, 328, 323–24, 313, 325, 316.
55 LSM to Langdon Cheves Jr., 5 February 1857, ibid., 393; Smythe, "Recollections," 19, quoted in A. V. Huff Jr., *Langdon Cheves of South Carolina* (Columbia, 1977), 244–45.
56 LSM to William Porcher Miles, 12 June 1848; LSM to Langdon Cheves Jr., 7 March 1856, in Lounsbury, *McCord: PDBL*, 274, 318.

11

TO HARDEN A LADY'S HAND

Gender politics, racial realities, and women millworkers in antebellum Georgia

Michele Gillespie

Michele Gillespie's essay examines a group much neglected by historians of the South, white women who worked for wages. While southern states lagged far behind New England in the development of a textile industry, Georgia, the subject of Gillespie's research here, did develop a significant industry by 1860, and its mill workers were mainly women from poor white families. Such women fit the stereotypes neither of contemporary southerners nor of most southern historians about women's lives in the Old South. The very existence of a force of low-wage, white, female workers contradicted the southern ideal of the "lady," but industrialists claimed that "There is nothing in tending a loom to harden a lady's hand." As Gillespie writes, industrialists and their apologists "used economic concerns about labor and race, social expectations about gender, and political fears about class not only to create a new workforce that was cheap and relatively tractable but to justify it as well." Poor white families supported these developments and in many cases relied on the wages their children earned in the mills, even though southern ideology also assumed that all white households should be supported by the work and incomes of "independent" men.

* * *

"There is nothing in tending a loom to harden a lady's hand," stated Chief Justice Henry Collier, a strong advocate for textile manufactures in the antebellum South. Like many promoters of southern industrialization in the decades before the Civil War, Collier recognized that the employment of white females in textile mills secured an inexpensive, quiescent labor force that not only did not compete with but indeed complemented the dominant agricultural economy and its key labor source—slaves. To compel southern society to embrace white women's employment in the mills, he manipulated the conventions of gender and race in the antebellum South by invoking the southern lady ideal with his statement. Thus Collier was contending that a white female employee could remain a "southern lady," despite the unprecedented experience of toiling for fourteen-hour days in massive buildings filled with noisy machines and choking fibers, because her hands would not be callused by her labors. Her mythical gentility, in other words, along with her virtue, would remain intact, making millwork an ideal pursuit for white women, an implicit contrast to slave women, who were perceived by whites to lack such critical character attributes and whose work was generally agricultural, often extremely arduous, and rarely gender-specific.[1]

When British traveler J. S. Buckingham passed through the region in 1842, he painted a very different picture of factory life in the Old South, one that did not include any reference to southern ladyhood. "The white families engaged in these factories live in log huts clustered about the establishment on the river's bank," he commented after meeting millworkers dwelling along the Oconee River in Athens, Georgia. "The whites look miserably pale and unhealthy; and they are said to be very short-lived, the first symptoms of fevers and dysenteries in the autumn appearing chiefly among them in the factories, and sweeping numbers of them off to death."[2] Even Henry Merrell, a Georgia industrialist who firmly believed in the importance of manufacturing for the welfare of the state and region, admitted factory work did not advance southern women's lot, nor promote her gentility. In speaking of the vagaries of the planter economy in general and the plight of the small planter and his kin in particular, he observed "The hard economy . . . condemns the females of a family to profitless drudgery at the loom." Merrell clearly understood that white female factory workers were all too frequently caught in a web of southern social relations that bound together family needs and commercial developments and left them with dreary lives over which they had too little control.[3]

The majority of factory workers in Georgia in the antebellum era were white women. The truth about their origins and experiences remains largely unexplored, despite the fact that their entry into wage work represented a significant new development in the antebellum era.[4] This essay explores the development of women as a mill labor force in Georgia, a key industrializing southern state in the antebellum period. It takes its cue from those scholars of nineteenth-century southern women's history, most especially Victoria Bynum and LeeAnn Whites, who have insisted on exploring the critical connections between the presumably private world of the home and family and the public world of politics and commerce.[5] In doing so, the essay highlights the interplay between seemingly straightforward economic concerns, perceptions about racial realities, uses of gender ideals, and new

273

constructions of working-class identity that worked together to make paid female labor socially and politically palatable in the Old South.

Women from all walks of life had always toiled in the South prior to the advent of female factory work. Indeed, the vast majority of southern women, white and black, slave and free, worked the livelong day, just not in a factory in front of mechanized looms for wages. Wives, daughters, widows, and spinsters managed the household, hen house, and vegetable and herb gardens, ran the kitchen and the dairy, did the spinning, knitting, and making of cloth and clothes, the cleaning and laundering, and the bearing and caring for children. These same women were invariably expected to work in the fields, pick cotton, serve as midwives to the livestock and each other, break horses and drive cattle, handle the plow, build fences, protect the homestead, and in some cases, work with slaves. Their experiences were framed by arduous and never-ending duties for which they received virtually no fiscal remuneration for their efforts (and, excepting the reality of the slave economy, were reminiscent of their preindustrial sisters in Europe and the North). Although growing evidence clearly indicates that antebellum southern women maintained an extensive system of informal trade networks and were employed in more sectors of the economy than previously appreciated, as this volume attests, much of their identity as documented in the historical record reflected their place in a patriarchal world rather than their identity as shaped by their skills, duties, and in some cases, even occupations.[6]

Slave women, whose very humanity let alone gender was ignored in the interests of augmenting property and production, failed to receive much recognition in the historical record either. Nor did most slave women secure any form of payment for their superhuman efforts, although recent research does indicate that some slave women hired out their own time, sometimes to their financial advantage, or engaged in informal economies of trade to improve the quality of their lives. Both these latter pursuits, one public, the other clandestine, were usually carried out beyond the master's purview, showing how their involvement in the developing commercial economy could give slave women a modicum of independence and choice as workers and consumers.[7]

Even the so-called southern lady was not immune to work, although often of a decidedly different nature than that of most white and black women in the South. The rewards she received were not necessarily immediately tangible and did not come in the form of wages. But the plantation mistress could revel in the symbolic power of her permanent pedestal in exchange for financial sustenance over the course of her lifetime (or at least until the Civil War), provided she generate a never-ending stream of emotional and religious succor to family, friends, and slaves, entertain her husband's business and political acquaintances, and manage the plantation household as well. All told, these were difficult and demanding duties, if not always physically exhausting or remunerative ones, and certainly required frequent removal of her proverbial white gloves.[8]

The rural world of women's work described here, that of white and black, slave and free, in the southern household during the antebellum period, has become an increasingly well documented subject. The introduction and maturation of industrialization in the antebellum South, along with the impact of the Civil War, slowly but surely brought an end to women's work as it once existed in this agricultural, slave-holding economy, yet this topic has not been a popular avenue for exploration. Southern women's transition from household to factory and market, and the shifts in social, economic, and political relations it created, has received critical attention from historians of the late nineteenth and twentieth centuries, however. These scholars have examined how once privileged women "got by" without paternal protectors and slave laborers. They have begun to analyze how share-cropping and tenant-farming women were confounded by the exigencies of their late-nineteenth- and twentieth-century rural lives, which forced them into new kinds of economic exchanges. Many of these postbellum women migrated to cities to earn less than adequate pay as domestics, store clerks, and even prostitutes, while others traveled to mill towns in search of factory work. Such experiences profoundly altered women's understanding of themselves and their place in the world.[9]

The origins of this transition, however, which stretch back into the antebellum era, have essentially gone unexamined. At first, industrialization in the South began as little more than a modest trickle of change in the early nineteenth century. At that time, new industrialists in the South were faced with a dilemma in a region ripe for industrialization. Who would work in the mills? Slaves were needed in the fields, and most white men considered wage work beneath them. The only remaining workforce was that of white women and children, who were perceived to be a readily available, cheap, and malleable source of labor. As Bess Beatty has argued in her work on antebellum industrialization in the North Carolina piedmont, textile mills were so new to the region that mill owners' ideas about who should labor in them and how that labor should be managed proved surprisingly flexible.[10] In this sense, industrialists were quite willing to forego gendered and racialized notions about who should and should not do manual labor in southern society in order to make their machines run and turn a handy profit from the fruits of their labor.

Although reliance on female labor in the fledgling textile industry involved relatively few numbers of women at the outset, especially when compared to the postbellum period, the movement of these women into the paid workforce and the rationales employed to explain this unique development in the region laid the groundwork for women's well-known participation in the southern textile industry after the Civil War (and through most of the twentieth century before most such jobs moved overseas). Mill advocates, largely using gender as explanation, over time carefully constructed the ideological and political frameworks for justifying textile workers' historically poor pay, indifferent treatment, and often dangerous working conditions.[11] While industrialization's beginnings in the North grew out of a regional agrarian economy in the throes of a commercial revolution, its beginnings in the South were firmly rooted in a more traditional agrarian economy dependent on slave labor and a trans-Atlantic market.[12] Originating with experiments in textile production at Pawtucket, Rhode Island, followed by the establishment of the Lowell Mills in Massachusetts, northern entrepreneurs, speculators, and politicians quickly came to embrace the textile industry as the key tool with which to break Britain's stronghold on the American economy. Domestic production of cloth and other manufactures meant the U.S. government could erect tariffs against importation and encourage a new measure of economic self-sufficiency nationwide. The Embargo Act and the War of 1812, which forced Americans to resort to home production rather than import manufactured goods from Europe, only served to hasten the industrial revolution's initial impact on New England, the mid-Atlantic and the Midwest; the South was not so eager by contrast. Although women laborers were important in easing the transition to a market economy, including those famous farmers' daughters who made up the first working class in the textile mills of Lowell, the diversifying economy quickly came to rely on male free labor as much and in some cases far more than female free labor.[13] As the market revolution's industrial manifestations began to take more permanent shape, men of means in the South grew increasingly disenchanted with the results. The advent of the cotton gin and the successful cultivation of short-staple cotton across the extensive southern piedmont—which stretched south from Virginia to Georgia and soon swung west across the up-country of the newer Gulf states—promised quick and impressive profits as long as planters could be assured competitive prices from both European and American buyers. The threat of tariffs augured badly for southerners, who feared that northern manufacturers would be able to buy their formerly lucrative crops at bargain-basement prices by forcing Europeans out of the picture. The rhetorical and legal battles that ensued because of these regional fears profoundly affected the national political discourse that led to secession and civil war. But long before these debates crescendoed into a terrible struggle between brothers, some southern speculators, entrepreneurs, and politicians considered fighting fire with fire. Why not, they pondered, build their own textile mills, thereby thwarting their northern competitors and securing increased economic independence for the region? This consideration led to the tentative beginnings of industrialization in the South and the first substantial movement of southern women into the paid workforce.

In many respects, Georgia led the way in this transformation. Although the state boasted a low-country population of wealthy planters, merchants, and plentiful slaves, the state's real growth and development were occurring in the up-country by the early nineteenth century. A burgeoning population of free whites and black slaves along with plenty of good land secured at Native Americans' expense proved the right recipe for economic expansion. As they migrated westward, farmers became planters and nonslaveholders became slaveholders, and many established thriving plantations and bustling market towns in their wake. In just ten years, from 1810 to 1820, the state's population (341,000) had increased by more than a third. By 1860, the population had more than tripled to over a million inhabitants, three out of five of whom were white.[14]

In Georgia, migration westward created strong demand for internal improvements in communication and transportation as early as the 1820s. Piedmont planters could not get their valuable cotton crop to market without adequate roads, river transport, and, eventually, railroads. Private banks mushroomed across the up-country to finance these ventures; regulated by the state and buoyed by the booming cotton economy, these banks proved surprisingly stable throughout the antebellum era.[15] Entrepreneurs eager to establish textile mills believed the energetic state of Georgia's economy and the increasing regional divisiveness between North and South in the political arena meant the time seemed ideal for introducing manufacturing. Although early investors had hoped to tie Georgia's future to New England's spectacular start by building two textile mills in the heart of the piedmont in 1810, their efforts proved premature. Unfortunately, the conclusion of the War of 1812 and the subsequent lifting of the embargo flooded the countryside with cheap imported cloth and forced them out of business.[16]

The textile movement that transformed Georgia into the Empire State on the eve of the Civil War took hold two decades later with the opening of two factories in reaction to the Tariff of 1828. Within ten years, fourteen more mills had sprung into operation. These factories claimed total capital investments of more than half a million dollars and employed roughly 800 people. By 1851, the state boasted forty mills and by some reports more than 2,000 operatives.[17]

Although scholars have long argued that industrialization lagged in the South, whether due to overinvestment of planter capital in land and slaves or the tenacity of the agrarian ideal, much evidence indicates that industrial development, despite its slow start, was very much on the ascendancy by the 1850s, only to be profoundly disrupted in the post-Civil War era. The cotton industry was a significant factor in this antebellum growth.[18] The expansion of the cotton mill industry was fueled for a variety of reasons. Many civic-minded up-country Georgians believed that the advent of the railroad would enhance the local economy and therefore hastened to ensure its passage through their community. Unfortunately, because the iron horse sped cotton almost directly to the sea, virtually bypassing much of the youthful urban piedmont altogether, it did not always leave new economic opportunities in its wake, despite initial expectations to the contrary. Because the railroad carried manufactured goods from the Northeast deep into the interior of the state for the first time, it actually damaged many local businesses and commercial ventures already in place since they could not compete with these cheaper imports. Town boosters argued that the establishment of textile mills would offset this damage because local manufacturers could use the railroad to ship their newly manufactured local goods across the piedmont. Some boosters even claimed up-country mills would substantially benefit area farmers who could become local suppliers of meat, vegetables, and dairy produce.[19] Thus the construction of new mills ultimately brought renewed hope for the economic viability of piedmont towns—a hope never fully realized until the late nineteenth century.[20]

The impetus for mills grew out of another set of concerns as well. State and local leaders quickly recognized that migration had not stopped at the Chattahoochee River, the state's westernmost border, but had spilled over into the newest plantation lands of Florida, Alabama, and Mississippi in the 1820s and 1830s. In fact, Carolina and Georgia families traveling west were such a common sight that one disgruntled Augusta resident simply referred to them as "the movers."[21] Georgia boosters recognized it would only be a matter of time before the rich cotton lands of Louisiana, Texas, and Arkansas siphoned off yet another generation of "movers" as well. The rapid drop in cotton prices in the 1820s followed by the constant stream of families westward convinced many politicians that industrialization offered an attractive alternative to the plantation economy and might help retain those Georgians who might otherwise look for better opportunities in the new Gulf states.[22] If measured by the spread of factories, the efforts of state and town leaders to generate industry proved quite successful. By 1850, the state led the way in manufacturing profits and output below the Mason-Dixon line. The up-country towns of Macon, Columbus, and

Milledgeville had become manufacturing centers. The up-country city of Augusta alone, which had recently resorted to canal building to ensure adequate water power and encourage more manufactures, had become home to nearly a dozen textile factories, and now sported the beguiling title "The Lowell of the South." During the decade that followed, increasing numbers of new textile plants spread even deeper into the Georgia hinterland. Powered by steam, these mills allowed owners to boast more spindles and higher production rates, and earned Georgia monikers such as "The New England of the South" and "The Empire State."[23]

Although the textile industry was brand-new in the 1830s and 1840s, and local mill owners unsure who in fact constituted the ideal laborer, white women and children quickly became the majority workforce. Census records indicate that by 1850 textile factories employed 873 male and 1,399 female hands (or a 2:3 male to female ratio). By 1860, they employed 1,131 male and 1,682 female hands (the 2:3 ratio of male to female hands remained unchanged). Moreover, many of those male hands were not adults.[24] A Milledgeville reporter offered a detailed description of labor specialization and some hints about its gendered and youthful nature based on his observations of the Eagle Textile Factory in Columbus in 1860. The mill, which employed approximately 250 hands, stood four stories high. Six hands, sex unspecified, operated machines in a picking room in the basement. On the first floor, twenty hands, "mostly bops," operated the carding machines. On the second floor, "70 girls, two overseers, and a few small boys" operated 136 looms, each of which could produce thirty to forty yards of cloth a day. On the third floor, seventy children, sex unspecified, operated thirty spinning frames and 5,000 cotton spindles, as well as rope, cotton yard, and sewing thread machines. On the fourth floor, twenty hands, sex unspecified, worked 140 woolen spindles, warping mills, frames, and beaming engines. The occupations of the remaining employees were not detailed.[25] Adult female laborers received an average of $10 a month in wages, and adult male laborers received an average of $20 a month at the profitable Eagle Mill, a clear indication why owners preferred female over male labor.[26] These unequal wages were not unusual. The Columbus Factory, for example, employed eighty operatives, "chiefly girls," paying them $10 to $12 per month, while men earned substantially more.[27] In 1850, women millworkers' average wage across the state was $7.39, while men earned an average of $14.57.[28] Children earned ten cents a day in the Richmond Factory in the 1840s. By 1859, children were earning $1.00 to $2.00 a week, and women from $3.00 to $5.00 in the nearby Augusta Factory.[29]

Mill owners also preferred women and children as laborers in Athens, a college town and market center in the upper piedmont serving

Georgia and Carolina farmers alike.[30] Four textile mills operated within seven miles of the town and were able to take advantage of new transportation opportunities with the arrival of the railroad in 1844. By the late 1840s, the Athens Manufacturing Company, the Princeton Manufacturing Company, the Mars Hill Factory, and the Georgia Factory produced a total of 4,400 yards of cloth a day. Their wares were sold in New York, Philadelphia, North and South Carolina, Tennessee, Georgia, Alabama, and New Orleans.[31] Together these mills employed over 200 operatives; every indication suggests that the majority of them were women. The Athens Manufacturing Company alone, the largest and most profitable of the four mills, employed eighty-five operatives, who were explicitly described by the owners as "mostly female."[32]

Information about these women and their families is sparse, but close analysis of the manuscript returns of the U.S. Census for Clarke County in 1860 suggests theirs was a complicated existence. Ninety-two women were identified as factory workers (an indication of the difficulties enumerators faced in including all residents, since it is all but certain that the number of female operatives was higher). Of these ninety-two, the oldest was forty-five and the youngest eleven. The average age of Clarke County female factory workers in the 1860 census was twenty-one. Over three-quarters (77 percent) of the women were native-born Georgians. The remaining 23 percent came from surrounding states, mostly South Carolina (19 percent), and a handful (4 percent) from Alabama, Tennessee, and North Carolina.[33]

The population schedules show that factory work was a family affair. Eighty-six percent of all female factory workers were joined in the mills by at least one other family member. In some of these households, male heads listed their occupations as farmers, while one or more family members worked in the factory. Yet farming was no longer a productive pursuit in a mature plantation economy like that surrounding Athens, where the high cost of land and slaves, along with taxes, and the ups and downs of the cotton market had hurt all but the wealthiest of planters. Yeomen families, in rough straits, needed additional income to make ends meet. As industrialist Henry Merrell observed, rural families in the Georgia piedmont sent their daughters to the new mills to help their families eke out a rather meager subsistence.[34]

The occupational identity of "farmer" undoubtedly allowed male household heads to save face, for many such "farm" families living in the factory district at the edge of town along the river listed no property in the census returns and hence could not have been truly farmers any longer. For example, N. Aumy, twenty-four, lived with her father, mother, and three brothers in the factory district alongside the Oconee.

Her father and oldest brother listed their occupations as farmers but owned no land. They may have hired themselves out as agricultural day laborers to make ends meet but clung to the "farmer" nomenclature despite their reduced circumstances. Another factory worker, Mary Bentley, sixteen, lived alone with her father in the factory district; he, too, claimed to be a farmer, however unlikely. The four Smith daughters, Louisa, Malinda, Mary, and Cornelia, ages sixteen to twenty-nine, lived with their father, also a so-called farmer, and a female boarder who worked in the factory with them. Male household heads who claimed to be farmers despite their lack of land probably had moved their families to the mill district only recently, having been unable to turn a profit on their crops and steer clear of debt in the turbulent agricultural economy of the late 1850s. This family migration pattern from farm to mill town is significant, for it precedes the more well known migration of rural farm families to mill towns in the 1890s and 1900s. In this sense, late-antebellum migration seems to have set an important social precedent for postbellum developments.[35]

In other male-headed households with millworking daughters, fathers often engaged in artisan occupations such as harness making, brick making, iron molding, and carpentry. In one instance, the father of the Hayes sisters—Becky, fifteen, Eliza, seventeen, and Cynthia, nineteen, all factory workers—was a schoolteacher (and was probably employed by one of the mills to educate their workers in evening classes, a not-infrequent practice at this time). Susan Saunders, twenty-two, worked in the factory with two of her seven siblings, while her father worked as a factory guard. With the exception of Mr. Saunders and Mr. Hayes, however, each of whose factory work was highly specialized, none of the fathers of daughters who worked in the factory were factory employees themselves.[36]

Herein lay the crux of the matter for many families. Men were reluctant to give up the independence that life on the farm or life as an artisan represented. As one critic stated about the impact of the textile industry, the arrival of the mills and the new economic order it represented undermined men's power and autonomy. "Labor-saving machines ... employ more women and children ... and with them must go a spirited and manly brother, husband, or father to cringe beneath the power of capital."[37] To perform wage work for capitalists was emasculating in a southern culture where men's social and political status was rooted in their independence—a legacy of Jeffersonian republicanism.

If antebellum men believed their identity was at stake if they succumbed to millwork, it helps explain why over half of the households (58 percent) containing female factory workers were headed by women. What is equally interesting in these female-headed households is how infrequently the female heads worked in the mills. Sarah and Eliza Giles, adult daughters of Mrs. Giles, worked in the factory, while their mother claimed the occupation of "house business." Anne and Martha Brazzleton, eighteen and sixteen, respectively, worked in the mills while their younger sister and their mother, the latter listing her occupation as "housework," apparently stayed home. It is certainly likely that a number of female household heads could not work in the factory because they had young children; factories generally would not hire anyone under the age of ten. But in many instances, this was not the case; instead, adult women appeared to be choosing "house business" while their children labored in the mills.

In other instances, single women factory workers in their teens and twenties, and in a few cases thirties, either lived with siblings, some of whom were factory workers as well, and no parents, or in a very few instances boarded with local families. The Pinterfield siblings, five daughters, ranging in age from thirteen to twenty, and one brother, eleven, lived without parents; all six children worked in the factory. Margaret and Nancy Williams lived with their three brothers, all brick masons, and no parents; in an unusual twist, their household included a male boarder named Ghee who also worked in the factory.[38]

These family structures suggest that widows and abandoned wives brought their children to these new factory towns in order to support themselves and their families—support that more often than not fell on the children rather than their mothers. It also suggests orphaned siblings looked to the mills for work. The prevalence of female-headed households corroborates the fact that Georgia industrialists, like southern industrialists in general, deliberately sought female workers and their children, as suggested by the following advertisement from the Eatonton Manufacturing Company: "White women, girls, and boys are such as will be wanted, aged ten years or upwards. Entire families may find it to their interest to engage in our service."[39]

The census records make it exceedingly apparent that the vast majority of female factory workers were young and single. Virtually all lived with family members and most in female-headed households. Without further evidence from other kinds of sources, it is dangerous to speculate further about the nature of these women's lives, except to conclude that for certain families in the piedmont, it was not unknown for young single women to work in the factory, mostly with sisters, sometimes with brothers. Their male family members were more likely to pursue agricultural and artisanal occupations than factory work; their female family members either worked in the factory, engaged in "housework," as was the case for many mothers, or employed themselves independently as milliners and seamstresses (114 Clarke County women listed their occupations as seamstresses or milliners in this same census). One final conclusion can be drawn from these records. Few of these households listed real estate holdings, and very few claimed personal property of any value, indicating that for most theirs was a marginal existence. Millwork attracted poor whites.[40]

The fact that in many of these families, men continued to seek independent work outside the mills and mothers stayed in the home suggests the broader power of southern culture to determine proper social roles for men and women regardless of class. These cultural dictates allowed poor men to retain their masculinity and independence and poor married women to retain their femininity and "ladyhood" despite their reduced circumstances. It would seem that these gendered expectations were such critical markers of social respect and status in the Old South that men and women were willing to forego earning wages, since they intimated weakness, vulnerability, and perhaps even unseemliness, and to have their empty purses filled by their children rather than themselves. Poor single women's identities, however, seem to have been more malleable and hence single women's lives viewed as more expendable.

Unlike the mill girls of Lowell, who lived without their families in boardinghouses and had some control over their social lives and wages, the young women in Athens who worked in the mills lived with their families. While this situation offered them some measure of support and protection, it also signaled family reliance on their wages and real limitations on their personal freedom. Given the financial woes these families faced, it seems unlikely that these women could secure much autonomy despite their role as a breadwinner, adding yet another significant contrast to female textile workers' experiences in the antebellum North, or even in the North Carolina piedmont. At the same time, the situation also has implications for understanding the connections between the antebellum and postbelluin South. Historians have stressed that in the late-nineteenth- and early-twentieth-century southern textile industry, employers justified paying male hands relatively low wages because working women and children were contributing to the household economy as well. The origins of this family wage system, however, seem more likely to have been forged in the antebellum period when adult males avoided engagement in factory work and factory owners explicitly sought the cheaper labor of women and children.[41]

While the evidence indicates that adult men and adult women skirted wage work in mills despite their straitened circumstances, sending their daughters to work in the mills in their stead—highlighting a significant degree of agency among parents in poor households, as well as their authority over their children—another interpretation remains equally plausible and even complementary. There is little question that mill owners preferred hiring white women and children over white males and slaves because they represented the cheapest labor source available. Cultural expectations about gender, age, and wage work, which compelled many white adults to avoid the factory, despite bad times, may in fact have aided industrialists in their search for bargain-basement laborers. Thus, familial roles and expectations worked in tandem with new economic developments to relegate white women, especially single white women, to subordinate status. As Bess Beatty has effectively argued ... individual women millworkers did find ways to resist that subordination, but that resistance occurred at the intersection of southern family culture and economic change, and as a product of racialized and gendered beliefs.[42]

By the 1840s, promoters of industry in Georgia and across the South argued rather vociferously that factory work saved poor whites from destitution. Preferring to overlook the economic exigencies that compelled industrialists to seek out white labor, factory owners insisted upon the benefits of factory employment for Georgia's growing class of landless white families. The industrialists also stressed their own unique role as benefactors in this situation. In the wake of the panic of 1837, the depressions in the 1840s, and the spread of the plantation economy, with its skyrocketing land and slave prices in the 1850s, leaders throughout the South expressed concern about the dangers of a burgeoning population of poor whites. Industrialists told worried citizens that more manufactories were the best solution. Stated Hezekiah Niles, editor of the *Niles' Weekly Register*, "We have regarded every cotton mill established in the South as a *machine* for the conversion of many to favor the domestic industry of the country—by seeing the good effects of such mills ... in affording employment to the labouring poor."[43] Throughout Georgia, industrialists contended that employing poor whites prevented their impoverishment and ruin. In a sense, some state and regional leaders were coming to recognize that Jeffersonian republicanism was no longer applicable when growing numbers of whites were destitute. The power of a racialized herrenvolk sensibility that had bound whites together across significant class differences for so long in the South no longer proved operable when poorer whites lacked even the vestiges of independence—a decent crop and arable land.

"[With] the factories built," wrote a Georgia editorialist in 1847, "there is at once an increased demand for labor, which will give profitable employment to hundreds and thousands of our own citizens who are now struggling for a meager subsistence by the cultivation of an almost barren soil."[44] The editor of the Columbus *Enquirer* celebrated the success of the Columbus mills that same year. "We love to contemplate the present improvement and future prosperity of our beautiful city. . . . Manufactories give employment and good wages, to a large number of the industrious women and children of the country, and add immensely to the independence and self-reliance of the people; hence we rejoice to see them sprung up in our midst."[45] Another writer urged planters to invest their capital not in land and slaves "but in the more profitable as well as more philanthropic business of manufacturing."[46]

Yet the actual use of textile mills as the solution to these growing numbers of impoverished whites had not been a foregone conclusion. Since the inception of the textile industry, politicians and promoters alike had debated whether to rely on white or black labor. In 1827, the Georgia legislature entertained a memorial to investigate the merits of supporting textile manufactures and, in particular, to evaluate "the practicability" of using slave labor in the mills.[47] J. S. Buckingham, a little more than a decade later, noted that three mills in Athens employed slave laborers alongside white laborers. One mill owned its own slave hands, while the other two hired their unfree workers from local planters on a monthly basis. Buckingham observed that slave laborers were as capable as free laborers of handling the looms and spindles but proved more expensive. Mill owners paid their hands, both free and slave, $7.00 per month, but they had to feed their slave laborers in addition to giving their owners their wages, making hired slaves too costly.[48]

Not surprisingly, as more and more mills established largely white labor forces, mill owners publicly intimated that all-white labor forces prevented poor white peoples' collusion with slaves. Although racism was certainly endemic in this society and the color line represented significant social hierarchies that some whites were loath to cross, blacks and whites had always worked together in a number of settings, whether on small farms, in artisans' shops, or on the waterfront, and the possibilities for challenging the power and authority of the planter class had always concerned many elites.[49] Blacks and whites could also work together in factories. Buckingham had found black and white factory hands working harmoniously in the Athens Manufacturing Company, the only Athens factory to own its slave hands. "There is no difficulty among them on account of color, the white girls working in the same room and at the same loom with black girls; and boys of each color, as well as men and women, working together without repugnance or objection," he reported. Few textile companies could afford to own slaves despite Buckingham's findings, however. More telling than the biracial workforce and these harmonious relations was the decision of the Athens Manufacturing Company to sell its handful of slaves in 1843. Although the reason for the sale is not explicit in the records, times were tight in the wake of the 1842 panic.

Owning slaves had required an initial outlay of cash to purchase them; it had also necessitated payment for ongoing expenses incurred in providing room, board, clothes, shoes, and health care. Selling these slaves not only eliminated those expenses but brought the company new capital at a rough time for the industry.[50]

The Athens mills notwithstanding, the Georgia textile industry as a whole relied far more on white than slave labor. Certainly a number of industry boosters penned editorials on the suitability of slave labor in Georgia manufactories, but these arguments did not sway general practice.[51] More frequently, newspapers of the period were filled with invective detailing how black competition with free labor undermined white men's independence, arguments that industrialists used to explain their preference for white labor. Of course, the reality was far simpler. In the Georgia piedmont, where these mills predominated, white women and children were cheaper to employ, more readily available, and more tractable than white men, who were reluctant to engage in factory work and were presumed more likely to protest and perhaps even strike like their northern brethren. Moreover, white women and children were cheaper than slaves, who were more expensive overall, tied to the agricultural calendar, and ultimately controlled by their owners if industrialists elected to hire rather than own slaves outright.[52]

The textile industry in Georgia was a difficult one in many respects. It lacked the extensive capital and economies of scale that made ventures in New England successful over long periods of time. Most Georgia mills manufactured similar products and competed for the same local and regional markets. About two-thirds of the goods were sold to merchants in the state; the remaining third were shipped to merchants in the Mississippi Valley, the North, and in some cases, China.[53] Moreover, the railroad had flooded cheap imports into local markets, which created added competition for homegrown goods. Frederick Law Olmsted was surprised to see the number of New England-made coarse and fine textiles sold alongside Georgia-made cotton during his trip through the state in the 1850s.[54] Many of these antebellum mills lacked adequate capital and after constructing their buildings found their enterprise stalled until they could find enough investors to allow them to buy the required machinery. Once in operation, mills had to contend with roller-coaster cotton prices and a series of panics and depressions, which often meant they could not sell enough goods to satisfy their investors. In some cases they were forced to close, in others to limp along undercapitalized, reducing the profitability of the textile industry throughout the state.[55]

The structural realities of the textile mill industry in Georgia forced owners and investors to cut corners wherever they could. Hiring the cheapest labor possible made good economic sense. Not surprisingly, although mill promoters argued to the contrary, factory wages in the Southeast in 1860 were lower than anywhere else in the nation, with the exception of Florida.[56] Textile mills in antebellum Georgia relied on a workforce of predominately white women and children because they were the cheapest available labor source.[57] Twenty years ago, Claudia Goldin and Kenneth Sokoloff showed that women and children comprised a significant portion of the antebellum manufacturing labor force in the Northeast. They also demonstrated that the wages of these laborers increased relative to that of men with industrial development.[58] Although women and children were the majority workforce in the manufacturing sector of the economy in the South, their wages did not rise relative to men's wages over the course of the antebellum era. Because poor white women and children had few options for alternative employment, and could not easily migrate elsewhere, they were forced to accept employers' terms.

The mill industry justified this system by stressing the value of an all-white labor force both for poor whites and, by implication, for the citizens of the state as a whole who would not be required to support them if employed.[59] These editorials skated around the fact that women and children were the bulk of their employees, however, rather than poor white men, whose growing presence was the stated cause for concern in the first place. They also ignored the hypocrisy of their rhetoric, labeling millworkers as worthy citizens and voters when in fact women and children, the bulk of these employees, were not entitled to the same privileges of citizenship as men. Although southern culture turned on the notion that male household heads secured citizenship and authority through their independence, and wore that badge of independence symbolically by boasting a house full of dependents (if not slaves, at least women and children), millwork profoundly altered the nature of that relationship, in some cases actually making the male household head dependent on women and children for support. Neither industrialists nor politicians could adapt this altered set of social relationships into their larger arguments about the value of mills for the Georgia economy and the laboring poor. Thus, the editor of the *Augusta Chronicle* could write in 1852 that employing white labor in factories was "for the benefit of society and the promotion of its great interests, by giving employment to the people, and affording them the facilities for rearing and educating their children, so as to fit them for the active and responsible duties of life, as citizens of this great and free Republic."[60]

Moreover, despite the rhetoric painting millwork as poor white people's panacea, gender notwithstanding, the operatives' experience appears to have been a mixed bag at best. Certainly some mill owners attempted to build a sense of community and create general goodwill by encouraging their workers to pursue their own advancement (and yet again setting precedents for structuring mill life in postbellum factory towns some decades later). The Princeton Manufacturing Company offered religious services to factory workers twice a month. It also created a library for use by its employees.[61] In nearby Graniteville, South Carolina, William Gregg, who embraced a decidedly paternalistic vision of owner-worker relations and whose opinions on wage labor are well documented, peopled his mills with white families from the South Carolina and Georgia up-country, the majority of whom were women. He also built a school with night classes, as well as a church to encourage moral virtue among his employees.[62] The Howard Manufactory in Columbus furnished churches and schools, too.[63] The *Augusta Chronicle* boasted that all Augusta mills offered "Sunday schools and evening schools, libraries, public lectures and public journals [as] no mean advantages for developing . . . intellectual and moral faculties."[64]

However successful these sporadic efforts to create camaraderie, promote education, and encourage piety were, and however committed employers' writings appeared on these issues, few owners showed much respect for the actual workers themselves and largely ignored the gendered realities of their workforce. Henry Merrell, who supervised several textile operations, including the successful Roswell Mills, reflected about his management days. "I have worried through. I had to 'make out' . . . with hands who looked upon their employer as their natural enemy."[65] He described these employees as "banditti."[66] In an 1847 article on Georgia manufacturing for the *New York Journal of Commerce*, Merrell publicly showed his disdain for his employees, as well as his belief in the value of millwork for their rehabilitation, by stating:

> [The mills] have forced into active employment, and into something like discipline, a very unruly and unproductive class of white population, who, when idle, are, to say the least, no friends of the planter. There are now no paupers, to speak of, in any county of Georgia where a cotton factory exists. By employing the children of such, factories preserve their parents from want. It may be estimated that during the late scarcity of food which has run through two years, the factories in Georgia have saved the state from a poor tax which would otherwise have exceeded all other taxes out together.[67]

For Merrell, industrialists proved philanthropists, saving the state from costly taxes and debt relief, all for a class of people he viewed as undeserving. Frederick Law Olmsted was equally unimpressed by the textile workers he encountered in Augusta, labeling them "a motley crew." His attitude may have stemmed from the stories he heard from local residents. A hotel manager, for example, warned him, "If you ride past the factory . . . you will see them loafing about, and I reckon you never saw such a meaner set of people anywhere. If they were niggers they would not sell for five hundred dollars."[68] The manager's comparison of these white workers with slaves is telling. So is his omission of the sex composition of the group, for it is not clear whether it is all male, all female, or mixed. His warning to Olmsted does suggest the making of a class identity based on a kind of resistance to their work, along with the public display of that resistance before the community, as suggested by the phrase "loafing about."

It is exceedingly difficult to present a true profile of these working people since it is largely their employers and an occasional traveler or local resident who has left us with these descriptions. Moreover, a literal social distance and a hefty measure of disdain clearly emanates from these writings, and personal ones in particular, in sharp contrast to these observers' public writings, which were more inclined to extol the virtues of the poor, or at the very least the potential for their salvation through factory work. Hence Daniel de Bruce Hack, charged by Augusta industrialist and politician William Schley with overseeing the construction and management of Schley's new textile factory on Spirit Creek outside the city, made fun of the rough "cotton crackers" who came thirty or forty at a time to watch the installation of the new machinery. He mocked the very language of these plain folk in letters to his Virginia friends that reported they called the mill equipment "fixments." Of the young mill women, he stated bluntly, "The girls are not very pretty," and in the same sentence added, "I am very pleased with the prospects of business." His employer, Schlep, did not evince much respect for his Augusta workers either. Writing Hack in 1845 about his visit to textile factories in Richmond, he concluded that in sharp contrast to his idle Augusta workers, the Richmond operatives "move like lamplighters, and you never see any two or more talking. Nor do you ever see one at a window—or otherwise idle."[69] One can only conclude that Augusta workers, whatever their sex, resisted their circumstances through their attitude.

Although what factory workers made of their employers and their situations is a shadowy subject at best, there are strong indications that wage work brought them as many troubles as they hoped to leave behind, and perhaps explains the bad behavior that managers and other observers complained about. J. S. Buckingham was appalled by the filthy log huts Athens factory workers resided in during the early 1840s. Locals reported that many factory workers were sickly and died prematurely. The Spirit Creek workers near Augusta dealt with successive bouts of influenza that left them weak and debilitated.[70] Even when living and working conditions did not encourage the spread of disease, operatives had to contend with the simple fact that wage work could not be guaranteed year-round. Many small factories failed within a few years, and in some cases within months, of their establishment. Many others slowed down production or stopped altogether in the summer because they either lacked the money to continue or payment for goods they had already produced remained outstanding.[71] Even the trustees of the Roswell Mill, a profitable enterprise in the 1850s, were less than sympathetic to their workers' welfare despite their success. When new state legislation required operatives' working hours be limited to from sunup to sundown, the board members voted that all Roswell employees, the majority of whom were women and children, could either work under the new laws but suffer reduced wages or work the old, longer hours for the same pay.[72]

Frederick Law Olmsted reported that Georgia factory owners had hired New England girls to run the looms but that they had left in haste after encountering sordid working conditions and rampant disrespect.[73] Millwork was a last resort for many poor white women in the piedmont, and not an opportunity for advancement. Chief Justice Henry Collier, in his bid to make textile labor respectable, stressed that factory labor did not "harden a lady's hand." The young white women (and children) who dominated the textile industry in antebellum Georgia may not have acquired calluses during their toil at the looms but little else about their experiences or circumstances was reminiscent of southern ladyhood. These factory laborers were generally poor white girls and women who helped support their families during periods of economic hardship. They were paid low wages, well below those of men, and were subject to the vagaries of the textile industry and the company that employed them. Industrialists stressed their own critical role as providers for poor white Georgians and advocates for their advancement. But the story is more complicated than that. The industry used economic concerns about labor and race, social expectations about gender, and political fears about class not only to create a new workforce that was cheap and relatively tractable but to justify it as well. Poor white families supported these developments and in many cases relied on these new working women to sustain them. Although the end of the Civil War would halt the industrialization movement in the South, it would pick up steam again. By the late nineteenth century, southern industrialists would rely once more on a predominantly white female labor force, dredging up the same sets of arguments and assumptions about gender and class employed a half century earlier to construct this working class, and in doing so, confirming the power of paternalism to prevail across time and place in the South.[74]

NOTES

1 *Monitor* (Tuscaloosa), 21 February 1846, cited in Richard W. Griffin, "Poor White Laborers in Southern Cotton Factories, 1789–1865," *The South Carolina Historical Magazine* 61, no. 1 (January 1940): 36. On the myth of the southern lady see ... Anne Firor Scott, *The Southern Lady from Pedestal to Politics, 1830–1930* (Chicago, 1970).

2 J. S. Buckingham, *The Slave States of America*, vol. 2 (London, 1842), 111–14.

3 James L. Sknner III, ed., *The Autobiography of Henry Merrell: Industrial Missionary to the South* (Athens, Ga., 1991), 406.

4 .... See Bess Beatty, "Gender Relations in Southern Textiles: A Historiographical Overview," in *Race, Class, and Community in Southern Labor History*, ed. Gary M. Fink and Merl E. Reed (Tuscaloosa, Al., 1994), 9–16.

5 Victoria E. Bynum, *Unruly Women: The Politics of Social and Sexual Control in the Old South* (Chapel Hill, 1992); LeeAnn Whites, *The Civil War as a Crisis in Gender: Augusta, Georgia, 1860–1890* (Athens, Ga., 1991).

6 For ... women's work in the South see Julia Cherry Spruill, *Women's Life and Work in the Southern Colonies* (Chapel Hill, 1938); [for] women's work in early modern Europe, Joan Scott and Louise Tilley, *Women, Work, and Family* (New York, 1978).

7 Jacqueline Jones, *Labor of Love, Labor of Sorrow: Black Women, Work, and the Family from Slavery to the Present* (New York, 1981); Deborah Gray White, *Ar'n't I a Woman: Female Slavery in the Plantation South* (New York, 1985); Betty Wood, *Women's Work, Men's Work: The Informal Slave Economies* of *Lowcountry Georgia, 1750–1830* (Athens, Ga., 1995).

8 Rich descriptions of the working lives of black and white women in the plantation world can be found in Scott, *Southern Lady* Catherine Clinton, *The Plantation Mistress: Woman's World in the Old South* (New York, 1982); Elizabeth Fox-Genovese, *Within the Plantation Household: Black and White Women of the Old South* (Chapel Hill, 1988); and Marli F. Wiener, *Mistresses and Slaves: Plantation Women in South Carolina, 1840–1880* (Urbana, Ill., 1998).

9 Jacqueline Dowd Hall, James Leloudis, Robert Korstad, Mary Murphy, Lu Ann Jones, and Christopher Daly, *Like a Family: The Making of a Cotton Mill World* (Chapel Hill, 1987); Cathy L. McHugh, *Mill Family: The Labor System in the Southern Textile Industry, 1880–1915* (New York, 1986); Linda Jean Frankel, "Women, Paternalism, and Protest in a Southern Textile Community: Henderson, North Carolina, 1900–1960" (Ph.D. diss., 1986, Harvard University).

10 Bess Beatty, *Alamance: The Holt Family and Industrialization in a North Carolina County, 1837–1900* (Baton Rouge, 1999), 53–57.

11 [For] southern labor and the textile mill industry in this latter period [see] Allen Tullos, *Habits of Industry: White Culture and the Transformation of the Carolina Piedmont* (Chapel Hill, 1989); David L. Carlton, *Mill and Town in South Carolina, 1880–1920* (Baton Rouge, 1982); and Melton Alonza McLaurin, *Paternalism and Protest: Southern Cotton Mill Workers and Organized Labor, 1875–1905* (Westport, Conn., 1971).

12 Gavin Wright, *The Political Economy of the Cotton South: Households Markets, and Wealth in the Nineteenth Century (New York, 1978)*; Eugene D. Genovese,

The Political Economy of Slavery: Studies in the Economy and Society of the Slave South (New York, 1967).

13 Thomas Dublin, *Women at Work: The Transformation of Work and Community in Lowell, Massachusetts, 1826–1860* (New York, 1979).

14 Kenneth Coleman, ed. *A History of Georgia* (Athens, Ga., 1977), 153, 413.

15 Coleman, *Georgia*, 153–54.

16 Ibid., 153–57.

17 Reported in "Industry and Commerce" manuscript, Georgia Writers Project, WPA, Box 57, File 7, Hargrett Library, University of Georgia, Athens, Georgia (hereafter HL).

18 On the backward nature of antebellum southern industrialization see Genovese, *Political Economy of Slavery*; Norris W. Preyer, "Why Did Industrialization Lag in the Old South?" *Georgia Historical Quarterly*, 55, no. 3 (Fall 1971), 378–96. On the developing nature of antebellum southern industrialization see Fred Bateman, James D. Foust, and Thomas J. Weiss, "Large-Scale Manufacturing in the South and West, 1850–1860," *Business History Review* 45 (1971), 1–17.

19 Editorial, *Augusta Chronicle*, 5 November 1846.

20 Michele Gillespie, *Free Labor in an Unfree World: White Artisans in Slaveholding Georgia, 1787–1860* (Athens: University of Georgia Press, 2000), ch. 3.

21 Daniel de Bruce Hack to an unnamed "Dear Friend," December 1834, in Daniel de Bruce Hack Letters, HL.

22 *Athenian* (Athens, Ga.), 24 March 1829; *Niles Weekly Register*, 31 August 1833, 4; 4 October 1834, 65.

23 Richard W. Griffin, "The Origins of the Industrial Revolution in Georgia Cotton Textiles, 1810–1865," *Georgia Historical Quarterly* 42 (1958), 361.

24 J. D. B. DeBow, comp., *Statistical View of the U.S., Being a Compendium of the Seventh Census* (Washington, D.C., 1854); *Manufactures of the U.S. in 1860, Compiled from the Original Returns of the Eighth Census* (Washington, D.C., 1865).

25 *Southern Recorder* (Milledgeville, Ga.), 13 March 1860.

26 George White, *Historical Collections of Georgia* (New York, 1854), 570.

27 George White, *Statistics of the State of Georgia* (Savannah, 1849), 446.

28 Eleanor Miot Boatwright, *Status of Women in Georgia, 1783–1860* (Brooklyn, 1994), 105.

29 Ibid., citing Augusta *Evening Dispatch*, 4 March 1819.

30 Ernest C. Hynds, *Antebellum Athens and Clarke County* (Athens, Ga., 1974), 54–55.

31 George White, *Statistics*, 182–83.

32 Ibid.

33 Manuscript returns, U.S. Census Bureau, Eighth Census, 1860, Clarke County. The census defined male operatives as those fifteen years of age and older and female operatives as sixteen and older.

34 Skinner, ed., *Henry Merrell*, 406.

35 Manuscript returns, 1860, Clarke County.

36 Ibid.

37 Editorial, *Augusta Chronicle*, 27 November 1847.

38 Manuscript returns, 1860, Clarke County.

39 *Federal Union* (Milledgeville), 3 September 1834.

40 Michael John Gagnon confirms my conclusions about Athens women millworkers in his dissertation, "Transition to an Industrial South: Athens, Georgia, 1830–1870" (Ph.D. diss., Emory University, 1999), 88–109. . . . See

[also] David C. Ward, "Industrial Workers in the Mid-Nineteenth Century South: Family and Labor in the Graniteville (S.C.) Textile Mill, 1845–1880, *Labor History* 28, no. 3 (Summer 1987): 328–48.

41 For a discussion of the family wage system and its larger implications in this later period see . . . Hall et al., *Like a Family*.

42 Bess Beatty, "I Can't Get Bored on Them Old Lomes: Female Textile Workers in the Antebellum South," in Delfino and Gillespie, eds., *Neither Lady Nor Slave*, 249–60.

43 Quoted in Griffin, "Industrial Revolution in Georgia," 361.

44 *Augusta Chronicle*, 7 December 1847.

45 *Columbus Enquirer*, 7 October 1847.

46 Editorial, *Augusta Chronicle*, 6 September 1841.

47 *Niles' Weekly Register*, 4 April 1825, 275, quoted in J. G. Johnson, "Notes on Manufacturing in Ante-bellum Georgia," *Georgia Historical Quarterly* 16, no. 3 (September 1932) 219, 225.

48 Ulrich B. Phillips, ed., *Plantation and Frontier*, vol. 2 of *A Documentary History of American Industrial Society*, ed. John R. Commons . . . (1910).

49 Timothy J. Lockley, *Lines in the Sand: Race and Class in Lowcountry Georgia, 1750–1860* (Athens, Ga., 2001).

50 Board Meeting Resolution, 16 February 1843, Chicopee Manufacturing Company Records, Box 27, HL.

51 See, for example, *Augusta Chronicle*, 24 April 1848.

52 In *The Cotton Mill Movement in Antebellum Alabama* (New York, 1978), 113–73, Randall Martin Miller makes a convincing argument for the economic advisability of using slave labor owned by the mills in textile factories, as opposed to hiring slaves, which was more expensive. . . .

53 Pamela Vadman Ulrich, " 'Plain Goods': Textile Production in Georgia, the Carolinas and Alabama, 1880 to 1920" (Ph.D. diss., University of Oregon, 1931), 38.

54 Cited in ibid., 40.

55 Skinner, ed., *Henry Merrell*, 133.

56 Fred Bateman and Thomas Weiss, *"A Deplorable Scarcity": The Failure of Industrialization in the Slave Economy* (Chapel Hill, 1981), 74. . . .

57 . . . . In contrast to the textile industry in Georgia, the iron industry relied heavily on a largely all-male workforce. . . . When white male ironworkers struck in 1847 at the Tredegar Iron Works in Richmond, Virginia, the owner systematically replaced them with slaves because they were cheaper and more tractable. See Patricia Schecter, "Free and Slave Labor in the Old South: The Tredegar Ironworkers' Strike of 1847," *Labor History* 35, no. 2 (1994), 165–86.

58 Claudia Goldin and Kenneth Sokoloff, "Women, Children, and Industrialization the Early Republic: Evidence from the Manufacturing Censuses," *Journal of Economic History* 42, no. 4 (December 1982): 741–74.

59 For example, *Augusta Chronicle*, 22 January 1848. . . .

60 *Augusta Chronicle*, 28 January 1852.

61 George White, *Statistics*, 182.

62 Ward, "Industrial Workers," 330–33; Johnson, "Notes on Manufacturing," 228.

63 Griffin, "Industrial Revolution in Georgia," 372.

64 *Augusta Chronicle*, 9 February 1849.

65 Skinner, ed., *Henry Merrell*, 133, 170.

66 Ibid., 152.

67 Ibid., 413.

68 Frederick Law Olmsted, *A Journey in the Back Country*, vol. 2 (1860; reprint, New York: 1907), 126–27.

69 Daniel de Bruce Hack to Miss Mary Fairfax, Dunfret, Virginia, [n.d.] December 1834; Hack to Michael Cleary, Richmond Factory, 18 April 1814; Wm. Schley to Hack, Richmond, Virginia, 26 November 1843, Daniel de Bruce Hack Letters, HL.

70 William Schley to Hack, Saratoga, New York, 5 August 1846, ibid.

71 Skinner, ed., *Henry Merrell*, 411, describes these difficulties in detail. . . .

72 Minutes of the Stockholders, Roswell Manufacturing Company, 30 October 1854, 44–45, DeKalb Historical Society, Decatur, Georgia.

73 Olmsted, *Journey in the Back Country*, 143.

74 The persistence of paternalism is a theme explored most recently in Edward J. Cashin and Glenn T. Eskew, eds., *Paternalism in a Southern City: Augusta, Georgia, 1790–1900* (Athens, Ga., 2001).

12

LAW, DOMESTIC VIOLENCE, AND THE LIMITS OF PATRIARCHAL AUTHORITY IN THE ANTEBELLUM SOUTH

Laura F. Edwards

Laura Edwards is one of a number southern historians who have found court records to be a fruitful source of evidence for the study of southern ideologies and of the social practices of ordinary people. In this essay, she uses local criminal court records for cases in which slaves and free women were charged with violence against masters and husbands. Formally, southern law (like law elsewhere) buttressed the patriarchal power of white men over their households; in many ways the laws governing relationships between parent and child, husband and wife, and master and slave overlapped, with all but adult white men being treated as "domestic dependents." In fact, she argues, the cases that came before courts in North Carolina and South Carolina demonstrate that patriarchal "power was neither complete nor stable." Both women and slave challenged white male authority, and poor white men, in particular, depended on the legal system "to uphold patriarchy." The cases thus reveal the limits, as well as the aspirations, of southern white patriarchs.

* * *

In 1846 a white man named James Meadows was murdered in Granville County, North Carolina. As his son later testified, three men dragged Meadows from his house in the middle of the night. After his Achilles tendon was cut so that he could not run away, he was beaten to death. Then, in what the court records cast as a final act of rage, his penis and testicles were "squeeze[d] and press[ed]." Despite the son's claim to have seen three men abduct Meadows, there were only two arrests: George, a neighboring slave, was charged with murder; and Mary Meadows, the murdered man's wife, was charged as an accomplice before the fact. Mary was acquitted. Evidence against George was equally thin and circumstantial, but he was convicted. In light of the

295

two different verdicts, one can safely assume that factors beyond trial testimony influenced the outcome. Antebellum gender conventions blinded court officials to the possibility that a white woman could participate in a brutal murder. Legal disabilities attached to the status of slaves prevented them from mounting as strong a defense as white southerners could, even though in this case the slave had very competent counsel. Thus, two years and two appeals later, George was hanged for the murder of James Meadows.[1] This compelling case speaks to central issues in antebellum southern history. The handling of the case and the outcome of the trial buttress the findings of historians who study slavery and the law. A white man's murder, a white woman's acquittal, and an African American man's conviction, all reinforce the racial and gender inequalities that these historians have found embedded in the southern judicial system. The two appeals made on George's behalf illustrate the evolution of and apparent contradictions within a legal framework that classified slaves as both people and property.[2]

In contrast to those southern historians who emphasize what the law did to people, recent scholarship uses the analytical lenses of gender, sexuality, and race to highlight fissures in southern society and the ability of ordinary southerners to disrupt the existing social order.[3] The hint of an illicit affair, such as the one that may have explained the conspiracy between Mary Meadows and George, would attract these historians; so, too, would the unconventional lives of the principals in the Meadows case.[4] Testimony in George's trial, for instance, reveals Mary Meadows as a foul-mouthed, quarrelsome woman who had boasted to her neighbors that she would have her husband beaten or killed. James Meadows, never far from a fight himself, supplied all sorts of people with all sorts of reasons for wanting him dead. His wife, whom he beat, was one of them; George may have been another. He and other slaves in his neighborhood had the opportunity to mix with James Meadows in a crowd of free blacks, slaves, and whites who drank, gambled, traded, fought, and no doubt drove respectable whites to distraction.[5] Obviously, the world of the Meadows case was not the orderly South prescribed in law. The fluidity, variety, and disorder of the Meadows's community emphasize issues that are central to recent scholarship—the contestation over racial, class, and gender roles endemic to southern society, the political content of matters that previous scholarship dismissed as merely "private," and the continual efforts of those in power to control what they saw as impending disorder.[6]

The Meadows case also moves beyond current scholarship by shedding new light on the process of constructing and reconstructing power in the antebellum South. It is clear that the judicial system asserted a racialized patriarchal order by executing George and acquitting Mary Meadows. It is also clear that James Meadows, Mary Meadows, and George had each disregarded rules of the established social order. In emphasizing either the affirmation or rejection of power, current scholarship tends to overlook both subtle differences in the ways that various people defined and reacted to authority and the complications in its institutional construction over time. It also ignores changes in the legal definition of authority at the state level—changes that are difficult to tease out of the sources because judges, in particular, explained their decisions in terms of legal continuity and the preservation of the status quo. Ultimately, the social and legal implications of cases such as the murder of James Meadows were both more indirect and more far reaching than existing scholarship suggests.

This article examines cases involving violence in order to reevaluate the operation of patriarchy at the local level and the legal definition of authority at the state level.[7] At first glance, records of these cases— from local courts and churches in antebellum North Carolina and South Carolina—may seem unrepresentative of southern society because of the bias toward conflict. Indeed, many criminal cases and church disputes involved not simply verbal disagreement, but physical violence of some kind. Yet the presence of so much violence in formal, public arenas is historiographically significant. Current paradigms link violent acts to a culture of honor that was supposedly at odds with law and other forms of institutional governance. Working from similar assumptions, many southern historians downplay violent behavior by white women and African Americans and locate the handling of violent acts against all domestic dependents (women, children, servants, and slaves) outside the formal legal system.[8] It is, then, interesting that many of the violent incidents mediated in local courts and churches involved two groups of domestic dependents—white women and slaves. That violence involving domestic dependents was so common and so public in the antebellum South but has left such little imprint on the historiography is the starting point for this analysis.[9]

The conflicts underlying these cases are as significant as their presence. In fact, the numbers are not that impressive relative to cases involving white-male-on-white-male violence. But cases involving women and slaves could never be typical of court business anyway, because the law worked to keep such cases out of court. Given the barriers, it is significant that these cases are there at all. Their real historical value lies in what they reveal about conflict over patriarchal power and how such conflicts were handled at law.[10] At issue were domestic dependents' assertions of their own ideas about the nature of power both within and without their households. These people did not intend to overthrow the existing social order; instead, they questioned the proper expression and substantive limit of patriarchal power. In so doing, some mobilized the full force of social custom and extensive community networks to support their claims. Yet, given the legal definition of domestic dependency—which emphasized the subsumption of dependents' identity under those of their heads of household and the resulting inability of dependents to act for themselves in law—actions and words of wives and slaves could also acquire political meanings that reached beyond the circumstances of specific cases and the intentions of those directly involved. Domestic dependents and their allies may not have intended to challenge the social order, but that was the effect if their cases made their way through the judicial system. When legal institutions intervened, they upheld the power of individual patriarchs over their households and returned dependents to the confines of domestic space.

But the legal affirmation of the existing order—which historians often take as the end of the story—was actually just a step in a much larger process. The law had to assert continually the power of white male household heads precisely because, in practice, that power was neither complete nor stable. Some white men failed to keep order themselves, and some dependents failed to remain quietly within their households; and the legal system acted in these circumstances to uphold patriarchy. James Meadows did not have the obedience of his wife or the respect of his neighbors, black or white; Mary Meadows was neither silent nor isolated; and George strayed so far from his appointed role that his neighbors identified him immediately as the only suspect in a murder that supposedly involved three men. Ironically, in this case, when patriarchy appeared strongest in law, it was weakest in practice. The Meadows case and others like it reveal the contingency and contestation that defined authority in the antebellum South, and that contingency and contestation of authority were precisely what the law sought to control, to diffuse, and to hide.[11]

The law defined domestic relations in terms of isolated households in which individual white male household heads exercised unchecked authority over their wives, children, servants, and slaves. But in reality, a dense web of social relations shaped the daily operation of domestic dependency in the antebellum South. The relative power of household heads and their dependents was deeply rooted within local contexts, shaped as much by kinship ties, community networks, and personal reputations as by gender, race, and class. At times, these factors converged to prevent white men from exercising authority and to allow wives and slaves to exploit their social resources in order to limit the authority of their husbands and masters. In these instances, domestic dependents acted independently, aggressively, and even violently. They also used available social networks to reinforce their claims and legitimize their actions.[12]

By all accounts, for instance, Mary Meadows was loud and demanding. She was particularly vocal on the subject of her husband. One year before his death, she complained about him to several neighbor women while grinding corn at John Duncan's house. In the course of this exchange, Mary Meadows offered to work for Duncan for one year without pay if he would kill her husband. Susannah Duncan substantiated her husband's story and expanded upon it. She had overheard a conversation between Mary Meadows and Thomas Murray. Murray had his own quarrel with James Meadows and had gone so far as to load a gun with which to shoot him but then decided against it. Mary Meadows reportedly said that "she wished that Murry had . . . blowed that load through him." She made a similar statement to Samuel Jackson. While arguing with her husband at a community gathering, she rebuked Jackson for not "knock[ing]" her husband's "brains out" when the two men had fought earlier. As her husband pushed her down the hill towards home, Meadows had yelled that if she "was a man," then she "would do it." Then, just one week before the murder, Mary Meadows told James Hobgood that she intended to have her husband beaten, boasting that he "would be the worst whiped man he [Hobgood] ever saw." The beating would be so severe, she claimed, that "his hide would not hold shucks."[13]

The willingness to be violent was not unusual among slaves and white women, particularly white women in poor families. The law defined domestic dependents, like Mary Meadows, as the recipients, not the instigators, of violence. Despite their position in law, most white women were not submissive enough to endure silently all kinds of abuse for the sake of their marriages. Nor were they so dependent that they were helpless without men, although class position shaped their responses to marital turmoil and determined the resources that they could summon.

White women could be as brutal as their menfolk. Even those in the planter class, supposedly paragons of refined womanhood, at least occasionally battered slaves and even their own children. Less restrained by class conventions, yeoman and poor white women also directed violence against other free adults for a variety of reasons: to defend themselves, to shame their antagonists, to retaliate for perceived wrongs, and to assert their own interests. A combination of these motives seems to explain the actions of Mary Hester, Nancy H. Pullam, and Rachel Hester, three women who assaulted a court official charged with seizing their property in default for a debt. Sometimes arguments involving women simply got out of hand, just as they did with men. Apparently, Abigail Guy's passion got the best of her when she "made an affray" at the Coe household in North Carolina, "wherein the persons of said Amos Coe & Betsy Coe was beaten & abused by . . . the said Abigale Guy." Violence perpetrated by women was at times simply an extension of drunken revelry. Patsy Dove and Fanny Davis of South Carolina were among such a group. Possibly looking for fun and diversion, they woke Hannah Green, let her chickens out of the hen house, and then chased her around the yard threatening to beat her.[14]

When necessary, wives used violence against their husbands. Of course, white women had a stake in their own dependency, which not only gave them rights to provision and protection but also grounded their racial and, in the case of wealthy women, their class privilege. This investment—combined with fear of physical force and other forms of retaliation—mediated their violence against men, particularly their husbands. But some did use force when they thought husbands had pushed the limits of their authority too far or expressed it inappropriately. Barbara Davis's reaction to her husband's abuse of his mother is typical. She stood by as her husband "dashed [his mother] against the floor" and threatened "to whip her," but when he got a gun to "blow her brains out," Barbara intervened. In fact, Mary Meadows may have acted similarly, feeling that her husband's abuse justified her own belligerence.[15]

Slaves, on the other hand, had little stake in their dependent status and frequently used violence to challenge the authority of their masters and other whites. Perhaps the most famous example is Frederick Douglass's fight with the man who was supposed to "break him in." In Douglass's narrative, the victory is an isolated triumph—another step towards personal independence, but not necessarily representative of the slave experience. As local court records indicate, however, such fights were common in the daily routine of slavery, part of the ongoing, often failed efforts of whites to maintain control over slaves. Joe, for instance, was "in the habit of scuffling" with Jacob Mathis, the white overseer of the South Carolina foundry where Joe worked. One day, after a fight that Mathis himself called typical, he filed assault charges against Joe. Apparently, the balance of power had tilted too far in Joe's favor, making it necessary for Mathis to bring in outside reinforcements. Even this effort failed to demonstrate Jacob Mathis's power because the court acquitted Joe.[16]

As Joe's experience suggests, threats and physical blows by slaves against whites allowed slaves to establish de facto borders around themselves that whites grudgingly acknowledged. When Lease, a South Carolina slave, threatened to strike Eunicey Guthrie, a white woman, for interfering with her children, the three other whites present did nothing to stop her. They may have already known better than to antagonize Lease. The experience of Violet, a slave given to the Burgess family by Thomas Burgess's father, is also instructive. As the Burgesses later explained, Violet had "generally done as she pleased" before. Polly Burgess, Violet's new mistress, decided to change that and struck at Violet with an ax handle in order to discipline her. Violet turned on her mistress, "took the weapon out her hand and knocked her down and struck her again. . . ." Wrestling Violet to the ground required several members of the family—one of whom was armed with a gun. The Burgesses then tied her up and whipped her. Still unable to control her, Thomas Burgess went for assistance. While he was gone, Violet untied her bonds, left, and stayed away for several days. She returned and "staid that week out," only to leave again. Defeated, the Burgesses filed charges against Violet for assault, hoping that the court system would succeed where they had failed. In court, both Lease and Violet were convicted and sentenced to whippings. Whites found it necessary to call on neighbors, churches, and the courts for assistance in protecting themselves from slaves. Such actions suggest slaves' persistence—if not always their success—in protecting themselves and in claiming control over their bodies. Violet's sentence could be interpreted as an indication of the futility of such efforts, but that interpretation discounts her previous success in controlling her life. After all, Violet is described as doing as she pleased and had every reason to believe that she might continue to do so.[17]

Wives and slaves also used social networks to limit their husbands' and masters' authority. Although Mary Meadows's efforts backfired, she actually followed a common pattern of publicizing husbands' and masters' excesses in the hopes of mobilizing outside aid. White women's ties to other families were particularly effective in disciplining their husbands. Wives in the planter class, for instance, fled abuse through extended visits or invited relatives and friends into their homes to moderate their husbands' behavior. Marion Singleton Deveaux Converse, a well-placed South Carolina widow, used both tactics in an effort to escape her second husband's tantrums, beatings, and heavy-handed pressure to sign over to him large portions of her estate. When Augustus L. Converse refused to alter his ways, Marion's sizeable, influential family closed ranks around her. Marion's welfare was not their only concern. Through his flagrant, public abuse, Augustus had embarrassed them and compromised their reputations. Worse, he threatened their patrimony by grasping at property entrusted to Marion's care. Ties that bound Marion to her father's and first husband's families gave her effective weapons to wield against a tyrannical but penniless and socially unconnected husband. With family support, Marion managed to procure a legal separation in a state where divorce was impossible. Her husband fared even worse in the court of public opinion, where Marion's family made him a social outcast and finally drove him out of South Carolina altogether. With every trace of Augustus Converse gone or suppressed, Marion dropped his name and lived the rest of her life as if he—and their marriage—had never existed.[18]

Poor wives did not have quite the same resources as women like Marion Singleton Deveaux, but they were also far less circumspect in publicizing marital disputes than members of the planter class. Like Mary Meadows, they made their husbands' failings known, requested shelter and provision, and even chided neighbors for failing to discipline their errant husbands. Complaining of her husband's abuse and neglect, Mrs. Woodruff of Spartanburg District, South Carolina, begged a neighbor woman for food and asked that word be sent to her father so that he could help her. Mrs. Littlefield, who also lived in Spartanburg District, regularly sought shelter with her neighbors to escape her violent husband. Mrs. Watkins of Laurens District did not suffer in silence either. She told at least two women that her husband "whipt" her. These women, in turn, told several others who, based on previous knowledge of Mrs. Watkins's husband, passed the story on as truth.[19]

The requests of poor white women often became demands, suggesting the extent to which they felt entitled to aid from neighbors and kin. Mary Meadows's efforts to have her husband beaten or worse may have been attempts to shame her neighbors into disciplining him. If so, her demands were not unprecedented. Community members regularly intervened when masters and husbands abused their power and abandoned their responsibilities, because surrounding social networks had to pick up the pieces of broken domestic relations, whether they liked it or not, as the above vagrancy cases indicate. Churches routinely mediated domestic disputes, seeing intervention as part of their mission to promote harmony among their congregants. So did family members, as North Carolina's Westley Rhodes discovered. Rhodes, who had long "indulged himself in the habits of intemperance and abuse to his wife," beat her "in a most cruel manner." Mrs. Rhodes "fled to her father's house," where her mother came to the rescue. Marching to Westley's house, his wife's mother "reprimanded him for his conduct" and "perhaps struck him with a tobacco stem which she had picked up on the road."[20]

Slaves could not use their social networks against masters in the same way, but they, too, had ties beyond their masters' households and the slave community. For instance, slaves occasionally fled to white neighbors' houses in order to evade beatings or to seek shelter afterward. In so doing, they expected more than temporary haven. Exhibiting the bloody results of their masters' brutality could prompt white neighbors to intervene. If direct action did not occur at that time, slaves still set the rumor mill in motion.[21]

The experience of Judy, a South Carolina slave, suggests how innuendo could work its way through the neighborhood and reappear on a master's doorstep. In 1823 Judy's master, Brother Johnson, charged her at their Baptist church with disobedience and lying. According to Brother Johnson, one of Judy's worst offenses was her assertion that she had "good backers in the church to do the Evel she had done, or Else she wood not have done it[.]" In her defense, Judy explained that she gave "ill Language" to her master and mistress "because she had not anough to Eat[.]" She "did not humble herself" afterward, because she feared that they would "tung lash her." While hedging on the question of whether she had threatened action against the Johnsons through her church allies, she finally admitted that she might have said words to that effect. Although "backers" may have been too strong a word, Judy effectively turned existing doubts about her master and mistress against them. Apparently the congregation knew enough about the abuse to make it impossible for the Johnsons to deny Judy's charges of ill treatment. Instead, Brother and Sister Johnson apologized for their past mistreatment of Judy. How the congregation knew about Judy's difficulties is unclear. Maybe some members saw or overheard for themselves. Or maybe Judy made sure that they knew. Either way, she stood firm in her refusal to admit any wrongdoing toward her master and mistress. Ultimately, Judy's recalcitrance resulted in her exclusion from the church, but the Johnsons' apology did not satisfy, either. The congregation continued to investigate and subjected the couple to ongoing scrutiny. Several months into the matter, Brother Harper complained of the church "leving him [Johnson] behind and working over his head." The church conceded that it had, and the issue cooled somewhat but not completely. Four years later the matter was still open and unresolved. Although Judy was not received back into fellowship, the cloud of suspicion over the Johnsons did not completely dissipate.[22]

Local courts could operate as extensions of community authority as well, although that did not always mean a favorable outcome for those who sought out the law. White women, who had more legal presence than slaves, challenged in court violent acts committed against them. These challenges arose particularly from poor and yeoman families. In 1833, for instance, Susannah Lansdale charged John Armstrong and Thomas A. Patrick with assault and battery. She claimed that they forced their way into her house, where they used "a great deal of very vulgar language and threatened her & did violently assault and abuse her by laying hands on her and dashing her across the house[.]" "[A]fter being frequently invited to leave," she continued, they "swore they would stay as long as they pleased[.]" The fight was over Susannah Lansdale's child, whom Thomas Patrick wanted to apprentice. Lansdale, however, refused either to relinquish her child without a fight or to accept silently the assault on her body.[23]

White women occasionally took their abusive husbands to court as well. A husband had the legal right to discipline his wife physically, and the courts, particularly at the appellate level, upheld that prerogative. But the law also allowed for the prosecution of husbands if their actions went beyond accepted discipline and disturbed the peace of the community. This provision allowed local legal officials to bypass legal practice at the appellate level and act on women's complaints. Mary Meadows, for instance, had intended to file charges against her husband just before his death. There is no record that she did so.[24] However, the complaints of women other than Mary Meadows are contained in court records. Usually wives swore out peace warrants, an action that brought their husbands under public scrutiny by forcing them to appear before a magistrate and post bond not to act violently toward their wives. Peace warrants were not an ideal solution. After posting bond, husbands returned home in no mood for a cheerful reconciliation. If they could not make bond and were jailed, wives could suffer economically. Still, peace warrants ensured public monitoring of husbands and penalties for further abuse. By implication, peace warrants also afforded wives a way out of the legal confines of domestic privacy, and the warrants legally transformed husbands' legitimate governance into illegitimate violence that endangered the public order. Occasionally, local officials went one step further: they prosecuted husbands for the criminal offense of assaulting their wives.[25]

Local officials did not relax the law in the same way for slaves, but their unwillingness to do so reveals as much about similarities as differences between wives and slaves. Local officials generally allowed wives to proceed with charges when the husband in question was poor and particularly troublesome. They acted in order to limit the rights of a husband, not to recognize a wife's claims to legal personhood. Similarly, slaves were acquitted of violence against a white person when the alleged victim was poor or otherwise socially marginal. In these instances, the courts protected masters by acquitting slaves. No one, for instance, was disposed to believe Lucressy Campbell, a poor white woman who charged a slave named Sam with rape. Campbell came alone to trial. She had no father, husband, or other male relative to prosecute her case. Nor did she have any witnesses to the crime or supporters to recommend her character. Her word amounted to little against the claims of six upstanding white citizens who lined up beside Sam's master to testify for Sam. Sam's acquittal did not result in greater legal rights for him or any other slave, but it spoke volumes

304

about Lucressy Campbell and, in a larger sense, the legal insignificance of a poor woman's word when she acted in her own name against the property of a wealthy, established master.[26]

Once the wheels of legal intervention were set in motion, wives and slaves often lost control and fell victim to the proceedings, even at the local level. Neighbors, kin, and local officials were not always sympathetic. Mary Meadows's repeated, increasingly desperate appeals for assistance fell on deaf ears. When assistance was forthcoming, it did not always promote the particular interests of those wives and slaves who complained. In South Carolina, neighbors resolved the problem of destitute and abused women by prosecuting their husbands for vagrancy. An open-ended charge that covered a wide range of "disorderly" conduct, vagrancy convictions gave communities leverage to force more responsible behavior from husbands and, by extension, their wives. In North Carolina, neighbors and local officials sent needy wives to the poor house instead of prosecuting their husbands for vagrancy.[27]

Wives and slaves found it even more difficult to articulate their views in terms recognized by law once their cases moved beyond the local level. Within the community, court officials could acknowledge the particular demands of individuals who were deemed worthy of special dispensation without altering the larger structure of the law. By contrast, at the appellate level, recognizing domestic dependents' claims meant universalizing them in ways that had the potential to fundamentally alter dependents' legal status.

In the antebellum period, legal recognition of bodily integrity and physical defense implied access to the full range of civil and political rights that came with legal personhood. In fact, the political implications of domestic dependency and its attendant denial of legal personhood were nowhere more apparent than in the legal treatment of violence, where the status of those involved defined the nature of the offense. The legal standing of physical violence committed by and against white men reflected their status as recognized members of the body politic with full civil and political rights. Antebellum law not only treated as criminal matters a wide range of violent acts against free white men but also gave these men great latitude to use violence against others.

This had not always been the case. In theory, even free white men had only limited legal recourse against physical violence during the colonial period. This was so because violence—except for death and maiming—was not a "public" crime unless it "injured" the King by breaching "his" peace. Otherwise, violent acts remained "private" civil matters. The distinction between "private" suits and "public" crimes was extremely important. In common law, criminal offenses were "public" because they endangered the social order to the point where the King or later, the state, prosecuted the suit. On the other hand, civil matters were "private" disputes that were limited in their impact to the parties directly involved. For instance, a criminal case in which Henry Jones had injured Jane Smith would be designated State v. Jones, while a civil case involving the same parties would be called Smith v. Jones. Before the American Revolution, the "private" nature of violent acts often took precedence over the "public" component. In his mid-eighteenth-century codification of English common law, for instance, Sir William Blackstone discussed assaults under the category "private wrongs." Following this logic, court officials in North and South Carolina prosecuted many incidents involving violence as civil rather than criminal matters even after the Revolution. Acting in the public's interests, they determined whether the incident was serious enough to constitute a breach of the public peace. Only then was it a criminal act.[28]

After the Revolution, when the body politic became the white male citizenry—and was no longer the King—a whole range of "private" injuries theoretically became "public" wrongs. The concept of "public" now comprised white men and their interests, and physical injuries to white men became, by definition, public wrongs. In practice, a series of procedural and doctrinal changes altered the treatment of violence against white men. Not only did the law begin categorizing as criminal matters a much wider range of violent acts against white men, but it also gave them greater latitude in using violence against others. The law treated violence against white men as more serious than violence against others because such acts affected the public order and therefore had criminal status. This allowed white men to mark off a large space around themselves and to defend that space from intrusion by others. These legal assumptions regarding public order gave standing to white men's new role of citizen, whose interests—not the King's—now collectively composed the "public."[29]

In contrast, all those who were supposed to be domestic dependents—all African Americans, white women, servants, and children—remained subjects of their fathers, husbands, and masters. As household heads, these men possessed property rights in their dependents' labor and bodies and possessed the political right to represent their interests in institutional arenas of public governance.

In studying categories of domestic dependency, historians have contrasted the position of slaves with that of white men, a method of comparison that minimized similarities in the status of domestic dependents. Generalizing from the experience of free white men to the free population as a whole, slaves' legal position appeared contradictory and the institution itself seemed anomalous. For the same reasons, legal recognition of slaves' humanity, particularly toward the end of the antebellum period, seemed like a liberalization of the law that brought slaves closer to the status of free people.[30]

Recent work uses gender analysis to reveal connections between the legal status of slaves and that of all who were supposed to be domestic dependents—particularly women of both races as well as African American men.[31] These connections cast the institution of slavery and the legal position of all domestic dependents in a new light. Only a small minority of the antebellum population, North or South, actually enjoyed the full body of rights that white men claimed. Domestic dependents, who composed a majority of the population, were subordinate to white men, legally recognized as "people," and yet denied "legal personhood." The legal residue of dependency also attached to white women and to African Americans who were not wives or slaves, because they were understood by virtue of their sex and/or race to be naturally dependent. Once this broadly conceived dependent majority becomes the point of comparison, the legal status of slaves begins to look less anomalous and contradictory in the context of the time. Indeed, from this perspective, it is clear that legal recognition of humanity did not imply legal personhood at all. Officially, slavery was a repressive extension of household heads' established rights over other domestic dependents. The institution of slavery magnified and even transformed that authority but did not create the legal concept.

Theoretical connections between laws relating to slaves and to wives did not mean that actual conditions or legal treatment of these two groups were the same or even resulted in similar outcomes. The legal position of slaves was far weaker than that of wives. Nineteenth-century southern political theorists regularly invoked theoretical links between marriage and slavery, but jurists increasingly avoided direct comparison of the actual situations of wives and slaves. Similarities in the legal logic governing free white women and enslaved African Americans were troublesome. Taken to its logical extreme, this reasoning might produce parallels in the lives of these two groups that would challenge jurists' commitment to the racial superiority of white women and, by extension, their belief in the inherent differences between all white and all black people.[32]

Nevertheless, the law did not recognize either wives or slaves as people who could act in their own names or bring their concerns directly to institutions of state governance. Even legal acknowledgment of their humanity did not give them access to the full range of rights that defined legal personhood. Wives and slaves were domestic dependents who were mired within the private sphere. Domestic relations were legally "private" in the same sense that civil issues were legally "private." This kind of privacy did not mean that domestic relations were wholly free from legal oversight. Rather, they were legally "private" in the sense that disputes between household heads and dependents were considered personal matters that should not, in theory, involve the public order. As a result, violence committed against them did not necessarily rise to the level of a "public" crime in law. By the same legal logic, a range of acts committed by them did rise to that level, because such actions harmed the bodies or property of citizens-that is, the public.

Mary Meadows, for instance, had accused her husband of physical abuse. In many such instances, violent behavior was recognized as problematic or even "criminal" by community standards, but it was not viewed that way in law. When husbands or masters beat their wives or slaves, the law considered it legitimate "discipline" necessary to household governance. In the case of slaves, courts also justified such actions in terms of masters' property rights in their slaves' bodies. Both husbands and masters could be tried for killing their wives and slaves. But usually, the charges were either reduced or dropped because the law defined legitimate discipline so broadly.[33] Antebellum southern courts routinely refused protection to dependents on the grounds that the sovereignty of a household head placed all of his actions toward his dependents beyond legal question. Even when "discipline" resulted in death, household heads could be convicted of murder only if they acted out of malo animo (wicked intent), which was nearly impossible to prove. As one influential nineteenth-century legal commentator explained, household heads were supposed to prevent the development of "vicious habits" in their dependents that might prove "a nuisance to the community." As long as they acted "from motives of duty, no verdict ought to be found against" them. Although writing about children and free servants, the point applied generally to all domestic dependents in the South. The law presumed that heads of household always acted in the interests of their dependents and the public. The same logic cast almost any act of defiance on the part of a dependent as "wicked intent." "Wicked intent" thus had a very different definition for domestic dependents than it did for free white men.[34]

Following these principles, courts in North and South Carolina allowed masters of slaves the most disciplinary discretion.[35] The experience of Warner Taylor, a particularly brutal North Carolina slaveholder, is revealing. In 1819 an inquest jury found him guilty of beating his slave Betty to death. But Taylor's responsibility for the killing was a different matter in a court of law. The grand jury did not find evidence of "wicked intent" and charged him with the lesser crime of manslaughter. He was acquitted at trial. Just six years later, however, Taylor admitted to beating another slave to death. Charged again with manslaughter, he was convicted this time. He asked for benefit of clergy, which was granted and resulted in his being burned on the hand instead of hanged, and, following the punishment, he went back home to his other unfortunate slaves.[36] Warner's treatment was well within the bounds of the law. The state supreme courts in both North and South Carolina upheld convictions against masters only when the agonizing details of "wicked intent" were so sadistic as to be, in one judge's words, "barbarities" that "did not belong to a state of civilization."[37]

When a woman was beaten by someone other than her husband, it was a crime. Even so, courts did not treat wives in the same way as other assault victims. In 1814, for instance, a county superior court in North Carolina indicted four people for riot against George Byers, even though he had not been directly assaulted. The defendants had actually assembled to give "great and gross abuse with foul and Blasphemous language . . . [to] Sally Byers the wife of the said George Byers." More than chivalry brought George Byers into his wife's case. Because wives were legally subsumed under their husbands, the law considered violence against them to be a crime against their husbands as well; technically, Sally Byers could not file criminal charges on her own behalf. Her husband could also initiate separate civil proceedings for any expenses incurred from her injuries and for damages sustained by the loss of her labor and sexual services.[38]

Despite these limitations, wives had more legal visibility than slaves. Where wives were recognized as parties in criminal offenses committed against them, slaves were not. In North Carolina, masters prosecuted their slaves' assault cases, as Benjamin Hester did in 1802 when he charged that Willie Howington "violently beat & also wound[ed] with a knife a Negro fellow belonging to the sd Hester." Hester's omission of his injured slave's name was unusual. More common was William Clay's 1815 complaint that Abington Kimbel "did commit an assault and battery on a certain negro man belonging to him . . . by the name of david."[39] Whether named or not, slaves were not legally recognized parties to the suit. Masters gave the injured slaves' names to clarify what property had been damaged, much as victims of burglary listed specific items stolen. Slaves' injuries, in other words, acquired status as criminal offenses only through their masters. They did not enter South Carolina courts as criminal matters at all. In the 1850s the South Carolina Supreme Court began interpreting a statute prohibiting "unjustified" abuse by masters to include violence by third parties as well. But for most of the antebellum period, South Carolina considered violent attacks on slaves to be merely civil offenses that entitled masters to sue for damages to their property. If the violence resulted in the slave's death, the state did allow the assailant to be charged with murder; the same was true in North Carolina, where the law also mandated that masters who killed slaves could face charges of manslaughter. But the legal standards of provocation discussed below meant that convictions were rare.[40]

As Mary Meadows and George discovered when they were arrested for the murder of James Meadows, the principle of domestic privacy did not remove the violent acts of wives and slaves from public view. Quite the opposite. Not only did antebellum southern courts consider virtually all violent acts committed by wives and slaves against their husbands and masters to be serious criminal offenses, but the courts also defined the category "violence" as applied to dependents' behavior broadly, in order to include speech and gestures. This double standard was based in the legal fiction that domestic dependents should not be public actors. Of course, southern jurists and lawmakers knew otherwise. It was very clear that slaves and wives had wills of their own and that they moved, spoke, and acted in public space. Recognition of the public nature of the action of dependents made the legal fiction necessary. By refusing to recognize within the theoretical structures of law the legitimacy of slaves' and wives' actions, antebellum court officials and politicians limited the possibility of a potentially troublesome population to affect public policy and institutions of governance. If the law did not recognize the capacity of wives and slaves to act, then it did not reckon with their actions and, more to the point, their actions left no imprint on the law.[41]

By implication, then, lawmakers categorized violent acts of wives and slaves as more serious than those committed by people—namely white men—who were already recognized legal actors. When wives or slaves imposed their wills upon legally recognized persons, whether directly or through dependents, they stepped out of their place and affected the public order. At these moments, they became legally visible and politically active, despite their official invisibility.

The legal definition of provocation suggests the lengths to which jurists went to maintain wives' and slaves' servile status. In fights among white men, nineteenth-century courts in North and South Carolina defined provocation as actual threats of violence, such as drawing a knife within striking range. If provoked, a white man could legally defend himself without bearing criminal responsibility for his acts. The definition of provocation was broader in altercations involving wives and slaves. Insults, disobedience, or suggestive gestures from dependents were sufficient provocation for violence from husbands, masters, and other white men and were legally considered "violence" in the sense that white men were entitled to use physical force in response to such actions. In 1821, for instance, Thomas Wright of North Carolina was indicted for the murder of his wife Anne, whom he had shot in the face at close range. Despite the evidence against him, he was acquitted. Anne Wright, it turns out, had been having an affair with Barnett Jones. A husband had a legally recognized, although "unwritten," exemption from murder charges when he killed his wife's seducer in the act. The judge and jury apparently expanded on this principal, finding Anne Wright's marital infidelity to be sufficient provocation for her husband's violence. Certainly that was the implication the court gave later, when it indicted Barnett Jones for adultery and noted that his partner in crime had been "killed by Her Husband for Bad treatment from Her & said Barnett."[42]

Neither wives nor slaves could adequately defend themselves against physical violence by those in authority over them. The law was particularly restrictive for slaves, allowing self-defense only when death or permanent injury was imminent. North Carolina's Justice Richmond Pearson explained the double standard operative in both states: "[I]f a white man, receiving a slight blow, kills with a deadly weapon, it is but manslaughter; if a slave, for such a blow, should kill a white man, it would be murder; for, accustomed as he is to constant humiliation, it would not be calculated to excite to such a degree as to 'dethrone reason', and must be ascribed to a 'wicked heart'."[43]

The legal institution of domestic dependency justified these restraints. Its effects were most visible in interactions of wives and slaves with their husbands and masters.[44] But the dependent status of wives and slaves also shaped cases in which husbands and masters were not involved. Most obviously, dependency muted their voices in court. Because they were legal extensions of another person, the law treated their oaths with suspicion and required corroborating evidence to establish their claims; limitations were most extreme against slaves, who were barred from testifying against whites.[45] Dependency also shaped the legal treatment of violence in more subtle ways, as Chief Justice Thomas Ruffin of the North Carolina Supreme Court revealed in an 1847 discussion of the legal limits of self-defense in relation to slaves. Ruffin argued that violence, in the form of corporal punishment, was essential to the subordination of all domestic dependents. Extending his legal argument, he reasoned that there was an assumption that domestic dependents responded to violence differently than did free white men and their violent acts were therefore judged by different standards. A child who killed a parent during punishment, for example, was guilty of murder because the act could be seen only as "a malignant and diabolical spirit of vengeance." Ruffin then expanded his logic to cover slaves' dealings with all free people. "[I]t is a just conclusion of reason, when a slave kills a white man for a battery . . . that the act did not flow from . . . uncontrollable resentment, but from a bad heart." Ruffin went on to demonstrate how dangerous the violent acts of domestic dependents were to his definition of public order. In his words, a slave with "a bad heart" was "intent upon the assertion of an equality, social and personal, with the white, and bent on mortal mischief in support of the assertion." Wives, whose domestic status also followed them beyond the household, could be viewed in the same light as slaves; but the evil intent revealed in wives' violent acts would be the "assertion of an equality, social and personal" with men.[46]

State supreme court justices sometimes pulled back from this logic and permitted domestic dependents to act in particular circumstances, when the abuse they had received was so extreme as to offend the judges' moral sensibilities. Wrestling with the theoretical balance of the dual status of slaves as property and people, for instance, judges placed limits on masters' and other whites' power over them. Though recognizing slaves' humanity, these decisions still denied them legal personhood. Whereas legally recognized people had the right to protect their bodies from others, the law defined slaves' acts of self-defense as a kind of "natural" response exhibited by all animals when their lives were endangered. The courts acquitted slaves on this basis only rarely. Like most cases in which slaves were accused of violence, George's alleged murder of James Meadows fell outside the legal category of self-defense. In the first appeal of his conviction, the state supreme court overturned the verdict on a procedural error. George was retried and convicted again. This time the court turned down his appeal, and George was hanged for the murder of James Meadows.[47]

The cumulative effect of the law was to erase from the public arena and, to a certain extent, from the historical record, both the existence and the effects of violence involving domestic dependents. The law confined the political implications of complaints from domestic dependents about unlimited, arbitrary power by categorizing them as "private" or "personal" issues, more the stuff of civil than criminal law. Legally defined violence committed by a domestic dependent was an isolated act caused by an evil, demented mind—not by legitimate grievances or systemic defects in the South's social structure. Therefore, the law limited the effects of fights between a husband and wife or a master and slave to the parties directly involved. Similarly, the law turned violent acts committed against dependents into regrettable but necessary means to keep subordinates in their place. By contrast, a fight between two white men was legally different. Here the law assumed that the dispute necessarily reached beyond the two parties, because they were constituent members of the public order. In such cases, the state intervened to regulate relations between public citizens, to ensure that their respective rights were maintained, and to set precedents involving other citizens' rights as well. In the process, the law made some categories of violence (i.e., between white men) more visible, more legitimate, and more political than other kinds.

Yet, the legal decisions of state supreme court justices, which established precedent for lower courts, suggest a degree of political disorder and a degree of political order that did not exist in practice. On the one hand, southern society was not as disorderly as the appellate cases decided in the state supreme courts implied. The wives and slaves involved in these cases were not actually asserting equality with white men. Some, particularly slaves, may have wanted to, but in the particular incidents that ultimately reached the appellate bench, their goals were more modest. They wanted limits on their husbands' and masters' authority. They wanted protection from physical abuse. They wanted access to public arenas that would enforce those limits. The courts, however, treated these cases as attacks on patriarchal authority because domestic dependents' claims would have undermined the structure of that authority if the courts recognized them as legitimate.

On the other hand, neither was southern society as orderly as the courts' assertion of patriarchal authority implied. The complaining voices of domestic dependents were audible—even at the higher levels of the court system—despite efforts to silence them and to force the aggrieved dependents into existing legal categories. Divorce petitions filed by husbands provide a good example. Hidden behind men's efforts to establish legal grounds for divorce were dissatisfied and obstinate wives who acted in ways not allowed in law and often discouraged in practice. John Moore, for instance, had "expected meekness and pliancy of disposition and temper" from his wife, Lovey. Instead, he "met with opposition" and had to "suffer the most continued and violent torrent of invective that ever flowed from the mouth of a female." In another case, eight neighbors claimed that they often heard Ann Jane Bryan abuse her husband "in a most extravagant and outrageous manner."[48]

Just as a wife's willfulness became "extravagant and outrageous" abuse for legal purposes in divorce, her decision to leave her husband became adultery or even prostitution in law. Exercising a time-honored form of what might be called self-divorce, some women left their husbands and started over as if they had never been married. This is exactly what Mary Ann Clawson did when she left James W. Mills after just fifteen days of marriage and returned to her father's house—apparently she had second thoughts about the marriage after she and her husband went to live with his parents. Mills tried to reconcile with her, proposing "to take her to the 'West' or any place she would choose for a residence." But Mary Ann Clawson was happy where she was. She "not only refused" to go with him, "but on the last occasion drew a knife from her bosom and said that if he insisted on his right to make her return she would cut his throat!" Other women entered new relationships that passed as marriages. John Farrow accused his wife Rebecca of "lewd and abominable actions" with several men, but Rebecca's last liaison was more stable than the petition initially implied. She had lived with this man, William O'Neal, for two years "as if they had been man and wife" despite being married to Farrow. Even women who claimed abandonment in their divorce petitions may not have been entirely truthful. By law, it was more difficult for wives to establish grounds for divorce if they were the ones who left. Mary Southwick, for instance, invoked the conventionally pathetic image of the abandoned, destitute wife in her divorce petition. Her husband countered with his own version of the story, claiming that she had left him, taking all the property that originally belonged to her and also a considerable part of his property.[49]

It is more difficult, however, to locate slaves' voices in the legal records. Trials usually went forward as if the accused slave were not there at all. George's trial for the murder of James Meadows was typical. The documentation of the case is extensive, including two appeals that produced lengthy opinions. But there is no record of any word uttered by George. Legally, nothing he said could have altered the outcome of his case. His fate rested entirely on the testimony of others. If anything, the appeals process marginalized him even more because it dealt with points of law, not the interpretation of the evidence.

The law's abstractions altered as much as they affirmed. By acting to buttress patriarchal authority, the courts acknowledged breaches in the social structure that required its reinforcement. In the process, the judicial system transformed what it sought to preserve, moving the formal definition of authority away from social practice. In order to clarify legal issues and weigh competing claims, the judiciary separated relations between household heads and dependents from other complicating social relations. This created the legal fiction of an isolated, self-contained household abstracted from social context. Demarcating the household as an individual man's private domain and refusing to intervene in his domestic governance, judges made each man sovereign at home and intervened only in his defense. In reality, however, no husband or master actually stood alone outside society; nor was any wife or slave completely isolated or silent inside a single household. To safeguard the position of the patriarch, the law overstated his authority in the abstract. These men were in actuality always subject to other men—and, sometimes, other women—in their families and communities. But the implications of these legal decisions fundamentally restructured the ways that authority, both inside and outside households, could be exercised.[50]

Patriarchal power was never as absolute in practice as it was in law.

In fact, the courts mobilized legal principles of domestic authority in situations where patriarchs' control had broken down—in cases where a household head abused his power over his dependents or proved unable to keep them under control. Such social and legal dominion gave men like James Meadows the upper hand in dealing with their domestic dependents. But James Meadows, for one, clearly faced a monumental task if he wished to play the patriarch. Ultimately, he and those like him failed because domestic dependents could and did fight back, demand consideration from the wider society, and push their way into the public realm in order to secure that acknowledgment. White men, particularly poor ones, struggled to defend their rights— powers granted to them by law—to govern dependents. In this contest, the law was a crucial, though often hidden, weapon that they used to assert authority and to distinguish themselves from those whom they sought to control. Indeed, those who were legally defined as "independent" were "dependent" on the law for their status.

NOTES

1 .... Information on the case comes from State v. George and Mary Meadows, 1847, Criminal Actions Concerning Slaves and Free Persons of Color, Granville County; State v. George, 1847, #4188 and State v. George, 1848, #4230, Supreme Court Original Cases . . .; see also Victoria E. Bynum, *Unruly Women: The Politics of Social and Sexual Control in the Old South* (Chapel Hill and London, 1992), 85–87. . . .

2 The literature on slave law has focused on how the law—or lack of access to the law—shaped slaves' lives. For work emphasizing racial inequality within the law and the arbitrary rules of masters see Michael Stephen Hindus, *Prison and Plantation: Crime, Justice, and Authority in Massachusetts and South Carolina, 1767–1878* (Chapel Hill, 1980); Philip J. Schwarz, *Twice Condemned: Slaves and the Criminal Laws of Virginia, 1705–1865* (Baton Rouge, 1988); Christopher Waldrep, *Roots of Disorder: Race and Criminal Justice in the American South*, 7–80 (Urbana, Ill., 1998). . . . For procedural protections for slaves see Daniel J. Flanigan, "Criminal Procedure in Slave Trials in the Antebellum South," *Journal of Southern History*, XL (November 1974), 537–64. Other scholars have emphasized that procedural fairness actually strengthened masters' direct power over slaves by legitimating the legal process. See Eugene D. Genovese, *Roll, Jordan, Roll: The World the Slaves Made* (New York, 1974), 25–49; and Edward L. Ayers, *Vengeance and Justice: Crime and Punishment in the 19th-Century American South* (New York, 1984), esp. pp. 132–36 . . . .; Recent studies have also stressed that class and gender as well as race and slavery determined the application of the law. See Peter W. Bardaglio, "Rape and the Law in the Old South: 'Calculated to excite indignation in every heart'," *Journal of Southern History*, LX (November 1994), 749–72; and Diane Miller Sommerville, "The Rape Myth in the Old South Reconsidered," *Journal of Southern History*, LXI (August 1995), 481–518. Thomas D. Morris, *Southern Slavery and the Law, 1619–1860* (Chapel Hill, 1996) is the most recent comprehensive work and addresses many of the above themes.

3 Eugene D. Genovese ... argues in *Roll, Jordan, Roll* [that] the institutional development of southern slavery depended on the actions of slaves themselves. Recent work in southern history, however ... [shows] how the law tried and sometimes failed to contain the agency of various people.... See Sharon Block, "Lines of Color, Sex, and Service: Comparative Sexual Coercion in Early America," in Martha Hodes, ed., *Sex, Love, Race: Crossing Boundaries in North American History* (New York, 1999), 141–63; Laura F. Edwards, " 'The Marriage Covenant is at the Foundation of all Our Rights': The Politics of Slave Marriages in North Carolina after Emancipation," *Law and History Review*, XIV (Spring 1996), 81–124. ...;

4 Was an ill-fated romance behind this case?.... There is ... no evidence to support such a theory....

5 For the social marginality of the Meadowses and their connection to free blacks and slaves see Bynum, *Unruly Women*, 90–92. Court cases involving Mary and James Meadows reveal the raucous behavior associated with those on the social margins. See State v. James Philpott and John Whitlow, 1819; State v. John Eastwood, 1830.... [See also] Charles C. Bolton, *Poor Whites of the Antebellum South: Tenants and Laborers in Central North Carolina and Northeast Mississippi* (Durham, 1994), chap. 3; and Bolton and Scott P. Culclasure, eds., *The Confessions of Edward Isham: A Poor White Life of the Old South* (Athens, Ga., 1998).

6 My analysis builds on recent work that uses the analytical categories of gender and sexuality to rethink the nature of power.... [T]his scholarship emphasizes the affirmation of patriarchal power and often fails to explain the lasting implications of the agency of those on the margins of power.... [numerous citations of work in this area have been omitted—ed.]

7 This paper relies on a range of local court and church records from various places in North and South Carolina. The bulk of the legal material comes from Anderson and Pendleton Districts in the upcountry of South Carolina (Anderson was created out of Pendleton in 1828), which contained a small slave population and a preponderance of white yeoman households, and Granville County, just south of the Virginia border in central North Carolina, which contained large plantations and a large slave population in the northern part of the county and white yeoman households in the southern part.... [S]econdary literature and supporting evidence from other areas in the two states indicate that the broad patterns of criminal prosecution and the kinds of cases in Granville County and Anderson and Pendleton Districts were not unusual....

8 Historians of the nineteenth-century South have tended to treat violent acts of all kinds as extralegal matters driven by a code of honor and generally resolved outside institutional structures of governance.... See Ayers, *Vengeance and Justice*, 106–37; Hindus, *Prison and Plantation*, 1–123; Waldrep, *Roots of Disorder*, 15–58.... The same presumptions also shape the work on southern honor: Kenneth S. Greenberg, *Masters and Statesmen* ... (Baltimore, 1985); Greenberg, *Honor and Slavery* ... (Princeton, 1996); Ted Ownby, *Subduing Satan* ... (Chapel Hill, 1990); Steven M. Stowe, *Intimacy and Power in the Old South* (Baltimore, 1987); and Bertram Wyatt-Brown, *Southern Honor: Ethics and Behavior in the Old South* (New York, 1982). Other work, including Wyatt-Brown's *Southern Honor*, emphasizes southerners' respect for the law and the law's power to shape southern society.... In *Double Character: Slavery and Mastery in the Southern Courtroom* (Princeton, 2000), which focuses on civil cases, Ariela Gross brings these two sides of the

historiographical debate together, arguing that a culture of honor and a southern legal culture coexisted. . . .

9 In "Keeping the Peace: Domestic Assault and Private Prosecution in Antebellum Baltimore," in Christine Daniels and Michael V. Kennedy, eds., *Over the Threshold: Intimate Violence in Early America* (New York, 1999), 148–69, Stephanie Cole has found similar patterns in the public handling of domestic violence in Baltimore.

10 Although such cases appeared regularly in the court records in significant clumps, figuring out the exact percentage is difficult, if not impossible . . . [since] local court records . . . are fragmented, voluminous, and largely unindexed. . . .

11 Here, I am asserting a different view of the relations between people and the law from that of most southern historians. I see the law as an imperfect, unwieldy tool whose application could produce results that were open to multiple meanings. . . . The classic statement of the law's hegemonic role in southern society is Genovese, *Roll, Jordan, Roll*, esp. 25–49. . . . Despite the voluminous literature debating the utility of hegemony, southern historians . . . tend to accept more uncritically than legal historians outside southern history the conception of the law as a hegemonic force. For discussion . . . see Michael Grossberg, *A Judgment for Solomon: The d'Hauteville Case and Legal Experience in Antebellum America* (Cambridge, Eng., 1996). . . .

12 Recent work has stressed connections between household authority and state power. [But] this scholarship overstates the authority of individual household heads because it relies heavily upon legal sources and official political pronouncements that abstract patriarchal power from social context. . . . At the same time, this body of work suggests the localized, particular nature of domestic dependency and the operation of power in southern communities generally. . . .

13 State v. George and Mary Meadows, 1847. . . .

14 State v. Mary Hester, Nancy H. Pullam, and Rachel Hester, 1813. . . . Cases involving women who acted violently are too numerous to list.

15 State v. Chesley Davis, 1819, Criminal Action Papers, Granville County (NCDAH). . . .

16 Frederick Douglass, *My Bondage and My Freedom* ([1855] Chicago, 1970), 180–92; and State v. Joe, 1841 . . . Spartanburg District. . . . Out of 34 recorded cases of violence by slaves against whites between 1824 and 1860, 9 cases involved someone who could be identified as a master, a member of the master's family, or an overseer. . . .

17 State v. Lease, 1841, #37, 2920, and State v. Violet, 1854 . . . Spartanburg District . . .

18 Marion Converse v. Augustus L. Converse, Sumter District Equity Court Records . . . ,

19 State v. James Woodruff, 1834, and State v. Marvel Littlefield, 1841, Vagrancy Trials, . . . Spartanburg District (SCDAH). . . . For abused women in similar social contexts—although very different time periods—mobilizing community ties or benefiting from such ties see also Susan Dwyer Amussen, " 'Being Stirred to Much Unquietness': Violence and Domestic Violence in Early Modern England," *Journal of Women's History*, VI (Summer 1994), 70–89. . . .

20 State v. Marvel Littlefield, 1841; Vagrancy Trials . . . Spartanburg District. . . .

21 See, for instance, State v. Jim, 1849 . . . Spartanburg District. . . .

22 For the dispute between Brother Johnson and Judy see Minutes, Big Creek Baptist Church, Anderson District . . . (SCL). . . .
23 State v. John Armstrong and Thomas Patrick, Fall Term, 1833, #1, Court of General Sessions, Session Rolls, Anderson District (SCDAH). There were 66 cases of violence against women in Granville County between 1800 and 1840. . . .
24 As James Blalock testified, Mary Meadows told him "about the treatment of her husband Jas. Medows [sic] towards her, and that she said that she intended to have him fixed at . . . court, so that he should not be scandalizing her." . . .
25 . . . Manuals for justices of the peace dating from the early part of the century clearly stated that wives could swear out peace warrants against their husbands. . . .
26 State v. Sam, 1830, case #50, 2916, Trial Records, Magistrates and Freeholders Court, Anderson District. . . . The same class concerns apparent in Sam's acquittal also shaped cases involving third-party violence against slaves. In these cases, the courts limited the ability of whites to use violence against slaves they did not own and delivered the occasional denouncement of vengeful and disorderly poor whites who sought to settle scores with their social betters by destroying slave property. . . .
27 . . . . South Carolina's vagrancy statute was passed in 1787. . . .
28 See Sir William Blackstone, *Commentaries on the Laws of England*, edited by St. George Tucker (5 vols.; Philadelphia, 1803). . . .
29 These changes took place on a number of different fronts, as the example of North Carolina indicates. . . . The laws underwent a similar transition in South Carolina and other southern states and also in northern states, although the timing and specifics varied. . . .
30 Many legal historians have noted that southern courts increasingly recognized the "human" status of slaves over the course of the antebellum period. . . . For a revealing discussion of the problematic relationship of women and slaves to legal personhood see Nancy Isenberg, *Sex and Citizenship in Antebellum America* (Chapel Hill, 1998), 103–54.
31 For the legal position of slaves as both persons and property as well as the absence of any sense of legal contradiction about that dual status see Thomas R. R. Cobb, *An Inquiry into the Law of Negro Slavery in the United States of America* (Philadelphia, 1858), esp. p. 83. Recent work that links slavery to other forms of domestic dependency indicates that this contradiction was not perceived as contradictory at the time. See Stephanie McCurry, *Masters of Small Worlds: Yeoman Households, Gender Relations, and the Political Culture of the Antebellum South Carolina Low Country* (New York, 1995) . . . .; historians of the nineteenth-century South have only begun to examine connections between slavery and other domestic relations. My argument builds on this work. See in particular Bardaglio, *Reconstructing the Household*; and Bynum, *Unruly Women*.
32 During the nineteenth century, the legal connections that once bound all domestic dependents together began to deteriorate and a separate body of law began to develop around each one. In decisions regarding the corporal punishment of slaves, even southern jurists usually analogized from the status of free servants or children and omitted wives from their discussions, although the same legal principles applied to them. . . .
33 The Puritans had criminalized wife beating in the colonial period as part of their mission to revise their laws and social governance and to create a

harmonious society. But these and other legal measures that limited husbands' authority over wives fell into disuse as religious enthusiasm weakened, the colonies grew, and the courts began to follow English common law more closely. . . . See Michael Grossberg, *Governing the Hearth: Law and the Family in Nineteenth-Century Am*erica (Chapel Hill, 1985). . . .

34 Quotations from Tapping Reeve, *The Law of Baron and Femme, of Parent and Child, Guardian and Ward, Master and Servant, and of the Powers of the Courts of Chancery* (3rd. ed., 1862; rpt. New York, 1970), 420. . . .

35 The basis of the two states' legal treatment of slavery, however, differed. North Carolina governed slavery through common law precepts. . . . South Carolina, by contrast, insisted common law principles did not apply to slaves because they were subjects of their masters, not the state. . . . Yet the outcome was much the same as in North Carolina because South Carolina legislators used the logic of domestic dependency in common law as the basic structure for its statutes.

36 State v. Warner Taylor, 1819; and State v. Thomas Huffand Warner Taylor, 1825; . . . Granville County. . . .

37 The quote is from State v. Hoover, 20 N.C. 500 (1839), 503. . . .

38 State v. Dicy Jones, Ben Wheeler, Winny Wheeler, John Stem, 1814 . . . Granville County

39 State v. Willie Howington, 1802 . . . Granville County. . . .

40 North Carolina allowed charges of murder and manslaughter to be filed in the cases where slaves were killed. South Carolina allowed only murder. . . .

41 Parham v. Blackwelder, 30 N.C. 446 (1848) contains a particularly revealing discussion about how servants and slaves can be at once legally subsumed within private space and yet have public consequences attached to their actions. . . .

42 State v. Thomas Wright, 1821; and State v. Barnett Jones, 1822; both in Criminal Action Papers, Granville County (NCDAH). . . .

43 Quotation from State v. Caesar, 31 N.C. 391 (1849), 400. . . . In South Carolina, the issue of provocation was resolved by statute and assumed wicked intent whenever a slave physically harmed a white person; killing was always murder and assault was never justified. . . .

44 A North Carolina court explained in a 1798 murder case: "[I]f a free servant refuses to obey . . . and the master endeavor to exact obedience by force, and the servant offers to resist by force . . . and the master kills, it is not murder, nor even manslaughter, but justifiable . . .": State v. Weaver, 3 N.C. 77 (1798) at 78. . . .

45 For slaves see Morris, *Southern Slavery and the Law*, 229–48. For women see Bardaglio, *Reconstructing the Household*, 74–78. . . .

46 State v. Caesar, 31 N.C. 391 (1849), 422 and 424. . . .

47 State v. George and Mary Meadows, 1847 . . . and State v. George, 1848. . . .

48 John Moore, 1801, and Jonathan Bryan, 1827–28, Divorce Petitions, General Assembly, Sessions Records (NCDAH). . . .

49 James W. Mills, 1827–28; John Farrow, 1801; Mary Southwick, 1810; Divorce Petitions, General Assembly, Sessions Records (NCDAH).

50 For the courts' construction of domestic dependency in the antebellum South see Bardaglio, *Reconstructing the Household*, esp. pp. 82–84 and 119–20; Bynum, *Unruly Women*, 35–58; Fox-Genovese, *Within the Plantation Household*, 37–99; and McCurry, *Masters of Small Worlds*, esp. pp. 85–91.

INDEX

Abbott, Sarah Ann 176, 178
abolitionism: female writers 259, 263, 267; freedom and progress 27, 30, 31; white slavery 196, 207, 209, 213; white women and party politics 223, 225
Aborigines 91, 93, 105
abortion 146
Adam, Barbara 86
Adams, John Quincy 232, 235, 241
An Address to the People of the United States (Kenney) 227
adultery 311, 313
Affleck, Thomas 49
African Americans: Gowrie plantation 58, 59, 60, 68, 70; historiography of slavery 1, 2; law and violence 296, 297, 307; Louisiana's sugar plantations 46, 50; property ownership 117, 118, 136–7, 138; time-consciousness 106; widow slaveowners 177
Africans 147, 148, 177, 204, 206, 207, 213
Aime, Valcour 41
Aiton, Thomas 95
alcohol: body politics 148, 150, 151, 156, 163, 164; law and violence 300; white slavery 201, 209
Alston, Sarah 178
American Bible Society 231

American Colonization Society 231
American Freedman's Inquiry Commission 185
American Revolution 13, 306
American Slavery As It Is: Testimonies of a Thousand Witnesses (Weld) 263
American Tract Society 231
Anderson, James 125
Andrew, James O. 60
Appeal to the Christian Women of the Southern States (Grimké) 259
Archer, Mary 178
Armageddon (Baldwin) 27
Arminianism 25, 32
Armstrong, Reverend George D. 25, 33
Armstrong, John 303
Arnold, Dr. Richard D. 67
Ascension Parish 49
Athens Manufacturing Company 280, 285
Atkins, Keletso 92
Augusta Chronicle 287
aural time 89, 95, 96, 100, 102, 103, 106
Avery, Robert B. 121
Axon, Tony 120

Bacon, Joseph 124
Bacon, Nancy 122
Bacon, Pompey 113–15, 118, 120, 121, 125, 135

Bacon, Samson 125, 128
Bacot, Ada 188
Bagshaw, A. R. 67
Baker, Everard Green 22, 23, 242
Baker, Paula C. 223
Baldwin, Samuel Davies 27
Ball, Charles 149
Ball plantation 63
Barbour, Benjamin Johnson 234
Barbour, James 229, 232, 235
Barbour, Lucy 235–6, 239, 240, 242
Barrow, Robert Ruffin 47
Basch, Norma 241
Beatty, Bess 275, 284
"Beauties of White Slavery" (article) 211
bells (time-consciousness) 95, 96, 100, 102, 104
Bennett, Susan 128
Bentley, Mary 281
Berlin, Ira 209
Berrien, John M. 20
Berry, Fannie 155, 176
Bibb, Henry 151
Bittle, Reverend David F. 24
"black blood" 200, 202, 204, 206
"blackness": body politics 145–6, 147, 148, 150, 158, 159, 165; whiteness and slavery 198–202, 204, 206, 208, 211
Blackstone, Sir William 306
Blair, Hugh 254
Blassingame, John W. 2
Bledsoe, Albert Taylor 25, 31
Blumenbach, Johann Friedrich 249
body politics 142–65; slave women 144–9, 153, 155–6, 158, 165; southern women 255, 265–6; whiteness and slavery 198, 199, 200, 213
Boston Cultivator 99
Bourdieu, Pierre 158
Bowman, James L. 45
Bowman, James P. 49
Bowman, Shearer Davis 43
Bradford, Lue 104
Bradford, M. E. 14
Brazil 45
Breaux, J. A. 204, 205
Brevard, Keziah 181, 183, 184, 189
Brown, Ebenezer 160
Brown, Kathleen M. 147

Brown, Thomas 238
Brown, William 104
Bruegel, Martin 91, 94, 96, 107
Bryan, Ann Jane 313
Buckingham, J. S. 273, 285, 289
Burge, Dolly 170, 171, 188
Burge, Thomas 170
Burgess, Polly 301
Burgess, Thomas 301
Burke, Caroline 173, 174, 175
Burke, John 174
Burnett, Midge 150, 152
Burnside, John 37
bush settlers 91, 92
Butler, Pierce 157
Byers, George 309
Byers, Sally 309
Bynum, Victoria 273

Calhoun, John C. 21
Calvinism 25, 26, 32
Camp, Stephanie M. H. 6, 142–65
Campbell, Lucressy 304, 305
Cannibals All! (Fitzhugh) 22
Cannon, S. N. 207
Capers, William 71, 72, 73, 74
capitalism: historiography of slavery 3, 4, 5, 6; Louisiana's sugar plantations 38, 39, 41, 43, 48, 51, 53, 54; moral progress 28, 29; time-consciousness 84–91, 93, 94, 97, 107
Carey, Henry 267
Carroll, Cora 104
Carter, George 95
Carter, Landon 95
Cartwright, Samuel 47, 211, 217
Carwardine, Richard J. 231
Cary, Virginia 175, 181–2
Cassell, Joshua 121
Cassels, William 122, 127, 133
Cassville Female College 256
Castera, L. 213
Cay Jr., Raymond 129
Cay Sr., Raymond 136
Charleston Courier 209
Chaulieu, Pierre 145
Cheves, Langdon 64, 258, 267, 268
childbearing 63, 121, 198
child labor 102, 121–3, 174, 275, 279, 281–8, 290
cholera 63, 64, 181, 186

322

The Christian Doctrine of Slavery
  (Armstrong) 25
Christianity: body politics 163;
  freedom and progress 22, 24, 25, 27,
  28, 31–3; historiography of slavery
  4–5; time-consciousness 88
churches 32, 89, 95, 96
civil law 305–8, 312
Civil Rights Movement 2
Civil War: gender politics 274, 275,
  276, 277, 290; historiography of
  slavery 5; Louisiana's sugar
  plantations 45; property ownership
  113, 115, 135, 137; whiteness and
  slavery 215; widow slaveowners
  183, 185, 187
Clagett, Ann 236
Clapp, Dexter 267
Clapp, Theodore 31
Clark, Anne 157
Clark, Gregory 88
Clark, Stephen F. 66
class 4, 8, 290
Clawson, J. B. 207, 212, 213
Clawson, Mary Ann 313
Clay Association 224, 236, 237, 238,
  239, 243
Clay, Henry 224, 231–6, 238, 239,
  240
Clay, William 309
Clingman, Thomas L. 20
clocks 48, 51, 85, 87–92, 94–7, 98,
  99–107
clothing: body politics 143, 144, 148,
  156–61; female writers 260; Gowrie
  plantation 60, 72; property
  ownership 125–6, 128
Cocke, James Powell 101
Cocke, Jane 178
Cocke, Martha 180
Coclanis, Peter 42
coercion theory 88
Colins, Bill 104
Collier, Henry 272, 273, 290
colonialism 145–6, 232
Columbus *Enquirer* 284
concubines 184
Constancia plantation 53
Converse, Augustus L. 301, 302
Converse, Marion Singleton Deveaux
  175, 178, 179, 301, 302
Cookshay plantation 179, 182

Cornelius, James 156
cotton 65, 133, 159, 179, 201, 276–8
*Cotton Is King and Pro-Slavery
  Arguments* (Elliott) 31
court cases: law and violence 295–8,
  303–6, 309–14; whiteness and
  slavery 196, 197, 201–8,
  214–17
Creel, Margaret Washington 59
Crimean War 20
Criswell, Robert 151
Cromwell, Elizabeth 186
Crump, Charlie 151, 152
Cuba 43
currency 120
Curtin, Philip D. 64

dances 143, 155–6, 209
Dandridge, Sarah Pendleton 227
Dandridge, Serena 235
Daniell, William Coffee 67
d'Aubigné, Jean Henri Merle 27
Davis, David Brian 13
Davis, Barbara 300
Davis, Fanny 300
Davis, Louise Penelope 250
Davison, Graeme 91–2
Deas, Anne 252
deaths *see* mortality rate of slaves
DeBow, James 22, 40
DeBow's Review 21, 40, 60, 211, 264
Declaration of Independence 16
DeLegal, Edward 119, 136
DeLeon, Edwin 20
Democratic Party 223–6, 230–5,
  237–40, 242, 243
Dennison, William 196, 212, 215
de Stael, Madame 262
Deveaux, Marion 175, 178, 179, 301,
  302
Dew, Charles 51
Dew, Thomas Roderick 15–19, 32, 252,
  253, 257
Dickson, Samuel Henry 15
A Digest of the Laws... (Dew) 15, 16,
  17
disease: Gowrie plantation 62–4, 65,
  66, 67–8; property ownership 122;
  white millworkers 289–90; white
  slavery 198; widow slaveowners
  173, 174, 180, 181
"Dissertation" (Dew) 252

divorce 301, 313, 314
domestic dependency 298, 305–8,
310–13, 315
Dominion (Baldwin) 27
Doswell, Susan 237
Douglass, Frederick 263, 300
Dove, Patsy 300
Downs, Mary 175, 182
doxa 158
Dred Scott v. Sandford 208, 217
dress *see* clothing
drinking *see* alcohol
Dryer, Jacob 132
Duncan, John 299
Duncan, Susannah 299
Dunn, Fannie 157
Dusinberre, William 43

Earle, Carville 43
"The Economics of Slavery in the
Antebellum South" (Conrad and
Meyer) (article) 3
Edisto Island 120
education of women *see* female
education
Edwards, Laura F. 7, 295–315
Edwards, Madaline 255
Elizabeth I 261
Elkins, Stanley 2
Elliott, E. N. 31
Elliott, Samuel 115, 123
Elliott, Toney 121
Embargo Act 276
"Enfranchisement of Women"
(McCord) 264
Engerman, Stanley 3, 46, 64
English Revolution 17
Eppes, Richard 100
Ervin, William Ethelbert 150
Evans, Augusta 251

Fagot, Samuel 53
fancy trade 198–9
Fanon, Frantz 145, 146, 148
Farmers' Register 103
Farow, John 314
Farow, Rebecca 314
Faust, Drew 5, 182, 183, 189
female body *see* body politics
female education 250–1, 253, 254, 256,
257, 263
Female Humane Association 236

female labor: body politics 157, 159;
female writers 261; millworkers
272–6, 279–82, 284, 286, 287, 290;
widow slaveowners 174
"The Female Slaves of London"
(article) 211
feminism 145, 146, 223, 243, 259, 263
fertility rates 63, 64, 68
Fields, Barbara Jeanne 211
Fitzhugh, George 4, 14, 15, 20, 22, 23,
211, 217
Fleischmann, Charles 44
Fleming, George 157
Flinn, Eliza 178
Flint, Timothy 45
flogging *see* whippings
Fogel, Robert William 3, 46, 51, 64
Follett, Richard 6, 37–54
Formisano, Ronald P. 231
Forstall, Edward 41, 45
Fox-Genovese, Elizabeth 5, 6
Franklin, Benjamin 99
Fraser, Charles 256
freedom: and progress 12, 13, 15–19,
23, 24, 28, 29, 33; runaway slaves 73,
74, 75
Freeman, Lucy 172–3, 175, 188, 189
Freeman, Theophilus 199
Frelinghuysen, Theodore 231
French Revolution 13, 14, 17, 26, 31
French, Sarah 237
Frogmoor Plantation 49
Fuller, Margaret 262

gambling 201, 209
gender: body politics 146, 156, 157,
159; female education 258; female
writers 261, 262, 263, 264, 265; law
and violence 296, 307; property
ownership 127; white women and
party politics 222, 223, 224, 229, 230;
white women millworkers 272, 276,
283, 290; widow slaveowners
171–2, 173, 180, 187, 189, 242
Genovese, Eugene D.: the dilemma
12–34; historiography of slavery 4,
5, 6, 7; Louisiana's sugar
plantations 39, 43, 50; time-
consciousness 97
George, Ceceil 50
Georgia: Gowrie plantation 58, 59, 62,
64; property ownership 137;

whiteness and slavery 202; white
women millworkers 273, 277,
278–80, 284, 286, 287, 288
Georgia Female College 253
Gibbon, Edward 27
Gillespie, Michele 6–7, 272–91
Gilmore, William 124, 126
Godlewska, Anne 143
Goldin, Claudia 287
Golding, William 131, 134
Gould, George 122
Gowrie plantation 59–63, 65–8, 71–5
Grimball, John Berkley 63
Graham, Senator W. A. 21
Grandy, Moses 104
Grant, Ulysses S. 115
Green, Hannah 300
Gregg, William 288
Grimball, John Berkley 63
Grimké, Angelina 258, 259, 261, 263,
264
Grimké, John Faucherand 259
Grimké, Sarah 250, 251, 255, 258,
259–60, 261, 262, 263
Grimké, Thomas 250, 257
Grimshaw, William 251
Guillory, Monique 198
Guthrie, Eunicey 300
Gutman, Herbert G. 2, 91, 94
Guy, Abigail 299–300

Hack, Daniel de Bruce 289
Hairston, Ruth 179
hairstyles 160
Halliburton, J. A. 196
Hamilton, Thomas 49
Hamilton, William 53–4
Hammond, James Henry 163, 189
Harland, Marion 234, 235, 242
Harmon, Jane Smith Hill 156
Harris, Dosia 154, 182
Harrison, Mark 89
Harrison, William Henry 224, 226,
227, 229, 230, 233, 238
Harris, Sam 132
Hart, Joel Tanner 239
Haynes, James 71
Hazzard-Gordon, Katrina 155
head wraps 160
health of slaves *see* disease
Heard, Bill 151
Henry, Jefferson Franklin 163
Hensley, Paul 90, 94

Herrenvolk 212, 284
Hester, Benjamin 309
Hester, Mary 299
Hester, Rachel 299
Hilliard, Henry 252
Hill, Jerry 183
Hillyer, Virgil 114, 115, 116, 129, 137
Hines, Benjamin 122
"The Hireling and the Slave" (poem)
210
A History of the Present Cabinet
(Kenney) 227
Hobgood, James 299
Hodge, Charles 30
Holmes, Jane 128
Hooper, Susan 228
Hopkins, Seaman 213
Howard Manufactory 288
Howard, Rev. C. W. 256
Howe, Daniel 231
Howington, Willie 309
Hutchison, Susan 174, 175
Hutson, William F. 25–6
Hutt, Andre 203
hybrid whiteness 198, 200, 203

industrial revolution 14, 24, 28, 29, 51,
89, 276
infant mortality 180
inheritance 123
Ireland 22
Irish workers 211
Islam 27
Izard, Alice 257

Jackson, Andrew 225, 230, 232
Jackson, Camilla 160
Jackson, Henry 179
Jackson, Martha 176, 177, 178, 179, 182
Jackson, Mildred Ann 199
Jackson, Samuel 299
Jacobs, Harriet 157
James, C. L. R. 145
James, Eliza 122, 126
James, Josephine 121
James, Paris 115
Jefferson, Thomas 251, 254, 256–7
Johnson, Brother 303
Johnson, Jonathan 95
Johnson, Michael P. 209
Johnson, Samuel 14, 22
Johnson, Walter 6, 184, 195–217

Jones, Barnett 311
Jones, Linda 132
Jordan, Winthrop D. 143
Joyner, Charles 59
June Days of 1848 26

Kames, Lord (Henry Home) 254
Kenney, Lucy 225, 227
Kerber, Linda K. 242
Kilpatrick, Judson 114, 115, 128, 134
Kimbel, Abington 309
Kincheloe Jr., Joe L. 231, 232
King, Roswell 157
Knowlton, Ephraim 47
Kohl, Lawrence 231
Kollock, Henry 259

Lansdale, Susannah 303, 304
Larken, Julia 162
Law, Tony 129
Lebsock, Suzanne 243
LeConte, Joseph 33
LeCounte, William 134
Lectures on the Restrictive System
    (Dew) 15
Lee, Elizabeth 181, 186
Lee, Grace C. 145
Lee, Lu 104
Le Goff, Jacques 88
A Letter Addressed to Martin Van Buren
    (Kenney) 225
Letters on Female Character (Cary) 181
Letters on the Equality of the Sexes and
    the Condition of Woman (Grimké)
    259–60, 261, 262, 263
Levine, Lawrence W. 2
Levy, Babette M. 94
Lewis, Catherine 174, 175, 182
Lexington Gazette 234, 237
Liberty County 114–15, 118–19, 121,
    123, 125–6, 129, 131–5, 137
Liddell, Moses 45
life expectancy of slaves 64
Life of Johnson (Boswell) 22
Lincoln, Abraham 215
Louisiana 37–54, 202, 209, 256
Love, Hunton 49
Lowe, Clarinda 125
Lowell 99, 100, 276, 283
Lumpkin, Joseph A. 20
Lyell, Sir Charles 50, 65, 69
Lynchburg Republican 237

Lynchburg Virginian 237, 244
Lyons, G. H. 207
Lyons, James 229

Madewood Plantation 47
Mallard, John B. 131
Mallard, Lazarus 136
Mallard, Robert Quaterman 124, 126
Mallard, Thomas 113, 122, 124
Malthus, Thomas 17, 32
Manigault, Charles 59–63, 66, 68–75
Manigault, Gabriel 73
Manigault, Louis 59, 61–3, 66–70, 72–5
Manly, Basil 255
Mansfield Female College 254
marriage: body politics 156; female
    education 256; female writers 260,
    262; law and violence 301–2, 307,
    313, 314; property ownership 121,
    126, 127, 128; widow slaveowners
    176
Martineau, Harriet 52–3, 262
Martin, W, J. 204
Marx, Karl 4, 8, 86, 105
Marxism 5, 8, 92, 93
Maryland Institute 22
Mathis, Jacob 300
Maury, Matthew F. 21
Maxwell, Prince 134
McAllister, Charity 157
McCollam, Andrew 45
McCord, David James 266
McCord, Langdon Cheves 267
McCord, Louisa 250–1, 258, 264–9
McCoy, Clara Cotton 183
McCulloh, R. S. 44
McCurry, Stephanie M. 212
McCutchon, Samuel 49
McDonald, Roderick 52
McDowell, James 226
McGerr, Michael E. 223, 241
McIver, William 121
Meadows, James 295–9, 310, 312, 314,
    315
Meadows, Mary 295–302, 304, 305,
    308, 310
Mention, Lisa 155
Merrell, Henry 273, 280, 288
Methodism 26
Mexican War 20, 27
Miles, William Porcher 255, 266, 268
Mill, John Stuart 264

Miller, Frances 161, 162
Miller, Perry 94
Mills, James W. 313
Minor, William 49
Missouri Compromise 225
modernism 14, 21
Montesquieu, Baron de 249
Moore, John 313
Moore, Samuel 257
moral philosophy 32
moral progress 13, 24, 25, 26, 27, 28
Mordecai, Ellen 238
Morgan, Edmund 13, 94
Morgan, Jennifer L. 147
Morgan, Philip D. 116
Morris, Christopher 156
Morrison, Alexina (Jane) 195–7, 200–6, 207–13, 214–17
Morrison, Mary 215
Morrison, Moses 203, 205, 206
Morrison v. White 197, 201–8, 210, 214–17
mortality rate of slaves: Gowrie plantation 63–8, 70, 75; law and violence 309–10; property ownership 122; white women millworkers 289–90; widow slaveowners 180
Motte, Mary 182
murder 295, 296, 297, 298, 310, 311, 312
Murray, Thomas 299
music 142, 143, 154–5

"Narrative and Testimony of Sarah M. Grimké" 263
Natal province, South Africa 84, 87, 92–3, 95–7, 103, 105–6
National Intelligencer 226, 229, 236
Nevitt, John 151
new economic history 2–3
New England 90
New Orleans Daily Crescent 211
New York Journal of Commerce 288
Niles, Hezekiah 284
Niles' Weekly Register 284
North: female education 256; freedom and progress 19, 22, 28–32, 34; time-consciousness 90–1, 93, 99, 107
"Northern White Slavery" 211
Northup, Solomon 46, 50, 199

Nott, Henry 253–4
Nottoway Plantation 45, 48

Oakes, James 39
Oaklands Plantation 49
O'Brien, Michael 6, 249–69
Olmsted, Frederick Law: body politics 158; gender politics 286, 289, 290; Gowrie plantation 66; Louisiana's sugar plantations 38, 44, 51
Olson, John F. 102
O'Malley, Michael 87
O'Neal, William 314
"On the Condition of Women in the United States" (Grimké) 260
Otey, Lucy 236
Outram, Dorinda 145

Palmer, Reverend Benjamin Morgan 27, 31
parties 142–5, 148, 150, 152–6, 159, 161–5
party politics *see* politics
paternalism: body politics 144, 150, 157, 164; gender politics 291; Gowrie plantation 59, 60, 62, 67–70, 72, 75; historiography of slavery 4, 5, 6, 7; Louisiana's sugar plantations 37, 39, 42, 51; widow slaveowners 176
Patrick, Thomas A. 303, 304
peace warrants 304
Peake, Martha 234
Pearson, Richmond 311
The Peculiar Institution (Stampp) 1
Penningroth, Dylan C. 6, 7, 52, 113–41
Perret, P. C. 207, 213
Petrigru, James Louis 251
Phillips, Ulrich B. 1, 2, 3, 4, 5
Pickens, Francis W. 21
Pierce, Franklin 240
Pierson, Vincent 182
Pitt, F. E. 27
plantations: body politics 143–4, 146, 148–54, 159, 161, 162; female education 256; gender politics 274–5; Gowrie plantation 58, 59, 61–3, 65–70, 72, 73, 75; historiography of slavery 1, 3, 4–5; Louisiana's sugar plantations 37–54; property

ownership 119, 133, 134, 135, 137; time-consciousness 100, 101, 102, 103, 104; widow slaveowners 187, 188
Planter's Banner 45
planter widows 171, 172, 175, 177, 178, 185
political economy 16, 17, 19, 28, 32, 33
The Political Economy of Slavery (Genovese) 4
politics 222–4, 226–8, 230–3, 235, 236, 241–4
Polk, James Knox 238
Porcher, Frederick Adolphus 21
Powers, Hiram 21
Preston, Louise Penelope 250
Preston, William Campbell 249–50
Primrose, Mary Ann 251
Princeton Manufacturing Company 280, 288
progress 12, 13, 15–20, 21–6, 28, 29, 33
property ownership 113–38
Protestant work ethic 84, 85, 86, 87, 93, 94, 107
Pryor, Sara 227
Pugh, Thomas 47
Pullam, Nancy H. 299
Puritanism 90, 94

Quakerism 259, 260
Quaterman, Jacob 119

race: gender politics 272; historiography 1; law and violence 296, 307; whiteness and slavery 197–8, 200–2, 204–7, 209–10, 212, 216–17
Randolph, John Hampden 45, 48, 53
Ransom, John Crowe 14
rape victims 184
Ravenel, Henry William 26
Rebeiro de Castro, Julian 45
reform 231, 232
religion: body politics 163; freedom and progress 21, 22, 24–8, 30–2; historiography of slavery 4–5; southern women 254, 255, 260, 262; time-consciousness 87, 89; white women and party politics 231
Remini, Robert V. 238
Residence Plantation 47
Rhodes, Westley 302

Ricardian theories 16, 32
rice plantations: body politics 146; Gowrie plantation 58, 59, 62, 63, 65–70, 72, 73, 75; property ownership 119, 133
Richardson, Martha 170
Richmond Crisis 230
Richmond Dispatch 244
Richmond Enquirer 231, 235, 236
Richmond Whig 229, 234, 235, 236, 237, 238
rival geography 143–4
Rivers, R. H. 15
Rives, Judith 224, 227
Rives, William Cabell 224, 226
Roark, James L. 209
Roberts, Linda 131
Robertson, James 38
Robinson, Solon 47
Roll, Jordan, Roll: The World the Slaves Made (Genovese) 4, 5
Roman, Andre 49
Rose, Willie Lee 60
Roswell Mills 288, 290
Ruffin, Eliza 187
Ruffin, Elizabeth 257
Ruffin, Thomas 311–12
Runnells, Eliza B. 225
Russell, William Howard 37–8, 49
Ryan, Mary P. 223

salt 120
Savage, Amey 63
Savage, Jack 70, 73, 75
Savage, Rep. John H. 21
Savannah River 59, 62, 63, 66, 75
Savannah River Anti-Slave Traffick Association 163, 164, 165
Saville, Julie 118, 137
Schley, William 289
Schwarz, Philip 186
Schweninger, Loren 117
Scott, Anne Firor 243
Scott, Reverend William A. 33
secession 25, 26, 244, 276
Semiramis 261
sexual exploitation: body politics 146, 148, 158; whiteness and slavery 213; widow slaveowners 172, 180, 184–5
sexuality: body politics 147, 148; historiography of slavery 3; law and violence 296, 307; southern

women 249, 255, 257, 260, 265, 266; whiteness and slavery 199, 200, 201, 205, 207, 208
Shakes, Celestia 227
Sherman, Gen. William T. 114, 134
Silbey, Joel H. 222
Silk Hope 59, 66, 74
skin color 197, 198, 205, 266
Skinner, K. Washington 66
slavery: body politics 142–4, 146–50, 152, 153, 156–8, 161, 163–5; female writers 259, 260, 263, 264, 265; freedom and progress 12–15, 17–23, 27–31, 33, 34; gender politics 273, 274, 275, 277, 285, 286; Gowrie plantation 58–61, 62–5, 66–8, 69–75; historiography 1–7; law and violence 295–8, 300–7, 308–14; Louisiana's sugar plantations 38, 40–3, 45, 47–54; property ownership 113–38; time-consciousness 85–8, 94, 97, 99–107; whiteness 195–200, 201–7, 208–13, 214–17; white women and party politics 225, 244; widow slaveowners 170–89
Smith, Adam 264
Smith, Charlie Tye 162
Smith, Elizabeth Oakes 264
Smith, Henry 179
Smith, Mark 6, 38, 51, 84–107
Smith, Neil 143
Smith, William A. 15
Sobel, Mechal 93
Solokoff, Kenneth 287
songs 2, 151, 154–5
South Carolina 59, 62, 64, 118, 146, 202
South Carolina Sea Islands 115, 137
Southern Agriculturalist 70, 100
Southern Claims Commission 115–17, 127, 128–9, 130, 132, 135–7
Southern Cultivator 99
Southern Literary Messenger 253
Southern Planter 99
Southern Presbyterian Review 33
Southern Quarterly Review 21, 264
Southwick, Mary 314
Stacy, Andrew 122
Stampp, Kenneth 1–2
Staunton Spectator 224, 225, 226
Steger, Mary 227, 228
Stephens, Marcus Cicero 251, 252

Stephens, Reverend Abednego 20
Stevens, David 131
Stevens, Henry 122
Stevens, Prince 128
Stevens, York 123
Stevenson, Brenda E. 156
Steward, Austin 152
Stewart, Annetta 121
Stewart, Charles 46
Stewart, Prince 127
Stroyer, Jacob 50
suffrage 239, 241–4, 257, 262
sugar plantations 37–54
Sumter, Natalie 175–6, 177, 178, 181, 186, 188

Taney, Chief Justice Roger 208
tariffs 276, 277
task system 70, 119, 120, 122
Taswell, Selena 160
Tate, Allen 14
Taylor, Harriet 264
Taylor, Miles 42
Taylor, Warner 308–9
Telfair, Edward 95
temperance 232, 233
Tennessee Baptist 27
textile industry 272, 275–7, 279–81, 285–90
The Theology of Christian Experience (Armstrong) 25
Thomas, James 103
Thomas, Philip 199
Thompson, Charlotte 123
Thompson, E. P. 88, 90, 91, 94, 103, 105
Thornton, Lucy 183
Thornwell, Rev. Dr. James Henley 15, 25, 26, 30, 31, 33
time-consciousness 48–9, 84–107
Time on the Cross (Fogel and Engerman) 3
time-thrift 86, 89, 93, 94, 97, 105
"Time, Work-Discipline and Industrial Capitalism" (Thompson) 88
"Tippecanoe and Tyler, Too" campaign 224, 226, 227, 230
tobacco 101, 178, 179, 201
Trentham, Henry James 159
Trescot, William Henry 255, 257
Tucker, George 15, 17, 32
Tucker, Henry St. George 15

Tucker, Nathaniel Beverley 15
Tucker, St. George 15
Tureaud, Benjamin 53

Uncle Tom's Cabin (Harriet Beecher Stowe) 264
Upson, Neal 151

Van Buren, Martin 225, 229
Varon, Elizabeth R. 6, 7, 222–44
Veblen, Thorstein 45
violence: body politics 146, 148, 156; female writers 263; law and patriarchal authority 295, 297, 299, 300, 302–6, 308–13; Louisiana's sugar plantations 50; time-consciousness 105; whiteness and slavery 200; widow slaveowners 172, 180, 182, 183, 184
Virginia 22, 223, 224, 226, 228–33, 244
Virginia Association of Ladies for Erecting a Statue to Henry Clay 224, 236, 237, 238, 239, 243

wages 52, 53, 279
Wallace, Annie 160
War for Southern Independence 12, 13
War of 1812 276, 277
Warrenton Female Academy 253
Washington Globe 230, 235
Washington, John 104
Washington National Intelligencer 226, 229, 236
watches 87, 89, 91, 94, 96, 98, 100, 102, 104
Weaver, Richard 21
Weber, Max 86, 92, 93, 105
Webster, Daniel 228, 229, 231, 232, 234, 250
Weld, Theodore 258, 259, 261, 263
West Indies 23, 43, 75
Westminster Review 264
Whig Party 223–9, 230–7, 238–44
Whig womanhood 223, 229, 230, 234, 235, 239, 242–4
whippings 61, 71, 102, 105–7, 149, 172, 180–5, 263
White, James 195–7, 200, 203, 205, 206, 212, 214
whiteness and slavery 196, 197–200, 201–7, 208–13

Whites, LeeAnn 273
white women: law and violence 296, 297, 299–301, 303, 304, 307; millworkers 272, 273, 284–7, 290
"wicked intent" 308, 309
widow slaveowners 170–89
Wilcox, Susannah 178, 179, 180
Wilkins, Eliza 179, 184
Williams, Nancy 142, 143, 154, 159, 161, 172, 187
Wills, James 180
Wilson, John 122
Winn, Peter 135
Winn, William 136
Wise, Henry 22
wives 301, 304, 305, 307–14
Woman and Her Needs (Smith) 264
Woman in the Nineteenth Century (Fuller) 262
women: body politics 142–65; gender politics 272, 273, 284–7, 290; historiography of slavery 6, 7; law and violence 296–301, 303, 304, 307, 309; party politics 222–6, 228–36, 239–44; property ownership 127, 128; southern women 249–54, 262, 265; suffrage 239, 241–4, 257, 262; whiteness and slavery 198, 199, 200, 212; widow slaveowners 170–89 *see also* female labor
women's rights 243, 256, 263, 264, 265, 266
Wood, Kirsten E. 6, 170–89
Woodruff, George 49
work ethic 51, 84, 86, 87, 93, 94, 107
Works Progress Administration Project 2
Wright, Anne 310, 311
Wright, Gavin 102
Wright, Thomas 310–11
Wyatt-Brown, Bertram 9, 98
Wyatt, Mary 161

yellow fever 66, 67
yeoman widows 171, 172, 175, 185
Young, Jeffrey R. 6, 58–76, 177
Younge, Rebecca 174

Zagarri, Rosemarie 241
Zulus 92, 93, 105

THE OLD SOUTH

"J. William Harris' *The Old South* brings together an impressive array of diverse social and cultural history of the pre-Civil War South as written by some of the most gifted scholars among the current generation of southern historians. It is broadly representative of much of the best work done over the past fifteen years. It successfully defines the cutting edge of southern social and cultural history for all who care to know."
— Lacy Ford, author of *A Companion to the Civil War and Reconstruction*

"With essays about plantation owners and slaves, labor and property, and many forms of politics, this collection presents the easiest way to encounter the most exciting scholarship on the antebellum South."
— Ted Ownby, author of *American Dreams in Mississippi: Consumers, Poverty, and Culture, 1830–1998*

"In this revised collection of essays, J. William Harris has provided teachers of southern history with an invaluable teaching tool that incorporates the newest and most exciting approaches to the social and cultural history of the Old South such as gender relations and political culture."
— Mitchell Snay, author of *Fenians, Freedmen, and Southern Whites: Race and Nationality in the Era of Reconstruction*

The antebellum South remains one of the most studied and written about periods of American history. For years, the terms of the debates were set in large part by the work of Eugene Genovese and Elizabeth Fox-Genovese. Recently, however, historians have moved past the classic debates and have taken the discussion into new territories.

In this new edition of *Society and Culture in the Slave South*, J. William Harris has chosen selections that present recent provocative viewpoints on the antebellum South, works that reveal both the focus and diversity of the ongoing revisions of historical thought. Including essays on paternalism, class, women and gender, culture and morality, *The Old South* offers readers selections that illustrate both the continuities and the new developments in historical scholarship on the antebellum South.

J. William Harris is Professor of History at the University of New Hampshire. He is the author of *Plain Folk and Gentry in a Slave Society* and *Deep Souths: Delta, Piedmont, and Sea Island Society in the Age of Segregation*.

REWRITING HISTORIES focuses on historical themes where standard conclusions are facing a major challenge. Each book presents eight to ten papers (edited and annotated where necessary) at the forefront of current research and interpretation, offering students an accessible way to engage with contemporary debates.

Series editor **Jack R. Censer** is Professor of History at George Mason University.

REWRITING HISTORIES
Series editor: Jack R. Censer

ATLANTIC AMERICAN
SOCIETIES: FROM COLUMBUS
THROUGH ABOLITION
Edited by J. R. McNeill and Alan Karras

DECOLONIZATION:
PERSPECTIVES FROM NOW AND
THEN
Edited by Prasenjit Duara

DIVERSITY AND UNITY IN EARLY
NORTH AMERICA
Edited by Philip Morgan

THE FRENCH REVOLUTION:
RECENT DEBATES AND NEW
CONTROVERSIES
Edited by Gary Kates

GENDER AND AMERICAN
HISTORY SINCE 1890
Edited by Barbara Melosh

GLOBAL FEMINISMS SINCE 1945
Edited by Bonnie G. Smith

THE HOLOCAUST: ORIGINS,
IMPLEMENTATION, AFTERMATH
Edited by Omer Bartov

THE INDUSTRIAL
REVOLUTION AND WORK IN
NINETEENTH-CENTURY EUROPE
Edited by Lenard R. Berlanstein

THE ISRAEL/PALESTINE
QUESTION
Edited by Ilan Pappé

MEDIEVAL RELIGION: NEW
APPROACHES
Constance Hoffman Berman

NAZISM AND GERMAN SOCIETY,
1933–1945
Edited by David Crew

THE NEW SOUTH: NEW
HISTORIES
Edited by J. William Harris

THE OLD SOUTH: NEW STUDIES
OF SOCIETY AND CULTURE
Edited by J. William Harris

THE ORIGINS OF THE COLD
WAR: AN INTERNATIONAL
HISTORY
Edited by David Painter and Melvyn Leffler

PRACTICING HISTORY: NEW
DIRECTIONS IN HISTORICAL
WRITING
Gabrielle M. Spiegel

REFORMATION TO REVOLUTION
Edited by Margo Todd

THE RENAISSANCE: ITALY AND
ABROAD
Edited by John Jeffries Martin

REVOLUTIONARY RUSSIA: NEW
APPROACHES TO THE RUSSIAN
REVOLUTION
Edited by Rex A. Wade

THE REVOLUTIONS OF 1989
Edited by Vladimir Tismaneanu

SEGREGATION AND APARTHEID
IN TWENTIETH CENTURY SOUTH
AFRICA
Edited by William Beinart and Saul Dubow

STALINISM: NEW DIRECTIONS
Edited by Sheila Fitzpatrick

TWENTIETH CENTURY CHINA:
NEW APPROACHES
Edited by Jeffrey N. Wasserstrom

FROM ROMAN PROVINCES TO
MEDIEVAL KINGDOMS
Edited by Thomas F.X. Noble